Acknowledgements

Art Direction
Michiel Schriever

Sr .Graphic Designer
Luke Pauw

Cover Image and 3D Models
Courtesy of Michael Sormann

Copy Editor
Erica Fyvie

Technical Editor
Alan Harris

Video Producer
Peter Verboom

Project Manager
Lenni Rodrigues

Special thanks go out to:

Roark Andrade, Mariann Barsolo, Carol Kelly, Travis Jones, Carmela Bourassa, Julie Fauteux, John Gross, Tonya Holder, Danielle Lamothe, Cory Mogk, Mary Ruijs, Carla Sharkey, Michael Stamler, and Claire Tacon.

We would like to extend a special thank you to Michael Sormann. This Book would not have been possible without his support.

Primary Author

Marc-André Guindon | NeoReel

Marc-André Guindon is the founder of NeoReel Inc. (*www.NeoReel.com*), a Montreal-based production facility. He is an Autodesk® Maya® Master and an advanced user of Autodesk® MotionBuilder™ software. Marc-André and NeoReel have partnered with Autodesk Inc. on several projects, including the Learning Maya series from version 6.0 to present. NeoReel was also the driving force behind the Maya Techniques™ DVDs, such as *How to Integrate Quadrupeds into a Production Pipeline* and *Maya and Alias MotionBuilder®*.

www.NeoReel.com

Marc-André has established complex pipelines and developed numerous plug-ins and tools, such as *Animation Layers for Maya* and *Visual MEL Studio*, for a variety of projects in both the film and game industries. His latest film projects include pre-visualization on *The Day the Earth Stood Still* (20th Century Fox), *G-Force* (Walt Disney Productions), *Journey 3D* (Walden Media), as well as visual effects for *Unearthed* (Ambush Entertainment), and *XXX: State of the Union* (Revolution Studios) among others. He also served in the game industry to integrate motion capture for *Prey* (2K Games) for the Xbox 360™, *Arena Football*™ (EA Sports) and the *Outlaw Game Series: Outlaw Volleyball*™, *Outlaw Golf*™, and *Outlaw Tennis*™ (Hypnotix).

Marc-André continues to seek challenges for himself, NeoReel, and his talented crew.

A 3D Roller Coaster Ride

Michael Sormann | Profile

Theme Planet is the labor of love of Austrian-born artist, Michael Sormann, who is a veteran of the computer games industry and a former employee of Rockstar Vienna. "I was fascinated by the thought of doing my own little project some day," he says. "So one day in a pub I was talking with my friends and, like nearly every evening, we talked about what kind of projects could be accomplished with 3D animations." After this conversation, Sormann began working steadily on designs in his spare time and importing them into Autodesk® Maya® software, where he developed them into fully rigged characters and locations.

As Sormann started sketching out concepts, the idea of a planet composed entirely of roller coasters began to emerge. "I wanted a world with a lot of very big structures and machines," says Sormann. "But I didn't want them to look too modern; more like machines from the time of the Industrial Revolution." The theme park, with its over-the-top environment seemed like a perfect fit. "I thought it would be a very interesting setting for cartoon characters to go to some funny adventures." In its final version, the planet has no surface, just one attraction piled on top of another—a landscape of rails, gears and levers, reminiscent of a Tim Burton movie.

The characters of *Theme Planet* couldn't be more different from the gritty, mechanical terrain they inhabit. Instead, they are whimsical and colorful, textured and shaded so that they look like stop-motion models. Sormann explains that the characters' exaggerated style stems from his passion for comics In particular, the work of André Franquin. "When I was in school I always wanted to become a comic artist and I always had a big collection of comics," he says. "I think these comics, mostly from France and Belgium, such as *Lucky Luke*, influenced me a lot and my drawing style reflects that."

Taught himself Maya

Self-taught in Maya through experimentation and online learning demonstrations, Sormann used the software for every aspect of *Theme Planet*. "I like Maya because it's a package that includes everything that you need," he says. "And you don't have to install tons of plug-ins to use it." To gear up for his first short film *Bunny Situation*, Sormann began using Maya to flesh out the world of *Theme Planet* and create small test animations.

Unlike most film projects, which start with the script or pitch, Sormann had already skinned, rigged and shaded the characters before he'd determined the final story. This meant that he had worked out a lot of the kinks before production began. Sormann's approach paid off—despite the fact that he was the only person working on the film, it only took three months to complete. "Normally it would have taken me a lot longer," he says, "but I already had most of the models and settings ready from *Theme Planet* renderings and animations I did before."

Bunny Situation follows a wily rabbit who finds himself on a conveyor belt, heading towards the "Smart-O-matic" brainwashing machine, run by *Theme Planet*'s Mad Constructor. With some help from Pig and Elephant, two good-natured repairmen, the rabbit manages to escape the Constructor's clutches. His plans foiled, the Mad Constructor climbs aboard the T.P. Barracuda, a hulking steam-powered train engine, for a showdown over the dilapidated tracks of *Theme Planet*.

Animating in Sync

At one point in *Bunny Situation*, the Mad Constructor steps into a "Body Enlargement Robot," which Sormann admits is his favorite sequence. "It was simply a cool challenge to animate a walking character that stands on top of another walking character, steering the robot's movements with his own. It was hard to keep so many moving bones, in two separate skeletons, in sync."

The bunny's ears were another difficult element to animate. "Surprisingly, it's not very hard to create these secondary animations by hand when the character is moving a lot," says Sormann. "But when the movements are more subtle, it's hard to get believable secondary animations on the long ears."

Sormann was able to achieve the sophisticated animation in the film with an innovative fix using Maya. "I simulated them with a spline Inverse Kinematics (IK)," reveals Sormann. "I converted the spline that controls the IK chain into a soft body. Then, I used the component editor for the particles that influenced the control vertices (CVs) of the spline and made them softer and softer depending on how far they were from the head."

Bunny Situation, along with other assets that Sormann has created for this project, is available on his website. The work has already attracted attention, garnering Sormann a Masters Award from Exposé 3 and articles in CG China, The Journal of Computer Graphics and the Swiss magazine *Heute*. *Bunny Situation* was recently screened at SIGGRAPH®, where Sormann also gave short demonstrations.

From Pencils to Pixels

Sormann credits some of his success to the fact that all of his designs begin as pencil on paper. He draws daily, both for his freelance work and his own projects. "I think that it helps a lot in 3D modeling if you are able to draw," he says, "especially characters, because it gives you an understanding of how structures and shapes have to look in 3D space."

"It's really cool to see a drawing coming into 3D space," he continues, "and then to finally see your characters animated." To achieve his vision, Sormann sketches six to ten versions of a particular character or location, then picks the parts he likes the most. He combines these into a final drawing to be scanned and imported into Maya as a plane in a scene. Keeping the drawing in the plane as a reference helps him make the model more faithful to the design. Once the shape is honed, he paints texture on the model, using bump maps to simulate natural texture on the skin.

Sormann is currently developing a longer story line for the characters of *Theme Planet* and he explains that this part of the process can be even more challenging than overcoming the technical hurdles. "You have to always keep in mind that the story is the most important thing," he says. "No matter how good the artwork looks, it's always important to have a good story behind it."

For more information on Michael Sormann or *Theme Planet* visit: **www.sormann3d.com**

Table of Contents

How to use this book

Thank you for choosing *Learning Autodesk® Maya® 2009 | The Special Effects Handbook*. This book builds on the projects begun in *Learning Autodesk Maya 2009 | The Modeling and Animation Handbook*. In some instances, you will have an opportunity to add details and effects to the scenes and characters you may have modeled and animated in the first half of this series. *Learning Autodesk Maya 2009 | The Special Effects Handbook* also covers important theories that apply to dynamics and rendering in Maya and mental ray for Maya. Within the pages of this book, you will work with and understand a wide variety of other workflows and theories.

The way you use this book will depend on your experience with computer graphics and 3D animation. This book moves at a fast pace and is designed to help intermediate-level users improve their rendering and dynamics skills and understand how they relate to one another in a production pipeline. In addition, you will learn to create Maya Fluid Effects, work with Maya nCloth and nParticles, create fur effects, and work with hair and dynamic curves. If this is your first experience with 3D software, we suggest that you begin with the *Learning Autodesk Maya 2009 | Foundation* book as the prerequisite before proceeding through the lessons in this book. If you are already familiar with Autodesk® Maya® or another 3D package, you can dive in and complete the lessons as written.

Updates to this book

In an effort to ensure your continued success through the lessons in this book, please visit our Web site for the latest updates available: *www.autodesk.com/learningtools-updates*.

Windows and Macintosh

This book is written to cover Windows and Macintosh platforms. You may notice that your screen varies slightly from the illustrations, depending on the platform you are using.

Things to watch for

Window focus may differ. For example, if you are on Windows, you have to click on the panel with your middle mouse button to make it active.

To select multiple attributes in Windows, use the **Ctrl** key. On Macintosh, use the **Command** key. To modify pivot position in Windows, use the **Insert** key. On Macintosh, use the **Home** key.

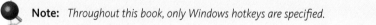

Note: *Throughout this book, only Windows hotkeys are specified.*

Autodesk packaging

This book can be used with either Autodesk® Maya® Complete 2009, Autodesk® Maya® Unlimited 2009, or the corresponding version of Autodesk® Maya® Personal Learning Edition, as the lessons included here focus on functionality shared among all three software packages.

Only the last project of this book reflects Autodesk® Maya® Unlimited 2009 features.

Learning Autodesk Maya DVD-ROM

The Learning Autodesk Maya DVD-ROM contains several resources to accelerate your learning experience including:

- Learning Maya support files;
- Instructor-led videos to guide you through the projects in the book;
- Autodesk Maya reference guides
- A link to a trial version of Autodesk® Maya®

Installing support files

Before beginning the lessons in this book, you will need to install the lesson support files. Copy the project directories found in the *support_files* folder on the DVD disc to the *Maya\projects* directory on your computer. Launch Maya and set the project by going to **File → Project → Set...** and selecting the appropriate project.

Windows: *C:\Documents and Settings\username\My Documents\maya\projects*

Macintosh: *Macintosh HD/Users/username/Documents/maya/projects*

Note: *The support files require Maya version 2009.*

Project 01

In Project One, you are going to explore in-depth shading networks. Shading networks are connections between nodes such as surfaces, materials, textures, utilities, etc., and are evaluated when Maya needs to render the scene. You will start by reviewing the basics of materials and then exploring some common texture nodes and utilities.

By the end of this project, you should feel comfortable creating various shading networks to enhance your scenes.

Materials

A material is a set of instructions that describes how the surface of an object will look when rendered. It is not just a collection of attributes you can texture-map, but also a mathematical description of how light will behave when it strikes the surface. A material's attributes allow you to fine-tune its look, whether it is a cartoon effect or photorealism.

In this lesson, you will learn the following:

- What an IPR render is
- The basics of materials and shading networks
- What a specular highlight is and how to use it
- What the following types of shaders are and how to use them

    anisotropic shaders

    layered shaders

    ramp shaders

    shading maps

    surface shaders

IPR

IPR stands for *Interactive Photorealistic Rendering* and is available for both mental ray and Autodesk® Maya® renderers. IPR is a type of software rendering that allows you to adjust shading and lighting attributes and see the updates in real-time. When you do an IPR render, it writes out a file (known as a deep raster file), that contains all the sample information for each pixel in the image. This file is written to the *renderData/iprImages* directory. It will have a name like *_ipr.iff*. This file is similar to the file that is written out when you do a normal render in the Render view, in that it is overwritten every time you do a new IPR render. As long as the current project stays the same, the file will be overwritten when an IPR render is started in that user session.

However, IPR does not prefix the camera name to the filename, as a normal render does. This means that if you change cameras and do an IPR render, the deep raster file will overwrite the same file. A regular render will add the prefix of the camera to the file and generate a new file. To save the Maya IPR file permanently so that it will not be overwritten, choose **File → Save IPR File** in the Render view window. This is useful if you are working on a large scene and the IPR file takes several minutes to generate. If this is the case, you can save out the IPR file and work on other things and still return to it at a later time. If you have saved out an IPR file, you can use **fcheck** to view the image component of the file. If you use the mental ray for Maya IPR, the IPR images will be saved in the Images directory.

Tip: *IPR files can be quite large and will consume large amounts of disk space. It is a good idea to delete these files if you do not need them.*

1 IPR rendering

- **Open** the scene file called *01-background.ma* from the *support_files/project1/scenes* directory on the DVD-ROM.
- Click the **IPR Render** button at the top of the main interface or in the Render view.

  The scene is rendered, and then a message appears at the bottom of the Render view that says:

  `Select a region to begin tuning`

- **Click+drag** to draw a region around the portion of the image you want to tune.

  You can now begin tuning lights and materials to see the IPR update automatically.

IPR running in Render view

Tip: *While the IPR is updating, you can add new lights, move lights, modify light attributes, and delete lights. You can also create, assign, and edit new materials and the render will automatically update. But, you cannot create, modify, or delete geometry or watch an animated object.*

• **Stop** the IPR by clicking the red stop sign button in the Render view.

Note: *The IPR for mental ray allows updating of raytracing attributes such as reflections and refractions.*

Shading networks

A shading network can be defined as a graph of connected nodes that can be used to shade objects. These networks generally contain what Maya classifies as materials and textures, but they do not have to contain only those nodes.

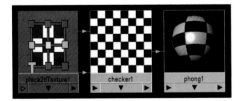

A phong shading network with checker color texture

The idea behind the Maya architecture is to have many simple nodes that can be connected in a virtually infinite number of combinations, rather than fewer and very complex nodes. For example, you will not find all of the conceivable light attributes on a single node; instead, you will have attributes for the light on one node, attributes for the light fog on another node and attributes for the light glow on a third node. While this may seem inconvenient at first, it will become apparent that this is a very powerful method for augmenting a shading network.

Shading groups

A *shading group* is a set of objects to be shaded with the shading network. Below is a diagram of a shading group called *phong1SG* (the SG stands for shading group). You can see a sphere connected to the shading group; these objects form the *set* that will be shaded by the shading network. In this case, the shading network is a phong material with a checker connected to it.

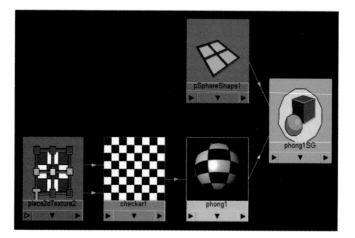

A shading group with attached shading network and surfaces

Note: *At render time, Maya determines which objects will be rendered by going to all of the shading groups and collecting all of the objects contained in each group. If an object is not a member of any shading group, it is not rendered.*

Connecting shading networks to shading groups

The shading network is connected to a *Port* attribute on the shading group. In a typical workflow, this connection will be made automatically. Below is a view of the **Attribute Editor** showing the three ports on a shading group:

The Attribute Editor for a shading group

Surface Material

This port is used to shade surfaces such as NURBS, polygons, and SubDs.

Volume Material

This port is used to shade volumes such as fogs and some particle types.

Displacement Material

This port is used for displacement mapping surfaces and is used in conjunction with the Surface Material port.

All shading groups have the same three ports; this generality allows any shading group to shade any type of object. Each port has a shading engine associated with it that will evaluate the network attached to it.

Bins

The **Hypershade** contains a **Bins** tab. Bins allow users to organize their networks into groups under specific headings. For instance, if you have several characters in a scene, each of which has a number of materials assigned to it, you may want to create a separate bin for each character to store all associated materials.

1 **Create a bin**

- Select **Window** → **Rendering Editors** → **Hypershade**.

- Click on the **Bins** tab.

- Click on the **Create Empty Bin** button or **RMB** on the **Master Bin** and select **Create** from the pop-up menu. A dialog box will pop up, where you can give your bin a name.

- Select the node to be part of that bin and then **RMB** on the name of the bin and select **Add Selected**.

Note: *In order to see the shaders in the bin, you must have the proper Hypershade tab selected.*

- To view the nodes that are part of a bin, make sure to view the top tabs from the **Tabs** menu, and then highlight a bin's tab.

  Only the nodes that are part of the highlighted bin are displayed.

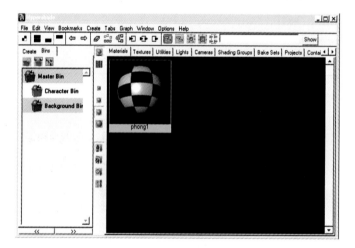

Bins displayed

Tip: *The **Text Filter** will allow you to type in a string or part of a string, and filter the top tabs accordingly. For instance, to see only phong materials, type in "pho*".*

Containers

You can arrange your Work area in the Hypershade or in the Hypergraph in a more efficient manner by assembling nodes into logical node groupings using container nodes. For example, if you have a complex shading network that appears multiple times within your scene, you can group each network into a container to obtain a simpler Work area.

1 Create a container

- Select **Window → Rendering Editors → Hypershade**.
- Select any object with a shading network assigned to it.
- Select **Graph → Graph Material on Selected Objects.**
- Select all the nodes that are part of the shading network except the shading group node.
- **RMB** on the selection and select **Create** container from selected.

The nodes will be collapsed into a container node.

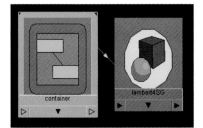

A container in the Hypershade

2 Expand a container

It is possible to expand a container in order to tweak its content.

- Select a container.
- Click the **Expand selected container(s)** button or select **Edit → Expand Container.**

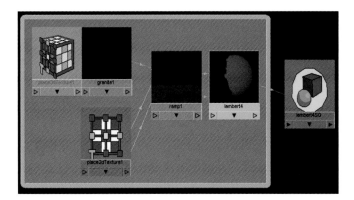

The expanded container

Note: *You can select nodes within a container and move them to organize the network display.*

- Click the **Collapse selected container(s)** button or select **Edit** → **Collapse Container** to collapse the network display.

 Tip: *You can also double-click on a container to toggle its display state.*

3 Remove a container
- Click the **Remove selected container(s)** button or select **Edit** → **Remove Container** to get the shading network out of the container.

The Maya Shader Library

After installing Maya, you can install the Maya Shader Library from the installation CD. This library is a collection of scene files consisting of over sixty shading networks, including materials and file textures. These networks can be used as-is or as a basis to create your own materials or shaders.

Once the Shader Library is installed, you can preview the library directly in the **Hypershade** via the **Shader Library** tab located in the top panel. To use one of the shaders from the library, simply **MMB+drag** it into the **Hypershade** or **RMB** on it and choose **Import Maya file**. Once you have dragged or imported the file, it will appear in the **Materials** tab and can be assigned or manipulated like any other material.

Note: *You cannot assign Shader Library materials directly from the Shader Library tab.*

Materials

A material is essentially a shading model that calculates the surface characteristics and determines how a surface will be shaded. The terms *shader* and *material* are used interchangeably; both are correct for this description. The common industry term is *shader,* and you will find this term throughout the book.

The single most important thing to do when creating an effective material is to concentrate on how the object's highlight appears. This one factor can dramatically improve the look of the material even before any textures are applied. Look around you and take note of the various ways light falls across surfaces. Notice how shiny objects have a bright small highlight and how a dull surface has barely any highlight at all.

You will now take a closer look at how light reflects off a surface. The following diagram illustrates how some portion of incident light is scattered as it reflects, and some portion of the light can be reflected at a more consistent angle. The light reflected at a consistent angle results in an intense bright region called a *specular highlight*. The scattered light is referred to as *diffuse* light.

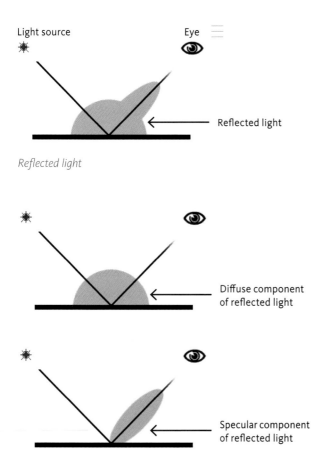

Reflected light

Light source

Eye

Reflected light

Diffuse component
of reflected light

Specular component
of reflected light

Components of refracted light

In reality, the specular component and the diffuse component of the total reflected light will vary depending on the characteristics of the surface.

In Maya, the diffuse component and the specular component are controlled separately, which gives you the flexibility to simulate virtually any real-world surface.

Lambert material

The *Lambert* material works well for matte surfaces. It simulates surfaces where most light rays will be absorbed by uneven, tiny surface imperfections. When light rays strike such a surface, they bounce around in the nooks and crannies instead of being reflected back from the surface. Any rays that actually are reflected will be scattered at close to random angles, so you will not see a specular highlight. There is very little correlation between the angle of incidence and the angle of the reflected rays.

The extent to which the scattered light is absorbed or reflected is controlled by the **Diffuse** attribute. This attribute exists on all of the basic materials.

Since light reflected from a surface is what gives you the sense of its color, low diffuse values close to **0.0** mean very little light is scattered, so the surface will look dark. A high diffuse value approaching **1.0** means that a lot of light is scattered, so the surface will look very saturated.

An example of a lambert surface with a low diffuse value is coal, where most light is absorbed by the surface imperfections. Examples of lambert surfaces with a high diffuse value are things like the surface of the moon or colored chalk. In this case, the surface imperfections cause the light to be scattered and some amount of it is actually reflected, giving these surfaces a strong sense of color.

The following image shows two lambert materials with different diffuse values; otherwise all of their attributes are identical.

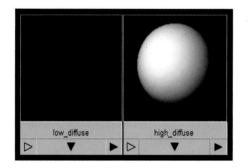

Different diffuse values

Tip: *The lambert shading model is used to compute the diffuse component of surface illumination. All other more complex shading models derive their diffuse component from lambert.*

Phong, phongE, and blinn

Very smooth surfaces such as glass, mirrors, and chrome will have a very low diffuse value, approaching zero. This is because they reflect very little scattered light. The light does not get scattered because there are few surface imperfections that would cause it to bounce at random angles. Instead, most of the light rays are reflected off the surface at a similar angle, resulting in a *specular highlight*. Because the lambert material does not simulate the specular component of surface illumination, for these types of surfaces you can choose from several other materials: *Phong*, *PhongE*, and *Blinn*.

Both phong and blinn shading models approximate the surface physics of incident light reflecting off a smooth surface. They are named after computer scientists Bui Tuong Phong and James Blinn.

The **Specular Shading** attributes on these three material types control how much the light rays cohere as they are reflected off the surface. If the light rays are reflected at close to the same angle, a tight highlight results. If the rays are more scattered, a bigger and softer highlight will result. If the rays were to become scattered enough, you would end up with the look of the lambert shading model.

At the other extreme, these shading models can simulate a mirror's almost perfectly smooth surface where very little light is absorbed and the reflected rays are very coherent.

Unlike the diffuse attribute, which is common to all of these materials, the attributes that control the specular highlight appearance have different names on each material.

Phong
Cosine Power affects the size of highlights on the surface. This attribute can be thought of as shininess. Low numbers create big highlights while high numbers produce small highlights, typically seen on very shiny surfaces.

PhongE
Roughness and **Highlight Size** work together to affect the size and look of the highlight.

Blinn
Eccentricity affects the size of highlights on the surface. Very shiny surfaces will need low values to produce a small and strong highlight, while surfaces like brushed metal will need higher values to produce a large highlight.

Using blinn, phong, or phongE?

While all three of these materials produce specular highlights, they each provide very different visual results. This visual impact is likely to be the determining factor in terms of which one to use, although it is worth noting that there is a slight increase in rendering time associated with using more complex materials such as blinn. The order of rendering performance from fastest to slowest is:

- phongE
- phong
- blinn

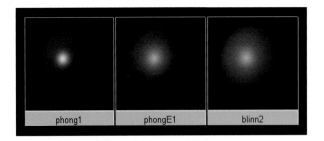

Comparison of materials phong, phongE, and blinn

Phong is less complex than blinn; it does not take into account changes in specularity due to the angle at which you are viewing the surface.

Blinn is a more sophisticated and true-to-life shading model, in which surfaces appear shinier at more severe angles. This can be controlled by the **Specular Roll Off** attribute on the blinn material. **Specular Roll Off** also allows surfaces to reflect more of their surroundings when viewed at glancing angles. The following images show the effect of this attribute on reflectivity:

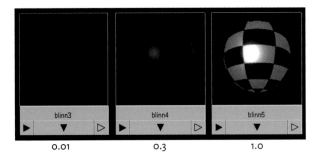

Effect of Specular Roll Off on reflectivity (Reflected Color mapped with checker)

> **Tip:** Use a **Specular Roll Off** value of **0.3** to simulate a wet surface, such as wet paint.

You will also see that the Specular Roll Off affects the transition between the Specular Color and the Diffuse Color.

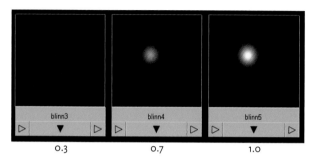

Effect of Specular Roll Off on transition from Specular Color to Diffuse Color

> **Tip:** The soft highlights on blinn surfaces are less likely to exhibit roping or flickering than the harder highlights on phong surfaces. Use the blinn material for surfaces with bump or displacement to reduce highlight roping or flickering.

Specialized surface materials

So far you have looked at the most frequently used materials. There are several other materials in Maya. These materials are:

- anisotropic shaders
- layered shaders
- ramp shaders
- shading maps
- surface shaders
- *Use Background* shaders

The anisotropic shader

The purpose of the *anisotropic* shader is to simulate surfaces that have micro-facet grooves when the specular highlight tends to be perpendicular to the direction of the grooves. If an anisotropic surface is spun against the grooves, the shape and location of the highlight will change depending on how the groove direction changes. Examples of uses for this material are satin, silk, nylon, CDs, etc.

Anisotropic material

Note: *The image shown above was rendered from the file 01-satinOrnament.ma from the support_files. There are also other anisotropic shaders for you to render in the Hypershade.*

In the following exercise, you will create and apply an anisotropic material to a falling CD, reproducing the rainbow highlights characteristic of a CD's underside. Later in this lesson you will complete the CD using a layered shader.

1 **Scene file**

- **Open** the scene file called *01-anisoCD_01.ma*.

  This file contains a NURBS disk that was animated as a rigid body colliding with a ground object. The simulation has been baked to allow scrubbing in the Time Slider. The CD geometry is made up of different pieces so different materials can be applied to the various sections. All pieces are parented under one rigid body node.

2 **Layout**

- Select **Panels → Saved Layouts → Hypershade/Render/Persp**.

- In the *Perspective* view, select **Panels → Perspective → camera**.

  The camera is already animated for this exercise. Make sure when you render that you are rendering this camera.

3 Create and assign an anisotropic material

- Use the **Create** menu in the **Hypershade** to create an **Anisotropic** material.
- **Assign** it to *mainCDbody* and *mediumRing*.

4 Tune the anisotropic material

- Set the following values:

    Diffuse to **0.05**;

    Angle to **180**;

    Spread X to **37**;

    Spread Y to **0.1**;

    Roughness to **0.4**;

    Fresnel Index to **8.4**.

Note: *The Diffuse value should be low because this material is meant to simulate the smooth plastic coating on the underside of a CD. Nearly all reflected light from a very smooth surface will be represented by the specular component. The microgrooves in this coating will produce anisotropic highlights controlled by the following attributes.*

Spread X

Controls how much the grooves spread out in the X-direction. The range is from **0.1** to **100**. (The X-direction is the surface's U-direction, rotated counterclockwise by the **Angle** attribute.) When this value is increased, the specular highlight shrinks in that direction, making the surface appear smoother. When the value is decreased, the highlight spreads out more in that direction, making the surface appear less smooth.

Spread Y

Controls how much the grooves spread out in the Y-direction. It ranges from **0.1** to **100**. (The Y-direction is perpendicular to the X-direction.) The effect of this attribute is similar to **Spread X**.

Roughness

Controls the overall roughness of the surface. It ranges from **0.01** to **1.0**, with larger values giving a rougher appearance. As this value is increased, the specular highlights are more spread out. This value will also affect the reflectivity of the material if the **Anisotropic Reflectivity** is turned **On**.

Angle

Defines the X and Y directions on the surface relative to the surface's intrinsic U and V directions. X is the U direction, rotated counterclockwise by the **Angle** attribute. These X and Y directions are used by the shader to place the microgrooves that control the anisotropic properties of the shader. This value ranges from **0** to **360 degrees**.

Fresnel Refractive Index

Affects the look of the anisotropic highlight. (If the material is transparent and you are raytracing, it does not affect the way light from other objects bends when passing through the material.) As you increase this attribute, the highlight becomes brighter.

For transparent objects, you may want to set the **Fresnel Index** to match the object's **Refractive Index**. This will give the most physically accurate result for the highlight.

If **Anisotropic Reflectivity** is turned **On**, the reflectivity of the material is calculated directly from its roughness. If this attribute is turned **Off**, the value in reflectivity is used instead.

5 IPR Render

- Go to frame **57**.
- Select **IPR → IPR Render → camera.**

  A variety of highlights will be clearly visible in the render.

- **Define** a tuning region that encompasses the entire CD.

  Note the quality and shape of the specular highlights. They are long and spread out across the surface, not round.

6 Map Specular Color

The colored highlights that occur on CDs generally run from the inside of the CD to the outer edge and are typically a variety of colors from the visible light spectrum. On real CDs, these rainbow colors are caused by the diffraction of light (diffraction is the term for light splitting into its individual wavelengths as it passes through a medium such as a prism). A colored ramp texture will be used to fake the appearance of diffraction.

- In the Hypergraph, show the top and bottom tabs.
- Select the **Textures** tab.
- **MMB+drag** the rainbowSpecRamp texture onto the *anisotropic1* material and select **Specular Color** from the drop-down menu.

7 Adjust the lighting

When working with the anisotropic material, controlling the direction, distribution, and intensity of the lighting is vital to the success of the look you are trying to attain. Normally, multiple lights are required at various angles to the surface to see the anisotropic highlights well.

- Increase the **Intensity** of the *spotLight2* to see the impact it has on the brightness of the highlights.
- **Move** the light to get a feel for the significance of its intensity and position relative to the surface.

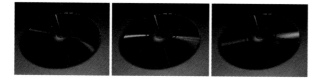

Position and intensity of spotLight2 modified

8 Save the file

- **Save** the file, as you will complete the CD in the next exercise.

> **Note:** *A movie file called ansioCD.mov is available in the support_files folder to show the final results.*

The layered shader

The *layered shader* can be used in two different ways. It can be used to layer materials, or to layer textures. Since there is a node specifically designed for layering textures that will be covered in the next lesson, you will experiment here only with the material layering capabilities.

When using the layered shader node, ask yourself if you need to see different material types on different areas of the same surface, or if you need to see different materials over the same area, such as a clear coat over car paint. If all you need is to overlay textures, you should use a layered texture rather than a layered shader. It is best to avoid using layered shaders unnecessarily because they are very expensive to render.

In this exercise, you will use the layered shader to combine two different materials.

1 Create materials to use as layers

Before you can layer anything, you will need some simple materials.

- In the **Hypershade**, create a *phong* and a *lambert* material.
- Set the *phong* material to **blue** and the *lambert* material to **red**.
- **Map** a checker to the **Transparency** of the *phong* material.
- Change the **Repeat UV** attribute to **8** and **8** on the *place2Dtexture* node for the *checker* texture.

2 Create a layered shader node

- **Create** a layered shader node.
- Open the **Attribute Editor** for the *layeredShader* node.

3 Connect the materials to the layered shader node

- **MMB+drag** the **red** *lambert* into the **Layered Shader Attributes** section.

- **MMB+drag** the **blue** *phong* into the **Layered Shader Attributes** section.

  *You will notice that each time you drag a material into the **Layered Shader Attributes** section, a new icon appears. These icons represent the layers.*

- Click on the small **x** under the green layer icon to **remove** it.

  The green icon is simply the default layer that you can get rid of once you have added your own layers.

4 Shuffle the layers

You now have a layered shader with two materials in it. However, the swatch for the layered shader will appear to be completely red. This is because the *red lambert* material (without any transparency) is on top of the *blue phong*. You need to change the order of the layers in order to see the phong on top of the lambert.

- In the **Attribute Editor** for the layered shader, **MMB+drag** the *lambert* icon to the right of the *phong* icon.

  You should now see both the layers in the swatch.

Tip: *The order of the layers from left to right in the Attribute Editor represents the layer order from top to bottom on the surface.*

5 IPR render the scene

- Create a **sphere**.

- Assign the *layeredShader* to the *sphere* and launch an IPR render.

  You will notice that the specular highlight falls across both the phong and the lambert regions of the surface (because even though the phong is transparent in those regions, its specular highlight is visible). This essentially defeats the purpose of using the layered materials.

  Because different parts of the surface show different materials, you will need to change the layers again.

6 Manipulate the layers

- With IPR still running, **break** the connection between the *checker* and *phong* in the **Hypershade**.

- **Create** a connection between the *checker* and the *lambert*'s **Transparency** attribute.

- In the **Attribute Editor** for the layered shader, swap the layers using the **MMB** as you did earlier.

  Notice how in the IPR render, the specular highlight no longer shows on both the red and blue regions.

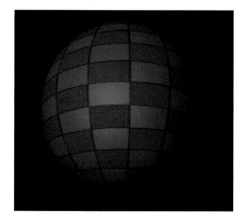

The IPR render

> **Tip:** *In more complex layered materials, you may need to apply a specular map to control the specular highlights on different layers.*

The shading network should look similar to the following:

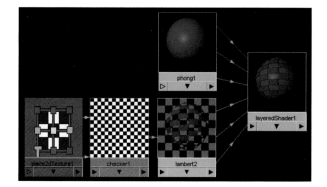

Layered shader shading network

Layered shader example

In this exercise, you will complete the CD that you started earlier in this chapter. You will use a layered shader to add the foil base visible under the clear grooved plastic on the underside of the CD.

1 Scene file

- Use the file you saved earlier.

   OR

- **Open** the file named *o1-anisoCD_o2.ma*.

2 Layout

- Select **Panels → Saved Layouts → Hypershade/Render/Persp**.
- In the *Perspective* view, select **Panels → Perspective → camera**.

3 Create a layered shader

- Create a **Layered Shader** material in the **Hypershade**.
- Assign the *layeredShader1* to *mainCDbody* and *mediumRing*.
- Open the **Attribute Editor** for the *layeredShader1*.
- **MMB+drag** the *anisotropic1* from the **Hypershade** into the **Layered Shader Attribute** section in the **Attribute Editor** for the *layeredShader1*.
- Click on the **X** under the green default layer icon to **remove** it.

4 Launch an IPR

- **IPR render** frame **57** for test rendering throughout this exercise.

5 Create a blinn for the foil coating

A blinn material will be used to create a silver/gold foil base coating on the CD. This layer will go under the anisotropic clear plastic coating.

- **Create** a **Blinn** material in **Hypershade**.
- **MMB+drag** the *blinn* into the **Layered Shader Attribute** section in the **Attribute Editor** for the *layeredShader1*.

   At this point, you will not be able to see the blinn layer because the anisotropic material has no transparency.

6 Adjust the transparency on the anisotropic material

- **Increase** the **Transparency** attribute on the *anisotropic* material to light grey for clear plastic.

   This will reveal the blinn layer.

7 **Tune the blinn material**
- **Adjust** the *blinn* attributes to get a silver look.

> **Tip:** *A good metallic material would use very low* **Diffuse**, *high* **Specular Roll Off**, *and low* **Eccentricity**.

8 **Add a reflection map**

Although the Diffuse, Eccentricity, and Specular Roll Off will be the primary attributes you tune on the blinn shader, adding a reflection map will enhance the visual impact of the foil.

- **Map** the **Reflected Color** attribute on the *blinn* with an **Env Chrome** from the **Environment Textures** section of the **Create Render Node** window.

This makes the CD appear to be reflecting a pseudo-environment.

- **Adjust** the **Reflectivity** attribute to increase or decrease the brightness of the reflection map.

- **Adjust** the colors on the *envChrome* texture if you do not want a blue look.

9 **Make final adjustments**

If you have been test rendering at the same frame, you should check some other frames throughout the animation to make sure the values you are using provide expected results.

The camera angle and lighting position are important parts of the overall effect in this example. Experiment with different lighting to see how it affects the overall image.

The layered shader lets you combine the features of the various shading models to produce one final result. This extra flexibility does come at the expense of increased render times, but it also gives you results that may be otherwise difficult to achieve.

10 **Save your work**
- The final scene file is called *01-anisoCD_03.ma*.

> **Tip:** *The file anisoCDBlendCol.mb demonstrates an alternate method of achieving a similar appearance in the shading, but with the use of a blendColors utility node rather than a layered shader.*

The ramp shader

The *ramp shader* allows extra control over the way color changes with light angle, brightness, or the viewing angle (facing ratio). You can easily give your objects a flat, toon-like look by using the ramp shader.

This shader shares many attributes with other materials. All the color-related attributes are controlled by ramps. There are also graphs for defining *Specular Roll Off* and *Reflectivity*, improving performance by avoiding complex shading networks and making toon shading easier to achieve.

In this exercise, you will use a ramp shader to give some bouncing balls a flat, toon-like look.

1   Scene file

- **Open** the *01-bounce_01.ma* scene file.

  This file consists of a number of spheres that use dynamics to bounce on a floor.

Note: *There is also a very large area light above the scene, which is why the illumination is so bright.*

2   Create a ramp shader

- Create a **Ramp Shader** material in the **Hypershade**.

- **Assign** the *rampShader* to all the spheres.

- Open the **Attribute Editor** for the *rampShader*.

  You will notice that many of the common material attributes are controlled by ramps.

3   Edit the ramp attributes to create a toon shader

- Under the **Color** section, create another ramp handle in the ramp field by clicking in the field.

- Set the **Selected Position** of this ramp handle to **0.15**.

- Select the *first ramp handle*, and change its color to a bright blue.

- Select **Interpolation** and change it to **None**.

  This will cause a crisp line between the different colors.

- Select the *second ramp handle* and set a darker blue.

- Select **Interpolation** and change it to **None**.

Note: *To set a color using RGB values, open the Color Chooser window and under the* **Sliders** *section, change* **HSV** *to* **RGB**. *You can now use the three sliders as R, G, and B values.*

- Change **Color Input** to **Brightness**.

4 **Test render the scene**

- **Play** the scene up to frame **85**.

- **Render** to see the results.

    Notice that there are no outlines, just flat bands of color.

Ramp shader so far

5 **Edit the Incandescence attribute**

- Under the **Incandescence** section, create another ramp handle.

- Set the **Selected Position** of this ramp handle to **0.3**.

- Select the *first ramp handle* and under **Selected Color**, change the **HSV values** to **-1,-1,-1**.

Note: *By setting the incandescence to negative values, you are forcing the light to be absorbed on the outer edge of the geometry rather than being emitted.*

- Change the **Interpolation** to **None**.

- **Render** the scene.

    Notice flat bands of color surrounded by a black outline.

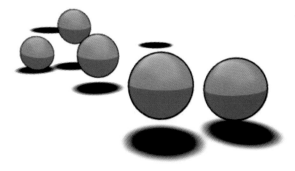

Ramp shader with outline

6 Add specular shading

- Under the **Specular Shading** section, change **Specularity** to **1.0** and **Eccentricity** to **0.06**.

This will change the size and brightness of the highlight.

Ramp shader with strong specular

Note: *The rectangular highlight is a result of the area light.*

7 Save your work

- The final scene file is called *01-bounce_02.ma*.

Note: *A movie file called bounce.avi is available on the accompanying DVD to show the final results.*

Shading maps

A *shading map* is a node that allows you to remap the output from a material to create custom shading results. Recall that a material is a mathematical formula or set of instructions on how to shade the surface. The purpose of the shading map is to allow you to control the final shaded results to go beyond what is possible with standard materials.

A shading map allows complete control over the transition from the highlight to the shaded area of a surface. For example, you could achieve a cartoon look by mapping a ramp texture to get simple banded shading.

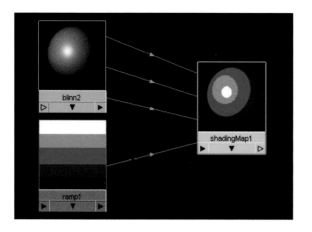

Shading map used with a ramp to produce toon-like blinn shading

Even more complex materials that have a translucent scattering layer can sometimes have a non-lambert falloff in diffuse intensity. This can be roughly simulated using the shading map to help get more natural-looking skin, for example.

This can be a very powerful feature because it allows you to remap the output of any shading model using a shading map. The remapped outputs of different shading models can then be recombined to create a new shading model.

Car paint exercise

Shading maps combined with a layered shader can be used to render realistic metallic paint. This allows for more variation in the look of the paint to avoid flat, monochromatic surfaces.

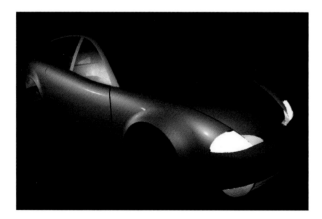

Clear coat and metallic highlight

Car paint can be represented in many ways. The purpose of this exercise is to show the use of a shading map for the control and placement of highlights on a car body.

1   **Scene file**

   • **Open** the file named *01-car_01.ma*.

2   **Create shaders**

   • In the **Hypershade**, create the following nodes:

      Layered Shader;

      Blinn;

      Shading Map.

3   **Add the shading map to the layered shader**

   • Open the **Attribute Editor** for the *layeredShader1*.

   • **MMB+drag** the *shadingMap1* material from **Hypershade** to the **Layered Shader Attributes** section of the *layeredShader1* node.

   • **Remove** the green layer from the *layeredShader1* node.

   • **Assign** the *layeredShader1* material to the car's *bodyGroup*.

4   **Tweak the shading map**

   • Select the *shadingMap1* material and open its **Attribute Editor**.

   In the **Shading Map Attributes** *section, you will notice two attributes called* **Shading Map Color** *and* **Color**.

   • **MMB+drag** the *blinn1* material from the **Hypershade** to the **Color** attribute of the **Shading Map Attributes** section of the *shadingMap1* node.

   • Set the following for *blinn1*:

      Color to **black**;

      Diffuse to **0.0**;

      Eccentricity to **0.45**;

      Specular Roll Off to **0.42**;

      Specular Color to **white**.

      Reflectivity to **0.0**.

5 Shading Map Color

- **Map** the *shadingMap1*'s **Shading Map Color** attribute with a **Ramp** texture.
- In the **Attribute Editor** for the new ramp texture, define four handles as follows:

    Handle at **Position 1.0, RGB 1.0, 1.0, 1.0**;

    Handle at **Position 0.9, RGB 0.71, 0.85, 0.85**;

    Handle at **Position 0.1, RGB 0.22, 0.25, 0.32**;

    Handle at **Position 0.0, RGB 0.0, 0.0, 0.0**.

6 Clear coat layer

Just as with a real car, a clear polished shader needs to be layered onto a matte base to create two separate highlight regions.

- In the **Hypershade**, create a **Blinn** material and set the following:

    Color to **black**;

    Transparency to **white**;

    Diffuse to **0.0**;

    Eccentricity to **0.09**;

    Specular Roll Off to **-10.0**;

    Reflectivity to **0.0**;

- **Rename** the new blinn to *clearCoat*.

Ramp attributes

7 Add the clear coat to the layered shader

- **MMB** the *clearCoat material* into the *layeredShader1* node's **Attribute Editor**.
- Use the **MMB** to reorder layers so the clear coat layer is in front of the base layer.

8 Reflection layer

Although reflections can be added to the clear coat layer, custom reflection effects will be isolated with their own layer.

- Create another **Blinn** shader.

    This shader will be used to control reflections.

- Set the **Color** to **black**.
- Increase the **Transparency** to **white**.
- Decrease the **Eccentricity** to **0.01** and increase the **Specular Roll Off** to **0.95**.

  This will ensure that the reflection will only be seen on angles oblique to the camera's eye.
- Click in the **Specular Color** attribute and set its **HSV** to **0, 0, 4**.

  This will set the specular color to superwhite, which will allow you to clearly see the reflections caused by the high Specular Roll Off attribute.
- Lower the **Reflectivity** to **0.05** to avoid washed out reflections.

Tip: *You must set* **Raytracing** *to* **On** *in the Render Settings to see reflections.*

- **Rename** the new blinn to *reflectivity*.

9 Add the reflection blinn to the layered shader
- **MMB** the reflection *reflectivity* into the *layeredShader1* node's **Attribute Editor**.
- Use the **MMB** to reorder layers so the reflection layer is in front of the clear coat layer.

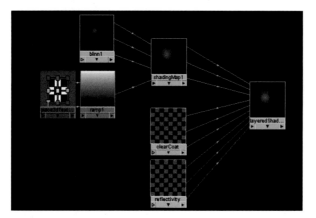

A layered shader network using a shading map for control of highlights

10 Set your Render Settings for raytracing
- In the **Raytracing Quality** section of the **Render Settings** window, turn **Raytracing On**.

11 Test render the scene.
- The final scene file is called *01-car_02.ma*.

The surface shader

The surface shader is a lightweight pass-through node that simply allows you to translate the names of any node's outputs to the names required for the shader to be a valid surface material.

What this means is that a node must directly connect to a surface material port of a shading group and have at least one of the following specially named output attributes to be a valid node:

- *outColor*
- *outTransparency*
- *outGlowColor*

If the node connected to the surface material port of a shading group does not have at least one of the above attributes, none of the objects assigned to that shading group will render.

> **Note:** *It does not matter which attribute of a node is connected to the surface material port of a shading group; only the* **outColor**, **outTransparency,** *and* **outGlowColor** *attributes of the connected node will be used.*

The surface shader node is simply a means to translate an arbitrary network of Maya or user-written nodes with randomly named output attributes into what the renderer will recognize as a shading network.

Use Background shader

The *Use Background* shader becomes important in workflows involving compositing in the production pipeline. It allows a surface to mask other objects behind it by using the background color. This will be covered in further detail later in this book.

Conclusion

Materials are the foundation for shading your surfaces. A material is a set of instructions that describes how the surface of an object will look when rendered. It is not just a collection of texture maps, but also a description of how light will fall across the surface. Maya provides a number of tools to help you define the materials in your scene.

In the next lesson, you will learn about procedural and file textures that can be used in shading networks.

Textures

One of the most important aspects of a scene is the look of the textures mapped to the various objects and surfaces. These textures give the objects relevance to their surroundings, enhancing the appearance and believability of the scene. It is important to keep in mind that this is a slower process than most would think; a certain amount of tweaking is involved in designing and applying textures.

In this lesson, you will learn the following:

- How to use textures to build shading networks
- Texture placement and conversion
- File texture filtering and the use of BOT (Block Order Texture) files
- Displacement mapping
- mental ray Bake Sets

Project 01

46

Layered texture

The layered texture node is designed to composite multiple textures using various blend modes directly inside Autodesk® Maya®.

It is important to understand the difference between the layered shader and the layered texture node. The layered texture node allows you to composite textures together using several blending operations such as add, multiply, subtract, etc., while the layered shader has only one level of transparency to blend textures.

In the following exercise, a *layered texture* node will be used to make your character dirty and add a bandage on the cheek.

1 Open the file

- **Open** the scene file called *02-layeredTexture_01.ma*.

2 Interaction and render optimizations

- Make sure to set the *smooth* attribute on the master node to **1**.

- **Hide** the *rigLayer*.

3 Graph the skin material

- In the **Hypershade**, graph the material already assigned to the face of the Constructor.

4 Create a layered texture node

- **Create** a **Layered Texture** by selecting **Create → Layered Texture**.

- **MMB+drag** *layeredTexture1* onto the Constructor's material and connect it to **Color**.

- In the **Attribute Editor** for *layeredTexture1*, click inside the **Layered Texture Attributes** section twice to create a total of **three layers**.

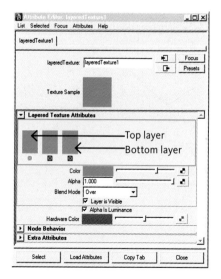

Layered texture attributes

> **Note:** *Just as in the layered shader, the top layer is farthest to the left and the bottom layer is on the far right. You can also rearrange the order of the layers at any time by* **MMB+dragging** *them in the* **Layered Texture Attributes** *section.*

5 Map the bottom layer

- Click on the bottom layer icon to make it the active layer.
- Make sure the **Blend Mode** is set to **None**.
- **Map** the **Color** attribute with the original file texture used to texture the Constructor.

  The bottom layer will not be visible yet because the middle and top layers are not set up.

- Temporarily make the top and middle layers invisible by clicking on the layer icon and then turning **Off** the **Layer is Visible** checkbox.

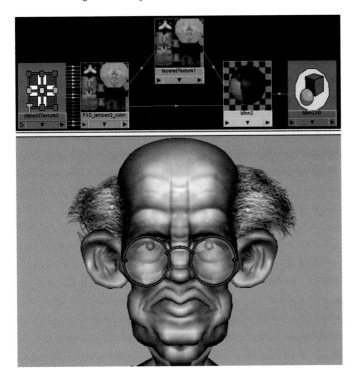

Bottom layer only

6 Map the middle layer

- In the **Attribute Editor** for the *layeredTexture1* node, click the *middle* layer icon to make it active.
- Turn the **Layer is Visible** checkbox back **On** for this layer.
- **Map** the **Color** attribute with a **Fractal** texture.

- Set the **Blend Mode** to **Multiply**.

  *This mode multiplies fractal1 and the skin texture. In areas where the fractal is white, the skin is unchanged because white is equal to **1, 1, 1**. Whichever color is multiplied by 1 gives the original color. Where the fractal is black, the skin becomes black because anything multiplied by **0, 0, 0** gives 0.*

- Set the *fractal*'s **Threshold** attribute to **0.5**.

  The fractal is now whiter with black spots of dirt. This will give a nice dirty look to the Constructor's skin.

Dirt layer multiplied with skin color layer

Note: *The hardware texturing might look very low resolution in the viewport since Maya will trade compositing quality for speed. The texture will be displayed appropriately in renders. To increase the display quality in the viewport, increase the **Texture Resolution** for the skin material.*

7   Map the top layer

- In the **Attribute Editor** for the *layeredTexture1* node, click on the *top* layer icon to make it active.

- Turn the **Layer is Visible** flag back **On** for this layer.

- Set the **Blend Mode** to **Over**.

  This mode will add the top layer over the other layers.

- Click the **Map** button for the **Color** attribute of the top layer.

- In the **Create Render Node** window, specify **As projection**, and then create a **File Texture**.
- **Browse** for the file called *bandage.tif* found in the *sourceimages* directory.

8   Tweak the texture projection

- **MMB+drag** the *projection1* onto the layered texture node and select **Other...**

  Doing so will open the Connection Editor.

- **Connect** the **Out Alpha** to the **Inputs** → **Inputs[0]** → **Inputs[0].Alpha** attribute.
- Turn **Off** the **Wrap** placement attributes in the **Effects** section of the projection node so the texture will not be repeated across the character when you place it.
- **Position** the *place3dTexture* node so the bandage is on the Constructor's forehead.
- **Test render** your scene to see the result of the shading network.

Texture placement for the bandage texture

- Set the **Default Color** attribute to **black** in the **Color Balance** section of the *projection1* node in the **Attribute Editor**.

  *This step is important because adjusting the **Coverage** attributes on the texture placement in the last step has exposed the **Default Color** surrounding the bandage. Because the **Blend Mode** is **Over**, setting the **Default Color** value to **black** leaves the layers beneath unchanged.*

Bandage layer adjusted

9 Save your work

- The final scene file is called *02-layeredTexture_02.ma*.

Using ramps to combine textures

Ramp textures are useful tools for developing textures. A ramp does not only blend colors, it also allows you to combine textures together and control how they blend.

If you look at a ramp in the Attribute Editor, it has position markers that define a specific U or V value along the texture. If you select one of these position markers in the Attribute Editor, there will be a color associated with it. You can then map that position marker's color and, depending on the interpolation settings, the texture will be blended with the other colors of the ramp.

The following example shows a couple of possibilities for using ramps to create texture effects in Maya.

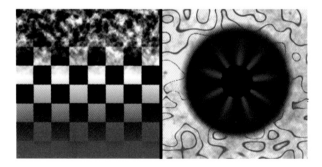

Ramp textures

> **Note:** *The ramp itself will not show the actual texture blend, but the swatch representing the ramp will.*

Dirty buggy

In this exercise, you will build a shading network for the Constructor's buggy. You will create a shading network using various connected nodes to achieve a dirty metallic look.

1 Open the file

- **Open** the file called *02-buggy_01.ma*.

2 Create a ramp shader

You will start by assigning a shader to the buggy in order to be able to use the IPR.

- **Graph** in the **Hypershade** the materials already on the buggy.
- **Create** a **Ramp Shader** and **rename** it *buggyShader*.
- **RMB** on the *blinn6* shader, which textures the wheels and bumper, and choose **Select Objects With Material**.
- **Assign** the *buggyShader* to the selection.
- Set the following for the *buggyShader*:

  Color to **light grey**;

  Color Input to **Facing Angle**;

  Specular Color to **white**.

- **Create** a new handle in the middle of the **Color** ramp attribute.
- Click the **map** button next to the ramp widget, then scroll at the bottom of the **Create Render Node** window and select a **Layered Texture**.
- **Rename** the new layered texture node to *buggyLayeredTexture*.

3 Create the base layer

You will now work up the base layer on the layered texture to create the look of uneven metal.

> **Note:** *Launch the IPR in order to see your changes.*

- In the **Attribute Editor** for *buggyLayeredTexture*, highlight the layer icon.

  This will be the base metal layer.

- Set the **Color** attribute of the selected layer to a **light grey**.

  The base layer could now use a fractal texture to break up the solid color.

- **Map** the new layer with a **Solid Fractal** from the **3D Textures** section.
- Set the following for the new *fractal*:

    Threshold to **0.4**;

    Amplitude to **0.5**;

    Color Gain to **light grey**.

The fractal texture on the buggy

4 Add a dirt layer

You will now add a new layer to the layered texture to create a dirty look.

- In the **Attribute Editor** for the *buggyLayeredTexture*, create a new layer.
- **MMB+drag** the new layer to the left of the other layers.
- Set the new layer's **Blend Mode** to **Over**.
- **Map** a **Granite** to the **Color** of the new layer.

5 Define an alpha for the dirt layer

The granite texture now covers the entire surface, but in this step you will define an alpha to make the granite look like dirt patches.

- In the **Attribute Editor** for the *buggyLayeredTexture*, **map** the **Alpha** attribute with a **Ramp**.

Tip: *Make sure to set the 2D texture creation mode back to **Normal** in the **Create Render Node** window.*

- Set the *ramp*'s **Type** to **V Ramp**.
- Set the bottom of the *ramp* to be **black** and delete the middle ramp handle.
- Highlight the bottom ramp handle, and then set the **Selected Position** to **0.7**.

- Highlight the top ramp handle, and then **map** the **Selected Color** with a **Solid Fractal**.
- Tweak the new *solidFractal* as follows:

    Threshold to **0.7**;

    Amplitude to **10.0**;

    Depth to **8.0, 8.0**;

    Invert to **On**;

The dirt layer

6 Bump mapping

In order to give a nice bumpy effect to the dirt, you will map the layered texture to the bump mapping of the ramp shader.

- **MMB+drag** the *buggyLayeredTexture* on the *buggyShader* and select **bump map** from the pop-up menu.
- Select the newly created *bump2d* node and set the **Bump Depth** attribute to **-0.2**.

The bump increases the texture's richness

7 Save your work

- The final scene is saved as *02-buggy_02.ma*.

Placement nodes

Because the shading networks created so far consist of 3D textures' placement, *place3dTexture* nodes have been created in the scene. These nodes can be manipulated to control the placement of the textures on the geometry.

1 Moving placement nodes

- To adjust a texture placement node, select a *place3dTexture* node in the **Hypershade** or a green 3D manipulator in a view.

- **Move**, **rotate,** and **scale** the 3D manipulator to see its effect on the surfaces.

> **Tip:**   *When the placement of textures is identical, it may be useful to share one texture placement for all 3D textures to make it easier to adjust them simultaneously. To do so, simply* **MMB+drag** *a place3dTexture node onto another 3D texture in the* **Hypershade,** *and select* **Default** *from the pop-up menu. This is also true for place2dTexture nodes.*

2 Parent 3D placement nodes

Since 3D textures have a *place3dTexture* node in the scene, the texture will slide on the surface of animated objects because the model will be moving through the 3D texture. For models that do not deform, it is a good idea to parent 3D texture nodes to the geometry in order to move both at the same time, thus preventing the texture from moving separately from the model.

- Select the *place3dTextures* and **parent** them to their respective surfaces.

> **Note:**   *In the case of deforming surfaces, you should use* **Texture → Create Texture Reference Object**.

Texture reference objects

When using 3D textures or projections on deforming objects, parenting placement nodes will not fix the crawling or swimming of the textures, so you need to consider using either a *texture reference object* or converting the textures to a 2D file.

A *texture reference object* is a templated copy of the original object that does not deform and is a reference for texture placement on the original object. The original object can then be deformed, and the 3D or projected texture placement information will be based on the non-deforming reference copy.

Some advantages of using this method are:

- It is quick to set-up.
- There is no fixed resolution, unlike converting to 2D file textures.
- You have the ability to animate 3D texture attributes.
- It does not require storing texture maps on disk.

Some disadvantages are:

- File size can increase because extra copies of geometry must be made.
- Noisy 3D textures can sometimes look like they are crawling or shimmering when animated.
- 3D textures can take longer to render than mapped file textures.

The following example demonstrates the need for special handling of the 3D textures due to deformations applied to the buggy. In the following steps, you will create texture reference objects to prevent swimming textures.

3 Scene file

- **Open** the scene called *02-buggyLattice_01.ma*.

> **Tip:** *In this file, the place3dTexture nodes are not parented to the geometry. Do not parent the place3dTexture nodes to animated transforms when you are planning to work with texture reference objects.*

- **Batch render** a small sequence or **test render** different frames in the animation to see the effect of the textures sliding on the model.

4 Create a texture reference object

- Go to frame **1**.

  This is the original position of the geometry used when texturing. You are guaranteed that the textures will look good at that position.

- Select the *buggy*.
- Select **Texturing → Create Texture Reference Object**.

  The texture reference objects are created and templated.

> **Tip:** *It is simpler to always create the texture reference objects after the texturing process and before animating the models.*

- **Batch render** a small sequence or **test render** different frames in the animation to see that the textures are now sticking to the surfaces.

Convert to file textures

Another option when dealing with animated or deforming geometry involves converting textures into file texture parametric maps. Once the conversion is done, the file textures are automatically saved to disk and mapped onto the surfaces.

Some advantages of using this technique are:

- It is possible to touch-up or otherwise manipulate a file texture in an Image Editor.
- It is generally much faster to render a file texture than a network of complex procedural textures.
- It is often easier to fix texture problems once the textures are converted to file textures.

Some disadvantages are:

- You can no longer animate texture attributes.
- The resolution is fixed.
- It can require large amounts of disk space to store image files.
- Very high resolution image files can require large amounts of memory during rendering.
- Converting to file textures for many surfaces will produce a separate material for each surface.

How to convert to file textures

- Select the texture, material, or shading group that you wish to convert.
- **Shift-select** the surface you want to create a file texture for.
- In the **Hypershade**, select **Edit → Convert to File Texture**.

   The options for this command allow you to specify the resolution of the new image file, whether or not anti-aliasing will be applied, and whether or not to bake the lighting into the resulting texture.

Converting textures on the buggy

In this exercise, you will convert the projected and 3D procedural textures to 2D file textures.

1 **Scene File**

- **Open** the scene called *02-buggyLattice_01.ma*.

   This is the same scene file as the previous exercise.

2 **Convert the texture**

- Select the *buggy* surface.
- Click on the **Graph Materials on Selected Objects** button in the **Hypershade**.

   This will display the shading network assigned to this surface.

- **Shift-select** the *buggyShader* material node.

  Both the surface and the material node are selected.

- Select **Edit → Convert to File Texture → ❑**.

- In the options, set the following:

   Anti-aliasing to **Off**;

   Background mode to **Extend edge color**;

   X and **Y resolution** to **1024**;

   File format to **Tiff**.

- Click the **Convert and Close** button.

> **Note:** *Baking may take a few seconds depending on system performance.*

The command will bake the 3D textures into one file per channel (color, bump, etc.), and they will be saved in the sourceimages folder of the current project. A new material is created and assigned to the surface. The original material remains intact and can be reassigned if needed.

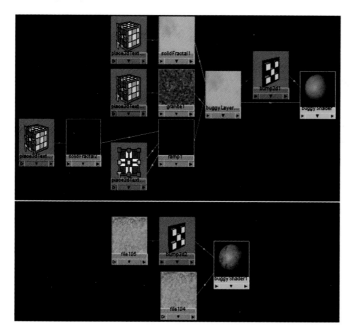

Old and converted shading network

Details about converting to file texture

- When you specify the shading node and surface to convert, depending on the shading node's type (i.e., texture, shader, shading group) and depending on how many surfaces are specified, the conversion command will run on each surface for each channel in the shading network.

> **Note:** *For example, if a blinn is chosen and there are connections to color and transparency, the command will run twice: once on the node connected to color and once using the node connected to transparency.*

- A discontinuity will be noticeable if normals are flipped and the **Double-Sided** option is turned On. The shading operates using camera normals, so the normal flip will occur around the silhouette of the surface as seen from the active camera. This is turned Off by default when converting.

- When the **Bake Shading Group Lighting** option is used, shadows are not included in the computed result. To include the shadow information, turn On the **Bake Shadows** option.

- **Bake Transparency** specifies whether to compute transparency when baking lights. This will sample both the color and transparency of the network.

- The options under **UV Range** specify how much of the surface to sample in UV space. For example, if you select one or more faces on a poly object, only the selected faces are sampled rather than the whole surface.

- Bump mapping has the effect of tweaking normals depending on a texture. You may want to convert a bump map, but be aware that the normals cannot be represented as a pixel map.

- When **Anti-alias** is turned on, the renderer doubles the resolution of the computed texture and averages four pixels to get the resulting pixel color.

- The active camera is important if sampling needs information from the normal camera. Most rendering nodes (for example, crater or marble) are not sensitive to the camera used but there are others (for example, camera projection and baked lighting) that will depend closely on the camera used. In these situations you should be aware that the active camera will be used.

- The conversion will name the output by combining the sampled node's name with the surface's name, such as *lambert1body.tif*. If this file already exists, the version number will be appended to the file. The file will be written to the *sourceimages* folder of the current project.

Limitations

- Depending on how the isoparms are positioned on NURBS surfaces, the samples could all be computed in a very small area of the surface.

- If polygons are used, the surface must have unique normalized UVs. If a polygon has non-unique UVs, or UVs are missing, no error messages are generated and the conversion will fail.

Disable initial load of file texture

To load scenes faster, you can disable the initial loading of a file texture from a disk. To disable the initial loading of a file texture, do the following:

- Select a file texture.

- In the Attribute Editor's **File Attributes** section, set the **Disable File Load** attribute to **On**.

  When the scene is loaded back into Maya, that file will be prevented from loading into memory, which will load the scene faster.

Test shading networks

The **Test Texture** command allows you to render a preview at any point in a shading network that uses shading nodes (including utility nodes). This will allow you to visualize a rendered result while building complex shading networks.

In order to test render any render nodes in a shading network, do the following:

- Select a render node, and then select **Edit** → **Test Texture** from the **Hypershade** menu.

  OR

- **RMB** on a render node in the **Hypershade** and select **Test Texture.**

  A rendered image showing the texture at that point in the shading network is displayed in the Render View window.

- Select **Edit** → **Render Texture Range** → ❑ from the **Hypershade** menu, and set the options to render a texture sequence and then open it with the fcheck image viewer.

Adobe® Photoshop® (.PSD) file texture

You can use PSD file textures in Maya to do compositing based on Photoshop layer sets and alpha information. The following example will use a simple scene to illustrate this capability.

1 **Create a plane**

- **Create** a primitive **NURBS plane**.

2 Assign a lambert material

- **Create** and **assign** a **lambert** material to the **NURBS** plane.

3 Create a PSD node

- Open the **Attribute Editor** for the new *lambert* and click on the **Map** button for the **Color** attribute.

- In the **2D Textures** section of the **Create Render Node** window, create a *psdFile* node.

> **Tip:** *Make sure the creation option is set to* **Normal***.*

- In the **Attribute Editor** for the new *psdFileTex*, **browse** for the Photoshop file called *PSDFileTex.psd* from the *sourceimages* folder.

PSD file loaded

> **Note:** *You will notice that both the* **Color** *and* **Transparency** *attributes of the lambert are mapped with the PSD file. Also notice that once you have loaded the PSD file, the attributes labeled* **Link to LayerSet** *and* **Alpha to Use** *are no longer grayed out.*

4 LayerSet and Alpha to Use

The **Link to LayerSet** and **Alpha to Use** attributes allow adjustment of Photoshop layers and alpha compositing inside Maya.

- Experiment with different settings; use hardware texture shading to see the results interactively.

5 **Convert to file texture**

It is possible to convert the PSD file texture to a standard file texture.

- In the **Hypershade**, **RMB** on the PSD file texture node and choose **Convert to File Texture**.

Create a PSD Shading Network

You can also create an entire PSD shading network, which lets you use layer sets in Photoshop to paint a material's channels.

1 **Create the PSD file**

- Select the object to paint.

- Select **Texturing** → **Create PSD Network** from the **Rendering** menu set.

  The Create PSD Network option window will be displayed.

- In the **Image Name** field, enter a meaningful name.

- At the bottom of the window, highlight and move the attributes you want to paint in Photoshop to the right column.

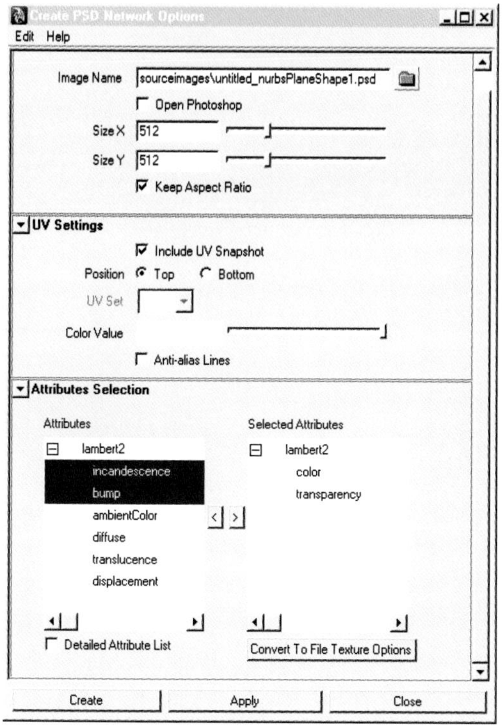

Create PSD Texture Options window

> **Tip:** *The **Include UV Snapshot** option can be very useful when you need to see the UVs in Photoshop.*

- Click the **Create** button.

2 Paint the PSD file in Photoshop

- Open the PSD file in Photoshop and paint the layers as required.
- **Save** the file.

3 Reload the file in Maya

- Select **Texturing** → **Update PSD Networks**.

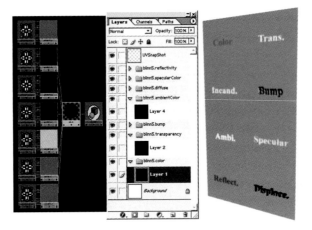

PSD shading network

File texture filtering

When rendering file textures, Maya applies texture filtering by default. The filtering is controlled by several attributes of file textures and contributes to the overall quality and speed of the final rendered image. In this section, you will look at one of the primary filter types, called *MipMapping*.

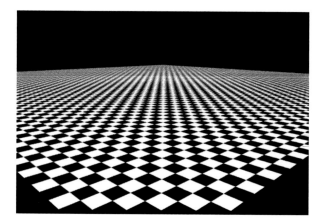

Checker filtering

Why filter file textures?

In the image shown above, a single pixel in the final image may correspond to thousands of pixels in the source checker pattern. Determining the final color for a single pixel would require an immense computation. To reduce the amount of work required to compute the final pixel color, a technique called *MipMapping* was developed to produce quicker filtering.

MipMap filtering means that Maya stores multiple resolutions of the same texture. For example, if you have a 512x512 image, Maya stores the 512x512, then 256x256, then 128x128, then 64x64, then 32x32, etc.

> **Note:** *It is most optimal for the MipMap to deal with square resolutions that are a multiple of 2. This is particularly true for bump maps, though close to square resolutions still produce very respectable results. Extreme non-square ratio textures may cause problems.*

The renderer chooses the appropriate level of file texture image to use based on how much screen coverage there is and how obliquely the object is being viewed. The further away or more oblique, the more the renderer tends to use a lower-resolution and blurry version of the texture.

How does it affect the image quality?

In terms of quality, the filtering acts like a form of anti-aliasing for textures. By using lower-resolution versions of a texture, filtering produces pixel colors that are an average of the surrounding colors on that texture map. This lends a somewhat blurry look to the receding parts of the textured surface in the rendered image.

However, the upside is that this *averaging* prevents detectable shifts in color for a single pixel from frame to frame. If the resulting distant pixel colors were precise at all times, you would see noticeable texture crawling or shimmering during animation because the same pixel could have different colors from frame to frame, depending on the viewing angle.

The trick is to strike the right balance between the sharpness of the texture you need in the final render and the amount of crawling you can tolerate in the texture during animation.

Tip: *When particular file textured surfaces are crawling, shimmering, or flickering, it is best not to experiment with the anti-aliasing shading samples first. The first choice should be to adjust the file texture's filter attribute values.*

The **Filter Size** is internally computed by Maya based on how much screen coverage there is and how obliquely the object is being viewed. The **Filter** and **Filter Offset** under the **Effects** section of the **Attribute Editor** are attributes that can be changed to alter the render.

Tip: *It is not recommended to set the **Filter** to **0**. Setting the **Filter** to **0** or a very small value will tell the renderer to ignore the internal filter size computation. This will force the renderer to use the highest level of the MipMap.*

As you can see, filtering textures provides two advantages. Instead of being very accurate about figuring out the color of a pixel far away from the camera, the renderer quickly gets texture values by interpolating between two levels of the MipMap. This makes it quicker to render. The other advantage is more aesthetic; using the filtering structure prevents noisy or shimmering texture problems.

Higher-order filter types

In some situations, adjusting the **Filter** attribute values will not help. When this occurs, the optimal solution is to employ a higher-order filter, such as the *Quadratic Filter*. The Quadratic Filter does more computations in projecting screen pixels to texture space, thus resulting in much cleaner results. This is the default filter type.

Pre-filtering file textures

The **Pre-Filter** and **Pre-Filter Radius** attributes, found in the **File Attributes** section of the **Attribute Editor**, are used to correct file textures that are aliased or contain noise in unwanted areas. When Pre-Filtering is On, the image file uses a Gaussian-type filter to get rid of noise and aliasing, contributing to a better quality image. The Pre-Filter Radius will determine the size of the filtering radius. The default value of **2.0** works for most images, but you can increase the radius to provide even smoother results. This can be particularly useful with bump or displacement mapping.

Block-ordered textures and caching

In the **Attribute Editor** for file textures, there is an attribute called **Use BOT**. This attribute can be used as an optimization if you find that your renders are running into swap space. Using swap is very slow, so you want to avoid this.

By setting **Use BOT** to **On**, you use a lot more disk space but less memory. This is because the renderer does not need to keep whole textures in RAM during the render. Instead, it uses tiles of the texture called *BOT* (Block Order Texture) files as it needs them.

BOTs are enabled by setting **Use BOT** to **On** for a file texture. If this flag is on and the file textures are not already BOT format files, Maya will automatically create BOT textures from the image files and store them in a temporary directory at render time.

The file textures can be pre-converted to BOT by using the `makebot` MEL command:

```
makebot -i "in _ image" -o "out _ bot _ file";
```

In this case, the resulting BOT files can be stored in a directory you specify. For example:

```
makebot -i "in _ image" -o "./sourceimages/out _ bot _ file";
```

Once the BOT files are created, you need to change the path and name in the file texture's **Attribute Editor** to point to the BOT files. If the textures are already in BOT format, this saves time at the start of the render. It also show you how much disk space is being taken up by the BOT files on disk before you start rendering.

Technical details

A BOT texture on disk is a compressed MipMap structure with 8x8 *texel* pages. A texel is a texture element derived in much the same way as pixel is a picture element. The textureCache is a 256 texel page cache in memory; that is, it can hold 256 of the 8x8 texel pages. There is only one textureCache for the entire rendering session and the cache is shared between all file textures.

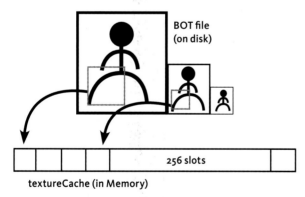

BOT file
(on disk)

256 slots

textureCache (in Memory)

BOT files and texture caching

The textureCache is loaded on demand. When part of a texture is required, if it is not already in the cache, it is loaded from disk. If the textureCache is full, the least recently accessed pages are removed and replaced with the pages being loaded.

BOT textures have the advantage of reducing the amount of memory required to keep textures in memory. If the image file has already been converted to a BOT texture file, the Maya renderer can use it much more quickly than when it has to convert the file to BOT texture on its own.

BOT textures do have some limitations as well. If multiple renderers/processors are using the same BOT file, there can be an I/O bandwidth problem which will cause all the renderers to slow down (having a copy of the BOT texture for each processor is the only work-around). If the image files are not BOT texture files to begin with, then the temporary directory can get full quickly with all of the temporary BOT files.

If different shading networks reference the same file texture image, a single copy of the image is kept in memory and shared by all the shaders.

Tip: Use **maya -optimizeRender -help** *for a list of flags and descriptions to use BOT files.*

Transparency mapping

If you map a file texture containing an Alpha channel to the *Color* channel of a material, you will notice that the *outTransparency* channel is connected to the material automatically. A material's transparency is the opposite of a file texture's Alpha channel, which is generally based on opacity:

alpha opacity, (0 = black = transparent; 1 = white = opaque)

material transparency, (0 = black = opaque; 1 = white = transparent)

There is no direct way for the Alpha of a file texture to act as a material's transparency. The *outAlpha* of the file texture would have to be sent through a *Reverse* utility node prior to connection to the material's *Transparency* attributes. Each channel (R,G,B) of the *outTransparency* attribute is the reverse of the node's *outAlpha* attribute. This makes it easier to define the opacity of a material by using only the Alpha channel.

Displacement mapping

Sometimes, rather than modeling the details of a surface, it is more convenient to use *Displacement Mapping*. Displacement mapping uses a texture to alter the shape of geometry. This is different than a bump map, which simply alters the way light hits the surface normals, creating the illusion of surface relief.

Normal

Bump mapping

Displacement mapping

Displacement and bump mapping

The displacement map is connected to the shading group node instead of the material node. This is because it is applied to the geometry rather than the shading. To see the connections in the Hypershade, select the material node and click the **Input and Output Connections** button. This will show the Displacement Map, the material node, and all of the geometry that belongs to the shading group.

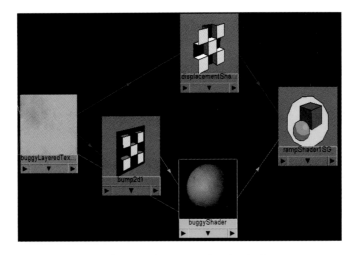

The displacement node is directly connected to the shading group

Displacement mapping adds detail to surfaces at render time in order to capture the small variance in a displacement texture. The renderer then generates high-quality displacement tessellation with minimum triangle counts.

The following exercise will use displacement mapping to texture the sole of a boot.

1 Scene file

- **Open** the scene called *02-bootDisplacement_01.ma*.

2 Graph the boot shading network

- Select the *boot* and click on the **Graph Materials on the Selected Objects** button in the **Hypershade**.

  At this time, the boot already has a sole texture assigned. You will use and modify that texture for both the bump and displacement.

3 Map the bump

- Open the **Attribute Editor** for the *soleShader.*
- **Map** its **Bump Mapping** attribute with a **file** texture.
- In the new file texture node, **browse** for the texture *bootSole.tif* from the *support_files.*
- **Test render** your scene.

  Notice how the sole appears to have relief, but the geometry was not affected.

4 **Connect the displacement**

• **MMB+drag** the sole file texture onto the *bootShader* material and connect it to **Displacement Map**.

This automatically connects the texture to the shading group node.

Tip: *Having both displacement and bump maps will make the geometry shading look more accurate.*

---

5 **Displacement amount**

In order to get a general idea of the amount of displacement needed to look good on the boot, you can change the **Alpha Gain** of the texture used for displacement.

• Set the **Alpha Gain** to **0.1** under **Color Balance** in the **Attribute Editor** for the boot sole texture.

• **Test render** the scene and change the **Alpha Gain** if needed.

The proper amount of displacement

Tip: *To reverse a displacement, you can set the **Alpha Gain** to a negative value.*

---

6 **Tune the displacement attributes**

The displacement attributes are found in the Attribute Editor for the geometry, not the texture map.

If the original tessellation triangle is large and the texture details are fine, then the **Initial Sample Rate** has to be large (from 30 to 50 or even higher). If the triangle is small and the texture details are not especially fine, then the **Initial Sample Rate** does not have to be very high (usually the default is good enough).

Observe how sharp the texture details are and if there are many clean lines or curved details. The sharper the features and the cleaner the lines, the higher the **Extra Sample Rate** needs to be.

- Select the *boot* and open its **Attribute Editor**.
- In the **Displacement Map** section, make sure the **Feature Displacement** flag is turned **On**.
- If the details in your test render look too rough, then increase the **Initial Sample Rate**.
- For now, set the **Extra Sample Rate** to o.
- **Test render** the boot to see the results of the displacement.

 Note: *It is not possible to use IPR to help tune the displacement attributes because the displacement map is applied to the geometry, not the shading. Changes in the shape of the geometry are not supported by IPR.*

- If not enough details are captured, increase the **Initial Sample Rate** some more.

 Tip: *Use the lowest acceptable value.*

- If the features are too jagged, increase the **Extra Sample Rate**.

  This attribute refines the displacement results. It is a good idea to try it at o and see if the quality is good enough. This will help to keep the triangle count as low as possible. Increase it until the edges of the texture details look acceptable.

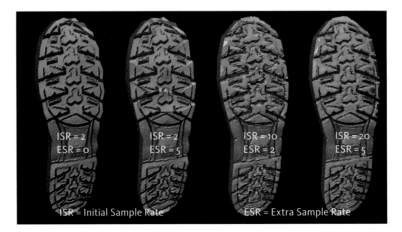

ISR = 2 | ISR = 2 | ISR = 10 | ISR = 20
ESR = o | ESR = 5 | ESR = 2 | ESR = 5

ISR = Initial Sample Rate   ESR = Extra Sample Rate

Variations of displacement attributes

 **Note:** *Displacement mapping especially affects the silhouette of the model.*

7 Using the Displacement to Polygon Tool

The **Modify → Convert** menu contains a tool called Displacement to Polygon. This useful tool bakes out the displaced surface as a polygon mesh, providing a great way to visualize the results without test rendering. The resulting polygonal object is created in the same location as the original and can be used instead of the original surface (in which case, the displacement map serves as a modeling tool). While the original surface is preserved, there is no history relationship between the original surface and the polygonal object. If changes are made to the original surface or any of its tessellation or displacement attributes, the Displacement to Polygon Tool must be used again to see the changes.

Tip: *In general, displacement will result in a very high number of polygons. This creates a very heavy file relative to the original surface. Use at your discretion.*

The following images show an example of the Displacement to Polygon Tool results:

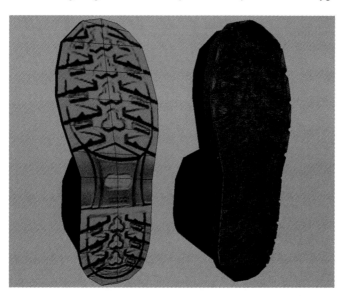

Conversion of displacement to polygons

Displacement mapping in mental ray

mental ray provides the opportunity to optimize a displacement by using the Displacement Approximation Editor. By default, mental ray will use the Maya tessellation settings for surface approximations. If you want to override this, use the **Window → Rendering Editors → mental ray → Approximation Editor**.

mental ray baking

To bake information (Convert to File Texture) with mental ray®, use *Bake Sets*. These allow users to bake a variety of objects with different baking options such as illumination, shadow, shading, and textures. You can also save different baking parameters, making it easier to re-bake when needed.

You can also bake objects that have not been assigned to a Bake Set. If this is the case, the objects are automatically assigned to the initial Bake Set, and the baking proceeds.

To do a simple batch bake using the mental ray renderer:

- Select one or more objects that you want to bake.
- Select **Lighting/Shading** → **Batch Bake (mental ray)** → ❑.
- Set the desired options and click **Convert**.

To create a mental ray Bake Set:

- Select one or more objects for which you want to create a Bake Set.
- Select **Lighting/Shading** → **Assign New Bake Set** → **Texture Bake Set**.
- Adjust the **Bake Sets** attributes in the **Bake Set Attribute Editor**.

  When you bake the objects, mental ray will use the Bake Set options they are assigned to.

Tip: *If you want to edit the Bake Set later,* **RMB** *on the object and select* **Baking** → **Baking Attributes**.

Memory mapped files

Using memory mapped texture files is recommended in most scenes as it reduces physical memory usage considerably. Without memory mapping, texture files are read into physical memory and are swapped to disk space in the event of memory running low. This is expensive in memory usage and time-consuming as texture files are swapped out to disk. Memory mapped files, however, do not use large blocks of memory. Instead, they reside in virtual memory. Memory mapping is particularly beneficial with large textures. However, any scene with more than a few hundred KB of file textures will benefit from memory mapping.

mental ray for Maya has a utility, `imf _ copy`, that is used for converting textures to memory mapped files.

The syntax is:

```
imf_copy (options) filename.tif filename.map
```

Note: *The* `.map` *extension does not have to be present; mental ray will recognize memory mapped files regardless. The extension is there as a matter of convention.*

Conclusion

Creating great textures is an important factor in producing a convincing image. Textures help determine the style you are reaching for, from cartoon style to extreme realism. If you have a strong grasp of the tools used to create textures, it opens the door to your artistic freedom.

In the next project, you will learn about lighting and cameras.

Project 02

In Project Two, you will learn about lights and cameras. Lighting a scene and setting up cameras will give ambience, depth, and realism to your renders. The topics outlined in the following lessons are a prerequisite for anyone who intends to create astonishing images.

Once you have completed this project, you should feel confident incorporating lights and cameras into your scene.

Lights

Lighting a CG scene is much like lighting for photography, film, or theater. As an element of design, light should be considered a basic influence at the beginning of the creative process and not something to be added later. This is especially true in computer graphics, where lighting is based on mathematical algorithms and creating real-world lighting effects requires a solid understanding of the software application.

In this lesson, you will learn the following:

- Lighting basics
- How to use decay rates and intensity curves
- How to use color curves and color mapping with lights
- How to link lights
- How to create mental ray area lights

Lighting concepts

The basic premise of good lighting is that when it is done right, objects and characters look like they fit and live in their surroundings. The design potential of light is inherent in its physical characteristics. As you control its intensity, color, and direction, light becomes a key factor in creating a scene. Lighter and darker areas help to compose the frame and guide the eye toward certain objects and actions.

Choosing light types

Once you have determined the direction and distribution of lights in a scene, you will also need to consider the type of light source.

Maya provides a selection of light types that all have attributes you can edit and animate to simulate real-world lighting. These lights can produce a range of qualities from soft and diffuse to harsh and intense because they each have different characteristics. While it is likely that your combination of lights and techniques will vary with each production, the design principles of combining sharp- and soft-edged light, different angles, intensities, and shadows remain the same.

Directional lights

Directional light

You will notice that the *directional light* icon depicts several parallel rays. This is because its purpose is to simulate a distant light source, such as the sun, whose light rays are coherent and parallel.

This type of light source will typically produce a harsher, more intense quality of light with harder edges and no subtle changes in surface shading because of its parallel rays with no decay. Directional lights are not very expensive to render because the angle is constant for all rays and decay is not computed.

Point lights

Point light

The *point light* icon depicts light rays emanating from a single point outwards in all directions. Its purpose is to simulate an omni-directional local light source, such as a light bulb or candle. This type of light does have decay and will typically produce more subtle, richer shading on surfaces.

Ambient lights

Ambient light

An *ambient light* is normally used as a non-directional light to simulate the diffused scattered or reflected light you see in real life.

However, you can adjust the *Ambient Shade* attribute, which gives directionality to the light. If set to 0.0, it acts like an RGB multiplier, allowing you to control the overall contrast levels in the scene. However, it is very difficult to determine the edges of objects at this setting with no other light source. The default is set to **0.45** to give a slight hint of shading on surfaces. If *Ambient Shade* is set to **1.0**, it is fully directional, (i.e., the location of the light is the source of the rays).

Ambient lights are quick to render because they have no decay and create no specular highlights. Often they are used as a secondary light source, supporting a stronger light source. Be aware that using only an ambient light for illumination has limitations. For example, bump maps will not show up.

Spot lights

Spot light

A *spot light* has a cone of influence in a specific direction. This is controlled by the *Cone Angle* attribute, which is measured in degrees from edge to edge. The spot light also has *Decay*, *Dropoff*, and *Penumbra* attributes, which will be covered later in the lesson.

Area lights

Area light

Point, directional, and spot lights are all abstract lighting models in the sense that they are zero-size lights that theoretically exist at a single point.

Because all lights in the natural world occupy some amount of space, *area lights* can help to produce a more realistic lighting distribution; an area light computation reflects the size and orientation of the light.

There are three effects that are difficult to achieve using light sources other than area lights:

- Straight, long, specular highlights (like those created by neon);
- Soft lighting distribution;
- Realistic shadows that vary from hard to soft.

Specular highlight size and orientation

Simply position and scale the light using IPR to see the specular highlight interactively.

Soft lighting distribution

The size, orientation, and position of the area light's manipulator in a view controls the lighting distribution.

- If you have a large area light, more light is emitted. The light can be non-proportionally scaled to modulate the distribution.

  A real-world analogy would be a window with a shade that pulls down; as you lower the shade, the size of the window opening gets smaller and the amount of light is reduced.

- The farther away the object is from the light, the less light is cast onto the object. Quadratic is the default type of decay.

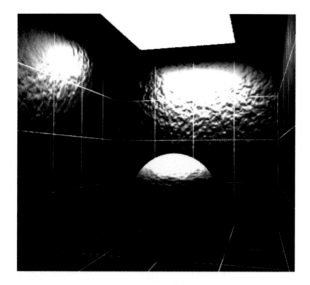

Highlight size and soft light distribution

Realistic shadows

The size and shape of an area light can help to create realistic raytraced shadows that dissipate as the receiving surface becomes more illuminated by the area light. This normally requires a relatively high number of shadow rays and can be expensive to render.

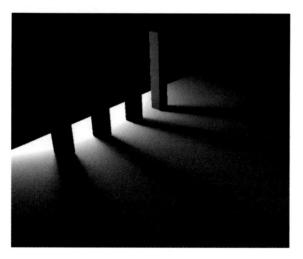

Realistic shadows using raytracing

Note: *Shadows will be discussed in greater detail in the next lesson.*

Optical effects

Any light that is visible to the camera lens has the potential to produce an optical effect, such as light glow or flare. Optical effects for an area light reflect the shape of its manipulator.

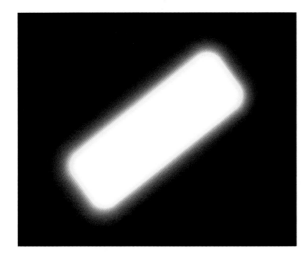

Optical light glow on an area light

> **Note:** *Optical effects like light glow and light glow occlusion will be covered in more detail in Lesson 8.*

Area light limitations

- Depth map shadows do not reflect the size and orientation of the area light.
- The specular highlight produced by an area light on an anisotropic shader is poorly defined.
- The specular highlight produced by an area light on plug-in shaders will not reflect the size and orientation of the area light. Enhancements have to be made to the architecture to support a proper specular direction.

Volume lights

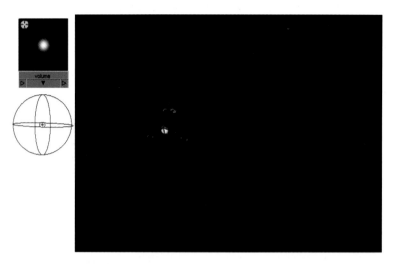

Volume light

The *volume light* illuminates objects within a given volume. Volumes can be spherical, cylindrical, box, or cone shaped. The advantage of using this type of light is that you have a visual representation of the extent of the light. In addition to the common attributes found in all lights, volume lights have attributes that allow greater control over the color of the volume. The **Color Range** section in the Attribute Editor allows the user to select one color or blend between colors within the volume. You can control the direction of a light within the volume by using the **Volume Light Direction** attributes.

Default lights

If there are no lights in a scene, Maya will create a directional light when the scene is rendered. This light is parented to the render camera and illuminates the scene regardless of where the camera is facing. After the render is complete, Maya removes the default light from the scene.

That same default light is used to shade models in the views (except when Use All Light (**7**) or **High Quality Rendering** mode is turned On).

Light intensity

Intensity can be defined as the actual or comparative brightness of light. Like most other render attributes, it can be modified either by using the slider or by mapping a texture to the channel.

Note: *It is possible to enter negative values for intensity. This will subtract light from the scene and can produce dark spots instead of hot spots on specular shading models.*

The **Emit Diffuse** and **Emit Specular** flags are **On** by default and will control the diffuse or specular shading results for the light. Ambient lights do not have these attributes.

Decay rates

Decay refers to how light diminishes with distance. It is possible to alter the rate of decay for point and spot lights by adjusting the **Decay Rate** in the light's Attribute Editor. The initial default is **No Decay**. The other settings are **Linear**, **Quadratic,** and **Cubic**.

> **Note:** *For computer animated characters or other elements that must match live action shots, it is very important to consider the decay rate. For example, if your character is moving toward or away from a light source, the intensity of the light cast onto the character must appear to increase or decrease as it would in real life, or it will not be believable when it is later added to the live shot. This is especially true if the character is placed next to a live actor who is also moving towards or away from the light source. For this reason you may choose to work with* **Quadratic** *decay for realism.*

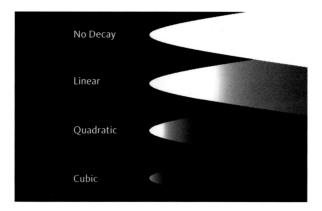

Light decay

No Decay - Light reaches everything.

Linear - Light intensity decreases in direct proportion to distance ($l=1/d$).

Quadratic - This is how light decays in real life ($l=1/d*d$)

Cubic - Light decays faster than in real life ($l=1/d*d*d$)

> **Note:** *The decay factor occurs only after a distance larger than 1 unit. Otherwise, with distances less than 1 unit, it could result in over-exposure in lighting.*

Precision lighting

While decay rates offer a mathematically accurate way to have light fall off over distance, they do not allow for any control in precision lighting.

Being able to do precision lighting is crucial to working on special effects, i.e., being able to interactively clamp lighting at an exact spot, or easily specifying the light intensity at an exact distance, etc. Currently, spot lights have all the tools to perform precision lighting.

Tip: *When beginning to work with decay on spot lights, it is best to use either the decay approach or the precision lighting approach, as mixing both may yield unexpected results.*

Decay regions

The primary purpose of *decay regions* is to allow regions to be lit or non-lit within the same cone of light. The decay regions can be used in conjunction with the decay rates to control effects, such as table lamps or car headlights, where the visible light beam emanates from a broad region rather than a single point in space.

The following steps show how to set-up decay regions on a spot light.

- Create a spot light.
- In the **Attribute Editor**, click the **Map** button for the **Light Fog** attribute.
- In the **Attribute Editor** for the *spotLight*, under **Light Effects** → **Decay Regions**, turn **On** the **Use Decay Regions**.
- Display the **Decay Region** manipulators by selecting **Display** → **Rendering** → **Camera/ Light Manipulator** → **Decay Regions**.

  You can interactively move the manipulator's rings in the views to define the regions of illumination.

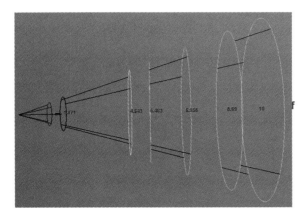

The Decay Regions Tool

- **Test render** the light.

  You should see the different regions because of the light fog.

> **Tip:** *An alternate way to adjust the regions is to open the **Region** subsections of the **Decay Regions** section in the Attribute Editor and enter values in the **Distance** fields. This tool can also be very useful as an interactive measuring tool to determine distances from the light.*

Intensity curve

At times it is important to be able to control the exact intensity of a light at a given distance from the light source. Intensity curves allow precise control over this effect.

- In the Attribute Editor for the *spotLight* , click on **Light Effects → Intensity Curve → Create.**

  A curve is created and connected to the light's intensity channel.

- With the light still selected, select **Window → Animation Editors → Graph Editor.**

- Press the **a** hotkey to frame all in the view or use **View → Frame All.**

  There will be a number of keyframes on the curve.

  *Notice that the vertical and horizontal axes represent **Intensity** and **Distance** for this curve.*

  You can edit this curve as you would edit any other animation curve in Maya by moving keyframes, adding or deleting keyframes, changing tangents, etc.

> **Tip:** *To try this with a point light, create a spot light and set-up the intensity curve, then convert the spot light to a point light through the Attribute Editor.*

Color curves

Similar to intensity curves, *color curves* allow you to individually control the red, green, and blue values of the light over distance.

- To create **Color Curves**, open the *spotLight*'s **Attribute Editor**, then click on **Light Effects → Color Curve → Create.**

> **Tip:** *Do not delete any of the color curves because this can give unexpected results. Instead, if you want to take out all of the green component, for example, delete the middle keys and set the remaining two keys to an intensity value of **0.0**.*

Dropoff

Spot lights also have a **Dropoff** attribute. Dropoff is similar to decay except that the light diminishes in intensity perpendicular to the light axis, instead of along that axis.

- Select a spot light and open the **Attribute Editor**.
- In the **Spot Light Attributes** section, adjust the **Dropoff** attribute.

You can watch the effect in the spot light panel in the Attribute Editor or in the IPR window.

Spot light dropoff effect

Note: *The results are computed as follows: cosine raised to the power of dropoff (where cos is the dot product of the light axis and the lighting direction vector).*

Penumbra angle

The penumbra is an area of diminishing intensity rimming the edge of the cone of light. The intensity of the light falls off linearly between the cone angle and the penumbra angle.

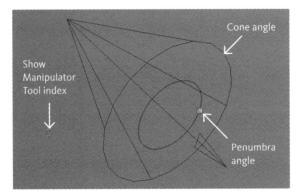

Spot light penumbra manipulator

> **Note:** *It is possible to enter negative numbers for **Penumbra Angle**. This will create a softening effect inward from the edge of the cone of influence.*

Color mapping lights

You will now specify a light color by mapping a texture onto the color channel. This essentially allows the light to act like a movie projector, projecting the texture onto the objects in the scene.

> **Tip:** *Mapping the color channel of a spot light with a water texture can create realistic-looking caustic patterns, especially when the texture is animated.*

In the following example, you will project a water caustic pattern on Leon by mapping a texture in a spot light **Color** attribute.

1 Scene file

- **Open** the scene file called *03-lights_01.ma*.
- Go to frame **110**.

2 Create a spot light and place it

- Select **Create → Lights → Spot Light**.
- Select **Panels → Look Through Selected**.

  You are now looking through the spotLight in order to help its placement.

- **Dolly** and **tumble** in this view to place the *spotLight* pointing straight on the Constructor, so the light appears to come from the dashboard.

  Make sure to place the character's face in the view circle, which defines the borders of the spot light.

- In the Attribute Editor for the spotlight, set the following:

    Decay Rate to **Linear**;

    Intensity to **10**;

    Cone Angle to **70**;

    Penumbra Angle to **20**;

    Dropoff to **10**;

    Depth Map Shadows to **On**.

Note: *Because a dashboard light should be a short-ranged and dimmed light source, the linear decay rate prevents the light and its texture from showing up on objects far away in the background. If you do not want to use this technique, you will need to use light-linking as seen in the next exercise.*

3 Map to the spot light

- Open the **Attribute Editor** for the *spotLight*, and then click on the **map** button to the right of the **Color** attribute.

- In the **Create Render Node** window, create a **File** texture.

- In the **Attribute Editor** for the new *file* texture, browse for the image called *dashboard. tif* from the *sourceimages* directory.

  This image contains random writing from a computer screen.

Tip: *You can position an image in the spot light by changing **Coverage**, **Translate Frame,** and **Rotate Frame** on the file texture's place2Dtexture node to position the image in the spot light.*

4 Test render

Texture mapped into spot light color

Light linking

Often when trying to solve specific lighting tasks, you will need to control which lights shine on which objects in your scene. This can be accomplished easily, using several methods. All of these methods will accomplish the same results, so it is really just a question of which one is the easier workflow for what you are trying to set-up.

Relationship Editor light centric

This method is the easiest to use when you are learning to use light linking, but it is not the fastest approach.

- Select **Windows** → **Relationship Editors** → **Light Linking** → **Light Centric**.

  The Relationship Editor is automatically configured for a Light Centric Light Linking task, and shows all of the light sets and individual lights in the scene on the left. In the right column, it shows all of the geometry and shading groups in the scene.

Light centric light linking

- Click to select a light or light set from the list on the left.

  Geometry illuminated by the selected lights is highlighted on the right.

- Toggle the highlight on the right side to specify the geometry to be illuminated by the selected light(s).

  Un-highlighted geometry will not be illuminated by the selected light(s).

Relationship Editor object centric

This method is the fastest approach to light linking since you can select the lights to affect the object you wish to change.

- Change the **Relationship Editor** configuration to **Object Centric Light Linking** or select **Windows** → **Relationship Editors** → **Light Linking** → **Object Centric**.

Object centric light linking

- Click to select an object or set of objects from the list on the left.

  Lights illuminating the selected objects are highlighted on the right.

- Click on the right side to choose which lights will illuminate the selected objects.

  Un-highlighted lights will not illuminate the selected objects.

Lighting/Shading menu

This workflow is the fastest method for setting up light linking. By default, a new light added to a scene illuminates all objects in the scene. This means that there is a link between the light and each piece of geometry to start with. The **Lighting/Shading** menu provides a simple way to break or make any of these links without needing to bring up the Relationship Editor.

- Select light(s), and then **Shift-select** object(s) you do not want the lights to illuminate.

- Select **Lighting/Shading → Break Light Links** from the Rendering menu set to break the link(s) between the selected nodes.

  Now the selected lights will not illuminate the selected geometry.

- Use the same workflow outlined above to recreate light links using **Lighting/Shading → Make Light Links**.

Note: *It does not matter whether you select the lights first or the objects first.*

Illuminates By Default

This workflow uses the menu actions described above and the **Illuminates By Default** feature. This method is recommended when adding a light that needs to shine on only one or a few specific objects in a scene, where there are many other objects and lights already set.

Using the Relationship Editor method, it would be time-consuming to turn off all the objects you do not want illuminated by the new light(s). Using the Lighting/Shading menu would also be time-consuming because again, you would need to select all the geometry you do not want illuminated in order to break all the links to the new light(s).

In this case, it is better to start out by telling the light(s) not to illuminate any geometry initially. Then it is just a matter of selecting the geometry you intend to illuminate with the new light(s) and making a link with the **Make Light Link** menu.

- Open the **Attribute Editor** for a *light*.
- Turn **Off** the **Illuminates by Default** checkbox.
- **Make Light Links** between the light and geometry.

Lights in mental ray®

All of the Maya lights will render using mental ray. As added features, some light types have extra mental ray attributes and support photon emission. Photon emission is necessary for effects such as *Caustics* and *Global Illumination*, which will be discussed in Project 4. Lights that are capable of this include *directional*, *point*, *spot*, and *mental ray area lights*. The other light types, *ambient*, *volume*, and *Maya area lights*, are supported but do not have mental ray attributes or support photon emission.

mental ray area light

The mental ray area light is slightly different than a Maya area light. The Maya area light can only be rectangular, whereas mental ray lights have a few more shape options.

Create a mental ray area light

- Create a point light or a spot light.
- Open the **Attribute Editor** for the light, then scroll down to the **mental ray → Area Light Editor** section.
- Set the **Area Light** checkbox to **On**.
- Adjust the area light as desired, using the options described below.

  The icon will let you know the direction the light will be emitted.

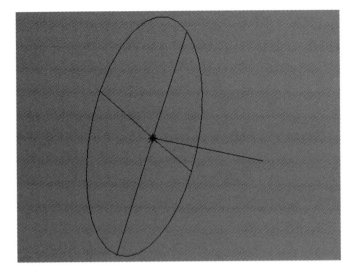

A disc-shaped mental ray area light

Type
Type refers to the shape of the area light source. Shapes available from the drop-down list include **Rectangle**, **Disc**, **Sphere**, and **Cylinder**.

Sampling
Sampling represents the number of sample points emitted from the light (X and Y). The default values are **3** and **3**. Increasing these values will reduce graininess, but will increase render time.

Low Level
If this value is greater than **1**, the light source will use the **Low Sampling** values as long as their sum is greater than the **Low Level** value. This affects reflection and refraction. The default is **0**.

Low Sampling
The defaults are **2** and **2**. Increasing this value may help where a lit edge looks grainy. This value will then be used as the minimum sampling value while the **Low Level** value is greater than **1**.

Visible
If you want the light object to be visible during a render, turn this **On**.

Conclusion

Lighting is an important aspect of the rendering process and having a good understanding of it can help you establish mood and atmosphere in your scenes. Understanding the technical aspects of lighting can help you create impressive renders.

In the next lesson, you will learn to create and control shadows.

Shadows

Some cinematographers say that the most important thing in lighting is what you do not light. They are referring to the relative effects of light and shadow. Shadows are involved in creating atmosphere and mood in a scene and help to define its look and feel.

In this lesson, you will learn the following:

- How to use depth map shadows
- About the different light types and their shadows
- How to create volumetric lighting effects
- How to use raytraced shadows
- How to use mental ray shadow maps
- How to motion-blur shadow maps with mental ray
- How to use mental ray raytrace shadows

Shadows

When lighting a scene, you need to take into consideration the type of shadows you want. For example, the elevation and direction of a light are important influences on the amount and shape of the shadow areas in the frame. Generally, shadows become more dominant as the angle of light incidence increases and as the lighting moves from front to back positions. This, in turn, affects the overall mood of the image; for a dark and gloomy scene you would want the lights behind your objects so the shadows are being cast into the frame.

Shadows also play an important role in rendering texture. To maximize texture, you use side lighting, also known as cross lighting. Side lighting creates long shadows that interact with the lit parts of the subject to yield good texture patterns. To minimize texture, you use frontal light, as it will create a very flat look because there will be fewer shadows.

By default, all objects have the ability to cast shadows as well as receive shadows. These abilities are controlled separately, using the **Render Stats** section of an object in the Attribute Editor.

Note: *The* **Receive Shadows** *attribute is ignored in IPR rendering.*

When rendering shadows in Maya, you have the option to use either **Raytrace Shadows** or **Depth Map Shadows**.

With depth map shadows, the depth maps are computed as a first pass before rendering, while raytraced shadows are computed during the rendering phase.

Note: *Use* **Lighting** → **Shadows** *to preview the position of your shadows when displaying hardware textures. This function is only possible with depth map shadows and only with certain graphics cards and drivers. See the Maya documentation for more information.*

Depth map shadows

The shadow depth map computation is done by rendering a *depth* image from the point of view of the light source; this image is later used during the rendering phase to determine if that light illuminates a given point. **Point**, **directional**, **volume**, **spot,** and **area lights** are the light types that can produce depth map shadows.

Note: *Depth map shadows are usually known as simply* **Dmaps**.

How Dmaps work

Similar to a topographical map, a Dmap is used to record distances between the light and objects in the scene. The Dmap is a square grid of pixels in front of the light. This grid is projected over the scene from the *light's* point of view, dividing the scene into sections.

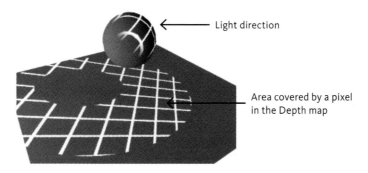

Light direction

Area covered by a pixel in the Depth map

Dmap grid example

A ray is cast through the center of each pixel in the Dmap. When the ray intersects the nearest shadow-casting surface, Maya records the distance from the light to that surface. These depth measurements make up the Dmap's pixel values. You can view the Dmap with **fcheck** by hitting the **Z** key. In this example, it would look like the following image:

Dmap viewed with fcheck

Depth mapping takes place at the beginning of the render process. The renderer later uses this depth information when creating the final image from the camera view. This process is described below.

In the following diagram, the shading is computed for points on the ground plane because the ground plane is visible to the camera. During this process, one of the necessary pieces of information is whether a point is in shadow or not.

In order to determine whether the point on the ground plane is in shadow, the renderer makes a comparison—it checks with all of the shadow-casting lights to see if the point being shaded is closer to or farther from the light than the point stored in the Dmap.

If the distance from the point being shaded (on the ground plane) to the light is greater than the stored depth value, then some other surface is closer to the light. This means that the point being shaded must be in shadow.

In this diagram, many points being shaded on the ground plane fall within the coverage region of a single pixel on the Dmap. This means that all of these points would be compared to the same stored depth value and hence, would be considered to be in shadow. Obviously, some of the points do not look as though they should be in shadow. The next section of this chapter looks at ways to resolve this type of inaccuracy.

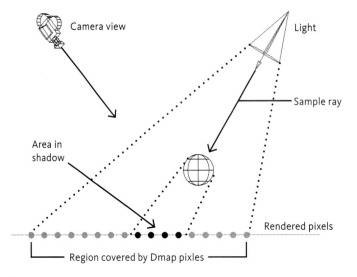

Dmap shadow computation

Self-shadowing

Self-shadowing refers to a surface casting shadows on itself.

Self-shadowing

Self-shadowing is caused by the specific shape of a surface, but Dmap can cause self-shadowing artifacts simply because of the finite resolution of the Dmap. Because only one depth value is stored per pixel, if you happen to be shading a point on a surface that lies between samples in the Dmap, there is the possibility that the averaged depth from the Dmap will incorrectly shadow the point being shaded. This self-shadowing will result in an undesirable moiré pattern or banding on surfaces facing toward the light.

The self-shadowing from Dmap shadows can be somewhat puzzling at first because it can happen even when there is nothing to cast a shadow.

The following rendered image shows self-shadowing artifacts on a single ground plane.

Banding caused by self-shadowing

The diagram below explains how this happens in the case of the plane shown above:

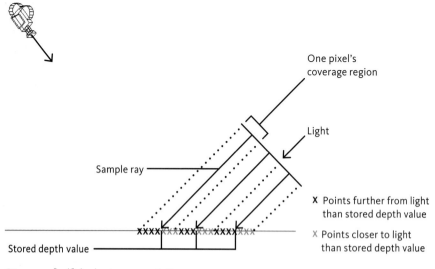

One pixel's
coverage region

Light

Sample ray

X Points further from light
than stored depth value

X Points closer to light
than stored depth value

Stored depth value

Diagram of self-shadowing computation

Even with a simple plane, self-shadowing can be caused by the limited number of depth samples stored in the Dmap. Each pixel on the Dmap covers a large region of the ground plane. As the image is rendered from the camera, any points on the plane that are further from the light than the stored depth value on the Dmap will be incorrectly thought to be in shadow from the plane itself.

The image below shows the moiré pattern that is also typical of self-shadowing:

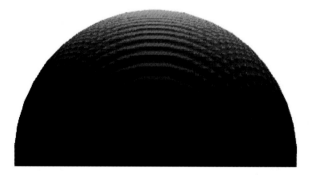

Moiré pattern caused by self-shadowing

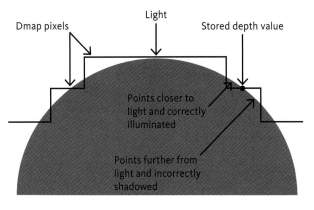

Diagram of computation

In the examples shown above, the **Resolution** of the Dmap is set intentionally low to exaggerate the self-shadowing artifacts. Increasing the resolution will not get rid of the artifacts, it will just make them smaller, sometimes giving a dull, dirty appearance to a surface.

Correcting self-shadowing with Dmap Bias

There are two shadow attributes available to help correct self-shadowing:

- **Use Mid Dist Dmap,** which will be discussed later. This feature is turned **On** by default and in many cases will prevent the self-shadowing artifacts shown above.
- **Dmap Bias** is another important Dmap shadow attribute that is used to correct self-shadowing.

The **Dmap Bias** attribute is very important when dealing with self-shadowing artifacts. The *bias* is a value by which the camera ray's intersection point is moved closer to the light source to avoid incorrect self-shadowing. In other words, it is a value that can be thought of as a *fudge factor* that is used for shadow purposes, to move the point being shaded closer to the light to bring it out of self-shadow.

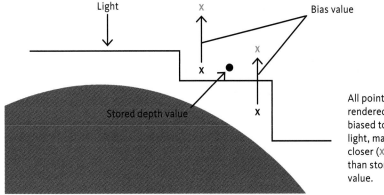

Dmap Bias moves the points to escape self-shadowing

While adjusting the **Dmap Bias**, take care to find the right value. Using too small a value may result in self-shadowing artifacts on the surface, as the previous images have shown. Using too large a value may lead to surfaces that should be in shadow not being in shadow. A large value might also lead to shadows that are detached from the casting objects, causing the object to appear to be floating (as shown below):

The object appears to float above the ground surface

> **Note:** The **Dmap Bias** *is not in world units. Here is how it is applied:*
> *Dmap Bias * current Z-depth = bias value*
> *The farther away the point is from the light source, the bigger the bias value. But, this value multiplies with the perspective Z-depth, so consider the user-entered* **Dmap Bias** *as a normalized bias value. Directional lights are the same, except that the bias is not multiplied by the Z-depth.*

Correcting self-shadowing with Mid Distance

Use Mid Dist Dmap is turned **On** by default to help prevent self-shadowing artifacts. It stands for *Use Middle Distance Depth Map*, which is a variation on the Dmap algorithm.

> **Note:** *If the Dmap is to be used for purposes other than shadowing, it is best to turn this option* **Off**.

Use Mid Dist Dmap attempts to eliminate the need for the Dmap Bias attribute by storing the midpoint between the first and second surface visible to the light source (rather than simply storing the distance to the nearest surface). Because this midpoint is normally farther from the light than any of the points on the surface itself, self-shadowing is less likely to occur. The diagram below shows how this works:

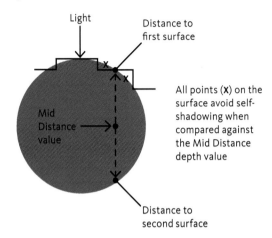

Mid Distance computation

Because **Use Mid Dist Dmap** is turned **On** by default, surfaces such as ground planes are not as susceptible to self-shadowing. The question often arises: What happens when there is only one surface that uses the *Mid Distance* algorithm? Answer: Since there is only one surface, Autodesk® Maya® uses the farthest bounding box among the receiving shadow surfaces.

> **Tip:** *When **Use Mid Dist Dmap** is turned **On**, there are actually two Dmaps created: the standard Dmap that stores the distances to the first surfaces and another one that stores the distances to the second surfaces. To see the difference, write the Dmaps to disk and **fcheck** them viewing the Z-buffer. The Dmaps are stored in the depth directory of your current project.*

Using both Dmap Bias and Use Mid Dist Dmap

The **Use Mid Dist Dmap** option can prevent some self-shadowing artifacts. However, depending on the model and the angle of the lights, a small **Dmap Bias** is normally required as well (the default is 0.001). The reason for this is that when surfaces are modeled close together, the mid distance is not significantly far enough from the first surface to allow the first surface to escape self-shadowing.

The following diagram shows the previous example of the plane. This time, a second plane is added slightly below the original. Because the planes are close together, the mid distance does very little to reduce the self-shadowing.

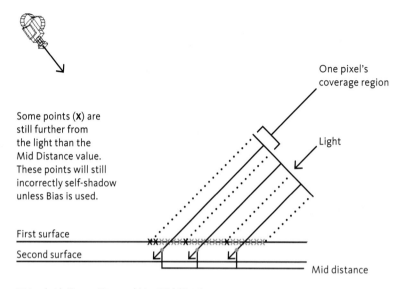

One pixel's
coverage region

Light

Some points (**X**) are
still further from
the light than the
Mid Distance value.
These points will still
incorrectly self-shadow
unless Bias is used.

First surface

Second surface

Mid distance

Using both Dmap Bias and Use Mid Dist Dmap

The following rendered images show the real effect of both **Use Mid Dist Dmap** and **Dmap Bias** working together to effectively remove all self-shadowing artifacts.

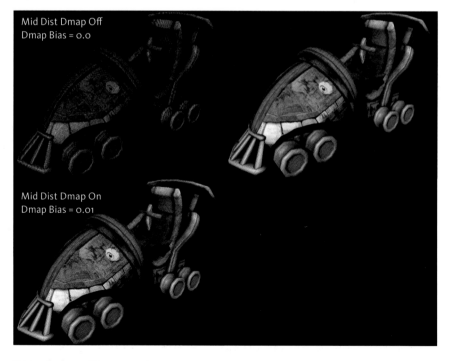

Mid Dist Dmap Off
Dmap Bias = 0.0

Mid Dist Dmap On
Dmap Bias = 0.01

Dmap shadow setting comparisons

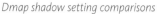

Angle of light and self-shadowing

The following diagram illustrates how the angle of light directly affects the likelihood of self-shadowing on a surface. Surfaces that are at an angle to the light are most likely to show self-shadowing because a single pixel's depth value is forced to approximate the shadows for a much larger region, which results in greater self-shadowing error.

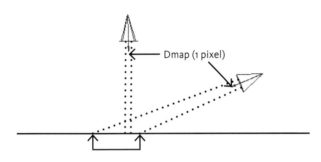

Angle of light impacts self-shadowing

Depth Map Resolution

Dmap Resolution defines the size of the Dmap rendered from a shadow-casting light. If it is set at 512, which is the default, the Dmap will be 512x512 pixels. As mentioned earlier, from the light point of view the map is a square grid of pixels in front of the light. This grid is projected over the scene, dividing it into sections. As a result, each section of the scene is represented by one pixel on the Dmap.

For example, let us say you have a scene that is 100 grid units by 100 grid units. There is a light casting shadows in your scene and the **Dmap Resolution** is set to **100**. Since the **Dmap Resolution** is set at **100**, one pixel from the Dmap will cover approximately one grid square of the scene. If there is a sphere that is 1 grid unit in size, the shadow for it will be calculated with the depth value of as little as one pixel in the Dmap. As you can see in the following image, there is not enough information in the Dmap to create a decent shadow.

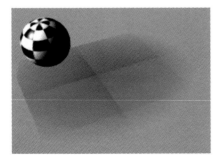

Low Dmap resolution

In the following image, the **Dmap Resolution** has been increased, resulting in enough information in the Dmap to create an accurate shadow.

High Dmap resolution

To automatically get the most detailed and accurate shadows out of a Dmap, there is an attribute called **Use Dmap Auto Focus** in the **Depth Map Shadow Attributes** section of the Attribute Editor. When this attribute's value is true, the renderer automatically computes the bounding volume for the shadow-casting objects in the view from the light source and uses the smallest possible field of view to render the shadow map. However, this can create artifacts over an animation if the bounding volume of the objects in your scene changes, possibly creating aliasing artifacts in your shadows, or unwanted softening or noise in the shadows.

Depth Map Filter Size

Dmap Filter Size helps control the softness of shadow edges. The softness of the shadow edge is a combination of the size of the shadow, the **Dmap Resolution,** and the **Dmap Filter Size**. If you have an object casting a shadow and the shadow is a little rough around the edges, increase the **Dmap Filter Size** to soften the edge. The following image shows the effect of **Dmap Filter Size**. Increasing **Dmap Filter Size** will increase render time, especially in conjunction with an increase in **Dmap Resolution**. For really soft and fuzzy shadows, try lowering the resolution and using a medium **Dmap Filter Size**. Be aware that the lower the resolution, the lower the accuracy of the shadow; using too low a resolution can result in flickering shadows in animation.

Dmap Resolution 128
Dmap Filter Size 3
Render time 1 second

Dmap Resolution 1024
Dmap Filter Size 10
Render time 5 seconds

Effect of filter size with various Dmap resolutions

Shadow Color

A phenomenon of color vision is the tendency of the eye to perceive the shadows cast from a colored light source to be the complementary color. It is not there in reality, but it is an optical illusion or color impression within the eye.

Lightening the shadow color also increases the transparency of the shadow. The following rendered images show this effect:

Lighting with a black and blue shadow color

Dmap Auto Focus

To avoid using very high resolution Dmaps wherever possible, it is important to keep the Dmap focused tightly on the shadow-casting objects. The **Use Dmap Auto Focus** feature allows the light to automatically determine the most optimal coverage region for the Dmap. The behavior of Auto Focus is shown in the examples below. The workflow when turning **Off** auto focus is described in the directional light example following the spot light example. In all examples below, the **Casts Shadows** flag is turned **Off** on the ground plane to help optimize Auto Focus.

For **Spot Lights**, the **Cone Angle** limits the size of the Dmap coverage when the light covers an area smaller than the shadow-casting objects. When the cone angle covers an area larger than the objects, Auto Focus keeps the Dmap tightly focused on the shadow-casting objects. When **Use Dmap Auto Focus** is turned **Off**, you need to set a specific angle to focus the Dmap. Care must be taken when setting this angle because if you set the **Dmap Focus** too small, the shadow may be cut off or may not appear at all.

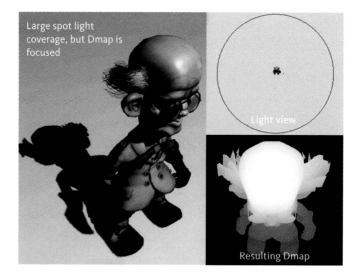

Use Dmap Auto Focus On

When the **Cone Angle** covers an area larger than the objects, **Auto Focus** keeps the Dmap coverage focused on the shadow-casting objects.

For **Directional Lights**, if **Use Dmap Auto Focus** is **On**, Maya will compute the vector for the light and the world bounding box based on all shadow-casting objects. The Dmap coverage will be fit to the width of the world bounding box looking through the light's Orthographic view. If you have a scene that scales a lot up or down or an object that crosses a large distance perpendicular to the light, the auto focus can cause flickering in animation. This is because the Dmap resolution remains constant but the coverage will keep changing, affecting the quality of the shadows. To avoid this, turn **Off** the **Use Dmap Auto Focus** option and manually set the **Dmap Width Focus**.

To determine the value to use as the **Dmap Width Focus**, look through the selected light and track and zoom until the shadow-casting objects are closely bounded by the view.
Select **View → Camera Attribute Editor**, and under **Orthographic Views**, the **Orthographic Width** is the value you should use as the **Dmap Width Focus** on the light.

Tracking and dollying the view of the light changes the position of the light. Normally, the position of a directional light is not important; however, when turning **Use Dmap Auto Focus** Off, you need to turn **On Use Light Position** on the light so that Maya knows the location from which you positioned the Dmap. Forgetting to turn On **Use Light Position** results in the default behavior where the Dmap is positioned at the origin. This may result in incorrect or offset shadows.

Directional light shadows

Directional lights have two possible behaviors with Dmap shadows. Since directional lights are assumed to be at an infinite distance from the scene (hence the parallel light rays), by default, they will cast shadows on the entire scene. The bounding box of the scene is taken and an orthogonal Dmap region is created, which contains the entire scene. This can result in shadow Dmap resolution problems if the scene is very large, but only if a small section of the scene is being viewed, or if the scene changes size dramatically over an animation.

Use Light Position is provided to limit the number of objects that are involved in a directional light's Dmap. Setting this attribute to **true** makes the directional light take its position (the location of the directional light icon in the view) into account. Objects in the half space defined by the light's position and direction are illuminated by the directional light and are used in the creation of the shadow Dmap. Any objects *behind* the directional light are not lit and do not participate in the generation of the shadow Dmap. The **Use Light Position** attribute is not on by default and can only be accessed when the **Use Dmap Auto Focus** is turned off.

The following explains how to create nice-looking shadows with a directional light.

1 Set the Dmap options

- Select the directional light that you are using to cast Dmap shadows.

- In the **Attribute Editor**, go to the **Dmap Shadows** section and set **Use Dmap Auto Focus** to **Off**.

- Set the **Use Light Position** to **On**.

2 Look through the light

- Make sure the directional light is selected, and then select **Panels → Look Through Selected.**

- Place this view so that all shadow-casting objects are closely bounded by it.

  *When you **Look Through Selected** on a light, a camera node underneath the light transform node is temporarily created. When you change the panel's view back to an Orthographic or Perspective view, the extra camera node is removed.*

3 Note the Orthographic values

- While looking through the directional light, select the **Camera** by going to **View → Camera Attribute Editor...**

- Open the **Orthographic Views** section and note the **Orthographic Width** value.

  The Orthographic Width value is the distance across the camera view. If you navigate around the scene until all the objects that will be casting shadows are contained within the view, the Orthographic Width will be the distance across the scene.

4 Set the Dmap Width Focus

- Select the light.
- Enter the value you recorded above into the **Dmap Width Focus**.

Tips for good directional light shadows:

- Render out the scene with **Disk Based Dmap** on **Overwrite Existing Dmaps** and **fcheck** the Dmap for the light. It will be in the *depth* directory of the current project. This will help troubleshooting. There is a *midmap* and the standard Dmap. You will need to press the **Z** key to see the depth information in these files.

- To help set-up accurate and detailed shadows without using huge Dmap resolutions, background geometry or ground planes may be able to have the **Casts Shadows** flag in the **Render Stats** section of the Attribute Editor turned **Off** so they will not be included in the auto focus. Another option is to use **Auto Focus Off** and **Use Light Position On** to manually tighten the shot.

- In the case where you have a problematic scene (where the world bounding box changes size dramatically or an object crosses a large distance perpendicular to the light), you may have to sacrifice speed and use a very high resolution Dmap and manually set the **Dmap Width Focus** to avoid flickering shadows.

Point light shadows

Point lights produce shadows by casting up to 12 Dmaps; a standard Dmap and a midmap are created in each of the cardinal axis directions (+X, -X, +Y, -Y, +Z, and -Z) from the point light's position in space. If there is no shadow-casting object in a particular cardinal axis direction, no Dmap for that direction is created. Be aware that if you specify a large shadow Dmap resolution, there can be 12 Dmaps of that large resolution generated. Maya does try to compact the Dmaps as much as possible, but large Dmaps can still occupy a great deal of memory and take valuable time to render. To further optimize your shadow Dmaps from point lights, you can turn individual directions off. For example, if there is nothing of interest to cast shadows on the ceiling of your room, you could disable the +Y Dmap by turning **Off** the **Use Y+ Dmap** attribute in the **Dmap Shadow Attributes** section of the point light's Attribute Editor.

Spot light shadows

Spot lights by default use only one Dmap. This approach has limitations when the angle of the spot light exceeds 90 degrees; the resolution of the Dmap must be increased dramatically to keep the shadow quality high. You can use up to six Dmaps for spot lights by turning **Off** the **Use Only Single Dmap** in the Attribute Editor. When this attribute is turned off, and the cone angle of the spot light exceeds 90 degrees, five or six Dmaps are created facing each axis directions of the spot light, much the same as for a point light. The only difference is that a spot light will only cast five Dmaps if the spot light does not shine onto one of the six faces. Just as cubic reflection maps avoid aliasing at the boundaries between faces of the cube, the cubic shadow map is also filtered to avoid artifacts.

Motion-blurred shadows

Shadows themselves do not motion-blur. To work around this limitation, render a shadow pass separately and process it to add blur before compositing. The other option is to use the mental ray® shadow maps.

Dmap shadows in IPR

There are some **Dmap Shadow** attributes that will update automatically in an IPR region, while others can only be previewed by selecting in the **Render View** window **IPR → Update Shadow Maps**. The shadow attributes are arranged in the light's Attribute Editor so that these attributes are grouped together.

Casting Dmap shadows example

In this exercise, you will experiment with casting Dmap shadows using the Constructor. The moon should be the only light source in the scene, so it should definitely cast shadows.

1   **Scene file**
    - **Open** the scene *04_moonLight 01.ma*.

2   **Create a directional light**
    - Set the light **Color** to be a **light blue**.

3   **Turn On Dmap shadows**
    - Select the light and set **Use Dmap Shadows** to **On.**
    - IPR render the scene and select a section that will allow you to see updates to the shadow.

    You will notice that the shadows do not look very good. They look blockish and the image contains many self-shadowing artifacts.

Moon light shadows

Note: *In this example scene, the Cast Shadows option of the skydome has been turned Off, otherwise the entire scene would be shadowed.*

4   Turn Off shadow casting

In this scene, the shadows are looking pixelated because the scene is large and the **Resolution** of the Dmap is at the default of 512. Before increasing the resolution of the Dmap, remember that the large ground planes do not cast shadows on anything so you can turn their **Cast Shadows** render attribute to **Off**. This allows **Dmap Auto Focus** to reduce the area that the Dmap covers, which improves the shadows in the scene.

- Set the *background:geoLayer* to be unreferenced.
- Select the *groundPlane* and open its **Attribute Editor**.
- In the **Render Stats** section, set the **Casts Shadows** flag to **Off**.

    The ground geometry will not be taken into consideration when computing the world bounding box.

- **Repeat** for any other background object that does not need to cast shadows.

Tip: *If you need to do this for many objects, use* **Window → General Editors → Attribute Spreadsheet...** *and look under the* **Render** *tab.*

- In the **Render view** window, use **IPR → Update Shadow Maps** to see the change in the shadows.

    The shadows will have tightened up.

5 Increase the resolution

You can see that the shadow quality is still blockish. The default resolution of 512 is not sufficient for this light shadowing the entire scene. You could just increase the **Dmap Filter Size** and have very soft shadows. However, some shadows from thin objects would become very faint and could flicker in animation with such a low resolution shadow map.

- In the **Attribute Editor** for *the directional light,* increase the **Dmap Resolution** until the blocky appearance is reduced and the level of shadow detail is to your satisfaction.

Tip: *Remember to use the **Update Shadow Maps** to see the results in IPR.*

Shadows with high resolution 4096 Dmap

Note: *Objects with transparency, such as the trees, will not cast proper shadows because the Dmap shadows do not take into consideration transparent pixels. In order to render semi-transparent objects with proper shadows, you will need to use raytraced shadows which will be covered later in this lesson.*

6 Adjust the Dmap Bias

At this point, the shadows are looking much better. However, you might notice self-shadowing artifacts. This can be solved using the **Dmap Bias** attribute.

- With IPR running, adjust **Dmap Bias** very slightly to values that are greater than **0.001**.

  The Dmap Bias will update in IPR automatically.

Note: *Too large a value may result in surfaces coming out of shadow that should be in shadow.*

7 Adjust the Dmap Filter Size

The final step is to smooth the rough edges of the shadows.

- Increase the **Dmap Filter Size** until the shadows have a nice soft look.

    A value of 5 should be enough to give nice smooth edges on the shadows. The higher you set this attribute, the softer the edges will look, but you will pay a significant price in the length of time it takes to render.

Shadows with Dmap Filter Size of 5

> **Tip:** For very soft and fuzzy shadows, sometimes it is better to use a low resolution Dmap with some amount of filtering rather than very high resolution Dmaps with very high filter sizes.

Optimizing Disk-Based Dmaps

The **Dmap Shadow** section contains settings to allow you to **Overwrite Existing Dmap(s)/ Reuse Existing Dmap(s)**. These settings cause the Dmaps to be written to or read from disk and should be enabled when doing iterative render tests on a scene with shadows that are finalized, or when there is only a camera fly-by/fly-through of the scene. Be aware that if you set these flags with animated moving objects, it will cause your shadows to remain stationary while the objects move.

- To help lower render times with **Disk Based Dmaps**, set **Disk Based Dmaps** to **Reuse Existing Dmap(s)**. The Dmap will be calculated the first time you render and saved to disk. During each subsequent render, the same Dmaps will be read from disk and the mid distance between them calculated.

Volumetric lighting effects

Another feature of Dmap shadows is the ability to cast volume shadows through fog. This is a very popular effect in movies and television. This effect is referred to as **Volumetric Lighting**.

In the support files, there is a scene called *04-volumetricLight_01.ma* **that** contains an example of volumetric lighting. Watch the movie *fogLightMoth.mov* for a rendered example of this effect.

Shadowing the fog is done by examining the shadow map a number of times across the fog volume.

The shadows are cast within the light fog

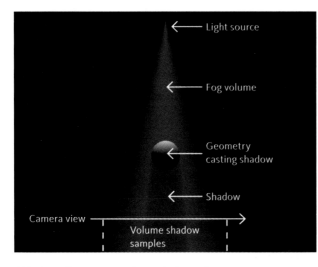

Side view of a ray penetrating a shadow volume

The number of times the fog is sampled is controlled by the attribute **Fog Shadow Samples,** located in the **Shadows** section of the light source. The higher the number of samples, the higher the quality of the shadows in the fog. Keep in mind, though, that this will increase render times. Also note that, internally, Maya does not use **Mid Distance** when fog shadows are being rendered.

To darken the shadows in the fog, the **Fog Shadow Intensity** can be increased. The effect of increasing the **Fog Shadow Intensity** and the **Fog Shadow Samples** is shown in the following images:

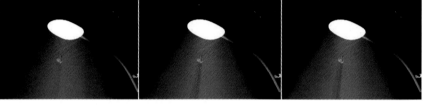

Samples: 20
Intensity: 1
Faint and grainy shadows

Samples: 20
Intensity: 3
More dramatic shadows, still grainy

Samples: 60
Intensity: 3
Dramatic and smooth shadows

Various fog shadow intensity and samples values

Light fog texture

Light fog is usually caused by small particles that scatter the light, giving an impression of volume. In order to recreate this effect, you can map a 3D texture in the fog and even animate the texture. It is very easy and pretty to add light fog texture to a scene, but it will cost some time to the renderer to calculate this effect.

In order to add a fog texture to a light, simply click on the **Map** button of the **Light Fog** attribute under the **Light Effects** section of the Attribute Editor. Doing so will create the nodes and connections required to render a homogeneous volumetric light fog. Map a 3D texture, such as a Solid Fractal, in the **Light Fog Color** attribute. Animate the texture to give the impression of fluidity.

In the support files, *04-volumetricLight_02.ma* contains the following scene, which uses volumetric textured fog.

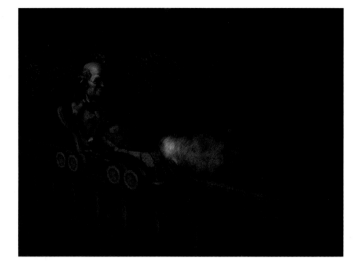

Light fog with 3D texture

Raytraced shadows

Raytraced shadows are slower to render than Dmap shadows and generally have quite a different look than Dmaps. However, there are several situations where you would need to use raytraced shadows:

- To render transparency-mapped shadow-casting objects where you want to see the details of the texture map in the shadow;
- To obtain colored transparent shadows from objects with a material that has color on the transparency channel;
- To obtain shadow attenuation where the shadow dissipates as it gets further away from the shadow-casting object (and for transparent objects, when a shadow's tendency to be brighter in the center);
- To create shadows from ambient lights, which have no Dmap shadows.

Detailed shadow through
transparency mapped surface

Shadow attenuation

Colored shadows from
colored transparent surface

Shadow from ambient light type

Various raytraced shadow effects

Note: *In order to use raytraced shadows, you must set the* **Raytracing** *option to* **On** *in the* **Render Settings.**

How to get soft attenuated shadows

The raytraced shadow attributes **Light Radius** and **Shadow Rays** help control the final look of the shadow. Increasing the **Light Radius** to a non-zero value will cause the shadow to begin to dissipate as it gets further from the shadow-casting object. To achieve a smooth appearance of raytraced shadows, the number of **Shadow Rays** will usually need to be increased. This can be seen in the following images:

Light radius: 0
Shadow rays: 1

Light radius: 3
Shadow rays: 1

Light radius: 3
Shadow rays: 10

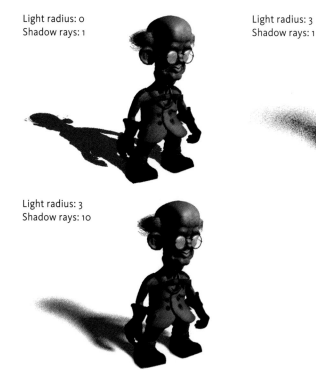

Attenuated raytraced shadow variations

> **Tip:** *The shadow of a transparent object tends to be brighter in the center, simulating a light's focus. On the material node of that object under the* **Raytrace Options***, there is a* **Shadow Attenuation** *control to simulate this property. A setting of 0 results in a constant intensity of the shadow, whereas a setting of 1 results in brighter shadows focused in the center.*

mental ray shadow maps

The shadow map computation in mental ray is similar to the Dmap shadow computation. Like Dmap shadows, this type of shadow can be imprecise, yet it is faster to compute than raytraced shadows.

In mental ray®, **Point, Directional, Spot,** and **Area Lights** are the light types that can produce shadow maps. To enable this option, select a light and turn **On** the **Use mental ray shadow map overrides** option in the light's mental ray section of the Attribute Editor.

> **Note:** *To use this technique you must render using the mental ray renderer.*

Dmap resolution

Resolution under mental ray **Shadow Maps Attributes** is the same as the Maya **Dmap Resolution** attribute. It defines the size of the shadow map rendered from a shadow-casting light. The larger this value, the more accurate the shadow map, resulting in more precise shadows. However, increasing this value will increase your render time.

Samples

Samples represent the number of samples the renderer will take to reduce the creation of artifacts. The higher the samples, the longer the render will take. In the examples below, you can see how increasing the samples' value gets rid of any artifacts. Note that increasing this value also increases render time.

Softness

Softness works the same as the Maya **Dmap Filter** attributes in that it controls the softness of the shadow edge. This often works best when used with a low resolution value.

Softness: 0   Softness: 0.3   Softness: 0.3
Samples: 0   Samples: 0   Samples: 30

mental ray shadow variations

> **Note:** *The mental ray shadow map algorithm attempts to resolve self-shadowing artifacts without user interaction. Therefore, parameters such as* **Use Mid Dist Dmap** *and* **Dmap Bias** *are not necessary and will not be used when the* **Take Settings from Maya** *button is used.*

Auto Focus shadow maps

The mental ray shadow map algorithm employs a similar **Auto Focus** feature to keep the shadow map focused tightly on the shadow-casting objects. Unlike Maya, however, mental ray does not allow a user to edit the placement of these maps.

Reusing mental ray shadow maps

You can re-use shadow maps to help speed up render times. Normally, mental ray will compute one shadow map per frame for an animation. If the light or shadow does not change over the course of an animation, you can reuse the same shadow map over and over, saving computation time and speeding up the render process. To reuse a shadow map, do the following:

- Open up the mental ray **Render Settings** and under the **Shadows** section, make sure the **Rebuild Mode** flag is set to **Reuse Existing Maps**.

- Open the **Shadows** section under the **mental ray** section of the light's **Attribute Editor**.

- Turn **On** the **Use mental ray shadow map overrides** option.

- Type a name for the shadow in the **Shadow Map File Name** field.

   This will be the name of the shadow map that is saved to disk.

> **Tip:** *You can also specify to add the* **Light Name**, **Scene Name**, *and* **Frame Extension** *to the shadow map name.*

- Do a render to generate that shadow map.

   The file will be saved in the mentalRay subdirectory of your current project directory under shadowMap.

- Leave the name in the field and mental ray will automatically reuse this map for every

Shadow map attributes

Motion blur shadow maps

In the real world, a photographer selects a camera with specific properties, adjusts the camera's settings (for example, the shutter speed), positions the camera to compose the shot, and then photographs the three-dimensional real world to produce a two-dimensional photograph. One of the properties the 3D computer graphics camera will attempt to reproduce is motion blur, the phenomenon of an object looking blurred as it moves quickly across a frame. With mental ray®, if an object has motion blur, its shadows can also exhibit motion blur. This effect is not possible with the Maya shadow types.

The following will take you through setting up motion-blurred shadow maps.

1 Scene file

- Open the file called *04-motionBlurredShadows_01.ma*.

  The file is very simple, consisting of a plane of light and an animated sphere.

2 Turn On Dmap shadows

- **Select** *directionalLight1* and turn **Use Depth Map Shadows** to **On**.

- Render frame **15** and click the **Keep Image** button in the **Render View** window.

3 Turn On motion blur

- **Open** *the mental ray Render Settings and* under the **Motion Blur** section of the **Quality** tab, choose **No Deformation** from the **Motion Blur** pull-down menu.

- Make sure the **Motion Blur By** is set to **3** to increase the amount of blur.

- Make sure that **Motion Blur Shadow Maps** under the **Shadows Maps** section of the Render Settings is **On**.

4 Render a frame

- Do another render at frame **15** in the Render view window.

- Keep this image and compare the shadows from the first image, which have no motion blur on them, to the current image.

5 Edit the motion blurred shadow

- If you find that your shadow exhibits artifacting or that the shadow itself is not soft or blurred enough, you may want to go to the shadow map settings under the light's **Attribute Editor** and increase the **Samples** and **Softness** parameters.

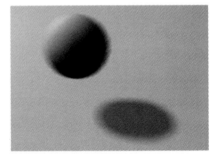

Motion blurred shadows with Samples set to 5 and Softness to 0.4

Tip: *If the blur on the object is relatively small, you may want to use only the Softness attribute to give the illusion of a motion-blurred shadow.*

Volumetric shadow maps

In order to cast shadows through a fog volume, you can use either shadow maps or raytrace shadows. If you use raytrace shadows, you will be able to cast transparent information through the shadow volume. Capturing transparent information through a volume is something that is not possible when using the Maya shadow options.

The following example shows how to create volumetric shadow maps.

1 Scene file

- Open the file called *04-volumeShadows_01.ma*.

  The file is very simple, consisting of a spot light and a sphere.

2 Turn On shadows and fog

- Select *spotLight1* and set **Use Dmap Shadows** to **On** and **Use mental ray shadow map overrides** to **On**.

- Select the map button next to **Light Fog** under the **Light Effects** section.

3 Edit the shadows

You may find that you either cannot see your shadows or there may be some artifacting. To get rid of this, do the following:

- Increase the **Samples** attribute under the **mental ray** section of the **Attribute Editor** to **2**.

- Slowly increase the value for the **Volume Samples Override** in the **Render Stats** section of the light's *coneShape1* node.

- To further alleviate artifacting, set the **Depth Jitter** option to **On**.

  This will randomize the samples of the volume by replacing banding artifacts with noise.

Volumetric shadows

mental ray raytraced shadows

Raytraced shadows in mental ray are the same to set-up and use as in Maya. If you are using the mental ray renderer with raytrace shadows, you will need to make sure **Raytracing** is turned **On** under the **Quality** tab of the mental ray Render Settings.

Reasons to use mental ray raytrace shadows include:

- Capturing transparency-mapped detail in a shadow that is cast through a volume;
- Rendering motion blurred shadows.

Note: *As you have seen earlier, you can also use mental ray shadow maps to get motion blurred shadows.*

Raytraced shadow methods

mental ray has three global shadow overrides. These modes affect all raytraced shadows in a scene. They can be useful for globally refining and adjusting the amount of information that is considered in the calculation of raytraced shadows. The controls are found in the mental ray **Render Settings** → **Quality** → **Shadows** section.

Shadow methods

Simple method

The distinctive feature associated with this shadow calculation mode is that the searching order for objects occluding illumination rays from a light source is unpredictable. This mode makes for faster shadow calculation.

Sorted method

This shadow mode is similar to simple mode with the exception that occluding objects are first listed and then sorted. Objects that occlude light rays from the light source are evaluated first.

Segmented method

This is the default. With this mode, shadow rays are sent from the illuminated point backwards toward the light source. This is the reverse of what happens with simple and sorted shadows. When a shadow ray hits an occluding object, its shadow shader is *called*. The occluding object's shadow shader then sends another shadow ray off towards the light source. This shadow mode allows the creation of volumetric raytraced shadows.

Disabled

As the name implies, this effectively turns all shadow calculations off. This is a handy global switch or override that turns all shadow calculations in a scene off.

Conclusion

Shadows are an important part of creating mood and atmosphere in a scene. There are a number of important concepts to understand in order to achieve the best shadows possible without compromising your render times.

In the next lesson, you will learn about cameras.

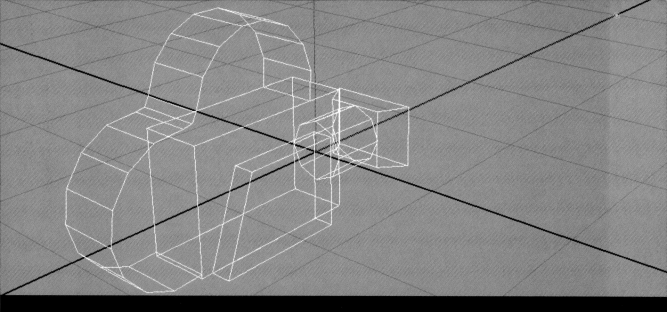

Cameras

A 3D camera is very similar to a motion picture or still camera. It mimics real-world settings to allow you to match images captured by real cameras.

In this lesson, you will learn the following:

- How to work with cameras
- How to work with film gates and film backs
- Aspect ratios
- How to do rotoscoping using D1 images
- mental ray camera attributes

Camera basics

The vast majority of your renderings will make use of the *Perspective* camera. While there is nothing technically wrong with using this camera for all of your animation and rendering, it is advisable to create a new camera to work with.

> **Note:** *The Perspective camera is treated differently because it is a static node. It is invisible to start with to discourage you from using it for your animation and rendering.*

There are two ways to create a new camera in your scene:

1 Creating a new camera

- In any view, go to **Panels** → **Perspective** → **New**.

  OR

- Go to **Create** → **Camera**.

  The Create menu method will place the camera at the origin, while using the Panels menu will place it away from the origin like the default Perspective camera. Other than the location at which the camera is created, there is no difference between these two methods.

2 Renaming the camera

- With the new camera selected, use the name field at the top of the **Channel Box** to give the camera a new name.

  This method of renaming will name both the transform node and the shape node.

Working with cameras

Once you have created a new camera or several new cameras, it is very easy to switch between them or change a view.

1 Switch between cameras

- In any view, select **Panels** → **Perspective** and choose from the list of cameras.

2 Positioning a camera

The main workflow for positioning cameras uses the following combinations:

> **Alt + LMB** to tumble the camera;
>
> **Alt + MMB** to track the camera;
>
> **Alt + LMB + MMB** or **Alt + RMB** to dolly the camera.

Additionally, Auotdek® Maya® has a suite of camera tools that can be used to achieve precise control over your camera's position and behavior.

- In the modeling window, select **View → Camera Tools**.

Note: *For more information on camera tools, see the Maya online documentation.*

3 Stepping back and forth between camera views

It is possible to step back and forth between your present and previous camera views.

- Use the **]** key to go forward and the **[** key to go backward though your recent camera views.

Tip: *You can change the animated camera transition speed in the* **Window → Settings/Preferences → Preferences,** *by changing the Total time value found under the Cameras category.*

4 Undo camera movements

The camera views are intentionally not included in the **Undo** feature. This is because you would be able to do many individual camera moves in order to get around your scene, which would cause the undo queue to get flooded with unhelpful undo's. If you would prefer them to be included, do one of the following:

- Enable **Camera Attribute Editor → Movement Options → Undoable Movements**.

  OR

- Select **View → Camera Settings → Undoable Movements**.

5 Camera bookmarks

Camera bookmarks can be very helpful when you need to return to a specific camera view. To create a bookmark, do the following:

- In the camera view, go to **View → Bookmarks → Edit Bookmarks...**

6 Selection and Frame Selection

There are two ways you can quickly dolly in on a selected object or group of selected objects:

- Use **View → Look at selection** to have the object centered in the window.
- Use **View → Frame Selection** to have the object centered in the window and close up to the camera.

These camera commands will also establish a new point of interest that the camera will orbit around. If you find that you cannot zoom in close enough on an object, try framing it with **Frame Selection** first.

> **Tip:** *You can do **Frame Selection** with the **f** hotkey to frame the selected objects. To frame all objects in the scene, press the **a** hotkey.*

7 Box dolly feature

To quickly dolly in on an area of the scene, you can use the box dolly feature.

- **Alt+Ctrl** and draw a marquee around the objects you wish to dolly in on.

    Left to *right* dollies **in**.

    Right to *left* dollies **out**.

Dolly vs. zoom

The difference between dolly and zoom is that when you dolly, you are physically moving the camera in space, while zoom refers to changing the camera's focal length.

What is the difference between moving the camera and changing the focal length? Why would you choose one over the other? The answer is that when you move the camera, the perspective changes. Objects far from the camera change in relative size at a slower rate than objects close to the camera. This is essentially what you see through your human eyes; as you walk around, your perspective changes.

When you zoom, you are changing the focal length of the lens; perspective does not change. This is something that your eyes cannot achieve, which creates an unsettling quality when used for heightened effect.

Perspective could be thought of as the rate that objects change in size in the frame as their distance from the camera changes.

> **Tip:** *In the camera's Attribute Editor, you can adjust the **Focal Length** in the **Camera Attributes** section to adjust the zoom, or use the **Zoom Tool** in the Camera Tools. If you look at a camera icon, you will see that the length of the lens is changing but the camera is not moving.*
> *Notice how this also changes the **Angle of View** attribute. It is not possible to animate the **Angle of View,** but it is possible to animate the **Focal Length** attribute.*

Hitchcock's Vertigo effect

Anyone who has seen the Alfred Hitchcock movie *Vertigo* may be familiar with the eerie camera effect in which some objects appear to move further away while others appear to move closer to the camera.

This is achieved by zooming in while dollying out or by dollying in while zooming out.

Cameras for batch rendering

For batch rendering, you will need to specify which camera you wish to render from.

- For most purposes, use **Render Settings** → **Image File Output** → **Renderable Cameras.**
- Select the camera from the **Renderable Camera** pop-up list.

Tip: *For more advanced users who need to render more than one camera at the same time, it is possible to use the* **Camera Attribute Editor** → **Output Settings** → **Renderable** *flag. In this case, the Render Settings will show more than one camera marked as renderable in the* **Camera** *pop-up list.*

Display options

When you are trying to frame a shot to render, you need to be able to see what area will actually be rendered. Cameras have some display mechanisms that allow you to see the rendering area very clearly.

1 Resolution Gate

- Within the camera view panel, enable **View** → **Camera Settings** → **Resolution Gate**.

  Doing so will display a green rectangle surrounding the renderable area in the camera view.

2 Overscan

- While in the **Attribute Editor** for the camera, go to the **Display Options** section.
- Increase the **Overscan** attribute.

  The **Overscan** *value does not change the rendered image. It is just a display feature to allow you to see parts of the scene outside of the region that will be rendered.*

Tip: *You can also modify the* **Overscan** *attribute for the camera to a value less than* 1 *to get a close-up of your scene without disturbing your camera position.*

3 Gate Mask

The area outside the resolution gate will not be rendered, so in order to focus only on what is visible to the camera, you can toggle the **Gate Mask** option.

- Within the camera view panel, toggle the **View** → **Camera Settings** → **Gate Mask**.
- Open the **Attribute Editor** for the camera and go to the **Display Options** section.
- Change the **Gate Mask Opacity** and **Gate Mask Color** to tweak the appearance of the gate mask.

Film gates and film backs

The following is a fairly extensive description of what *film gates* and *film backs* are on real cameras and in Maya. If you are creating an entire shot in Maya and have complete artistic license over the view from the camera, there is no reason to be concerned with film backs. As you have already seen, the default settings will ensure that everything inside the resolution gate will be rendered. If you are trying to match the look of a real shot, film backs become important.

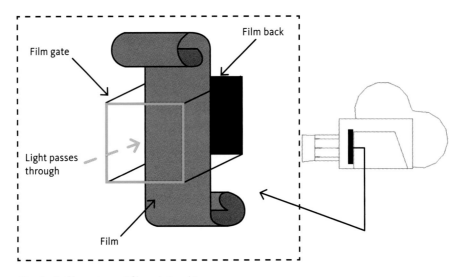

Film back, film gate, and film relationship

The *film back* corresponds to the size of the film negatives and is measured in millimeters. Because of this, when people talk about a 35mm camera, for instance, they are referring to the size of the film back and the film negative.

The *film gate* is a metal plate that sits in front of the film negative to hold it in place. The plate overlaps some portion of the film so only the region inside the gate is actually exposed to light. It is this region that you are simulating in Maya in order to match the real footage. It is expressed as the **Camera Aperture** attribute.

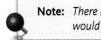

Note: *There is no attribute to specify the entire size of the film back separately as this would just represent unexposed wasted portions of the film in real life.*

The **Film Gate** attribute in Maya is presented as a list of presets. In the list you will see five settings for 35mm. This is because, as you can see from the above discussion, for all 35mm cameras the film back and film negative sizes will be the same. However, the size of the region inside the film gate will differ depending on how big the opening is in the gate. Keep in mind that it is the exposed region of the film that you are simulating when you render an image in Maya.

Film Back		
Film Gate	35mm 1.85 Projection ▼	
Camera Aperture	0.825	0.446
Film Aspect Ratio	1.85	
Lens Squeeze Ratio	1.000	

Film back attributes

Another attribute that is used to describe the region inside the film gate is the **Film Aspect Ratio**. The following diagram shows the meaning of **Film Aspect Ratio**. It is simply the **Camera Aperture** attribute represented as a ratio.

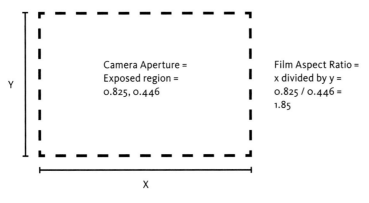

Camera Aperture =
Exposed region =
0.825, 0.446

Film Aspect Ratio =
x divided by y =
0.825 / 0.446 =
1.85

Y

X

Film aspect ratio

Film back with focal length and angle of view

The following steps demonstrate the relationship between the film back, focal length, and angle of view.

1 **Change the film gate presets**

• Use the pop-up list of presets to switch between various **Film Gates**.

*Notice that the **Angle Of View** changes, but the **Focal Length** does not.*

2   Adjust the focal length

- Adjust the **Focal Length** and notice that the **Angle Of View** changes.

  As you extend the focal length, the angle of view gets narrower. As you shorten the focal length, the angle of view gets wider.

The following diagrams illustrate these relationships.

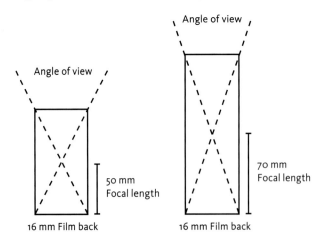

Effect of changing focal length without changing film back

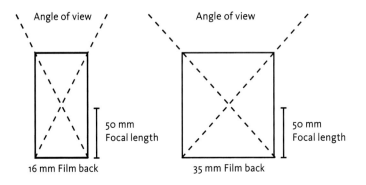

Effect of changing film back without changing focal length

Tip: *The **Focal Length** of a lens is defined as the distance from the lens to the film plane. Lenses are identified by their focal length expressed in millimeters. By this you can see that a 50mm lens has a focal length of 50mm.*

Most people are familiar with the effect of changing the focal length in real cameras. This amounts to switching to different lenses or adjusting the zoom to lengthen or shorten the lens you are using. You can see how this affects the angle of view in the first diagram above.

The second diagram above illustrates what will happen if you keep the same lens, but switch to a different-sized camera.

The process of switching to a different camera size while keeping the same size lens is exactly what you are doing when you switch the **Film Back** in Maya. The result is that the angle of view changes, but the focal length does not.

Now you can see why changing to different film backs without changing the focal length seems to cause the camera to zoom in and out.

> **Note:** *The camera aperture is related to the focal length in that different film backs have different normal lenses. A normal lens focal length is not telephoto or wide-angle. It closely approximates normal vision. As the size of the camera aperture increases, a longer focal length is required to maintain normal perspective. That is why a 35mm camera uses a 50mm lens as a normal lens. On a 16mm camera, the same 50mm lens would appear to be telephoto. A normal focal length for a camera is a focal length that equals the diagonal measurement of the camera aperture in millimeters, which means you have to find the hypotenuse.*

Film gate and resolution gate

Now that you have looked at the meaning of film backs and film gates, you need to understand how this relates to the **Resolution Gate** for rendering.

1   **Create a new file**

2   **Turn on the Resolution Gates**
    - Set both the **Resolution Gate** and **Film Gate** checkboxes to **On** in the camera's **Display Options** in the Attribute Editor.

3   **Change the Overscan**
    - Set the **Overscan** value to **1.3**.

      Notice that at this point the gates do not match. This is because they do not have the same aspect ratio.

4 **Fit Resolution Gate**

The **Fit Resolution Gate** attribute controls how Maya fits the film gate to the resolution gate. By default, the **Fit Resolution Gate** attribute is set to **Horizontal**.

- In the camera's **Attribute Editor**, change the **Fit Resolution Gate** attribute in the **Film Back** section to **Vertical**.

Notice how the film gate is drawn differently relative to the resolution gate.

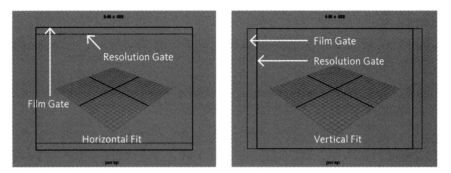

Fit/resolution gate difference

Because the two gates have a different aspect ratio, Maya can only match them in one dimension —either horizontally or vertically, but not both.

In the case of **Horizontal Fit**, the width of the film gate is matched to the resolution gate's horizontal dimension. This means that the gates will not match vertically.

In the case of **Vertical Fit**, this ensures that the height of the film gate is matched to the resolution gate's vertical dimension. In this case, the horizontal width of the gates will not match.

Safe action and safe title

Now that you understand the different gates, you will learn about the safe action and safe title. These options can be of interest depending on your production type, such as TV shows, publicity or films, since clipping may occur around your images to fit the media resolution.

- Within the camera view panel, enable **View** → **Camera Settings** → **Safe Action**.

Turn this option on to display a box defining the region that you should keep all of your scene's action within if you plan to display the rendered images on a television screen.

- Within the camera view panel, enable **View** → **Camera Settings** → **Safe Title**.

Turn this option on to display a box defining the region that you should keep all of your scene's text (titles) within if you plan to display the rendered images on a television screen.

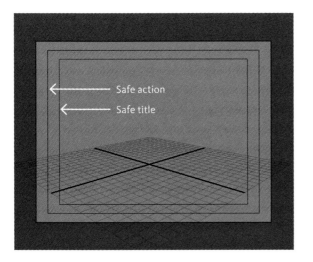

Displayed safe action and safe title

Match the resolution gate and film gate

If you are working with film gates, chances are you are trying to match a real camera, so you want your rendered images to match the real film gate exactly.

The only way that the film gate and resolution gate can match exactly in both dimensions is if they share the same aspect ratio. This will be covered later.

Note: *Again, this matching of aspect ratios is only required when aiming for the look of a specific real camera. Otherwise, film backs do not need to be considered at all.*

Image planes

Image planes are 2D texture-mapped planes connected to a camera, perpendicular to the lens axis. They can be used for purposes such as creating environments or tracing concept sketches in the early phases of modeling. In this lesson, you are going to look at how to use them to match live action.

Matching live action refers to the process of positioning and animating objects in a scene relative to a live action background sequence of images. The specific case that will be covered involves working with NTSC digital video footage.

Note: *NTSC is the only video format that will be covered. The workflow itself is the same for other formats, like PAL; only the specific numbers differ.*

Non-square pixels

Using *NTSC Digital Video*, or *D1*, as it is commonly referred to in the industry, poses a unique challenge that is often misunderstood. The challenge surrounds the fact that digital video is generated by devices that typically use *non-square pixels*. However, computer monitors display only square pixels. To compensate for this, Maya has a workflow to allow your objects to match-up correctly with the background plates.

Aspect ratios

The key to successfully matching live action is to understand the meaning of several different aspect ratios.

Image aspect ratio

This is the aspect ratio of the image you will render and is represented by the *resolution gate*. Image aspect simply represents the resolution of an image as a ratio.

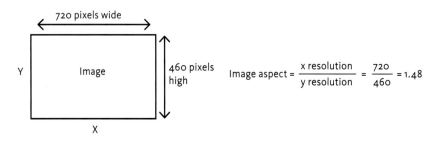

Image aspect ratio

The above diagram illustrates how a digital video image does not satisfy the 1.33 aspect desired for television viewing, until you take into account the *pixel aspect ratio* as described in the next section. This is the special case of image aspect differences you encounter when working with digital video that needs to match computer generated imagery.

Pixel aspect ratio

Each image is made up of pixels. The pixels themselves have an aspect ratio, called the *pixel aspect ratio.*

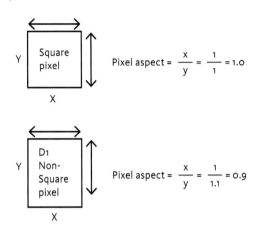

Pixel aspect = $\dfrac{x}{y} = \dfrac{1}{1} = 1.0$

Pixel aspect = $\dfrac{x}{y} = \dfrac{1}{1.1} = 0.9$

Pixel aspect ratio

With digital video, the pixels have an *aspect ratio* of **0.9**. They are slightly taller than they are wide.

Device aspect ratio

Up until now, all of the aspect ratios you have looked at have followed the same equation of *x* divided by *y* equals *aspect ratio.* The device aspect ratio is calculated differently.

device aspect = image aspect x pixel aspect
= 1.48 x 0.9
= 1.33

Film aspect ratio

Another attribute that is used to describe the region defined by the film gate is the **film aspect ratio**. It is simply the **Camera Aperture** attribute represented as a ratio.

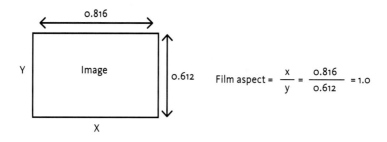

$$\text{Film aspect} = \frac{x}{y} = \frac{0.816}{0.612} = 1.0$$

Film aspect ratio

You will see where these aspect ratios fit in as you go through the workflow.

Workflow to match live action digital video

1 Open a new scene

- Start with a new scene by selecting **File** → **New Scene**.

2 Set the Resolution

- Open **Render Settings** and under the **Common** tab, set **Image Size** → **Presets** to CCIR 601/Quantel NTSC.

3 Set the camera attributes

- Open the **Display Options** in the camera's **Attribute Editor** and set the **Resolution** and **Film Gates** to **On.**

- In the **Film Back** section, set the **Overscan** to **1.3**.

  Recall that this is only a display mechanism that will allow you to see the gates entirely.

- While in the **Film Back** section, chose the preset **Film Gate** → **35mm TV Projection** which has a **Film Aspect** of **1.33**.

  You will need to know which real camera the video footage was shot with in order to know which film gate to choose for an accurate match.

> **Tip:** *The important thing here is that the **Film Aspect** is **1.33**, which matches the device aspect of **D1** video. As long as these two aspect ratios match, the resolution gate and the film gate will match precisely.*

4 Create the image plane

- In the **Environment** section of the camera's Attribute Editor, click on the **Create** button to create an **Image Plane**.

This will build the nodes and the connections required for the image plane.

5 Bring in D1sphere.iff

For this workflow example, bring in the D1 image of a sphere. The sphere makes it very obvious that you are seeing an image distorted by the non-square pixels.

- In the **Image Plane** attributes, browse the **Image Name** and select *D1sphere.iff.*

The image comes in looking slightly stretched horizontally.

- In the **Placement** section of the Attribute Editor, set the **Fit** to **To Size.**

*The **To Size** fit method on the image plane will alter the original aspect ratio of the D1sphere.iff image to make it fit the aspect ratio of the film gate (by default, the image plane is fit to the film gate).*

Notice that as soon as you fit to size, the sphere looks correct.

6 Animate the D1 sequence

If you had a sequence of images, you would need to animate them on the image plane. The easiest way to do this is to select the **Use Image Sequence** attribute in the file node's Attribute Editor.

7 Match the live action

At this point, you can go ahead and model, position, and animate your objects using the image plane as your guide.

> **Note:** *An image plane is intended to move along with your camera. If you want to disable this feature, you can change Image Plane to Fixed in the Image Plane Attributes section of the Attribute Editor.*

8 Turn off the display of the image plane

By default, an image plane will render with your scene. The following will hide the image plane.

- Once the animation is done, set the **Display Mode** to **None** in the **Image Plane Attributes** section.

This ensures that the image plane will not be rendered in your final images.

9   **Render the sequence**

- In the **Render Settings** under the **Common** tab, set the **Frame/Animation Ext** pop-up list to one of the settings that has a **#** in it.

  This will enable the rendering of an animation.

- Set the **Start** and **End** frame numbers.

- **Batch Render** the sequence using **Render → Batch Render...**

10 **Composite the images**

Once the images are rendered, you will be able to composite them with the D1 footage and everything will match perfectly.

Clipping planes

Clipping planes are used to determine which objects will be rendered in your scene. There is a near clipping plane and a far clipping plane, and all visible objects between these clipping planes will be rendered. The position of these clipping planes is found under **Camera Attributes** in the Attribute Editor. The clipping planes can be seen in the modeling views if they are turned On.

- To turn **On** clipping planes in the view, use **Display → Rendering → Camera/Light Manipulator → Clipping Planes**.

- Adjust them interactively in the view or from the **Attribute Editor**.

Maya outputs a **Z-depth buffer,** which can be used to determine the depth at which a pixel makes first contact with geometry in a scene. The Z-depth values will be between **-1** and **0** depending on how far the geometry is from the near and far clipping planes. Those intersections clipped by the near or far plane will be given a depth of 0. If the clipping planes have a fairly large separation distance in units, precision will be lost when comparing depths that are similar to one another.

For example, if your clipping planes are set far apart and you have a number of objects clustered together, each object will have a depth value that is very similar to the others. If these depth numbers are rounded-off, the values can become identical, resulting in artifacts.

These rendering artifacts will look like background objects showing through foreground objects.

> **Tip:**   *When manually changing the near and far clipping plane values in the Attribute Editor, remember to set these values to the shortest range possible. For instance, attempting to set the near clipping plane to 0.0 and the far clipping plane to 1 000 000, will result in artifacts in the viewport.*

Auto Render Clip Plane

If you select a camera and open the Attribute Editor, you will notice that **Auto Render Clip Plane** is **On** by default. This allows Maya to automatically set the near and far clipping planes optimally, depending on where objects are in the scene. This approach tries to minimize the likelihood of the artifacts mentioned above.

With **Auto Render Clip Plane** turned **On**, the clipping planes can change from frame to frame in an animation. So, if you are outputting Z-depth information for some other purpose, you may wish to turn the Auto clipping **Off**.

If you turn **Off** the **Auto Render Clip Plane**, the values shown in the camera's Attribute Editor will be used in the render.

Optimize renders using clipping planes

- To see the camera's **frustum** use **Display** → **Rendering** → **Camera /Light Manipulator** → **Clipping Planes** or **Display** → **Show** → **Camera Manipulators**.

Note: *The frustrum is the area visible in the camera view, and located beween the clipping planes.*

- Geometry that penetrates the **near** clipping plane will be clipped to the near clipping plane. Any part of the geometry nearer to the camera than the near clipping plane will not be rendered.
- If a piece of geometry spans the **far** clipping plane, it will be rendered in its entirety.
- If a piece of geometry is beyond the far clipping plane, it will not be rendered at all.

  The type of clipping occurring at the far clipping plane is at the object level, not at the triangle level.

The following diagram shows this clipping relationship. Object 1 will be cut by the near clipping plane so that only the portion beyond the near clipping plane is rendered. Object 2 will be completely rendered because part of it is nearer to the camera than the far clipping plane. Object 3 will not be rendered since it is beyond the far clipping plane.

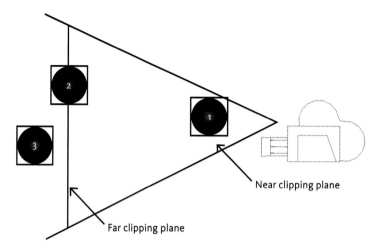

Near clipping plane

Far clipping plane

Near and far plane clipping: object 1 is partially rendered, object 2 is rendered, object 3 is not rendered

Camera output settings

The camera's Attribute Editor contains a section related to what the selected camera will output at render time. Switches can be found here that control whether the camera is renderable and whether or not it will output mask, depth, or color (image).

You can also select how the camera will derive depth information for use in post-process rendering effects such as Paint Effects and depth of field.

The default setting for camera depth lookup is **Furthest Visible Depth**. This is the setting necessary for proper handling of camera to object depth sorting when working with Paint Effects' element rendering.

The **Furthest Visible Depth** setting can have a detrimental effect on other depth-based effects such as depth of field. If you find this to be the case, set this attribute to **Closest Visible Depth**.

mental ray cameras

When rendering using mental ray, you can map shaders to the camera to get interesting effects. The following shows some of these special shaders.

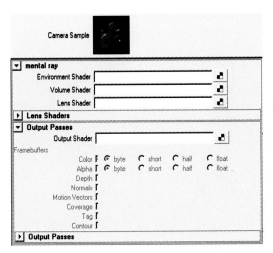

mental ray section of Attribute Editor

Output shader

Allows post-processing of a file prior to it being written. These are plug-ins written in C/C++ that allow custom compositing, motion blurring, depth of field, halo, color correction, and file grain. These custom effects may be preferable to what is in the base package.

Volume shader

In the simplest case, this is a uniform fog that fades objects in the distance to white. It can also be used for smoke, clouds, and fur items that normally would be difficult to model. For Global Illumination, use the photon volume shader.

Lens shader

By allowing modification of the ray direction and origin, more realistic paths through the camera can be achieved instead of passing through a precise path. It can be used to achieve custom depth of field effects.

Environment shader

This option attaches an environment shader to the camera and maps a texture on an infinite theoretical shape.

Conclusion

Camera attributes are important for understanding the rendering process. In order to be able to use them effectively, it is essential to have a complete understanding of the topics covered in this lesson.

In the next lesson, you will learn about raytracing features.

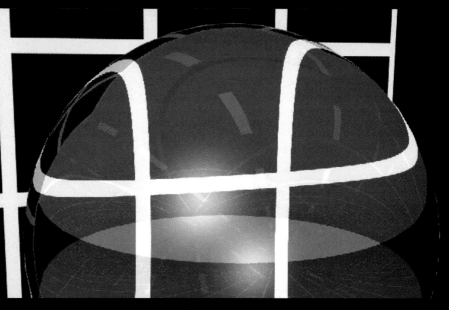

Raytracing

Raytracing is a method of rendering in which rays originate from the camera/ eye and are sent out into the scene. Depending on what they encounter, they can spawn other rays. For instance, if a ray hits a reflective surface it will spawn another ray that will bounce off the surface, and if it encounters another object, you will get a reflection.

Raytracing enables you to cast accurate shadows through partially transparent surfaces and allows you to see real reflections. If you do not raytrace, you can still get the look of reflections through the use of texture maps on the reflected color attribute. However, this can amount to a lot of work and still cannot produce self-reflections, which are important for realism. Raytracing also enables your scene to have refractive surfaces.

In this lesson, you will learn the following:

- How raytracing works

- About reflection, refraction, and shadow limits

- About chromatic aberration

- About environment textures

- About memory requirements

Raytracing

The Autodesk® Maya® rendering architecture is a **hybrid** renderer. It uses an **EAS (Exact Area Sampling)** or **A-buffer algorithm** for primary visibility from the eye, and then raytraces any secondary rays.

When an object is encountered that requires raytracing to compute some component of its shading (raytraced shadows, reflections, and refractions), the raytracer is invoked. An important distinction to make here is that not all objects in a scene will need to be raytraced. If you had a transparent surface with a **Refract Index** of **1.0** (meaning no bending of light will occur), you would simply leave the **Refractions Flag** turned **Off** for that material. In order to use raytracing in Maya, you will need to enable it through the Render Settings window.

 Note: *Keep in mind that raytracing is memory intensive and will increase rendering time.*

1 **Enable raytracing**
  - Select **Window** → **Rendering Editors** → **Render Settings** and open the **Raytracing Quality** section of the **Maya Software** renderer.
  - Click the **Raytracing** checkbox to turn it **On**.

    You have now enabled raytracing for the entire scene.

2 **Set which objects will not be raytraced**

    There is a further level of control in choosing which objects you want raytraced in a scene. By default, all objects have **Raytracing** turned **On**. You will want to turn **Off** raytracing for objects that do not need to be raytraced to cut down on rendering time.

  - Select an object you do not want raytraced and open the **Attribute Editor.**
  - Open the **Render Stats** section.
  - Turn **Visible in Reflections** to **Off**.
  - Turn **Visible in Refractions** to **Off**.

3 **Start rendering**

    You can now render into a view or batch render the scene file.

Reflections, refractions, and shadows

Once you have turned **Raytracing** to **On** in the **Render Settings** and the appropriate **Render Stats** are set, when you render a scene it will have reflections and refractions depending on the materials assigned to the surfaces. If you have turned **Raytrace Shadows** to **On** for the lights in your scene, you will also get raytraced shadows. Notice when you turned **Raytracing On** in the Render Settings there are three sliders: **Reflections**, **Refractions**, and **Shadows**. These sliders correspond to limits that are associated with the rays being used in raytracing. Because shooting many reflection, refraction, or shadow rays increases rendering time, there needs to be a way to limit the number of such rays being shot, and Maya provides two locations where these limits are available. The first is in the Render Settings, which affect everything. The other is in the material's Attribute Editor for reflections and refractions, and in the lights' Attribute Editor for raytraced shadows. The lower set of values of the two will determine the limit for each surface. If you have your limits set too low, you will not get the desired results.

For example, if you have light passing through a transparent sphere, then on a plane, and back again through the sphere, you need to make sure that you have enough reflection rays to pass through all those surfaces. The same goes for shadows. If you have the shadow limit set at 1 and you want to cast a shadow through a transparent surface, you will not see a shadow. You would need to increase the shadow limit on the light.

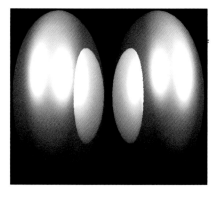
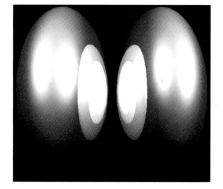

Reflection limit set to 1   *Reflection limit set to 3*

Reflectivity

In the case of transparent surfaces such as glass, the level of reflectivity depends on the angle at which the glass is viewed. Standing in front of a storefront window looking straight in, you will see a very faint reflection. However, if you look at the window from an angle, the reflections will be more pronounced. This is controlled by the **Specular Roll Off** attribute on the blinn material.

There is a physical property called *Total Internal Reflection*. This is when light tries to pass from a dense medium to a less dense medium at too shallow an angle and bounces off the boundary of the two media. This effect is the basic mechanism behind optical fibers. Light bounces along the inside of the optical fiber, unable to escape because whenever it tries to leave, all of it is internally reflected.

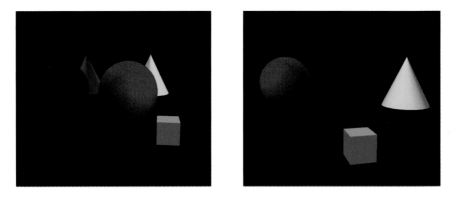

Reflection at an angle and from the front of a blinn material

Refractions

There is an additional control for refractions called **Refraction Index.** This can be defined as the ratio of the speed at which light is traveling in the object compared to its speed in a vacuum. If the index of refraction is 1.0, there is no distortion or bending of the light as it travels through the surface. For example, water (20° Celsius) has a refraction index of 1.33.

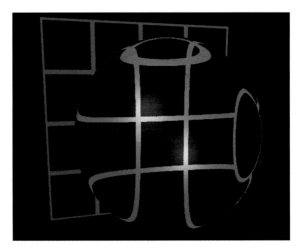

Refraction effect for a transparent object

> **Tip:** *To make objects viewed through a refracting surface less jagged, try increasing the shading samples on the refracting surface. If it is just a single object that causes you trouble, you should increase the shading samples on a per object level.*

Reflection specularity

This helps control the contribution of the specular highlights in reflections. Sometimes you can encounter artifacts in the reflections of highlights.

Light absorbance

This will describe how light-absorbing a material is. Transparent materials usually absorb an amount of light that passes through them. The thicker the material, the less light gets through.

Surface thickness

This simulates a surface thickness in world space of transparent objects created from a single surface. This works well when the edges of the surface are not visible (e.g., a car windshield).

Chromatic aberration

Different wavelengths of light refract at different angles when passing through a transparent surface during raytracing. Chromatic aberration only affects light rays as they pass through the second surface of a transparent object.

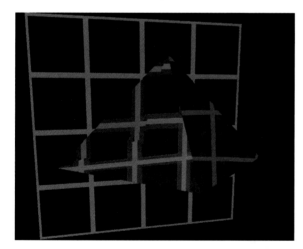

The chromatic aberration effect

You can enable the **Chromatic Aberration** option under the material's **Raytrace Options** in the Attribute Editor.

Reflected Color

An important feature to be aware of with reflections and raytracing is the ability to map the **Reflected Color** of a material and also get reflections from objects in the scene. This means reflection maps and raytraced reflections can be used together. Basically, if a reflection ray coming off a surface strikes an object, it will reflect that object, and if the ray goes off to infinity, it will use the reflection map. This can be used to get the environment to show up on a reflective surface.

One common usage of the Reflected Color attribute is to fake an environment reflection using an Environment Chrome or an Environment Sky texture, or to use a real reflection with the Environment Ball texture.

1   Create a reflective material

- Create a *blinn* material.
- Set **Reflectivity** to **1.0**.
- Assign the *blinn* to a sphere.

2   Create an image plane

- Select the camera and open the **Attribute Editor**.
- Go to the **Environment** section and click **Create** beside **Image Plane**.
- **Map** the image plane with any background picture, such as the *environment.jpg* found in the *sourceimages* folder.

3   Position camera and render

- Make sure you have turned **On** the **Raytracing** in the **Render Settings**.
- **Add** a light to your scene.
- **Render** the scene.

  You will notice that the image plane is not reflecting off the sphere. This is because an image plane is set to be invisible in reflections and refractions by default, and because image planes are not intended to be a surrounding environment.

4   Map a fake environment onto the shader

- Select the *blinn* material and open the **Attribute Editor**.
- **Map** an **Environment Chrome** texture from the **Hypershade** onto the **Reflected Color** of the *blinn* material.

  This environment texture uses a fake environment to mimic reflections.

5   Render the scene

  You should now see a fake reflection on the sphere.

Note: *Alternatively, you could map the reflected color with an Environment Ball and then map it with the image used in step 2. Doing so would reflect the image properly, but in order to create adequate reflection, the image would need to be spherical.*

6 Add other objects

- Create a **cone** and move it beside the sphere.

- **Render** your scene.

  Notice that other objects will be reflected in the sphere as well as the environment chrome.

The reflected color effect

Note: *If you have a number of objects in your scene that need to reflect the environment, you will need to map the environment texture onto each one. Another workaround for this is to create a large sphere and map your environment texture onto it, then place all your objects inside of it. When you raytrace, the reflections of the environment will come from the large sphere.*

Memory and performance options

In the Render Settings, if you open the **Memory and Performance Options** tab, you will find a **Raytracing** section. This section has several controls that the renderer uses to define what will happen when you start a render with **Raytracing** enabled.

The first thing you need to know is that when a raytrace is invoked, it breaks the bounding box of the scene up into cubes that are called voxels. The **Recursion Depth**, **Leaf Primitives,** and **Subdivision Power** attributes are used to determine the size and number of the voxels used. If there are too many objects in a voxel, the renderer subdivides the voxel into smaller voxels, all contained in the big voxel.

Why does the renderer *voxelize* the space? One of the primary performance problems in raytracing is *surface intersection*. If the renderer can limit the number of objects participating in the calculation, it can speed up the algorithm. As a ray is traced through the scene, the renderer can immediately and efficiently know which voxels are intersected and which ones are not. The renderer can safely ignore those objects contained in voxels that *do not* intersect the ray. That way, the renderer has limited the number of objects participating in surface intersection.

Recursion depth

With a fixed resolution for voxels, it is possible that a voxel may contain many triangles, causing raytracing to be very slow if this voxel is hit because the ray will need to intersect against many triangles. When there are many triangles, the renderer can further subdivide the voxel into another 3D array of voxels occupying the space of the parent voxel. Thus, each of those voxels should contain pointers to fewer triangles, reducing the amount of work for the raytracing. The **Recursion Depth** attribute determines the number of levels on which this occurs. It is recommended that this value stay at **2**, because there is a trade-off of voxel *traversal time* vs. *triangle intersection time*. Larger does not mean better. Larger also means more memory used by the voxels.

Tip: *In cases where the raytrace is running out of memory to the point where it cannot complete the render, it is possible to lower the **Recursion Depth** to 1. This will take much longer to render, but will use less memory.*

Leaf Primitives

This attribute determines the number of triangles in a voxel before you recursively create voxels.

Subdivision Power

This determines the *X,Y, and Z* resolutions of the voxels. So, when it is determined that a voxel needs to be subdivided, the **Subdivision Power** is used to determine how many voxels will be created.

A problem that arises with raytracing is that of the *large floor*. If you have a large plane in a scene with a small concentration of detailed surfaces in one area, it will be slow to render with raytracing. The problem here is that the entire bounding box of the scene will be used to create evenly sized voxels. What you get is a bunch of voxels that are empty or have only one surface in them and you get one voxel with the bulk of the geometry. Even if the voxels are recursively subdivided, you still end up with lots of geometry in few voxels. This will slow down the renderer. One way around this is to turn **Raytracing Off** for the large floor. With the large floor out of the way, the bounding box for raytracing is centered around the concentrated geometry and you get a much better voxel/geometry distribution.

mental ray rendering

mental ray is a raytrace renderer. To determine pixel colors, the raytracing algorithm sends rays into the scene from the position of the render camera. These rays will either hit an object or go through empty space. If a ray hits an object, the corresponding material shader is referenced or *called*. If the material shader is reflective or refractive, secondary rays will subsequently be sent into the scene. These secondary rays are used to calculate reflections and refractions.

Shooting rays into a scene can become expensive in terms of rendering efficiency. mental ray ensures render efficiencies through the initial use of the scanline rendering algorithm. The initial scanline rendering phase entails sorting of the scene elements with respect to their relation to the camera.

> **Note:** *It is important to note that the scanline algorithm is not used if distorting lens shaders are used. An example would be a physical _lens_dof shader.*

If a scanline ray encounters a material shader that requires reflections or refraction, secondary raytraced rays are then sent out from the sampled point. The ray then continues until it encounters either a diffusive surface or infinity.

> **Note:** *Infrasampling is a term used to describe the condition where there are fewer samples than pixels in the rendered image. Oversampling implies more samples than pixels.*

Shadow method calculation is a function of which rendering algorithm is used. The scanline renderer calculates shadow information using pre-computed depth maps. These shadow depth maps describe whether a given point is in shadow. This scanline shadow calculation is fast, but has limitations in the area of shadows from transparent objects. The raytrace algorithm does support transparent shadows.

Conclusion

Some interesting effects can be achieved using a raytracing renderer. With a general understanding of limits and memory requirements, you will be able to optimize raytracing and achieve great results.

Project 03

In Project Three, you will learn about renderers and rendering tasks. At the end of this project, you will understand what rendering involves, and you should be comfortable launching and controlling rendering processes. You will also experiment with creating different non-realistic renders, such as cartoon-style images and Web-style images. You will also work through some Paint Effects tasks.

Controlling Renders

An important consideration when rendering in production is the time it takes to render a frame. Fortunately, there are a number of options that allow you to get the best performance from the Autodesk[®] Maya[®] renderer. This chapter will focus on how to set-up renders to get the best quality and shorter render times.

In this lesson, you will learn the following

- About anti-aliasing
- About tessellation and how to control it
- About memory requirements and optimizations
- About render diagnostics

Anti-aliasing

Part of the philosophy of a renderer is to attempt to solve each part of the rendering process independently, using the best method for each rendering problem. For this reason, when it comes to anti-aliasing, geometric edge anti-aliasing is solved completely before the shading is solved. The following takes a closer look at what this means.

> **Note:** *Anti-aliasing is the smoothing of jagged stair step effects in images by adjusting pixel intensities so there is a more gradual transition between the color of a line and the background color.*

In some renderers, both the edge anti-aliasing and the shading anti-aliasing are affected by the same controls. In the Maya software renderer, these two processes are controlled separately. There is a significant benefit to separating the anti-aliasing controls, which will become clearer as they are defined.

Separate controls for edge anti-aliasing and shading samples

Edge anti-aliasing

When the renderer goes to render a pixel, one of the things it needs to know is what geometry is visible in that pixel. When the renderer determines what geometry is visible in a pixel, it subdivides the pixel into a grid much denser than the pixel and then checks whether a triangle is visible in any section of the pixel. This gives very accurate information about the visibility of objects within the pixel. The renderer uses this information to compute edge anti-aliasing. The algorithm used to determine edge anti-aliasing is called Exact Area Sampling (EAS).

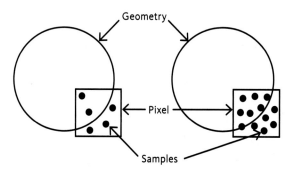

Edge anti-aliasing

As you can see in the diagram above, a small number of visibility samples will not provide very much information about the edge of the geometry in the pixel. However, if there are many visibility samples, there is a lot more information and the renderer can more accurately determine the object's edge in a pixel. The appearance of the edge becomes much cleaner and smoother in the rendered image as the number of visibility samples increases.

The number of visibility samples the renderer looks at in a pixel is controlled by the **Edge Anti-aliasing** attribute in the Render Settings.

1   **Scene file**

   • Open the scene file *07-antialiasing_01.ma*.

   This is a very simple scene with a NURBS plane in it.

2   **Adjust the edge anti-aliasing**

   • Open the **Render Settings** and in the **Anti-aliasing Quality** section, set the **Edge Anti-aliasing** to **Low Quality** and render the scene.

   Notice how the edges of the plane look rough and jagged.

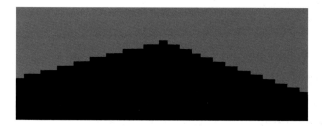

Close-up of the rendered image

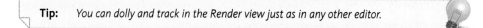

Tip: *You can dolly and track in the Render view just as in any other editor.*

- Use the **Keep Image** feature in the **Render view**.
- **Repeat** the above steps with the edge anti-aliasing set to **Medium** and **High Quality**, keeping the image after each render.

3 Compare the results

- Use the slider at the bottom of the Render view to step through the images for comparison.

  Notice how the edges of the NURBS plane get smoother as the quality is increased.

The actual number of visibility samples used at each quality level is as follows:

Low Quality

The fastest anti-aliasing setting. For each pixel being rendered, **2 samples** are analyzed, producing low-quality edge anti-aliasing. This setting is mostly used for quick test renders of complex scenes.

Medium Quality

For each pixel being rendered, **8 samples** are analyzed, producing medium-quality edge anti-aliasing. This quality is a little slower and gives moderately good edge anti-aliasing.

High Quality

For each pixel being rendered, **32 samples** are analyzed, producing high-quality edge anti-aliasing.

Highest Quality

This quality setting also uses **32 samples** per pixel. However, it also enables something called *adaptive shading*, covered in the discussion of shading anti-aliasing later in this lesson.

Small geometry edge anti-aliasing

Often in animation, the silhouette edges of very small objects will appear to flicker; this is caused by inaccurate determination of their visibility. In this scenario, even the 32 samples used on **High** or **Highest Quality** are not sufficient to prevent this flickering. However, there is a way to solve this problem.

1 Increase edge anti-aliasing

- In the Render Settings, set the **Edge Anti-aliasing** to **High** or **Highest**.

  *The geometry **Anti-aliasing Override** does not take effect unless the **Edge Anti-aliasing** is set to **High** or **Highest Quality**.*

2 Turn On Geometry Anti-aliasing Override

- Select the flickering geometry.
- Open the **Attribute Editor** and go to the **Render Stats** section.
- Turn **On** the **Geometry Anti-aliasing Override** flag.

  You will notice that the **Anti-aliasing Level** *attribute is no longer greyed.*

Note: *The* **Geometry Anti-aliasing Override** *switch and the* **Anti-aliasing Level** *are also available from the Rendering Flags window and from the Attribute Spreadsheet.*

3 Set the Anti-aliasing Level

- Set the **Anti-aliasing Level** to **2**.
- Render to see if the flickering has stopped.
- If the flickering remains, increase the **Anti-aliasing Level** to **3** and render.
- Keep increasing the level until you are happy with the results.

There are currently five anti-aliasing levels defined, with **1** being the **default**, and **5** being the **Best** anti-aliasing quality. A higher anti-aliasing level setting will take longer to render the object. Anti-aliasing level 2 or 3 should be sufficient for most problems.

The following are **Geometry Anti-aliasing Override** level settings:

Level 1 *takes* **32 visibility samples** *per pixel;*

Level 2 *takes* **96 visibility samples** *per pixel;*

Level 3 *takes* **288 visibility samples** *per pixel;*

Level 4 *takes* **512 visibility samples** *per pixel;*

Level 5 *takes* **800 visibility samples** *per pixel.*

One important thing to note is that the cost to render the rest of the image does not change. It is only more expensive to render the geometry with the **Geometry Anti-aliasing Override** turned **On** and with higher anti-aliasing levels. So, it is important to switch on the **Geometry Anti-aliasing Override** for only the flickering geometry.

This feature is useful only for objects without 3D motion blur. If 3D motion blur is enabled and there is no camera animation, a non-moving object's anti-aliasing level can be overridden and set to some higher value. A moving object's anti-aliasing level setting will be ignored. If moving an object's edge anti-aliasing is a problem, try increasing the **Max 3D Blur Visibility** samples in Render Settings when rendering on **Highest Quality** mode.

> **Tip:** *If the flickering is caused by small geometry that is a few pixels in size, it is best to switch on multi-pixel filtering. Sometimes it is theoretically impossible to fix the flickering problem without multi-pixel filtering. This is because without the filtering, the edge anti-aliasing is done with respect to one pixel, and roping artifacts will appear even if the most accurate answer for that pixel's edge anti-aliasing is given. When multi-pixel filtering is used, it filters more than one pixel's results (the ideal pixel width being **2**). Also note that sharp television cameras have the same problem—even though each pixel is resolved completely, thin, high-contrast lines (such as the white lines on sports fields) can exhibit the same artifacts, so the problem is not limited to computer graphics. The best multi-pixel filtering options can be one of the default 3x3-width gaussian filters or a 3x3-width quadratic, but if it is too soft, try a 2x2-width triangular filter.*

Shading anti-aliasing

As you may have noticed, working with edge anti-aliasing has allowed you to clean up the edges of the example plane, but what about the rough looking circle of light on the plane? The *jaggies* at the edge of the circle of light are affected by **Shading Anti-aliasing**.

The renderer tries to shade each object only once per pixel. However, this is not always a high enough sampling frequency to properly anti-alias some shading events like thin specular highlights, shadow edges, or complex textures.

In the Render Settings, there is a section that deals with **Number of Samples**. This allows you to control the shading anti-aliasing.

Notice that when the **Edge Anti-aliasing** is set to **High Quality**, the **Max Shading** attribute is greyed-out. This means that the **Shading** attribute value will determine the number of shading samples per object per pixel. The **default** is **1**. This means only one shading sample per object per pixel.

Anti-aliasing Quality section

You will now look at how changing the shading samples will affect your image. Focus on the region illuminated by the spot light on the plane.

1 **Scene file**

   • Continue working with the scene file *07-antialiasing_01.ma*.

2 **Increase edge anti-aliasing**

   • **Render** the file with the **Edge Anti-aliasing** set to **High Quality** and the **Shading** set to **1**.

   • **Keep** the image.

   • Change the **Shading** value to **8**.

   • **Render** the image again.

   Notice how this time the image takes a lot longer to render.

   • **Compare** the images.

   The images should look like this:

Edge Anti-aliasing set to High Quality, Shading samples set to 1

Edge Anti-aliasing set to High Quality, Shading samples set to 8

Setting the **Shading Samples** to **8** smoothed the edge of the lighting on the surface, but rendering time increased significantly. For this reason, increasing this value is not recommended, because it will increase the number of shading samples globally for *every* pixel, whether needed or not. This can amount to a lot of wasted render time.

A more efficient approach to improving shading anti-aliasing is to use **Adaptive Shading**. This adaptive feature is enabled by setting the **Edge Anti-aliasing** to **Highest Quality**. Notice that the **Max Shading** attribute is no longer greyed.

> **Note:** *As discussed earlier, the* **Edge Anti-aliasing** *is resolved separately and ahead of the shading anti-aliasing. Setting the* **Edge Anti-aliasing** *to* **Highest Quality** *is the switch that enables the adaptive shading capabilities.*

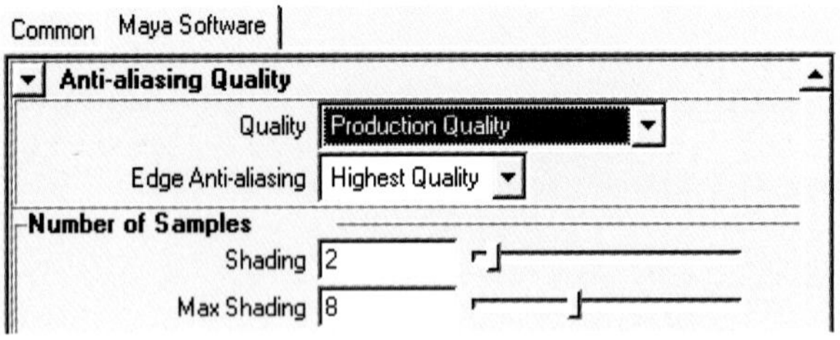

Adaptive shading enabled

Both **High** and **Highest Quality** will use **32** visibility samples to compute the edge anti-aliasing, so the edges of the plane will anti-alias the same whether on **High** or **Highest**.

3 **Set edge anti-aliasing to highest quality**

- Set the **Edge Anti-aliasing** to **Highest Quality**.

- Set the **Shading** attribute back to a value of **1**, and the **Max Shading** attribute to a value of **8**.

- **Render** the scene again.

    You should notice that this time the circle of light looks very smooth, but the render time did not increase as much as before.

The reason the shading quality looks much better but did not take longer to render is that the renderer only used more shading samples on the pixels where that was needed, around the edge of the circle of light. Because the renderer was able to adapt to the needs of the shading, this method is called *adaptive shading*.

Adaptive shading

To do this adaptive process, the renderer examines the contrast between a pixel and its five already computed neighboring pixels (the next scanline in a tile is not yet rendered, so all eight neighboring pixels cannot be examined). The following diagram shows the five neighboring pixels involved in the contrast computation:

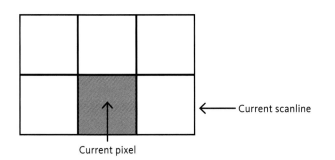

Current scanline

Current pixel

The five neighboring pixels used to compute contrast

Once the renderer knows how much contrast there is between a pixel and its five neighbors, it compares this value to a **threshold** value specified in the Render Settings.

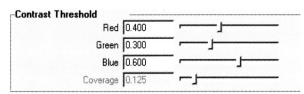

Contrast Threshold

Red	0.400
Green	0.300
Blue	0.600
Coverage	0.125

Render Settings contrast threshold

If the contrast between the current pixel being shaded and any of its neighbors exceeds the **Contrast Threshold** in the Render Settings, additional shading samples are used.

The number of additional shading samples used is determined by a simple linear function. The following diagram shows a chart of how this mechanism works:

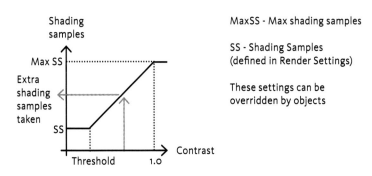

MaxSS - Max shading samples

SS - Shading Samples
(defined in Render Settings)

These settings can be
overridden by objects

The number of extra shading samples for highest quality is computed

The number of samples starts at the **Shading Samples** value (SS) and remains at that number until the **Contrast Threshold** is exceeded. At this point, as the distance above the threshold increases, so does the number of shading samples taken until the full contrast of **1.0** is reached and **Max Shading** samples are taken.

There are several examples of how you can use this mechanism to your advantage:

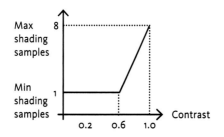

Shading samples vs. contrast threshold

Low-contrast scene

Suppose there is a low-contrast scene, either all lowlighting or all evenly brightly lit. When the renderer looks at the difference between two pixels, it will likely find very little contrast. When this difference is compared to the **Contrast Threshold** in Render Settings, it is very likely to slip under the threshold (i.e., the contrast between the two pixels is less than the threshold).

The result is that the minimum number of shading samples will be used to shade the current pixel.

If you look at the default **Contrast Threshold** settings in the Render Settings, you will see that they are:

> **Red** *to* **0.4***;*
>
> **Green** *to* **0.3***;*
>
> **Blue** *to* **0.6**.

These settings were chosen because they roughly correspond to the human eye's responsiveness to these wavelengths of light.

Note: *The human eye is very sensitive to changes in green, but not very sensitive to changes in blue.*

Shading samples override

In cases where a particular object requires a very high number of shading samples, it is possible to override the adaptive shading range set in the Render Settings.

- Select the object.

- Open the **Attribute Editor** and go to the **Render Stats** section.

- Turn **On** the **Shading Samples Override** flag.

- Enter the required **Min** and **Max** shading samples for that object in the **Shading Samples** and **Max Shading Samples** fields.
- **Render** the scene.

This is much more efficient than increasing the shading samples in the Render Settings.

Image plane aliasing

If your image plane appears aliased, increasing the **Global Shading Samples** will not help. The only way to improve the anti-aliasing of the image planes would be to increase the values of the **Shading Samples** and **Max Shading Samples** in the Attribute Editor of the image plane. If the image of the image plane matches the resolution of the rendering, additional anti-aliasing will not be required.

Tessellation

Tessellation is the process of approximating a NURBS surface with triangles. Tessellation is a required step because the renderer only knows how to render triangles and volumes, not NURBS surfaces. Tessellation generally applies only to NURBS surfaces, but in the case of displacement mapping, it can also apply to poly meshes.

You need to be aware of tessellation since it determines how smooth an object will look when you start getting close to it. When objects are poorly tessellated and close to the camera, they will look faceted (like the model on the right in the following image). If an object in your scene never approaches the camera, you can probably leave the tessellation controls at a lower setting. In the following diagram, there are three images of the same object in different positions. The tessellation setting is the same for each image and you can see that the closer you get, the more it is a factor in the smoothness of your object. If the object never gets any closer than the small image on the left, you can leave the tessellation at its default setting. As it comes closer to the camera, you need to start increasing the amount of tessellation to smooth out the surface. At its closest position, the tessellation controls need to be set quite high to ensure that the surface is smooth.

Object approaching camera

In the pre-production phase of a project, the models needed in the scene will be decided upon. Based on storyboards, you will know their positions in the scene and distance to the camera. You need to determine which objects will never get close to the camera and which ones will. Once that information is determined, it is easy to define how the tessellation controls need to be set. If an object is far from the camera at all times, leave it at the default. If an object is mid-distance from the camera, increase the tessellation slightly. If the object gets very close to the camera, increase the tessellation more. The only way to determine how much tessellation is needed is to do test renderings. These tests can be done very early in the process, since tessellation has nothing to do with the material that is assigned to the surface (unless the surface has a displacement map). As soon as an object is modeled, you can set the tessellation attributes.

Note: *If you are tessellating a surface that will have a displacement map, you need to have the displacement map assigned to the surface to determine good tessellation levels.*

The next image has the same objects as the previous image, but the tessellation has been improved so the surfaces appear nice and smooth.

Improved tessellation

Display Render Tessellation

The following shows how to display the Render Tessellation on NURBS objects.

1 NURBS plane

- **Create** a NURBS plane.
- Set **PatchesU** and **PatchesV** to **2**.

2 Display Render Tessellation

- In the Attribute Editor for the plane, open the **Tessellation** section and set **Display Render Tessellation** to **On**.

3 Change U and V Divisions Factor

- Set **U Divisions Factor** to **1**.

- Set **V Divisions Factor** to **2**.

According to the above equation, the surface should have 6 isoparms in the V direction and 3 in the U direction.

*number U = 1 * (2 + 1) = 3;*

*number V = 2 * (2+1) = 6;*

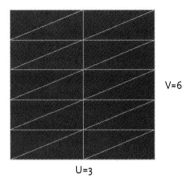

V=6

U=3

Plane with Display Render Tessellation On

Tessellation methods

There are two ways to set tessellation in Maya. One way is to select the object and look in its Attribute Editor under the **Tessellation** section to find the attributes for tessellating that particular object. Another way to set tessellation is by going to **Render → Set NURBS Tessellation**.

Tessellation controls

You can apply tessellation on a per surface basis or set a number of attributes and apply those to all objects. If you choose **Automatic**, Maya will evaluate the tessellation based on coverage and the distance of the surface from the camera. Because of the manner in which this is evaluated, if the surface or camera is animated, this relationship will change over time. When the surface is closest to the camera, you will require the best tessellation. Maya will compute this for you for a specified frame range set under **Use Frame Range**. The tessellation will be evaluated at each frame, and the tessellation attributes will be adjusted to provide optimal tessellation.

If you choose **Manual**, you can use a number of controls that will allow you to evaluate the best tessellation. There are two levels of tessellation control—the first level is **Basic**.

Basic tessellation controls

This first level of tessellation control is a good starting point in determining the tessellation of your surfaces. It allows you to change the tessellation of your surfaces using a pull-down menu. The first thing you should do is go to the object's Attribute Editor and set **Display Render Tessellation** to **On**. This is an invaluable tool in helping you to determine tessellation. If you are in wireframe mode and enable this feature, it will put you in shaded mode so you will be able to see how the surface will be tessellated when it is selected.

Surfaces with Display Render Tessellation set to On

> **Tip:** *Use the* **Attribute Spreadsheet** *to change all the surfaces at the same time.*

Curvature Tolerance has a pull-down menu that allows you to change tessellation criteria from **No Curvature Check** up to **Highest Quality**. When you change these values, the software is actually changing the **Explicit Tessellation Attributes** for you. Maya is trying to give you one menu where you can control a number of different settings that affect tessellation.

The **Curvature Tolerance** setting in the top part of the **Tessellation** section has several options, which correspond to the **Primary** and **Secondary Tessellation** attributes. For the **Primary Tessellation** attributes, modes U and V are set to **Per Surf # of Isoparms in 3D**. The **Secondary Tessellation** attributes are affected by **Chord Height Ratio**. They correspond to the following:

- **Curvature Tolerance - Low Quality** = Chord Height Ratio of **0.987**;
- **Curvature Tolerance - Medium Quality** = **0.990**;
- **Curvature Tolerance - High Quality** = **0.994**;
- **Curvature Tolerance - Highest Quality** = **0.995**.

U Divisions Factor and **V Divisions Factor** allow you to further increase the surface tessellation. These numbers act as a multiplier on the **Per Surf # of Isoparms in 3D** as per the following equation:

```
Number U/V = U/V Divisions Factor* ((#spans U/V) + 1)
```
where the number of spans can be found at the top of the NURBS shape's Attribute Editor.

Smooth Edge

Depending on the surface you are tessellating, you will often have sections that are over-tessellated. This happens when you are trying to increase the tessellation to improve the smoothness of one area and the control causes another area to be over-tessellated. One way to control the tessellation of edges without affecting the surface is to use **Smooth Edge**. It allows you to increase the tessellation along the edge of a surface without having to add extra tessellation over the entire surface. This can help keep tessellation values down for a surface when extra tessellation is only needed along the edge. For example, you might trim a hole out of a plane. When you render the object you might need to use **Smooth Edge** in order to increase the tessellation along the trim edge. By using **Smooth Edge**, you avoid having to increase the tessellation for the entire surface. In the following images, the surface is a plane with one corner pulled up. The image on the left has Smooth Edge **Off** and the image on the right has Smooth Edge **On**. You can see that along the curved edge there is more tessellation on the image on the right, but the flat areas of the surface have the same tessellation.

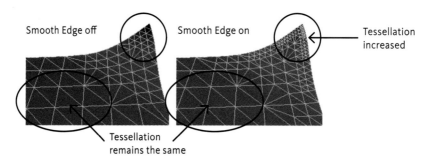

Smooth Edge off   Smooth Edge on   Tessellation increased

Tessellation remains the same

Smooth Edge

The **Smooth Edge** option lets you increase the tessellation quality (the number of triangles) only along the boundary of an object to avoid faceting artifacts along the edges, without incurring the high rendering time cost of increasing the tessellation level uniformly across the entire object.

To control **Smooth Edge** and how finely it tessellates a boundary, use the attribute called **Smooth Edge Ratio**. It is a ratio between the length of the tessellated triangle and the curve of the boundary. The closer this value approaches **1**, the more triangles will be tessellated along the boundary.

There are some situations when the **Smooth Edge** attribute should not be used. In the following diagram, when **Smooth Edge** is turned **On,** you will notice some artifacts in the highlights along the curved parts of the surface. What has happened is the surface was tessellated normally everywhere except the edge, where more triangles were used to get a smooth edge. This caused the curvature in the surface to be slightly different closer to the edge.

To correct the problem, you need to turn Smooth Edge **Off**, and rely on tessellating the entire surface. This ensures that the same number of triangles are used along the entire curved section. It will give you an even highlight.

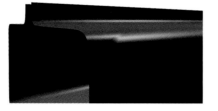

Smooth Edge On causing artifacts

Smooth Edge Off with Explicit Tessellation attributes

> **Note:** *When using **Smooth Edge**, it is important to note that when you increase tessellation along the edge, it can also increase tessellation further into the surface to prevent cracking and T-junctions within the surface.*

Explicit tessellation attributes

If you have set **Curvature Tolerance** to its highest setting and are still not satisfied with the smoothness of your surfaces, then you need to turn **On** the **Explicit Tessellation** attributes. The explicit tessellation attributes are grouped into **Primary Tessellation** and **Secondary Tessellation** attributes.

The **Primary Tessellation** attributes describe how the overall surface will be tessellated. **Mode U** and **Mode V** tell Maya how to tessellate the surface. The U and V values represent the U and V parametric dimensions of the NURBS surface. These values can be set differently so you could have different tessellation for each direction of your surface.

There are four settings for Modes U and V:

- **Per Surf # of Isoparms** lets you specify the number of isoparms you want to create on your surface, ignoring the surface's isoparms. This lets you put fewer isoparms on your surface than there are spans on your surface.

- **Per Surf # of Isoparms in 3D** also lets you specify the number of isoparms you want on your surface, but attempts to space the isoparms equally in 3D space (as opposed to parametric space). This is good for converting NURBS to polygons. This mode produces more evenly distributed triangles than other modes.

- **Per Span # of Isoparms** lets you specify the number of subdivisions that will occur between each span, no matter how large or small. Therefore, very small spans are divided into the same number of subdivisions as very large spans. This is the most common mode. The default setting is **3**. The per span settings are important as they can help a lot in avoiding cracks between joined surfaces where the spans match. This is particularly important for building characters with multiple surfaces.

- **Best Guess Based on Screen Size** creates a bounding box around the NURBS surface, projects it into screen space and calculates the number of pixels in the space. Maya uses this number to guess at the per-surface number of isoparms. The maximum value is **40**. The more screen space the object uses, the higher the number that is set by using this mode. This mode would not be ideal for animation if the camera or the object is moving, since the bounding box would be changing constantly. If the bounding box changes, so does the tessellation—this will cause textures to jitter. You may also experience problems with specular highlights.

> **Note:** *Be careful when using **Best Guess Based on Screen Size** when **Display Render Tessellation** is **On**. If you have a complicated NURBS surface, it can take some time to update the display.*

Secondary Tessellation attributes give you the best control for fine-tuning the tessellation of your surfaces. They allow you to have adaptive tessellation. This means you can have more tessellation on a curved part of your surface than a flat part. There are three options to choose from:

- **Use Chord Height** is the first option and it is a physical measurement based on units. A surface curve will have triangles that will try to approximate the curve. The chord height is the perpendicular distance at the center of a triangle edge to the curve that defines the surface. If the actual distance measured is greater than the chord height value, then the triangle is subdivided again. Once it is subdivided, it will be checked against the same criteria again, and if it still does not meet the criteria, it will continue to be subdivided until it does. Since chord height is based on a default unit, it does not always work well for very small models as the chord height values on a small model will be smaller still.

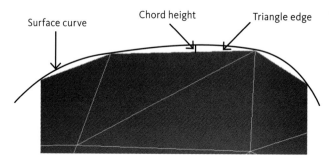

Chord height

- **Use Chord Height Ratio** is the second option and is the option used by the **Curvature Tolerance**. It is a ratio based on the chord height divided by the triangle edge length and subtracted from 1.

```
Chord Height Ratio = 1 - (Chord Height / Triangle Edge Length)
```

*The diagram shows what the chord height is. The triangle edge length is the length of the edge defined by the two points on the triangle that intersect with the surface curve. The default value is **0.983**, which means the chord height is very small compared to the triangle's edge length. The closer this control is to 1, the tighter the fit of the triangle to the surface.*

- **Use Min Screen** is the third option. It bases the tessellation on a minimum screen size for which the default value is 14 pixels. All triangles created during tessellation must fit within this screen size. If they do not, they are further subdivided until they do. This option is good for still images with a setting of **11.0** for **Min Screen**. It will render out nice and smooth surfaces. It is not recommended for animations, because the tessellation will constantly be changing when an object is moving. This will cause textures to jitter or jump, because the shading for a particular pixel will have different tessellations to deal with on each frame.

> **Note:** *Be careful when* **Display Render Tessellation** *is* **On** *and you are using* **Min Screen***, as the display can take a few seconds to update.*

It is possible in the Secondary Tessellation attributes to turn on more than one option. Do not do this, as the renderer will go through each option and check the tessellation of the surface. This will cause the renderer to slow down with no improvement in visual appearance.

Tessellation and displacements

Displacement maps are a special case since the surface does not know how the displacement map will displace it. It is very difficult to detect curvature changes effectively based on the displacement, so a higher initial tessellation is needed. By default, when you add a displacement map to a surface, the tessellation is increased by a factor of **6**. You should also avoid using the **Secondary Tessellation** attributes as you want to make sure the surface is evenly tessellated all over for the displacement map.

> **Note:** *It is possible that you will have a surface that is hard to smooth out using the tessellation controls. One possibility is to rebuild the surface with more isoparms and use the setting* **Per Span # of Isoparms***.*

Scene optimization

To help optimize your scene, there are two commands you can run. In the **Hypershade** window, select **Edit → Delete Unused Nodes,** or from the main window select **File → Optimize Scene Size**. These commands can help optimize the size of your scene by cleaning up unused nodes and other things.

Edit → Delete Unused Nodes will delete any unused nodes in the Hypershade window, such as duplicate shading groups that are not being used, extra placement nodes, extra utility nodes, etc.

File → Optimize Scene Size will clean up the following:

- Invalid NURBS surfaces and curves;
- Empty sets, partitions, and transforms;
- Unused nodes;
- Duplicate shading networks.

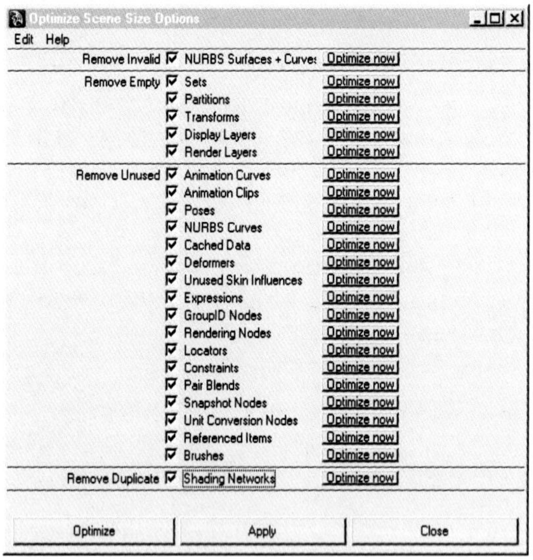

Optimize Scene Size options

Make a habit of optimizing your scene size before you save. Optimizing your scene size before saving can:

- Improve overall performance of renderers;
- Improve use of memory;
- Reduce unnecessary waste of disk space.

Use the following steps to optimize scene size:

1 Optimize Scene

- Select **File → Optimize Scene Size → ❑**.

  The Optimize Scene Size options window opens.

- Select the items you want optimized.
- Click **Optimize**.

2 Save Settings

- Click **Save** in the window to save the settings.
- When you select **File → Optimize Scene Size**, the saved settings are used.

3 Save your work

Pre-render optimization

Pre-render optimization is a command you can run that will create a smaller and more efficient Maya binary (*.mb*) file reserved for rendering. By deleting information not relevant to the renderer, the new leaner file can help reduce overall memory usage and decrease render times. When the command is invoked, your file is run through **Optimize Scene Size** with all flags checked **On**, and then additional information is deleted (history, UI settings, datablocks, static actions, and animation caching). BOT files are also created and relinked to existing textures. It is a good idea when using file referencing to **Export All** first; otherwise, some optimizations might be missed. The usage of this pre-render setup is straightforward. See the `maya -optimizeRender -help` message for a list of flags to use.

> **Note:** *You will get optimal results when using BOT files for large resolution textures. When using the* **-botRes** *flag, you will specify the resolutions that will be relinked with BOT files. If you specified* **-botRes 1024**, *all textures bigger than 1024x1024 will be relinked to use BOT files.*

This script searches for the following scenarios:

Motion blur limitations;

Output image file format restrictions;

By frame setting of o causing hang;

Fractional by frame setting requiring modify ext.;

No renderable cameras;

Ortho camera rendering artifacts.

The following warnings may be issued:

No lights warning;

Composite rendering warning.

Warnings for the following scenarios which affect performance:

Suggestion of using 2D motion blur instead of 3D motion blur;

RT warning and RT limits;

High shading sample warning.

Conclusion

When everything else is completed in a scene and you are ready to render, you need to be aware of how to control the render. This means paying attention to image quality, memory requirements, and render times. In this lesson, you learned the tools to be prepared for your next render.

In the next lesson, you will look at special effects rendering and compositing.

Special Effects and Compositing

Once you have modeled, textured, and added lights to your scene, there are a number of special effects you can include to enhance the quality of your render before and after rendering.

In this lesson, you will learn the following:

- How to control glow
- How to use motion blur
- How to use mental ray motion blur
- How to use depth of field
- How to render for compositing

Special effects

OpticalFX lets you add glows, halos, and lens flares to lights. Those effects can be used to simply brighten up a light source or to create explosions, rocket thrusters, and other special effects. Shader glow can be used to brighten up a material with a luminous radiance. It can be used to create lava, neon lights, and other glow effects.

Light glow

In the real world, when light shines directly into an observer's eye or into a camera's lens, the light source may appear to glow. If the light passes through a mesh (for example, a star filter on a camera) or through hair or eyelashes, the light will refract, producing a star-like glow. In some cases, the light may reflect off the surface of a camera's compound lens and produce a lens flare. These are all examples of optical light effects.

When lights appear to glow, it is purely a retinal effect in the eye. To see this, look up at a light source such as a street light and squint. You will see a glow around the light. Now use your finger to block only the light source; the glow disappears. Notice also that if you cover only part of the light source, the glow is still visible and will in fact appear in front of your finger. The light glow in Maya simulates this real world effect of blocking the light source, called occlusion.

Light glow occlusion

The most common issue that arises when working with light glow in Autodesk® Maya® is the need to control **Light Source Occlusion**. Often people will animate the position of objects that pass in front of glowing lights and will find that the glow shows right through the objects. This is because the light needs you to specify how big or small the light source actually is in order to know when it is completely covered by an object.

Note: *The light glow feature is only supported by the Maya software renderer.*

1 **Create a light glow**

- Open a point light's **Attribute Editor**.

- In the **Light Effects** section, click on the **map** button beside the **Light Glow**.

  An opticalFX node is automatically created, connected to the light node, and displayed in the Attribute Editor. Also, a new icon has appeared, surrounding the light source in the views.

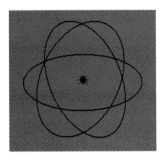

Point light OpticalFX icon

2   Set the size of the light source

Now that you have created a glow effect, you need to consider how you want this glow to behave. Recall that the light glow is only going to shut off completely if the entire light source is occluded. If the light is going to pass behind an object, the size of this *sphereShape* icon, relative to the size of the object, will determine whether you see the glow though the object or not.

- Select the light glow icon in one of the views.

  Notice that a new tab appears in the Attribute Editor, called sphereShape.

- Click on the *sphereShape* tab.

- Select **Render Sphere Attributes → Radius**.

- Use this **Radius** attribute to adjust the size of the icon in the scene.

Note: *Adjusting the **Radius** attribute will not affect the appearance of the light glow. It is only used to determine occlusion.*

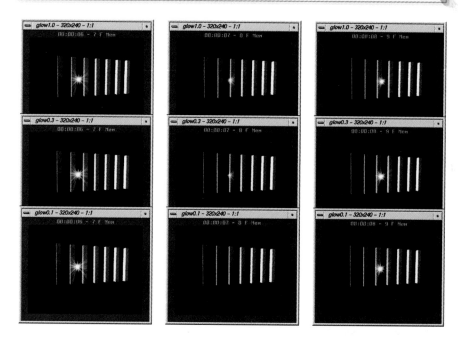

Comparison of different radius values

In the images shown above, a glowing point light moves from left to right behind the columns. In the middle images, the glow is partially dimmed with a radius of **1.0**, increasingly dimmed with a radius of **0.3**, and fully occluded with a radius of **0.1**.

185

Shader glow

Unlike light glow, shader glow in a scene is controlled by a single *shaderGlow* node. This node can be found in the **Hypershade** window, under the **Materials** tab.

1 Scene file

- **Open** the scene file called *08-glow_01.ma*.

  This scene contains a Theme Planet ride with pre-created shading network and a textured background.

> **Tip:** *To better see transparent objects in the viewport, enable the view's* **Shading** →
> **Polygon Transparency Sorting.**

2 Add a glow effect

- Select the *ride* geometry.
- In the **Hypershade**, click the **Graph materials on selected objects** button.

  The object already has a shading network with a texture mapped into the **Incandescence** *of the material.*

- Select the *rideLambert* material.
- In the **Attribute Editor**, scroll to the **Special Effects** section and set **Glow Intensity** to **0.4**.
- **Render** the scene.

  You should see a glow where the material is not black. The glow is bluish because it inherits the color of the stars. Also, the stars are connected to the incandescence of the material, so they will be visible even if there are no lights in the scene.

The star material with glow

3 Shader glow

By modifying a scene's shader glow, you will affect how the glow renders for your entire scene. You can achieve some very interesting effects by tweaking this specialized shader.

- In the Hypershade, select the **Materials** tab.
- Open the Attribute Editor for the *shaderGlow1* node.
- Try to change the **Glow Type** and **Halo Type** to different values, and then render your scene.

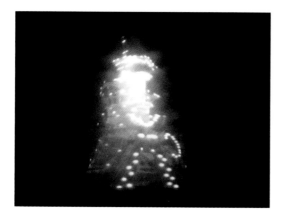

Modified shader glow

4 Hide the source object

- Open the **Special Effects** section and set **Hide Source** to **On**.

  *The **Hide Source** attribute will render the glow without the geometry, giving an interesting ghosting effect.*

- **Render** the scene.

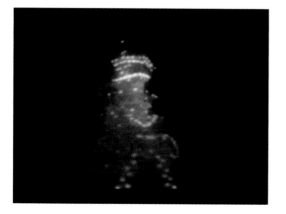

The hide source effect

Creating a neon effect

Neon tubes are the quintessential shader glow example. Try this to create a realistic neon effect.

1 Create the shader

- **Create** a **Surface Shader** material and **assign** it to any object.
- Set the **Out Color** attribute to a bright color.
- Set the **Out Glow Color** to a darker complementary color.

  Notice how you are able to set the glow color directly.

2 Render the effect

Surface shader glow

With other material types, there is no attribute to control the shader glow color directly. It is derived from the glow color on the *shaderGlow* node and the color of the material. With the surface shader material, it is possible to experiment with different combinations of glow color and surface color. Also, because the surface shader has no sense of a shading model, it renders as though it is self illuminating—perfect for neon tubes, L.E.D. displays, etc.

Motion blur

Motion blur simulates how a real camera works if objects are moving while the camera's shutter is still open. This technique is very common in the entertainment industry for creating photorealistic images and animation involving quick motions.

With the Maya software renderer, there are two types of motion blur: **2D** and **3D**. The shutter angle determines the blur length, but this can be overridden in the Render Settings. This matter will be discussed later in the lesson.

Understand the shutter angle

Whether using 2D or 3D motion blur, it is important to understand the shutter angle. The motion blur algorithm uses a **shutter open**, **shutter mid,** and **shutter close** sample for every frame to determine the change in position of a given triangle.

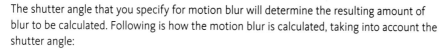

Note: *Triangle refers to a tessellation triangle on a surface.*

The shutter angle that you specify for motion blur will determine the resulting amount of blur to be calculated. Following is how the motion blur is calculated, taking into account the shutter angle:

Take the **Shutter Angle** value (the default is **144)**, and divide it by **360** degrees.
For example, 144 / 360 = 0.4.

0.4 represents the interval in time between the shutter open and shutter close samples. Shutter mid is always the frame time itself. For example, for motion blur at frame **1**, shutter open would be at frame **0.8** and shutter close would be at frame **1.2**. However, when we calculate motion blur for mental ray, we calculate forward only.

By this, you can see that a shutter angle of 360 degrees would give shutter open and close samples that are exactly one frame apart (i.e., 360/360 = 1).

You will notice that by setting the shutter angle to 360, we increased the amount of motion blur. This is because the longer the shutter is open (i.e., the further apart the shutter open and shutter close samples are taken), the blurrier a moving object will appear to be.

How to change the shutter angle

- Open the **Attribute Editor** for the camera.
- Open the **Special Effects** section.
- Adjust the **Shutter Angle** attribute.

mental ray® motion blur

In mental ray, there are two types of motion blur: **Linear (transformation)** and **Exact (deformation)**. Motion blur in mental ray blurs everything: shaders, textures, lights, shadows, reflections, refractions, and caustics. The shutter angle determines the blur path length, but this can be adjusted by the mental ray motion blur attributes in the Render Settings.

To turn on motion blur in mental ray, go to the mental ray **Render Settings** and under the quality tab, open up the **Motion Blur** section. From there, you can select one of the options from the calculation drop-down menu.

Blurred shadows and reflections using mental ray

 Note: *Motion blur in mental ray is calculated forward only.*

Linear vs. exact motion blur

As it is with the software renderer's motion blur, the decision whether to use linear (2D) or exact (3D) mental ray motion blur depends on the type of motion of your object, as well as the time available to render the animation. Linear motion blur is faster to calculate than exact motion blur.

Linear motion blur only takes into account an object's transformation, rotation, and scale. The object's deformation will not be considered. For example, if you have blend shapes or a skeleton that deforms a piece of geometry, the resulting motion would not be considered when calculating this type of motion blur.

Exact takes into account all the transformations as well as the object's deformations. This type of blur is more expensive to render.

 Note: *An object's motion blur can be turned off in its* **Render Stats** *section of the Attribute Editor.*

Editing mental ray motion blur

Motion Blur By is a multiplier for the **Shutter Angle.** The larger this value, the longer the shutter remains open, resulting in more blur.

Shutter represents the length of time the camera's shutter is open. The longer a shutter is open, the more blurry an object will be. However, unlike a real camera, the shutter value does not affect the brightness of an image. If the shutter is set to 0, there will be no motion blur. Larger values increase the length of the blur.

Shutter Delay represents the normalized time that a shutter remains closed before opening. For instance, if the shutter delay is set to 0, the shutter opens at the beginning of the frame. If the shutter delay is set to .5, it opens halfway through the frame.

There are four separate controls for **Time Contrast**: **Red**, **Green**, **Blue,** and **Alpha.** If you have a fast-moving object, these values can usually be set high. Motion blur tends to make sampling artifacts less noticeable, so you can get away with higher contrast values (in other words, lower quality settings). However, if you find that your motion blur is grainy, you can smooth it by decreasing your time contrast values. The lower the time contrast values, the greater your render times.

> **Tip:** *Always try fixing the quality of motion blur by decreasing* **Time Contrast** *values first and* **Number of Samples** *last. This way, you can increase render performance while not compromising non-blurred anti-aliasing.*

Motion Steps can create motion paths from motion transforms. The image on the left represents a value of **1** for motion steps. The image on the right represents a value of **8** for motion steps. Notice the rounder blur on the outer edges of the blade on the right

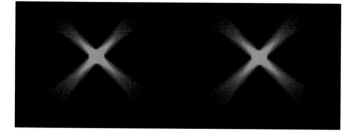

Different amount of motion steps

2D vs. 3D motion blur

The decision whether to use 3D or 2D motion blur is really a matter of determining which one is more appropriate for a given scene and the time available to render the animation. 3D motion blur is usually slower and more memory intensive. However, there will be times when 3D motion blur is required because of some limitations of 2D blur (discussed in the next section). In general, it is recommended that you try to use 2D motion blur because it is very fast and produces excellent results in most cases. All of the motion blur attributes, other than **Shutter Angle**, are found in the Render Settings under the **Motion Blur** section. If it is desirable for motion blur to be Off for some objects, open the Attribute Editor for those objects and toggle **Off** the motion blur in the **Render Stats** section.

The following example compares the results of 2D vs. 3D motion blur.

Comparison between 2D (left) and 3D (right) motion blur

There was quite a difference in rendering time for the above images. The 3D motion blur image took about four times as long as the 2D motion blur image to render, but notice how the 2D motion blur also blurs the background, while the 3D blur does not.

 Note: *Motion vector files can be used by other programs to generate blur.*

Limitations of 2D motion blur

2D motion blur does not work well in these situations:

Moving transparent objects with a background

The background will also be blurred in this case. The solution is to blur the transparent object separately and composite it into the rest of the scene.

Detailed background behind moving objects

Some details might be lost since the renderer has to make assumptions about the background area occluded by the moving objects. The solution is to blur the moving objects without the background and then composite the results.

Fast rotating objects

A motion vector can be thought of as the direction of a pixel in 3D. This vector does not contain any rotation values, so the rendered image will show a linear movement because it does not know about the arc motion of the pixel in between the first and last positions.

Objects entering from outside the image or leaving the image

The renderer does not know the object color outside of the image and has to make assumptions. The solution is to render a slightly larger image, which covers the original image, and then crop it to the desired size.

Volume objects (particles, fog) and image planes

Motion vectors are only calculated for moving triangles (tessellated NURBS and poly meshes).

Note: *The rendered results from 3D and 2D are quite different. It is not a good idea to mix the rendered images from these two kinds of blurring operations.*

Depth of field

Depth of field is a photographic effect in which objects within a certain range of distance remain sharply focused. Objects outside this range appear out of focus. You can simulate this using the camera's Depth of Field attribute. This is not a post-process effect in mental ray, but true depth of field.

1 Setting up the camera for depth of field

- Open the file *08-depthOfField_01.ma*.

- In a *four-view* layout, set *camera1* to replace the *Perspective* view.

- In the *top* view, select *camera1* and press **t** to show the *camera*'s **Manipulators.** Place the **Center of Interest** at the location you want to remain in focus.

- Select **Window** → **General Editors** → **Connection Editor**.

- Load the camera shape into both sides of the **Connection Editor**.

- Connect the **Center of Interest** to the **Focus Distance**.

Note: *Another alternate but equally useful workflow in setting up depth of field is to use the **Distance Tool**. This can be found under **Create** → **Measure Tools** → **Distance Tool**. This will allow you to measure the distance between the camera and the point in your scene that you want to use as the focus distance.*

193

2 Enable depth of field

- In the Attribute Editor for the camera, open the **Depth of Field** section.

- Set the **Depth of Field** flag to **On**.

- Adjust the **F Stop** to control the amount of depth of field.

  *The **F Stop** value represents the distance in front of and behind the focus distance that will remain in focus. A low value represents a short distance that will be in focus; a very high value F-stop will result in very little blur because a deeper range is in focus. In essence, the lower the F-stop value, the smaller the region in focus will be.*

Image rendered with depth of field

Tip: *It is possible to use Render Region to test render depth of field.*

Limitations of depth of field

Transparent surfaces can cause problems with depth of field. The technical reason for this limitation is that the transparent surface is at a certain depth from the camera. The renderer only stores one depth per pixel, and it chooses to store the nearest point to the eye. For transparent surfaces, the depth of the transparent surface will determine the blur, so the background will show through, un-blurred. The background, when seen through the transparent object, will be blurred at the same depth as the transparent surface. This limitation is not limited to Maya and has led to the industry accepted practice of rendering components separately and compositing them.

Reasons to render for compositing

Compositing is the process of merging multiple layers of image information into one image to create a final look. A common misconception is that compositing is for large productions with many artists. However, smaller production facilities and individual artists can also benefit from the opportunities and advantages offered by compositing. For example, with compositing you can:

- Have the flexibility to re-render or color-correct individual elements without having to re-render the whole scene.

- Increase creative potential and achieve effects with the 2D compositing package that are not possible with the renderer.

- Take advantage of effects that are faster and more flexible in 2D, such as depth of field and glow, rather than rendering them in 3D.

- Combine different looks from different renderers, such as hardware and software particle effects.

- Combine 3D rendered elements with 2D live action footage.

- Save time when rendering scenes where the camera does not move; you only need to render one frame of the background to be used behind the whole animation sequence.

- Successfully render large complex scenes in layers so that you do not exceed your hardware and software memory capabilities.

Set-up a render for compositing

Rendering in layers refers to the process of separating scene elements so that different objects or sets of objects can be rendered as separate images. The first step is to determine how to divide the scene into layers. This may be very simple or incredibly complex and will depend entirely on your needs for any given project. Once you have decided how you want to separate your scene elements, there are several workflow approaches you can use to render them separately.

Rendering with render layers

A typical approach to separating your scene elements is to use *render layers*. You can assign objects to render layers using the same workflow as you would when working with display layers.

Render layers allows you to organize the objects in your scene specifically to meet your rendering needs. The most basic approach might be to separate objects into foreground, midground, and background layers. Or, you may decide to divide the scene elements by specific objects or sets of objects.

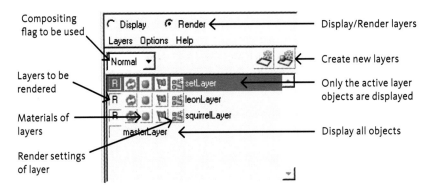

Compositing flag to be used

Layers to be rendered

Materials of layers

Render settings of layer

Display/Render layers

Create new layers

Only the active layer objects are displayed

Display all objects

Render Layer Editor

If you need very precise control over the color of your rendered objects separate from the shadows on them, you can further break down your shot by rendering separate passes within any render layer. The term *render passes* generally refers to the process of rendering various attributes separately such as color, shadows, specular highlights, etc. The Render Layers Editor allows you to set this up.

The following images were rendered with different render passes: specular highlights (left) and diffuse (center). The last image on the right shows the resulting composited image.

Specular and diffuse rendered as separate render passes and composited

Tip: *Render passes are not limited to the example above. You can easily render beauty, shadow, specular, color, and diffuse passes by setting simple checkboxes to On.*

The alpha channel

When rendering objects for compositing, one of the most important requirements is an *alpha channel*. The alpha channel, sometimes called a *mask* or *matte*, contains information about the coverage and opacity of objects in an image. This information is later used by the compositing application to combine the images.

In the alpha channel, opaque regions of objects are white, and fully transparent objects or empty spaces are black. The grayscale regions in the alpha channel mean semi-transparent objects.

The following image shows the alpha channel for the Constructor and the boat.

Alpha and RGB channels

Matte opacity

There are many cases where compositing the separate elements of even a simple scene can be tricky and require careful planning.

The following image depicts the compositing of two separately rendered objects. A problem exists where, for example, the Constructor stands in the boat, and his geometry is both in front of and behind some of the boat's geometry. This is because the alpha channel does not contain any information about what part of an object goes in front or behind other objects. For this reason, the compositing application does not know this information either.

The **Matte Opacity** feature provides one way to resolve this dilemma.

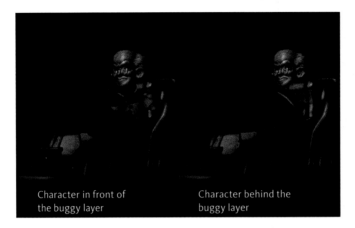

| Character in front of | Character behind the |
| the buggy layer | buggy layer |

Separately rendered objects that will be difficult to composite correctly

Note: *In some cases, it is possible to affect the alpha channels later, in the compositing application, to allow images to composite correctly. Another possible approach is to render the images with a depth channel for use in compositing packages with depth compositing capabilities. However, there are limitations to depth compositing techniques, so it is a good idea to learn these other methods as well.*

To ensure that the objects composite properly, you can use an attribute called **Matte Opacity,** found in the Attribute Editor for all materials. This allows you to manipulate the rendered alpha value on a per-material basis.

▼ **Matte Opacity**		
Matte Opacity Mode	Opacity Gain ▼	
Matte Opacity	1.000	⌐————————⌐ ▪

Matte opacity found in any material's Attribute Editor

The **Matte Opacity** feature has three modes:

Black Hole

To solve this particular compositing problem, the **Black Hole** mode is useful. This mode will set the RGBA values to exactly (0,0,0,0), resulting in images with cutout regions that allow the objects to fit together correctly. The image below shows the alpha of the Constructor once the boat materials have been set to **Black Hole**.

Black hole used to hide parts of the objects

Opacity Gain

This is the default mode for **Matte Opacity**. Alpha values are calculated in the normal way, and then multiplied by the **Matte Opacity** value. Because the **Matte Opacity** attribute has a default value of **1.0**, the rendered alpha values remain unchanged ($1.0 * x = x$). However, you can adjust the matte opacity value to achieve the following effects:

- Animate the matte opacity value from 0-1 or vice versa to create fade-in or fade-out effects when composited.

- Texture map the matte opacity attribute to create interesting compositing effects, especially if you use an animated texture or sequence of images.

Solid Matte

When **Matte Opacity** is in **Solid Matte** mode, the normally calculated alpha values are ignored in favor of the matte opacity setting. The entire matte for the object is set to the value of the matte opacity attribute. This can be useful if you need an object to have a specific alpha value. For example, if you have a transparent object, the normal alpha value calculated by the renderer will be 0. Solid matte can be used to set a non-zero value for the alpha on the transparent object. If you were rendering a view through a window and wanted to composite that into another scene, setting the matte opacity value to 1.0 (in solid matte mode) on the window's material would help you achieve this.

> **Note:** *Opacity gain and solid matte modes will not change the RGB component of your image. They will only change the alpha value generated by the shader.*

Altering the mattes in a compositing application

Depending on what effects will be used at the compositing stage, it is sometimes important to render the whole object rather than having parts cut away with black hole. This gives you greater flexibility for effects such as blur, or overcoming moiré patterns on edges. Under these circumstances, you would need to use techniques in the compositing application in order to composite the elements correctly. This can involve manipulating a combination of the alpha values themselves, or creating custom masks to reveal/conceal objects as they are layered together.

mental ray blurred reflections and refractions

Typically, raytraced reflections and refractions exhibit very sharp definition. In reality, there are always inaccuracies in surface finishes and impurities in material structures that cause light rays to be reflected and refracted slightly off the original ray direction.

mental ray reflection and refraction blur of a material

You can adjust mental ray reflection and refraction blur in the **mental ray** section of the material node.

Reflection and refraction blur

These attributes determine the amount of reflection and refraction blur. A good starting point is between 0.1 and 0.3.

Reflection and refraction rays

When reflection and refraction blur have been enabled, ray direction is not exactly determined by the raytracing algorithm. Reflection and refraction rays will randomly deviate as specified by the blur attributes. This attribute is used to control the amount of *supersampling* required by the random deviation of the ray direction. Generally, higher reflection and refraction rays are required with more blur.

Use Background Shader

You can also use the **Use Background Shader** to make 3D geometry look like it is part of a real image. For example, if you want to place the Constructor over a background shot of a desert, you will need his shadows to be on the sand. Doing so would greatly help to enhance the integration of CG elements into the background image.

1 **Scene file**
   - **Open** the file called 08-rollercoster_01.ma.

2 **Image plane**
   - Create an **Image Plane** for the *camera1*.
   - **Browse** for the image called *photo.tif* from the *sourceimages* directory.

3 **Environment**
   - **Model** a stand-in geometry that represents the content of the image plane.

   If you model a geometry similar to the content of the reference image, your shadows and reflections will perfectly match upon compositing.

   - **Assign** a **Use Background Shader** to the stand-in geometry.

   This will make the geometry disappear seamlessly into the background image, but it will catch shadows and reflections.

4 **Lights**
   - Create lighting similar to the one in the reference image.
   - Turn **On** shadows on the lights.
   - **Render** the scene.

   The stand-in geometry will receive shadows, creating the illusion that the Constructor is actually part of the image.

Stand-in geometry blocks geometry, but receives shadows and reflections

> **Tip:** *The same approach can be used to make a 2D image on an image plane look like it is part of a 3D scene. Use the same technique for modeling stand-in geometry: Assign a Use Background Shader to the stand-ins. With the stand-in geometry casting shadows and raytraced reflections of other geometry in the 3D scene, it is very convincing.*

Camera projection

The Use Background technique described above reaches its limit in a case where, for example, you decide you want to be able to animate something that is getting its color from part of a 2D image plane. This might be a case of making a dog talk or a cat's eyes bulge open, where the dog and cat exist in a live shot behind stand-in geometry. In this case, you can use the **As Projection** method of texture mapping to project the 2D image onto the stand-in, making sure that the **Projection Type** on the projection node is set to *perspective* and the **Link to Camera** attribute is set to the appropriate camera. Then you would do a **Convert Solid Texture** to create parametric texture maps on the surfaces. Once this is done, you can animate the stand-in geometry and render it so that it can be composited with the original images.

Composite rendering

If you find yourself in a situation where you are rendering an object over a background that is any color other than completely black (0,0,0), you should set **Premultiply** to **Off** in the Render Settings under the **Render Options** section.

What this feature does is prevent the edges of geometry from being anti-aliased against the background color. For this reason, the RGB component of the image will look badly aliased. However, the mask channel is perfectly anti-aliased. The mask channel is what is used to blend the rendered element into the background of choice at the compositing stage. Because the composite rendering flag prevented the edges from including any of the rendering background color, you will not get an unsightly rim showing in the rendering background color after compositing.

Premultiply Threshold is mainly a games feature. This is a normalized [0,1] alpha threshold; the foreground is registered only if the alpha value is above the composite threshold.

Conclusion

Adding effects enhances a scene's quality and produces some interesting results. Compositing involves rendering a scene in separate components and then merging those components together.

In the next lesson, you will review hardware rendering.

Hardware Rendering

In the past, the Hardware Render Buffer was used to create fast, low-quality previews of animations or to output hardware-rendered particles. However, modern graphic cards have become more sophisticated and are able to support more advanced features. You can now use the hardware renderer to get fast, high-quality images.

In this lesson, you will learn the following:

- Hardware renderer basics
- How to use the hardware renderer
- How to hardware-render particles
- How to adjust and optimize hardware renders

The hardware renderer vs. the Hardware Render Buffer

There are two ways to do a hardware render in Maya. One is to use the *Hardware Render Buffer* and the other is to use the *hardware renderer*. Both methods use the power of graphics cards to create bitmap images, but the hardware renderer delivers much more in terms of quality and features.

The Hardware Render Buffer uses the graphics buffer and graphics memory of your computer to draw an image to the display and then take a snapshot of it. The snapshot is then written to a file as a rendered image. This technique has the advantage of being very fast, but also the limitation of few rendering perks like shadows, reflections, and post-process effects such as motion blur. To access the Hardware Render Buffer go to **Window → Rendering Editors → Hardware Render Buffer**. The Hardware Render Buffer has its own Render Settings, and the window will assume the size of the selected resolution format.

Note: *It is important to note that since the Hardware Render Buffer is taking screen grabs of the image on your monitor, you will need to make sure that there are now other windows visible in front of this window when you are rendering. It is also advisable to turn Off your screensaver for renders that may take a while.*

Unlike the Hardware Render Buffer, the hardware renderer will allow you to output features like shadows, per-pixel specular highlights, bump maps, and reflections for materials. The quality of particles is much better than when using the Hardware Render Buffer. The other advantage to using the hardware renderer is the user can output images in batch mode. This means you can create images in the background or offline and work in Maya or other applications at the same time. For a full list of supported hardware render features, check the documentation of the current release.

Note: *To see which graphics cards are qualified to use with Maya, see the qualification charts on the following Web site:*
http://www.autodesk.com/maya-qualified-hardware

Using the hardware renderer

The speed and quality of the hardware-rendered image depends on the scene. When you first start up your render, it may take a while for the first frame to render. The reason for this is that the hardware renderer must translate the scene into a data structure that is optimized for the graphics' hardware. This is handled in the software by the CPU and includes the translation of geometry into a format optimized for drawing, loading file textures, and evaluating and baking shading networks, if necessary. If the data does not change, it is cached for subsequent frames, which is probably the reason why the first frame seems to take longer to compute than other frames.

You can control image quality and optimize your scene by:

- Using lambert and phong materials.

  Other shading models will work, but lambert and phong are the best because their appearance in the hardware renderer is similar to that of the software renderer. Note that this will not actually speed things up, but will make tweaking easier.

- Using polygons.

  Try to model with polygons or tessellate NURBS surfaces by using **Modify → Convert → NURBS to Polygons**. *Something to keep in mind is that the hardware renderer uses the same tessellation settings as the software renderer.*

- Be aware of the UV mapping of your polygon.

  For example, you may notice that the quality of your specular highlight is poor. A reason for this can be the spacing between UVs. Try to avoid overlapping triangles, thin triangles, or triangles that cover small UV areas. These could impact image quality. Note that if UV coordinates are not specified, the hardware renderer will create them on the fly for specular highlights and bump mapping. It will take some time to compute this, although it is usually quite small.

- When possible, bake your textures.

  Use the **Edit → Convert to File Texture** *command in the* **Edit** *menu of the Hypershade or the* **Lighting/Shading → Batch Bake** *command in the* **Render** *menu to bake your textures to files.*

Hardware Render Settings

There are several ways to access the hardware renderer. One way is to go to **Render Settings** and set **Render Using → Maya Hardware**. Another way is to select **Render → Render Using → Maya Hardware**.

There are two sections in the **Maya Hardware** tab: **Quality** and **Render Options**.

Quality Settings

Presets

These presets will change the quality of the hardware rendering.

Number Of Samples

This defines the number of samples per pixel. This attribute influences the render time dramatically. The higher the value, the better the anti-aliasing, but the longer it takes to calculate.

Transparency sorting

This attribute defines two different ways to detect and draw transparent objects: per object and per polygon.

Per object

Objects are sorted from farthest to closest in depth from the camera. The object's bounding box is used to determine its position relative to the camera. If an object has different shaders assigned to it, each part of the object gets its own bounding box with respect to the assigned shader. This option provides faster results, but may not render complex transparent objects correctly because each object's polygons are drawn in arbitrary order. However, in most cases this option gives you a proper result.

Per polygon

Each object's polygons are sorted and drawn from farthest to closest in distance from the camera. This option provides more accurate transparency representation, but it takes longer to process. Only use this option if **Per object** delivers incorrect results.

Color and Bump Resolution

The hardware renderer automatically bakes 3D textures into 2D textures, and you can define the resolution of the resulting files with the **Color** and **Bump** attributes. This process is comparable to the Hypershade command **Edit → Convert to File Texture**, but processed automatically. The baked channels may include color, diffuse, bump, incandescence, specular color, cosine power, and ambient color.

Render options

Culling

This option controls how the rendered polygon is rendered, dependent on its normal direction to the camera.

Per object

The setting in the Attribute Editor **Render Stats** section of each individual object is used by the hardware renderer.

All Double-sided

Both sides of the polygons in the scene are rendered. This is a global effect.

All Single-sided

Only polygons with normals facing to the camera are rendered. This is a global effect.

Motion Blur

The hardware renderer supports motion blur if this option is On. If you render particles with motion blur, it is recommended to create a particle disk cache for proper calculation and to bake simulations before rendering. Failure to do so will result in incorrect particle positions. Motion blur requires the scene to be evaluated both forward and backward in time; if there is no disk cache for dynamics, the image will be rendered with the wrong particle positions when the scene is evaluated backward in time.

Motion Blur By Frame

The hardware renderer calculates motion blur by evaluating the object at different positions and blending them. With the **Motion Blur by Frame** option, you can modify the start and end points of the motion blur calculation. This attribute is related to **Number of Exposures** and the **Shutter Angle** attribute in the camera's Attribute Editor.

Number of Exposures

This attribute defines how many samples are calculated to create a smooth motion blur. It divides the given time range into specific frames. The final image is the accumulated average of all the exposures.

Geometry Mask

This option is typically used when rendering hardware particles. It renders the geometry of the scene just as if there was a **Use Background Shader** assigned to all the geometry, with the alpha channel of the geometry set to black. Thus, you can easily composite the particle images right on top of the normal color render of the scene.

Hardware render

In this exercise, you will learn some methods to manipulate the output settings and general look of your hardware rendering.

1   Changing the output filename

- **Open** the file *09-hardwareRender_01.ma*.

- Go to the **Render Settings** window and make sure the option **Render Using** is set to **Maya Hardware**.

- **Rewind** to frame **1**; then **play** the animation and **stop** where you see particles emitting from the buggy.

- Make sure your **Playback Speed** is set to **Play Every Frame**.

> **Note:**   *When a scene contains dynamics, it is recommended to always do a runup from the first frame to the current frame.*

- **Render** a frame where you can see the particles.

By default, particles cast shadows

2 Light linking

You will notice that all objects in the scene cast shadows, including the particles. To avoid this, break the light link for the particles.

- Select the *directionalLight* casting the shadows, then **Shift-select** the *smoke* particle object and select **Lighting/Shading → Break Light Link** from the **Rendering** menu set.

- **Render** the scene.

  The particles no longer cast shadows.

Hardware render without shadows on particles

3 Rendering with motion blur

- Go to the **Render Options** section of the Hardware **Render Settings**.

- Enable **Motion blur**.

- **Render** the scene.

  You will notice that the motion blur looks blocky and incorrect. The problem is that for the relatively slow motion, there are not enough motion exposures to create the blur.

Motion blur artifacts are noticeable

4 Motion blur length and exposures

- Go to the **Render Options** section of the Hardware **Render Settings**.

- Gradually **increase** the **Number of Exposures** until you get an acceptable motion blur quality.

  Increasing this attribute will give more definition to the motion blur, but it will also increase the render time.

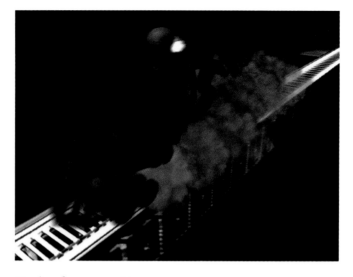

Number of exposures set to 15

5 Caching particles

If you render with motion blur and your scene contains particles, it can be necessary to create a particle cache before rendering the entire scene. To do so, go to **Solvers** → **Create Particle Disk Cache** from the Dynamics menu set.

 Note: *Dynamics will be covered later in this book.*

6 Performing a batch command

You can use the Render view window to see single-frame hardware-rendered results. To render an animation, define the frame range in the **Render Settings** as usual, and then choose **Render** → **Batch Render**.

To batch render outside Maya, you have to run Maya from the command window. The command is:

```
maya -prompt -file filename -command hwRender
```

In this case, you can type:

```
maya -prompt -file 09-hardwareRender_01.ma -command hwRender
```

If you need to specify additional options, such as frame range, use the **setAttr** command to set attributes on the Hardware Render Settings node before running the **hwRender** command. Multiple commands can be specified in the **-command** flag by enclosing the commands in quotes and separating the individual commands by semicolons.

Conclusion

The hardware renderer and Hardware Render Buffer both use the power of the graphics card to render images. Despite the fact that they offer a lower image quality, they are very fast and efficient for rendering geometry and particles.

In the next lesson, you will look at the Maya vector renderer.

Vector Rendering

In computer graphics, there are two principal ways of storing graphic elements: bitmap images and vector images. Both techniques satisfy different needs and have their own advantages and disadvantages. In this lesson, you will render vector images using the Autodesk® Maya® vector renderer.

In this lesson, you will learn the following:

• The difference between bitmap and vector images

• How to render vector images

• How to change the vector renderer options

• How to view a vector image or animation

Bitmap images

Bitmap images are largely used to display photographs, textures, or computer-generated images. A bitmap image has two main characteristics that define the quality: resolution and the number of bits per pixel. The resolution is defined by the number of pixels in the X and Y directions. The number of bits per pixel defines how much information can be stored per pixel. Both attributes together define the file size of an image. The biggest advantage of bitmaps is their ability to carry the necessary information to display photorealistic content. The biggest disadvantage is that the resolution directly affects image quality. Scaling a bitmap image always has an impact on the image quality, and high-quality bitmaps need a lot of disk space and memory. These are some of the drawbacks that limit the use of bitmaps.

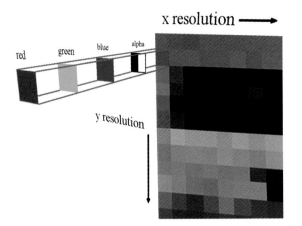

A bitmap image

The most common type of image format output by a renderer is 32-bit (24 bits for the color information (red, green, blue) and 8 bits for the alpha channel (RGBA)). This means you have 24 bits of color information per pixel and 2 to the exponent 24 = 16,777,216 colors. The alpha channel contains an additional 8 bits of information that are used for compositing.

Vector images

Vector formats are chiefly used for print publishing, especially diagrams, logos, and typography. Web vector formats are also very common because they have a relatively small file size and are scalable. Vector images handle curves and closed shapes that can be filled with solid colors or color ramps. A vector graphic is described by two color properties: *outline* and *fill*. These two properties are a mathematical description of the shape and color, and because of this, the quality of a vector image is independent of the resolution. That means you can scale a vector graphic to any size you choose without losing quality or detail. As well, vector graphic formats do not take up as much disk space as bitmap images.

Also, the individual elements can be easily animated and used for interaction with the user. The disadvantage is that it is hard to get realistic results with a vector graphic.

A scaled vector graphic

The above vector render was viewed through a web browser. It illustrates a vector graphic in four different scales.

The vector renderer is based on RAViX Technology (Rapid Visibility Extension). This technology detects the lines and vertices that make up a 3D model and converts 3D models into 2D vector-based imagery. Because of this, animated objects like menu icons or characters can easily be created in Maya. Animation can also be rendered in vector format and later reused and edited in software packages like Adobe® Flash® or Adobe® Illustrator®.

The vector renderer supports the most common vector formats: Adobe Flash (.swf), Swift 3D Importer (.swft), Encapsulated Postscript (.eps), Adobe Illustrator (.ai), and Scalable Vector Graphics SVG (.svg).

You can use software like Adobe® Flash®, Adobe® GoLive®, Adobe® Freehand, Adobe® Illustrator®, or CorelDraw® to edit in these formats, or you can simply view them in a web browser.

In addition to the vector formats, the vector renderer can output from the vector graphic the bitmap file format commonly used. By using these image formats, you can create non-realistic effects and compose them with any other rendered images.

The vector renderer is not designed to create a vectorized copy of the software rendering. Because of this, it does not support all features that are available with a traditional renderer, like the software renderer or mental ray. For a full list of unsupported features, check the online documentation on the vector renderer.

Tip: *It is recommended you work with polygonal objects when using the vector render, but you are not limited to them. NURBS and subdivision surfaces are supported as well.*

Render Settings

This section describes the options in the Render Settings window and their impact on the output image. It is important to understand these attributes as they affect render time, file size, and image quality.

To see the vector renderer options, open the **Render Settings** window and under **Render Using** select **Maya Vector**.

Note: *If you do not see this option, you will need to go to* **Window → Settings/ Preferences → Plug-in Manager** *and load VectorRender.mll.*

Tip: *You can experiment with the different options on the scene file called 10-leonVector_01.ma.*

Image format options (swf)

Under the **Common** tab in the **Image File Output** section, notice the default **Image Format** is **Macromedia SWF (.swf)** format. If you choose the **Maya Vector** tab, you will get attributes that accompany that format, in this case Macromedia SWF.

Frame Rate

The frame rate measured in frames per second for the output animation.

Flash Version

The version of the rendered Flash Player file.

Open in Browser

If enabled, the vector image or animation is displayed in your default browser after it is rendered. The browser gives you information about the image name, location, file size, and the time it took for rendering.

Combine Fills and Edges

When **Combine Fills and Edges** is **On**, outlines and fills for a surface become a single object. When it is **Off**, outlines and fills for a surface become separate objects. The size of the rendered file will be smaller when **Combine Fills and Edges** is **Off**.

This option can usually remain disabled. The optimization of the file size typically happens in Flash. When using Flash, it is important to have easy access to all parts of the vector graphics. This option really only includes fills and outlines. If you add highlights and reflections, these effects are treated as separate objects in Flash.

Image format options (svg)

Under the **Common** tab in the **Image File Output** section, if you choose the SVG format, the **Maya Vector** tab will show attributes that accompany that format, in this case SVG.

Frame Rate

The frame rate measured in frames per second for the output animation.

Svg Animation

If **Svg Animation** is **Native**, the renderer creates one svg file containing the frames of your animation and the scripting that drives it. If **Svg Animation** is **Script**, the renderer creates an svg file containing the frames of your animation and an HTML file containing the JavaScript that drives it.

If your animation is long, file size increases when **Svg Animation** is **Native**.

Compress

Only use this option if you plan to publish the rendered svg file directly to the Web. If you plan to import the svg file into another application like GoLive or Illustrator, the **Compress** attribute must be disabled, because you cannot edit a compressed svg file.

Appearance options

The following options control the complexity of the final vector image.

Curve Tolerance

A value from **0** to **15** determines how object outlines are represented. When Curve Tolerance is **0**, object outlines are drawn by a series of straight line segments (one segment for each polygon edge). This produces an outline that exactly matches the outline of polygons, but also produces larger file sizes.

When Curve Tolerance is **15**, object outlines are represented by curved lines. This produces an outline that may appear slightly distorted compared to the original object's outline, but also produces smaller file sizes.

Secondary Curve Fitting

This option provides more control over the conversion of line segments into curves by adding a second pass. Typically, this results in more linear segments converted to curves. While this option increases render time, it can help produce better results and smaller files.

Detail Level Preset

Predefined settings for the **Detail Level** attribute.

Detail Level

Determines the level of detail in the rendered image. High values produce more detailed images and more accurate renders than low values, but they take longer to render and increase file size.

A value of **0** sets **Detail Level** to **Automatic** to allow the renderer to choose the appropriate level of detail for your scene.

With a higher detail level, the vector renderer generates more edit points for the single objects. The best way to see this is to compare the vector images in vector editing software.

Low Detail Level   High Detail Level

Detail level comparison

The image on the left was rendered with a **Curve Tolerance** of **2** and a **Detail Level** of **1**. The file size is 5 KB and took 30 seconds to render. The image on the right was rendered with a **Curve Tolerance** of **2** and a **Detail Level** of **20**. The file size is 15 KB and took 2 minutes to render. As you can see in the images above, there are additional details in specific areas when the detail level is high, but the influence to the overall look for this object is not so dramatic.

Note: *Low detail level will cause flickering in animation due to the different calculations on each frame.*

Fill options

Choosing to use the **Fill Object** attribute has a major impact on file size, as well as render time. Keep in mind that if you really need a photorealistic rendering, a bitmap format is the better choice.

All fill styles, except single color, respond to point lights and get the final color from the color attribute in the assigned material of the object. All other light types and most of the material attributes are ignored by the vector renderer. If your scene does not contain point lights, a default point light is automatically created, which is located at the camera and will be deleted after rendering. Also, light linking and all attributes except primary visibility in the Render Stats section of the objects are ignored by the vector renderer.

In the following description of the attributes, the terms face, surface, and triangle are used. Face is used to describe a polygonal face, *surface* represents a single NURBS surface, and *triangle* refers to the triangulated version of a polygonal face or a NURBS surface.

> **Note:** *To better see the character, edge outlines are used in all the following images.*

Single Color

If **Single Color** is selected, the fill color behaves similarly to a surface shader. The objects appear flat-shaded and independent from lighting. They get the color from the **Color** attribute of the assigned shader. Internally, an ambient light is calculated to shade the surfaces, so the final color may vary slightly from the material's **Color** attribute.

Single Color fill

Two Colors

This attribute uses two solid colors to achieve a shaded, 3D-like look on the surface. This doesn't mean that the final image only contains two tones of a color. An object with a blue material can have various tones of blue, depending on the view angle and lighting.

Four Colors

Works like the attribute Two Colors, but uses four solid colors to shade a surface.

Two Color fill

Four Color fill

Full Color

Shades each triangle with a solid color. You can achieve a similar look when using **Shading** → **Flat Shading All** in the panel menu of a view. This option creates a big file and takes a long time to render because the color must be calculated for each triangle. This means that the tessellation for NURBS objects is also taken into account.

Full Color fill with different model resolutions

Average Color

With Average Color, each face and surface is shaded with one solid color. The definition of a face is driven by the smoothing angle between them. By making edges hard with **Edit Polygon → Normals → Soften/Harden**, you can influence the look of the shaded object.

Average Color fill

Area Gradient

This attribute fills each face and surface with one radial gradient. Using it, you can create a nice 3D effect with only a slight increase in file size. Flat faces and surfaces get a more even fill, smooth surfaces and faces a gradient fill.

Mesh Gradient

This is the most expensive option available in this section and creates the biggest files. However, it gives you a vectorized look that is the closest to a regular software rendering.

Mesh gradient fills each triangle with a linear gradient based on the material color and lighting. A similar look can be achieved inside Maya when selecting **Shading** → **Smooth Shade All** from a view menu.

Area Gradient Color fill *Mesh Gradient Color fill*

Show Back Faces

If this option is enabled, the vector renderer also renders faces whose normals are facing away from the camera. This option is equivalent to the attribute **Double-sided** in the **Render Stats** section of an object. Disabling this attribute reduces the file size in some cases.

SWF options

Shadows, highlights, and reflections have a global influence to the scene. As mentioned above, the **Render Stats** in the Attribute Editor are ignored. You can only control the shadows, highlights, and reflections for the whole scene, not on a per object basis.

If you render with these attributes enabled, each feature appears as one part in the vector graphic. If you import it into vector editing software, you will get the whole image on one layer. But, each part is separate and you can select it as one piece, making it easier to apply each *feature* to one layer.

Shadows

If selected, it enables all objects to cast and receive shadows. Only shadow-casting point lights are rendered. Both Dmap and raytrace shadows will work. When raytraced shadows are used, the **Light Radius** attribute in the *light*'s Attribute Editor is also ignored.

> **Tip:** *There are two other restrictions when rendering shadows with the vector renderer: transparent objects cannot receive shadows, and the shadow color is ignored.*

Four Color fill and Shadows

Highlights

This option is only available when **Fill Style** is **Single Color**, **Average Color,** or **Area Gradient**. With this attribute, a highlight is calculated. The highlight appears as a number of concentric solid color regions. The number of rings is driven by the **Highlight Level** attribute. The highlight is a separate, semi-transparent layer that lies above the fill and edges. Therefore, objects appear brighter than without the highlights.

The following material attributes influence the look of the highlight:

Anisotropic	**Roughness**;
Blinn	**Eccentricity**;
Phong	**Cosine Power**;
PhongE	**Roughness**.

If the **Specular Color** is mapped with a texture, the materials' default color is used to compute the color of the highlight.

Reflections

This attribute enables the vector renderer to render reflections. If you select this option, all objects show up in reflections. The attribute **Reflection Depth** controls how often a reflection is traced. This attribute is comparable to the Reflection Depth attribute for a material.

Single Color fill and Highlights

Single Color fill and Reflections

Edge options

Enable this option to render your objects with an outline.

Edge Weight

This option lets you control the thickness of the outline. It is measured in points. If you render to a vector format, you can modify the line thickness later in vector editing software. The option **Edge Weight Presets** provides you with some presets.

Edge Color

Controls the overall color of the outline.

Edge Style

Controls the placement of the outline. If set to **Outlines**, the object's contour is rendered as an outline. If set to **Entire Mesh**, the object's triangulation is vectorized.

 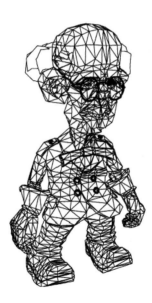

Different edge styles

Hidden Edge

If this option is enabled, the vector renderer displays all edges. This gives a wireframe-like look.

Edge Detail

If this option is enabled, sharp edges between polygon edges are rendered as outline. The **Min Edge Angle** attribute acts as a threshold and gives you global control over where a line is drawn inside the object. An edge line will be drawn at angles greater than this threshold but not below it. The appearance of a line is also influenced by the smoothing angle. This means you can force the renderer to add and delete lines with **Polygon → Normals → Soften/ Harden**. This workflow allows local control and works for single parts of an object.

Hidden Edges   *Outlines and Edge Detail*

Render layers

Objects on different render layers are rendered to different files. To compose them, these files can be imported into the vector graphics software.

Tip: *Remember that when working with render layer passes, features such as shadows and reflections are calculated only for objects on the same layer.*

1 Create render layers

- In the **Layer Editor**, switch to **Render Layers**.

- Create new layers and assign objects to them.

- If you select **Render → Batch Render,** the renderer will output each layer to a specific vector file.

Command Line vector rendering

You can also render your scene through the **Command Line**. Open a command window and type:

```
mayaVectorRender -help
```

This command will show you the options for using the vector renderer via the Command Line. Simply, to render a scene, go to the directory containing your scene file and type:

```
mayaVectorRender -file filename
```

This command launches a vector render with the Render Settings that were saved in the scene file.

Conclusion

In this lesson, you explored the various outputs of the vector renderer. By using vector rendering, you will be able to render cartoon-style images and animation, or fulfill tasks like generating vector content for a Web site.

In the next lesson, you will learn about some Paint Effects and Toon features.

Maya Paint Effects

Autodesk® Maya® software Paint Effects offers a wide variety of brushes that let you add real-time effects to a scene. With this toolset, you can work on either a 2D canvas or in a typical 3D scene. This makes it possible to create either bitmap images or integrated brush strokes that can be viewed and animated in 3D. Paint Effects' vast library of presets makes it easy to add effects to your scene with a few brush strokes. As you learn more, you can also enhance the existing brushes and even add your own to the library.

In this lesson, you will learn the following:

- About Maya Paint Effects
- How to paint brush strokes
- How to render Paint Effects
- How to convert Paint Effects
- How to use Toon

Paint Effects brushes

When you create Paint Effects, you first need to select a *brush* and then paint *strokes* either in your 3D scene or on a 2D canvas. A brush defines how the Paint Effects look is generated (*spawned*) from a stroke. A stroke is usually user drawn, defining a path along which the Paint Effects will be assigned.

Paint Effects works by creating a series of dots along a curve, which can take basically any shapes, with any colors. When you paint, the closer the dots are together, the smoother the brush stroke will look. Brushes can be almost anything you want. Included in Autodesk® Maya® is a group of default brushes such as grass, trees, lighting, fur, and much more.

Rendering Paint Effects

Rendering Paint Effects involves a post-process in the Maya software renderer. This means that you cannot render Paint Effects with another renderer. The way to work around this is either to render a separate pass with only Paint Effects, which will be composited with your other layers, or you can convert Paint Effects to NURBS or polygons.

When you convert Paint Effects to geometry, the history of the brush and stroke is maintained. By doing so, you can render fully animated brushes in any other renderer.

In the following example, you will see how to use Paint Effects and convert it so it can be rendered into the vector renderer.

1 Scene file

- **Open** a new scene.

2 Paint strokes

- In the Rendering menu set, select **Paint Effects → Get Brush**...
- In the Visor, select the **flowers** directory, and click on the **sunflower.mel** brush preset.

  Doing so will automatically load the brush preset and will activate the Paint Effects Tool.

- Paint directly on the grid in your scene.

  Sunflowers will spawn along your stroke path.

Sunflowers painted directly in the view

3 Share one brush

Each time you click and draw a line in the viewport, a stroke and brush are created. This lets you customize each stroke individually, but doing so also makes it difficult to change the look of all the strokes at the same time. Fortunately, you can specify that all the strokes share the same brush, which will allow you to tweak only a single brush for all your strokes.

- Open the **Outliner**.

  You should see all the different strokes you have just drawn.

- Select all the strokes.
- Select **Paint Effects → Share One Brush**.

  Now all the strokes use the same brush. Modifying this brush will change all the strokes at the same time.

4 Render

- Render the scene using the Maya software renderer.

Maya software render

Converting Paint Effects

In order to be able to render Paint Effects into another renderer, you must convert the strokes to geometry. Doing so will conserve the history of the strokes, so you will still be able to tweak the look of the strokes, modify their animation, and change the conversion resolution.

1 Scene file
- Continue using the scene created in the last exercise.

2 Convert to polygons
- Select all the strokes.
- Select **Modify** → **Convert** → **Paint Effects to Polygons**.

  The strokes are now converted to polygons.

3 Change the resolution of the geometry
- Select the geometry and open the **Attribute Editor**.
- Select the *sunflower1* tab.

  This is the original brush used to paint the sunflowers.
- **Tweak** the brush attributes and see how the polygonal geometry is updated.

Note: *Any attributes controlling the shaded look of the strokes will not be updated. This is because materials were created to shade the geometry and these materials are not connected to the strokes.*

4 Play back the scene
- **Play back** the scene.

  Notice that the original Paint Effects stroke is animated, so the geometry is also animated because of construction history.

5 Render using the vector renderer
- **Render** the scene using the Maya vector renderer.

Paint Effects is now renderable with other renderers

Toon

The Toon menu under the Rendering menu set allows you to give a cartoon look to your geometry. Through this menu, you can control the fill color of the geometry along with its outline. As you will see in this exercise, you can assign Paint Effects strokes to the outlines, thus giving a more refined cartoon look.

1   Scene file

- Open the scene file called *11-toonRender_01.ma*.

2   Assign an outline

- Select all the geometry.
- Select **Toon** → **Assign Outline** → **Add New Toon Outline**.

   A new pfxToon node is created, allowing you to customize the outline of the geometry.

Tip: *Toon outlines are quite heavy. To speed up the view, toggle off **Show** → **Strokes** in the viewport.*

3   Change the camera background color

- Select **Toon** → **Set Camera Background Color** → **Persp**.
- In the displayed **Color Chooser**, select white as the background color.

4 **Assign a Paint Effects brush**

- Select **Paint Effects → Get Brush...**

- In the Visor, select the **pencils** directory and click on the *pencilScribbleDark.mel* brush preset.

- Select the *pfxToon1* node from the **Outliner**.

- Select **Toon → Assign Paint Effects Brush to Toon Lines**.

  The Toon outline is now made of the selected Paint Effects brush.

5 **Tweak the Toon outline**

- Select the *pfxToon1* node from the **Outliner** and open its **Attribute Editor**.

- Under the *pfxToonShape1* tab, open the **Screenspace Width Control** and set the following:

  Screenspace Width to **On**;

  Distance Scaling to **0.8**.

  Enabling the Screenspace Width option sets the width of the Paint Effects strokes relative to the rendered image size rather than scene size. This means that the size of the strokes will stay the same even if the character walks away or comes close to the camera.

6 **Render the scene**

- Set the renderer to **Maya Software**.

- Render the scene.

7 **Change the fill color**

As you can see, you have only specified the outlines of the geometry, and not the fill color.

- Select all the geometry.

- Select **Toon → Assign Fill Shader → Solid Color**.

  A new white surface shader will be created and assigned to the geometry.

Toon outline

Note: *You can optionally create various fill shaders. Experiment with them if you wish.*

- **Render** the scene.

8 Tweak the outlines

There are several options you can tweak to customize the Toon outlines.

- Select the *pfxToon* node.
- Open the **Attribute Editor**.
- Change the various settings that control the different line types.
- Change the fill color if wanted.
- **Render** your scene to see the effects of your changes.

Toon outline and white fill color

Toon outline and three-color tone fill

Conclusion

In this lesson, you experimented with some simple Paint Effects and Toon features. Paint Effects enables you to create good looking scene content very quickly. On top of the extensive library of brush presets already included with Maya, you can edit presets to create new customized brushes. You also learned how to render Paint Effects into other renderers by converting Paint Effects to geometry. Lastly, you used the Toon features, along with Paint Effects, to quickly give a full cartoon style to your geometry.

In the next project, you will learn how to create photorealistic images by using the mental ray® renderer.

Project 04

In Project Four, you will overview some advanced features of the mental ray renderer. Some of the features you will experience here can greatly improve your renders and add that certain quality that makes photorealistic CG images believable.

Caustics and Global Illumination

Caustics are light patterns formed by focused light. They are created when light from a source illuminates a diffuse surface by way of one or more specular reflections or transmissions. Examples of Caustic effects include the hot spots seen on surfaces when light is focused through a refractive glass or reflected off metal, or the patterns created on the bottom of a swimming pool from light shining through the water.

In this lesson, you will learn the following:

- How to use Caustics
- How to fine-tune Caustics
- How to use Global Illumination
- How to fine-tune Global Illumination

Direct and indirect illumination

Direct illumination occurs when a light source directly illuminates an object or objects in a scene. *Indirect illumination* occurs when light illuminates objects by reflection or transmission by other objects. Global Illumination is the technique used to describe indirect illumination. Indirect illumination includes Global Illumination, Final Gather, and effects such as Caustics. Since Global Illumination and Caustics cannot be simulated efficiently using standard raytracing methods, mental ray uses a mechanism based on *photon maps*. Light is emitted from the source in the form of energy, called photons. Photons are followed as they bounce around a scene until they are either absorbed or escape to infinity. The absorbed photons are then stored in a Photon Map and used at render time to calculate illumination in a scene. Photons can be emitted from standard light sources, as well as from user-defined photon-emitting shaders.

Caustics

In this exercise, you will learn to enable Caustics and fine-tune the effects.

1   **Scene file**   *cauo tics.01.mb*
    * **Open** the scene file called *12-cognacGlass_01.ma.*
    * **Render** the scene to see the initial results using software rendering.

    This is a simple scene consisting of a glass and a spot light. The glass and its contents have refractive materials, and the spot light casts raytraced shadows. You can see that the shadows cast by the glass are properly colored and transparent, but the image lacks the hot spots usually seen when light shines through glass.

Initial software render

2 Enable Caustics

- Open the **Render Settings** window and change **Render Using** to **mental ray**.

- In the **mental ray** tab, go to the **Quality Presets** setting found under the **Quality** tab, and select the **Preview Caustics** preset.

- Scroll to the **Raytracing** section and increase the settings as follows:

  Refractions to **6**;

  Max Trace Depth to **8.**

  The Refractions value is the number of times the ray must go through a transparent surface before it stops. The Max Trace Depth value should be equal to the reflection rays plus refraction rays.

- Scroll to the **Caustics** section under the **Indirect Lighting** tab.

  Note that the **Caustics** *option is enabled because of the quality preset.*

- Under the **Photon Tracing** section, increase **Max Photon Depth** and **Photon Refractions** to **6**.

  The photon in this example goes through six transparent surfaces and then stops, hitting a diffuse surface, in this case the wall. Therefore, the default value of **5** *would not produce proper results.*

[handwritten annotation: where is this?]

> **Tip:** *In the* **Translation** *section under the* **Options** *tab, you can set* **Export Verbosity** *to* **Progress Messages** *in order to check rendering progress messages in the Output Window.*

3 Enable photon emission

In order to use Caustics, at least one of the light sources in your scene must emit photons. Each photon emitted by the light source is traced through the scene until it either hits a diffuse surface or has been reflected or transmitted the maximum number of times indicated by **Photon Trace Depth**. The Caustic photon map holds just those photons that have been specularly reflected or refracted, before hitting a diffuse surface where they are stored.

> **Note:** *It is also possible to use custom mental ray shaders as photon emitters.*

- In the **Hypershade**, select the **Lights** tab.

- Select *spotLightShape1* and open its **Attribute Editor**.

- Scroll to the **mental ray → Caustic and Global Illumination** section and set **Emit Photons** to **On**.

- Make sure **Photon Intensity** is set to **8000**.

Photon Intensity is the amount of light distributed by the light source. Each photon will carry a fraction of the light source energy and distribute it into the scene.

- Make sure **Caustic Photons** is set to **10000**.

The number of Caustic Photons emitted by the light source will determine the quality of the generated Caustics. More photons produce higher-quality results, but also increase memory usage. A suggested workflow is to use the default number of photons or fewer while tuning your image, to produce quick, low-quality Caustics. You can then increase the number of photons to produce higher-quality images.

- Make sure **Exponent** is set to **2**.

This attribute acts like decay; the intensity increases as the value decreases. The default value of 2 simulates quadratic (realistic) decay.

Caustic and Global Illumination light attributes

4 Test render the scene

You should now see Caustic effects around the glass, but the brightness and quality will not be very good; the Caustic effects will be spotty. Further tuning is needed to improve the appearance of Caustics.

Initial results of render with Caustics

5 Fine-tuning Caustics

You may find that the Caustic effects are not bright enough. Raising or lowering the **Photon Intensity** of your light source will increase or decrease the brightness of your Caustics.

[handwritten: Indirect Lighting tab]

- Open the **Attribute Editor** for the *light* and scroll to the **Caustics** section.
- Set **Photon Intensity** value to **25000**. *[handwritten: Window > Indirect Lighting Quality tab > Preview Caustics]*
- In the **mental ray** tab of the **Render Settings**, scroll to the **Caustics** section.

The appearance of Caustics can be fine-tuned using the Caustic Accuracy and Radius settings.

- Under the **Caustics** section, increase **Radius** to **1.5** or **2** by small increments and **test render** to see its results.

Radius controls the maximum distance at which mental ray considers photons. For example, to specify that only photons within 1 scene unit away should be used, set Radius to 1. When Radius is left at the default value of 0, the renderer will itself calculate an appropriate radius based on your scene size. However, this default result is not always acceptable, as in this case. Increasing the Radius will generally decrease noise but give a more blurred result. To decrease noise without blurring details, it would be necessary to increase the number of photons emitted by your light source.

- Set Accuracy to 100 and increase it by small increments and test render to see its results.

Accuracy controls how many photons are considered during rendering. Larger numbers make the Caustics smoother. For example, to specify that at most 100 photons should be used to compute the Caustic brightness, set Accuracy to 100. You can also use greater values for more accuracy.

Radius 2.000, Accuracy 100, Photon Intensity 25000

- In the **Caustics** section of the **Render Settings**, change **Caustic Filter Type** to **Cone**.

*Changing the **Caustic Filter Type** to **Cone** can produce smoother results.*

Results using Cone filter

- In the **Caustic and Global Illumination** attributes for the *light*, increase **Caustic Photons** to **20000**.

  In order to further improve the quality of Caustic effects, you can increase the number of emitted photons. This will slow down your rendering time but improve image quality.

- Further improvements to Caustics generally require experimentation with the light's **Intensity**, **Caustic Photons**, and **Exponent** values, as well as the Render Settings **Accuracy** and **Radius** values.

20000 Caustic Photons, Accuracy 200, Radius 1.5

6   Save your work

- The final scene file is called *12-cognacGlass_02.ma*.

Light's Photon
Intensity = 25000
Exponent = 2
Caustic Photons = 20000

Global Illumination

In this exercise, you will enable Global Illumination and fine-tune the results.

1 Scene file

- **Open** the scene file called *12-global_01.ma*.

  This scene consists of the buggy in a garage. The garage door is animated open, allowing indirect light to spill into the scene and illuminate its contents.

- Go to the last frame of the animation, where the illumination will be at its fullest.

- **Render** the scene to see the initial results using software rendering.

Software render

2 Enable Global Illumination

- Open the **Render Settings** window and change your selected renderer to **mental ray**.

- Select the **Quality** tab.

- Go to the **Quality Presets** and select **Preview: Global Illumination**.

  *If you select the **Indirect Lighting** tab and scroll to the **Global Illumination** section, you will see that **Global Illumination** is now enabled.*

3 Enable photon emission

As with Caustics, at least one of the light sources in your scene must emit photons.

- From the **Outliner**, select the *spotLight* and open the **Attribute Editor**.
- Under the **Spot Light Attributes** section, set **Intensity** to **0.3.**

  This means that most of the illumination in the scene will come from photons.

- Scroll to the **mental ray** → **Caustic and Global Illumination** section and set **Emit Photons** to **On**.
- Leave **Photon Intensity** at the default **8000**.
- Leave **Exponent** at its default value of **2** for now.
- Leave **Global Illum Photons** at the default number **10000**.

4 Test render the scene

There is very little, if any, illumination in the scene. Further tuning is needed.

Note: *If you get a message stating "no photons stored after emitting 10000 photons," it means that photons emitted by the source do not hit any energy-storing object. One reason this can happen is that the photon-emitting source is emitting photons in the wrong direction.*

5 Change the Exponent value

As mentioned in the previous exercise, the **Exponent** attribute represents decay.

- To increase the chances of photons reaching the back of the garage, decrease the **Exponent** attribute to **1**.
- **Render** the scene.

6 Change the Photon Intensity values

You can now see the effect of the Global Illumination at the back of the garage and on the floor a little more clearly but, you may find that overall the scene is still not bright enough.

- Change the **Photon Intensity** value to **15000**.
- **Render** the scene.

Exponent 1, Photon Intensity 15000

7 Change the Global Illumination Radius

The scene is bright enough, but now you need to further fine-tune the photons.

- Under the **Indirect Lighting** tab of the **Render Settings** window, open the **Global Illumination** section.

- Set the **Radius** to **1** and **test render** the scene.

  Increasing this value will help smooth out the photons and reduce blotchiness.

- If you still find that your photons are not smooth enough, increase the **Radius** to **2**.

> **Tip:** Using the **Keep Image** *button in the Render view window menu bar will allow you to compare current renders to previous renders.*

- Continue increasing the radius until you see little or no change in image quality.

  *When you reach the point where changing the **Radius** has little effect on the image, start increasing your **Accuracy** value.*

8 Increase the Accuracy

- Increase the **Accuracy** value to about **900**.

  This will further refine your photons, helping to smooth them.

Radius 2, Global Illumination Accuracy 900

9 Further refinements

Most illumination in this scene comes solely from photons. You may find that the shadow information created this way is either weak or absent. The following image was rendered using soft raytraced shadows. This helps add depth to the scene and separate the boat from the background.

Global Illumination and shadows

10 Save your work

- The final scene file is called *12-global_02.ma.*

Conclusion

Adding Caustics and Global Illumination to your scenes can help create more subtle and realistic light effects.

In the next lesson, you will learn about Final Gather and HDRI, which can also be used to boost image quality.

Final Gathering and HDRI

Final Gather in mental ray is a process that can be used with Global Illumination to obtain a finer level of diffuse detail resolve, or it can also be used by itself as an independent rendering alternative.

In this lesson, you will learn the following:

- How to use Final Gathering
- How to set up Final Gather rendering
- How to combine Final Gather with Global Illumination
- How to use high dynamic range images (HDRI)
- How to use image-based lighting

Final Gathering

With Final Gathering (FG), mental ray calculates the scene irradiance or total incoming illumination in the scene. Every object in your scene is, in effect, a light source. It is possible, therefore, to render a scene without any lights. This can be a very useful technique.

It is important to note that one ray generation is used in the Final Gather process. This differs from Global Illumination photon mapping, where photons bounce around many times. The Final Gather method allows for one Final Gather ray emission and then contact with a surface to determine whether there is a diffuse light contribution to the emitting surface point's color value. Final Gather does not allow for multiple diffuse light bounces. It will calculate color bleeding and diffuse contributions from the first surface, but not from a secondary surface.

With Final Gather, a semi-hemispherical area above the point to be shaded is sampled to determine the indirect and direct illumination. This semi-hemispherical area is defined by the **Min Radius** and **Max Radius** values found in the **Final Gathering** section of the Render Settings.

Not all points are sampled with this approach. Rather, an averaging of nearby points is calculated, and this value is used for the sampled point. This technique is used because Final Gather ray generation is too expensive to calculate for all sampled points.

The final result of the FG process is a set of values for how much light is incident upon each point in the scene.

Final Gather is useful in the following situations:

- In very diffuse scenes where indirect illumination changes slowly;

- To eliminate low frequency noise when using Global Illumination, as well as low photon emission values;

- With finer detail resolution;

- When combined with Global Illumination, a more physically accurate solution is possible;

- For convincing soft shadow techniques;

- To help eliminate dark corners.

Final Gather default Render Settings

The Final Gather options that most directly affect visual quality are **Accuracy** and **Min** and **Max Radius**.

Accuracy

This is the number of rays that are sent out from each sampled point. The default value is **100**. When rendering out for production, more **Accuracy** will be required.

Min Radius and Max Radius

The **Min Radius** and **Max Radius** attributes control the size of the sampling region within which the Final Gather rays search for irradiance information from other surfaces.

With the default **0.0** values, mental ray will calculate values that seem appropriate based on scene dimensions. This will speed things up. However, using the default values does not allow for the complexity of a specific scene's individual geometry. Ultimately, you will want to enter your own scene-specific Min Radius and Max Radius values for optimal Final Gather results.

Typically, a good rule is to take 10% of your scene's overall dimension in units for the Max Radius, and then take 10% of that value for the Min Radius. Again, this is a starting point, as a particular scene may contain geometry that requires lesser or greater values for proper detail resolution.

Min Radius and Max Radius are functions of scene geometry detail level and how it is arranged in the scene. Every scene will be different and will require some initial adjusting for optimum results.

> **Note:** *In the tutorial on combining Global Illumination and Final Gather later in this lesson, the interior architectural scene benefits from adjusting the default Min Radius and Max Radius values. This adjustment creates better diffuse detailing between the duct work and ceiling and along the stairs.*

Speeding Up Final Gathering

There are two options you can control to help speed up the Final Gathering operation.

Rebuild Final Gathering

The Rebuild option is enabled by default and will ignore any Final Gather map that has been generated previously. Turning this off will force Final Gather to use the results from a previous Final Gather render if an FG map was created. Use of this toggle will speed the Final Gather considerably.

It is important to note that if the number of rays has changed, the Final Gather map will be ignored and new Final Gather rays will be emitted. A glance into the Output window will reveal the following message in such an event:

```
RCFG 0.2  info : finalgMap/test1: final gather options differ from
ones currently used, content ignored

RCFG 0.2  info : overwriting final gather file "finalgMap/test1"
```

If you are rendering out a still image and are not changing the Final Gather settings, turning **Rebuild** off can save considerable time.

When rendering out a camera animation sequence, it may be possible to get away with the Final Gather calculations of the previous frames. This will depend on how the irradiance changes during the course of the camera animation. In such an event, considerable time can be saved if **Rebuild** is disabled. However, if there are objects in the scene that are moving, the irradiance values for the scene will have to be recomputed for each subsequent frame.

Final Gather File

This option allows Final Gather results to be stored in a file—the Final Gather map described for the previous option. This map allows later frames to reuse Final Gather results from a frame rendered earlier. The file is saved into the current project's *mentalRay\finalgMap* directory.

To create a Final Gather map, do the following:

- Set **Rebuild** to **On**;
- Enter a file name in the **Final Gather File** field;
- **Render** the scene.

Irradiance

Irradiance can most easily be defined as total incoming illumination. It is an environmental lighting parameter that determines the amount of light that is incident upon a surface. The following attributes are found on each material's Attribute Editor, under the **mental ray** section.

Irradiance

This attribute is used to map an incoming *illumination map*, such as one created using Convert to File Texture, mental ray, or another texture map that may have been created. With this shader attribute mapped, the Final Gather solution takes the irradiance information from the texture map and not from surrounding surfaces.

Irradiance Color

This attribute controls the effects of photon mapping and Final Gather on a surface. For example, if a red ball is sitting on a white diffuse plane, the plane will acquire a red tinge from the ball. Irradiance Color allows for the control of this color bleeding effect.

Using Final Gathering

With the following series of workflow examples illuminating and rendering Leon's buggy, you will discover that Final Gather can be affected and adjusted in several ways. The Final Gather solution can be affected by:

- The number of Final Gather rays;
- The Min Radius and Max Radius;
- The camera background color;
- Colored incandescence in the scene;
- Ambient color in the scene;
- Irradiance contributions from shaders;
- Irradiance color mapping contributions from shaders;
- Whether there are lights in the scene and their locations.

Another technique for overall illumination when doing a Final Gather render includes the use of *High Dynamic Range Images(HDRI)* , or using a dummy surface (light card) out of the camera view with an Incandescence value. (HDRI will be covered in greater detail later in this lesson.)

1   Scene file

- **Open** the scene file called *13-finalGather_01.ma*. ~~Final_gather Project . 01~~

   The scene file consists of the buggy sitting on a ground plane. There is one directional light in the scene. The dome shader has a slight incandescence value. This is the illumination or irradiance contribution in the scene.

> **Note: Incandescence** *could be supplanted with* **Ambient Color** *to get the same effect.*

2   Disable Illuminates by Default

   It is important to turn off the directional light's **Illuminates by Default**, since all illumination will come from Final Gather rays.

- Go to the *directionalLight*'s **Attribute Editor** and under the **Directional Lights Attributes**, set **Illuminates by Default** to **Off**.

> **Note:**   *Color bleed, which we will add in a later step, will not occur in your scene if there are no lights, colored incandescence, or ambient color.*

(handwritten: glossary: Diffuse / Incandescent / Irradiance Color)

3 Final Gather rendering

- In the **Render Settings**, change **Render Using** to **mental ray**.
- Under the **Indirect Lighting** tab, scroll down to the **Final Gathering** section and set **Final Gathering** to **On**.
- Make sure **Accuracy** is set to **100**.

  This will speed up the render time up considerably. This is a good starting point for test renders.

- **Render** the scene.

Finalgather.01.jpeg

Final Gathering render—no lights

Notice the soft shadows on the underside of the buggy. The points being shaded under the buggy are hidden from the scene irradiance, and also from the illumination contributed by the incandescence on the dome shader. This results in a soft shadow effect.

> **Note:** *The scene will render out black if there are no lights or irradiance contribution from other surfaces in the scene. Try increasing and decreasing the dome shader's incandescence value. With a low value, the scene will render out dark because there is little irradiance in the scene from any source. With a high value, the scene will render brighter because it has more irradiance.*

> **Note:** *With this scene, the default Final Gather Min Radius and Max Radius values of 0 are sufficient for good image quality. With the complex interior architecture scene in our second example, adjusting these values will give better image quality.*

4 Color bleeding

Even with no lights in the scene, it is possible to achieve a nice color bleed effect.

- Adjust the **Ambient Color** or add colored incandescence to the buggy's shaders. *Car's*

- **Render** again.

Notice the color bleed, which is now everywhere underneath the buggy.

Final gather.02. jpeg

Final Gathering color bleed—no lights

> **Note:** *Another technique for contributing lighting levels in a Final Gather rendered scene is changing the camera's background color to a value other than black. Go to the camera's Attribute Editor to change the Environment Background Color to gray and render the scene.*

5 Using lights

Now you will enable back the directional light in the scene to contribute to the Final Gather process.

- Set the **Illuminates by Default** checkbox for the *directionalLight* to **On**.

- **Render** out the scene.

Notice that the color bleed from the buggy onto the floor is much brighter. This is because the light is brightening the sides of the buggy, thus contributing to color bleeding.

259

jpeg.03 (handwritten)

Final Gathering with lights

- Go to the **mental ray** section of the floor shader's **Attribute Editor**.
- **Decrease** the **Irradiance Color** slightly.
- **Render** out the scene.

  Notice the decrease in color bleed and the darkening of the floor.

Tip: *Another technique that can be useful is mapping the **Irradiance Color** attribute of a shader with a file texture.*

6 Shadows

- Enable the **Raytraced Shadows** checkbox for the *directionalLight*.
- Set **Light Angle** to **2** and **Shadow Rays** to **15**.

  Doing so will smooth out the raytraced shadows.

In the Attribute Spread Sheet (handwritten)

- **Decrease** the **Intensity** to **0.5**.
- Turn **Off** the **Cast shadows** option of the sky dome to make sure the entire scene is not in shadows. *We'll go over this in class (Attribute Spread sheet)* (handwritten)
- **Render** out the scene and notice the realism of the shadows.

Shadows along with Final Gathering

[handwritten: jpeg.04.]

[handwritten: Type this]

Final Gathering and Global Illumination example

Using Final Gathering and Global Illumination together results in very fine resolution of diffuse details. The technique is particularly useful for interior architectural shots where lighting definition is a function of light contribution from interior and exterior sources.

[handwritten: scene]

In this exercise, you will set-up daylight lighting in a loft and then set-up Global Illumination. Once the scene is correctly illuminated using photon mapping, you will add Final Gathering.

1   Scene file

[handwritten: architecture]

- **Open** the scene file called *13-FgGi_01.ma.* *[handwritten: week11.01.mb]*

  The scene contains an interior architectural shot with attendant lights and shaders. There are pre-positioned lights in the scene: three linked spot lights for the translucent panels over the kitchen area, one linked directional light for exterior lighting, one spot light on the outside for interior direct illumination and shadows, and two spot lights for the lampshade over the dining area.

[handwritten: Open this & then assign provided textures. Render a still & save it. use 'Keep Image!]

2   Set-up the exterior light

- Select *spotLight5* and change the **Decay Rate** to **Quadratic** and the **Intensity** to **2500**.

  This light is used for direct illumination and primary shadow generation. With the Quadratic Decay, light interacts with surfaces based on real world physics.

- Enable **Raytrace Shadows**.

[handwritten: Scroll down to the Shadows section, and...]

> **Note:** *When setting up Global Illumination and Final Gather, use the quadratic decay rate. This ensures that light levels in the scene decrease in intensity based on the inverse square law, just as light behaves in the real world.*

[handwritten: Render a still + compare it]

3 The translucent panels

The three translucent panels in the kitchen generate warm light effects. The three spot lights overhead need to be linked to the translucent panels.

- Select **Window** → **Relationship Editor** → **Light Linking** → **Light Centric**.
- Link the three spot lights to the translucent panels as follows:

  spotLight1 linked to *panel1*.   (look in the loft group)

  spotLight2 linked to *panel2*;

  spotLight3 linked to *panel3*.   Render use 'Keep Image'.

> **Note:** You will have to turn Off the Illuminates by Default option for each light that you will link to specific objects.

4 Exterior lighting

- Link *directionalLight1* to the exterior *wall1* geometry.

5 The lampshade

There are two spots lights in this lampshade arrangement. The top spot light needs to be linked to the lampshade geometry. The bottom spot light that fits just inside the lampshade is used for direct illumination, shadow generation, and photon emission.

- Link *spotlight6* to the *lamp1* geometry.

  Doing so allows for controlled illumination of the warm light effect on the lampshade geometry.

- Select *spotLight4* and change the **Intensity** to **45** and **Decay Rate** to **Quadratic**.

  The intensity of spotLight4 will be increased later, when Global Illumination and Final Gather are enabled.

6 Render set-up

- Open the **Render Settings** and make sure to render using **mental ray**.
- **Render** the scene.

  Because there is no Global Illumination occurring in the scene, the render is only using the direct illumination from the lights in the scene for illumination. If you render this scene out using the software renderer, the result will be almost the same.

No Global Illumination, no Final Gathering

Global Illumination

You will now enable Global Illumination in the scene.

[handwritten: Am in the Indirect Lighting tab,]

1 Enable Global Illumination

- Open the **Render Settings** and set **Global Illumination** to **On**.

- Set the following:

    Accuracy to **450**;

    Radius to **6.0**.

[handwritten: + go to its Attribute Editor. In the Caustic + Global Illumination area,]

2 Photon emission

- Select *spotLight4* and set **Emit Photons** to **On**.

- Set the following:

    Photon Intensity to **2000**;

    Exponent to **2.0**;

    Global Illumination Photons to **25000**.

3 Render

- **Render** the scene.

    Notice how the scene gets a warm tone from the yellow lighting.

[handwritten, top right: need interior Archit— stairsMetal. jpeg]

[handwritten: jpeg.01]

02.
jpeg

Global Illumination, no Final Gathering

Final Gathering

You will now disable Global Illumination and enable Final Gathering in the scene.

1 **Disable Global Illumination**

   • Set **Emit Photons** to **Off** in the **Attribute Editor** of *spotLight4*.

   • Set **Global Illumination** to **Off** in the **Render Settings**.

2 **Enable Final Gather**

   • Set **Final Gather** to **On** in the **Render Settings**.

3 **Adjust the Final Gather accuracy**

   • In the **Final Gather** section of Render Settings, change the **Accuracy** to **125**.

   *This is a good value for test rendering. For a higher quality render, **400-600** rays will give very fine detailing.*

4 **Adjust the Min Radius and Max Radius**

   The Min Radius and Max Radius define the search area, within which Final Gather rays will look for irradiance information from neighboring surfaces. The areas above the ducting, in the far corner, and along the wall on the left are good examples of where the default o Min Radius and Max Radius values are not sufficient for optimum image quality.

   Tracings   Indirect Lighting tab,

   • Under the **Final Gathering Options** section of the Render Settings, enable the **Use Radius Quality Control** option.

   • Set **Min Radius** and **Max Radius** to **8** and **20,** respectively.

   • **Render** the scene.

03 jpeg

Final Gathering, no Global Illumination

> **Note:** *Results may vary from the image shown here.*

> **Tip:** *If your render is too bright, try adjusting the intensity of your lights. If you notice splotchy areas, enabling **Jitter** will sometimes further assist with the removal of these areas.*

Final Gathering and Global Illumination

You will now render the interior architectural scene out using both Global Illumination and Final Gather.

1   **Enable Global Illumination**

- In the **Global Illumination** section of **Render Settings**, set **Global Illumination** back **On**.

2   **Pre-compute Photon Lookup**

The **Pre-compute Photon Lookup** toggle arranges irradiance to be stored with the photon map when Global Illumination is enabled. This toggle is used only if Global Illumination is turned on, i.e., photon emission is occurring in the scene. Fewer Final Gather points are required with this option, as the photon map will carry a good approximation of the irradiance in the scene. This is because irradiance can be estimated with a single lookup instead of using a large number of photons. Enabling this feature will slow the photon mapping phase, but will speed up the Final Gather process. Ultimately, the render will be faster with this feature enabled.

- Go to the **Final Gathering Map** section of Render Settings and turn **Pre-compute Photon Lookup** on.

- Turn back **On** the *spotlight4*'s **Emit Photons** attribute.

3 Render the scene

Notice that the areas under the table are now correctly illuminated.

Final Gathering and Global Illumination

 Tip: *To increase or decrease the overall lighting levels, adjust the* **Photon Intensity** *value of spotlight4.*

High Dynamic Range Image

The Final Gather process can also make use of a *High Dynamic Range Image* (HDRI), as the basis for illumination information in a scene. This is known as *image-based lighting*.

High Dynamic Range Image nappaValley.tif

An HDRI has an extra floating-point value that is used to describe the exponent or persistence of light at any given pixel. This overall illumination information is used in the Final Gather process. A Low Dynamic Range Image (LDRI), the kind of image that everyone is familiar with, has limitations when it comes to describing the range of colors necessary to correctly describe light values precisely. Think of a dark cathedral with strong light spilling through a stained glass window—the range from dark to bright is too broad for a conventional LDRI. Such an LDRI will have areas that are overexposed and others that are very black.

Pixels that have a high floating-point value (exponential value), are not affected very much by a darkening of the overall image. Pixels that have a lower persistence of light would be affected more by this same darkening operation.

Creating your own HDRI involves taking several shots of the same subject matter with different exposures (bracketed *f stops*) and then assembling the images into a floating-point tiff HDRI. There are applications available for this purpose.

HRDI example   ~~Type this over the weekend~~

In this exercise, you will use the HDRI *nappaValley.tif* as the source of illumination and reflection for the buggy.

1 **Scene file**
   - **Open** the scene file called *13-HDRI_01.ma.*   *HDRI project.01.mb*
   - *Render the scene and keep the image in the Render view.*

     The scene contains the Constructor's buggy, a ground, and a giant dome surface. Note that there is only a very dim light source in the scene.

2 **Create and apply the HDRI shading network**
   - In the **Hypershade**, select the *dome* shader.
   - **Map** a **File** texture to the shader's **Ambient Color**.
   - **Browse** for the *nappaValley.tif* file found in the *sourceImages* directory.

   > **Note:** *When loading an HDRI into Maya, you will see a warning message specifying that Maya cannot read the HDRI. Ignore this message since mental ray can handle that type of file correctly.*

3 **Render Settings**
   - In the **Render Settings**, set **Final Gathering** to **On**.
   - Make sure the number of **Accuracy** is set to **100**.

     This is sufficient for testing purposes. Leave the other attributes at their default settings.

4 Render

- **Render** the scene.

  Notice the yellow highlight on the left of the buggy while the other side has more blue. These colors are coming from the HDRI.

HDRI used as background and illumination source

 Tip: *You may need to increase the **Accuracy** to obtain good shadow quality.*

5 Adjust the effect

- To adjust the effect of the HDRI irradiance contribution, go to the **Color Balance** section of the HDRI's file texture node and change the values to your needs.

  Increasing the brightness of the image will increase the amount of light contribution in the scene.

6 Save your work

- **Save** the scene as *13-HDRI_02.ma*.

Image-based lighting

In the previous HDRI exercise, you enclosed a scene using a dome surface and mapped it with an HDRI texture. While this workflow is appropriate if a finite distance to the environment is required, it can cause problems when the environment is infinitely distant. Because the sphere is geometry, mental ray processes it as such (i.e., it is tessellated), and this can, at times, slow down a render significantly.

With image-based lighting (IBL), you can use the HDRI to simulate light from an infinitely distant environment. This is a much quicker and easier method for setting up HDRI, and is also faster to render and more effective for distant environments, such as sky. Virtual lights can be derived from the environment image to cast shadows and contribute to Final Gather and Global Illumination simulations.

1 Open the scene file

HDRI project.01.mb

- **Open** the scene file called _13-IBL_01.ma._

This is the same scene as you used for the HDRI exercise, except that there is no sky dome, Final Gather is disabled, and there is no light source.

2 Create the IBL sphere

- **Open** the mental ray Render Settings.

- Under the **Indirect Lighting** tab, scroll to the **Environment** section and click the **Create** button next to the **Image-Based Lighting** option.

A mental ray infinite environment sphere will be created.

3 Map the image

- In the **Attribute Editor** for the mentalrayIblShape1 node, under **Image-Based Lighting Attributes**, map nappaValley.tif file to **Image Name**.

- **Render** the scene.

Render using image-based lighting

Super white
V = ☒ 1   *black*

> **Tip:** *Experiment with different values for* **Color Gain** *and* **Color Offset** *to achieve the effect that you desire.*

4 Adjusting illumination

You may find the scene is lacking shadows. The **Emit Light** option will further illuminate your scene.

- In the Attribute Editor for the mentalrayIblShape1 node, under the **Light Emission** section, set **Emit Light** to **On**.

  This will allow for the emission of light from the infinitely distant IBL environment.

- Set both **Quality U** and **Quality V** to **16**.

  These values represent the resolution for a control texture for light emission. Every pixel in that texture corresponds to a virtual directional light. The higher these values, the longer it will take to render, so it is best to start with low values and gradually increase them.

5 Adjust samples

To sample all the directional lights in the control texture would be very expensive. The **Samples** attribute allows you to control the sampling of the strongest lights. The first parameter specifies the number of important lights that must be sampled. The second parameter quasi-randomly selects a certain number of remaining lights. The higher the sample values, the longer the render.

- Set the first **Samples** parameter to a value of **10** and the second to a value of **4**.

- **Render** the scene.

Image-based lighting results with Emit Light option

> **Tip:** *If you find that the **Emit Light** option is slowing down your render too much, you can add regular lights into the scene for illumination instead.*

6   Save your work

- **Save** the scene as *13-IBL_02.ma*.

Conclusion

Final Gather and HDRI both allow precise diffuse light contributions in your scene and can help to create photorealistic images.

In the next lesson, you will learn about some of the mental ray shaders.

mental ray Shaders

mental ray® supports all Autodesk® Maya® shaders, textures, and lights, but it is also possible to use custom mental ray shaders.

This lesson presents several examples showing how to use custom mental ray shaders to create complex effects that may not be easily reproduced using any other renderer.

In this lesson, you will learn the following:

- mental ray's shader library
- How to use mental ray material shaders, photon shaders, shadow shaders, volume shaders, and light shaders
- How to create a mental ray double-sided shader
- How to assemble a mental ray bump map

The shader library

mental ray includes an extensive library of custom mental ray shaders. In addition to standard shaders, user-defined shaders written in standard C or C++ can be precompiled and linked at runtime, or can be both compiled and linked at runtime.

You can create mental ray custom shaders the same way you create Maya shading nodes: within the Hypershade **Create** bar, the Hypershade **Create** menu, or the Create Render Node window.

mental ray shader nodes are available by default in the Hypershade. If the Hypershade does not include the **mental ray** section in the Create Render Node window, the mental ray plug-in is probably not loaded. Use the **Window** → **Settings/Preferences** → **Plug-in Manager** to load the *Mayatomr.mll* plug-in.

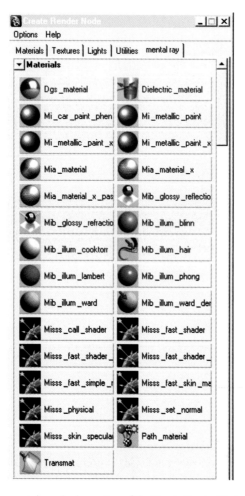

mental ray shader section of the Create Render Node window

Note: *It is possible to load and unload the mental ray libraries selectively, using the Shader Manager. This handy interface is located under* **Window → Rendering Editors → mental ray → Shader Manager**.

mental ray Shader Manager

Material shaders

The mental ray material shaders are similar to the Maya surface materials.

Two mental ray material shaders will be discussed here: *dgs_material* and *dielectric_material*. These two shaders implement different physically based models of reflection and refraction.

The *dgs* in *dgs_material* stands for diffuse-glossy-specular. The *dgs_material* shader can simulate mirrors, glossy paint or plastic, anisotropic glossy materials such as brushed metal, diffuse materials such as paper, translucent materials such as frosted glass, and any combination of these.

The *dielectric_material* shader is a physically based material shader that can be used to simulate dielectric media such as glass or water and other liquids.

In this exercise, you will learn to use these mental ray material shaders.

1 Scene file

• **Open** the file called *14-crystalBall_01.ma*.

This scene has been set-up for rendering with mental ray using Caustics. There is one point light in the scene and it has been set to emit photons. The objects in the scene use regular Maya shaders.

• **Render** the scene.

Crystal ball render with Caustics

2 Assign a mental ray material shader

You will use mental ray custom shaders to replace the regular phong shader on the crystal ball.

- Select the *crystal ball* surface.
- Open the **Hypershade** and click the **Graph Materials on Selected Objects** button.

  This will display the phong1 material and the phong1SG shading group.

- Select *phong1SG* and open the **Attribute Editor**.
- In the *phong1SG* tab, expand the **mental ray → Custom Shaders** attributes section.
- Open the **Create mental ray Nodes** bar in the **Hypershade** and expand the **Materials** section.
- **MMB+drag** a *dielectric_material* node to the *phong1SG*'s **Material Shader** attribute.

> **Note:** *The dielectric material has built-in absorption fresnel reflection. It simulates dielectric media very well. Technically, a dielectric material is a poor conductor of electricity but is a good supporter of electrostatic fields. Dielectric materials are generally solid. Some examples include porcelain, ceramic, plastics, and glass.*

3 Assign a mental ray photon shader

The regular Maya shaders, such as phong, lambert, and blinn, have photon attributes by default. This is not the case with mental ray material shaders; in order to use photonic effects such as Caustics with a mental ray material shader, you must have a photon shader connected to the shading group.

- Select *phong1SG* and open its Attribute Editor.

- In the *phong1SG* tab, expand the **mental ray → Custom Shaders** attributes section.
- Open the **Create mental ray Nodes** bar in the **Hypershade** and expand the **Photonic Materials** section.
- **MMB+drag** a *dielectric_material_photon* node to the *phong1SG*'s **Photon Shader** attribute.

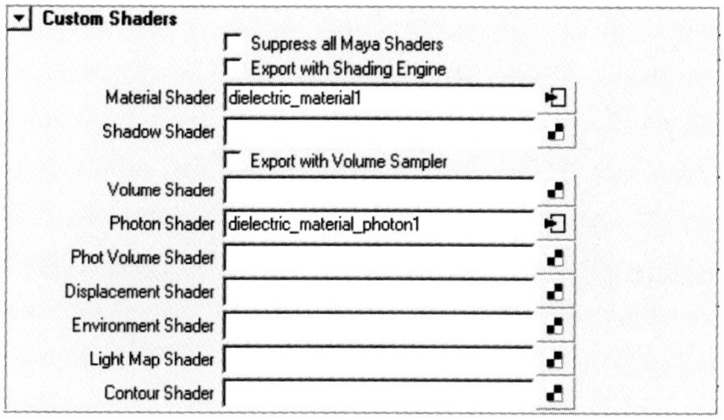

Custom material and photon shaders

4 **Change the settings for the custom shaders**

The various settings for the custom mental ray shaders are at zero by default; they must be changed in order for the shaders to render properly. You can read more about the settings for these custom shaders in the mental ray shader reference section of the Maya documentation.

- Select *dielectric_material1* in the **Hypershade** and open its **Attribute Editor**.
- Set the **Col** attribute as follows:

    H to **198**;

    S to **0.13**;

    V to **1.0**.

- Set the **Index of Refraction** attribute to **2.0**.

    2.0 is the refractive index of crystal.

- Set the **Phong Coefficient** attribute to **140**.

    *This setting is used to compute normalized phong highlights. It is similar to the **Cosine Power** attribute of a regular phong shader.*

> **Tip:** If **Phong Coefficient** is zero, only reflected rays will create highlight effects. Therefore, **Phong Coefficient** could be left at zero if Final Gather or a mental ray physical light was being used to light the scene. This is not the case in this scene, so the **Phong Coefficient** attribute must be set in order for there to be highlights on the material. If the **Outside Color** is different from the color for **Col** and the **Index of Refraction** value is non-zero, the reflected color will be a combination of the two colors (**Outside Color** and **Col**).

- Select the *dielectric_material_photon1* node and open its **Attribute Editor**.
- The settings for the *dielectric_material_photon1* shader should match the *dielectric_material1* shader:

    Col to **pale blue**;

    Index of Refraction to **2.00**;

    Phong Coefficient to **140**.

> **Note:** If the **Outside Color** color is different from the color for **Col** and the **Index of Refraction** value is non-zero, the color of the Caustics will be taken from **Outside Color**.

5 Render the scene

You may notice that it renders faster than it did at the beginning of this exercise.

Crystal ball with dielectric shader

6 Save your work

- **Save** your scene as *14-crystalBall_02.ma*.

Shadow shaders

It is possible to use mental ray shadow shaders to further customize the appearance of your object's shadows.

> **Note:** *If photon effects such as Caustics or Global Illumination are used, shadow shaders are generally not recommended because light effects are properly determined by the photons. Shadow shaders used with Caustics or Global Illumination will not produce physically correct results, but they can be used to fake certain shadow effects.*

1 Scene file

- **Continue** with your own scene.

  OR

- **Open** the scene called *14-crystalBall_02.ma*.

2 Assign a shadow shader

- Open the **Hypershade** and select the *phong1* material.
- Select **Graph → Output Connections**.

  This will display the phong1SG shading group.

- Select *phong1SG* and open its **Attribute Editor**.
- Under the *phong1SG* tab, expand the **mental ray** section.
- Expand the **Shadow Shaders** section of the **Create mental ray Nodes** bar in the **Hypershade.**
- **MMB+drag** a *mib_shadow_transparency* node to the *phong1SG*'s **Shadow Shader** attribute.

3 Adjust the shadow shader

- In the **Channel Box** for the *mib_shadow_transparency1* node, set **Mode** to **3.**

  Doing so will remove light dependency. You will not get any shadows if you leave this at 0.

- Set the **Color** attribute as follows:

  H to **198;**

  S to **0.3;**

  V to **0.8.**

  Doing so will determine the shadow color.

Tip: *You can soften your shadows by enabling area light in your light's mental ray attributes in order to convert it to a mental ray area light. This may slow down rendering time.*

4 Render the scene

Transparent blue shadow shader

5 Save your work

- **Save** your scene as *14-crystalBall_03.ma*.

Volume shaders

Volumetric materials scatter light to a certain degree, and they can realistically simulate effects such as fog, smoke, translucent glass, etc. A volume shader can be assigned to a particular object by connecting it to an object's shading group.

In this exercise, you will apply a volume shader to the crystal ball from the previous exercises.

1 Scene file

- **Continue** with your own scene.

  OR

- **Open** the scene called *14-crystalBall_03.ma*.

2   **Assign a volume shader**

• Open the **Hypershade** and select the *phong1* material.

• Select **Graph → Output Connections**.

This will display the phong1SG shading group.

• Select *phong1SG* and open its **Attribute Editor**.

• Under the *phong1SG* tab, expand the **mental ray** section.

• Expand the **Volumetric Materials** section of the **Create mental ray Nodes** bar in the **Hypershade.**

• **MMB+drag** a *parti_volume* node to the *phong1SG*'s mental ray **Volume Shader** attribute.

> **Note:** *Make sure you connect the volume shader to the shading group's* **Volume Shader** *attribute, found in the* **mental ray** *attribute section. Do not connect it to the Volume Material attribute found in the Shading Group attributes section.*

3   **Assign a photon volume shader**

In order for the Caustic effects in this scene to work, the volume shader needs an equivalent photon volume shader as well.

• Expand the **Photon Volumetric Materials** section of the **Create mental ray Nodes** bar in the **Hypershade.**

• **MMB+drag** a *parti_volume_photon* node to the *phong1SG*'s mental ray **Photon Volume Shader** attribute.

4   **Adjust the volume shader**

In order for the volume shaders to render properly, their settings must be adjusted. In this scene, the volume shader and the photon volume shader will use identical settings.

• In the **Hypershade**, select the *parti_volume1* node and open the **Attribute Editor**.

• Set the following settings:

    Set **Scatter** to be aqua.

Scatter *is the color of the scattering medium.*

    Set **Extinction** to **0.3**.

Extinction *determines how much light is absorbed or scattered in the medium. The higher the value, the denser the medium, and the more light is scattered. A value of* **0** *would indicate clean air or a vacuum.*

    Min Step Len to **0.03;**

    Max Step Len to **0.1.**

Min Step Len and **Max Step Len** determine the step length for rays marching in a non-homogeneous medium. In other words, they regulate accuracy.

- Select the *parti_volume_photon* node and give it the same settings.

Tip: *You can also try experimenting with different settings.*

5 Adjust the light energy

Adjust the photon energy to get a nice Caustic effect.

- In the Hypershade's **Lights** tab, select *pointLightShape1* and open its **Attribute Editor**.
- In the **mental ray** → **Caustics and Global Illumination** section, change the **Photon Intensity** values to between **400** and **1000.**

6 Increase Caustic photon radius

If you render the scene now, you may see dots scattered throughout your image— these are the photons. Increasing the photon radius is one way to correct this effect.

- Open the **Render Settings**.
- Click on the **mental ray** tab, then scroll to the **Caustics and Global Illumination** section.
- Set **Caustic Options Radius** to **2.000**.

7 Render the scene

Your crystal ball should now be uniformly translucent.

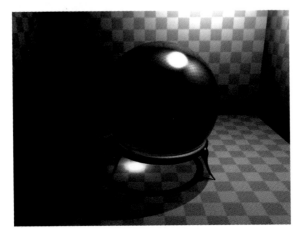

Volume shader creates translucent glass effect

8 Save your work

- **Save** your scene as *14-crystalBall_04.ma*.

Volume noise

You will now use some Maya textures and utility nodes to further enhance the appearance of the volume shader.

1 Scene file

- **Continue** with your own scene.

  OR

- **Open** the scene called *14-crystalBall_04.ma*.

2 Create a volume noise texture

A volume noise texture will be used to color the volume shader's scatter attribute.

- In the **Create Maya Node** bar of the Hypershade, scroll to the **3D Textures** section and create a **Volume Noise** texture.

- Adjust the texture's attributes as follows:

  Amplitude to **0.86;**

  Frequency Ratio to **1.37;**

  Frequency to **10.0;**

  Noise Type to **Wispy;**

  Color Gain to **dull yellow;**

  Color Offset to **dark blue-green**.

3 Connect the volume noise texture to the volume shaders

- Select the *parti_volume1* node in the **Hypershade** and open its **Attribute Editor**.

- **MMB+drag** the *volumeNoise1* texture to the *parti_volume1*'s **Scatter** attribute.

- **Repeat** the above steps with the *parti_volume_photon1* node.

4 Adjust the volume shaders

If you render the scene now, you should see a wispy color effect inside your crystal ball, but the smoke is still uniformly distributed. You can increase the **Non-uniform** attribute of the volume shaders to randomize the distribution of the volumetric material. The **Non-uniform** attribute can be set to any number between 0 and 1.

- Select the *parti_volume1* node and increase the **Non-uniform** attribute to **0.95**.

- **Repeat** the above steps with the *parti_volume_photon1* node.

5   Restrict the height of the smoke

Currently, the volumetric material fills the entire sphere. You can use the volume shader's **Height** attribute to limit the height of the material. When the volume shader's **Mode** value is set to **0**, the volumetric material fills the entire volume. When **Mode** is **1**, there will be clear air or vacuum anywhere above the **Height** setting.

- Select the *parti_volume1* node and open its **Attribute Editor**.
- Set the **Mode** attribute to **1**.
- Set the **Height** attribute to **3**.
- **Repeat** the above steps with the *parti_volume_photon1* node.

Note: *To see more clearly the effect of changing the height attribute, try setting the* **Index Of Refraction** *attribute to* **1** *and the* **Transp** *attribute to* **1**. *The glass will now render, making the volumetric effect much more evident.*

6   Randomize the smoke height

A noise texture will be used to make the height a little less even.

- In the **Create Maya Nodes** bar of the **Hypershade**, scroll to the **2D Textures** section and **create** a **Noise** texture.
- Adjust the *noise1* texture's as follows:

   Amplitude to **0.79**;

   Ratio to **0.32**;

   Frequency Ratio to **1.97**;

   Noise Type to **Wispy**.

- Open the **General Utilities** section of the **Hypershade** and **create** a **Set Range** node.

The noise texture's output will return a value between 0 and 1, but the **Height** value for the smoke in the crystal ball should be higher than that. The Set Range utility will allow you to specify a new output range.

- **MMB+drag** the *noise1* texture onto the *setRange1* node and choose **Other** from the pop-up menu.
- In the **Connection Editor**, connect *noise1*'s **Out Alpha** attribute to *setRange1*'s **Value X** attribute.
- Select *setRange1* and open its **Attribute Editor**.
- Set the following:

   Min X to **2.0**;

   Max X to **4.0**;

   Old Min to **0.0**;

   Old Max to **1.0**.

- **MMB+drag** the *setRange1* onto the *parti_volume1* node and select **Other** from the pop-up menu.
- **Connect** *setRange1*'s **Out Value X** attribute to *parti_volume1*'s **Height** attribute.
- **Repeat** the previous steps to connect *setRange1*'s **Out Value X** attribute with the *parti_volume_photon1* node's **Height** attribute.

7 Render the scene

The smoke inside the crystal ball now has uneven distribution and height.

Smoke effect

8 Save your work

- **Save** your scene as *14-crystalBall_05.ma*.

Double-sided shaders

The mental ray custom *mib_twosided* shader can be used to create a surface material with different properties for each side of the geometry to which it is assigned (e.g., specular, diffuse, bump). This is known as a double-sided material.

In order to achieve the double-sided shader effect with mental ray, you will have to use a different workflow than the one used with Maya.

1 Scene file

- **Open** the file called *14-doubleSided_01.ma*.

2 Create the required shaders and textures

- In the **Create All Nodes** bar of the **Hypershade**, create a **blinn** and a **lambert** shader.
- Change the *blinn* **Color** to **gold** and the *lambert* **Color** to **deep blue**.
- Scroll to the **2D Textures** section of the **Hypershade.**
- **MMB+drag** a **Bulge** texture on top of the *blinn* shader and choose **Bump Map** from the pop-up menu.
- Open the **Attribute Editor** for the **2D placement** of the *bulge* texture and set the following values:

    Coverage to **0.675, 1.0**;

    Translate Frame to **0.06, -0.065**;

    Repeat UV to **22.0, 22.0.**

- From the **Create 2D Textures** section of the Hypershade, **MMB+drag** a **Grid** texture on top of the *lambert* shader and choose **Bump Map** from the pop-up menu.
- Open the **Attribute Editor** for the *grid* texture and set the following values:

    U Width to **0.0**;

    V Width to **0.12.**

- Open the **Attribute Editor** for the *grid*'s 2D placement node and set the following values:

    Repeat UV to **0.0, 50.0.**

3 Create a mib_twosided

- **Assign** the *blinn* material to the *goblet* surface.
- With the *blinn* and *lambert* selected, select **Graph → Input and Output Connections** in the **Hypershade.**

    This will display the shading group node used by the materials.

- Select *blinnSG* and open its **Attribute Editor**.
- Make sure the *blinnSG* tab is selected.
- Open the **Create mental ray Nodes** bar in the **Hypershade** and expand the **Sample Compositing** section.
- **MMB+drag** a *mib_twosided* node onto the **Material Shader** port of *blinnSG*. ∧ *located in the Custom Shaders Section*

    Doing so will break the existing connection to the blinn material, which is what you want.

4 Assign materials to mib_twosided

- Open the **Attribute Editor** for the *mib_twosided* node.
- **MMB+drag** the *lambert* material onto the **Front** attribute of *mib_twosided*.
- **MMB+drag** the *blinn* material onto the **Back** attribute of *mib_twosided*.

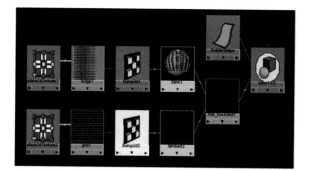

mib_twosided shading network

5 Render the scene

- In the Render Settings, set **Render Using** to **mental ray**.
- **Render** the scene.

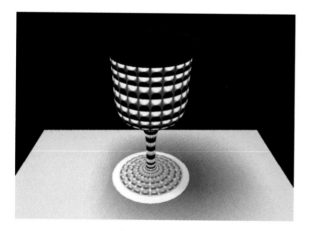

mib_twosided used to create a double-sided shader effect

Light shaders

The mental ray light shaders can be used to replace the regular Maya lights at render time. This workflow will be illustrated in this exercise.

1 Scene file

- **Open** the file called *14-lightShader_01.ma*.

2 **Create a mental ray light shader**

- In the **Create mental ray Nodes** bar in the **Hypershade**, expand the **mentalRay Lights** section and create a *mib_light_spot* node.

- Open the **Attribute Editor** for the *spotLight* in the scene and scroll to the **mental ray → Custom Shaders** section.

- **MMB+drag** the *mib_light_spot* node into the **Light Shader** port of the *spotLight*.

- In the Hypershade, select the *spotLight* node and display its **Input and Output Connections**.

- Open the **Attribute Editor** for the *coneShape* node and expand the **Render Stats** section.

- Set the following under the **Render Stats** section:

    Volume Samples Override to **On**;

    Depth Jitter to **On**;

    Volume Samples to **12**.

3 **Adjust mib_light_spot node**

- Set the **Color** attribute of the *mib_light_spot* to a pale yellow.

- Make sure **Shadow** is set to **On**.

  This will result in volumetric shadows.

- Make sure **Attenuation** is set to **On**.

  *If **Attenuation** is **On**, the light will start from the **Start** value and will fade at the **Stop** value.*

- Set the **Cone** value to **4**.

Note: *If **Factor** is different than **0**, you will not get a volumetric shadow.*

4 **Render the scene**

- **Render** the scene using mental ray.

Light shader with shadows

Tip: *Increase the **Color** of the mib_light_spot node to get brighter lighting.*

Bump maps

mental ray bump maps work a little differently than the Maya bump maps. The workflow is not initially intuitive. The following workflow is for a bump map based on a file texture. If a procedural bump map is required, either convert the texture to a file or use normal bump mapping.

The mental ray bump network makes use of the following mental ray custom shader nodes:

dgs_material;

mib_color_mix;

mib_passthrough_bump_map;

mib_bump_basis;

mentalrayTexture;

mib_texture_remap;

mib_texture_vector.

1 Scene file

- **Open** the file called *14-bumpmap_01.ma*.

  The file contains a NURBS sphere and directional light.

2 Create a dgs_material

- In the Hypershade, go to the **Materials** section of the **Create mental ray Nodes** bar.

- **Create** a *dgs_material* and **assign** it to the *sphere*.

- Set the following on the newly created node:

    Shiny to **20.0**;

    Diffuse to **white**;

    Glossy to **grey**.

3 Create a mib_color_mix node

- Go to the **Data Conversion** section of the **Create mental ray Nodes** bar.

- **Create** a *mib_color_mix* node and **connect** its **outValue** attribute to the **Specular** attribute of the *dgs_material*.

Note: *The mib_color_mix node is required to return problematic surface normals back to normal prior to color calculation.*

Project 04

290

4 **Create required mental ray textures**

- Go to the **Textures** section of the **Create mental ray Nodes** bar.
- Create the following nodes:

    mib_passthrough_bump_map;

    mib_bump_basis;

    mib_texture_remap;

    mib_texture_vector.

5 **Connect the bump network**

- Make the following connections:

    mib_texture_vector1.outValue to *mib_texture_remap1.input;*

    mib_texture_remap1.outValue to *mib_passthrough_bump_map1.coord;*

    mib_passthrough_bump_map1.outValue to *mib_color_mix.colorBase;*

    mib_bump_basis.u and .v to *mib_passthrough_bump_map.u* and *.v.*

6 **Create the mentalrayTexture node**

- Select the *mib_passthrough_bump_map1* node and open its **Attribute Editor.**
- Click on the **mental ray Texture map** button.

    A new node will be created that allows for the file texture information to be input.

- Select the *mentalrayTexture* node and open its **Attribute Editor.**
- Click the **browse** button, then select *scratches.tif* as basis of the bump map.

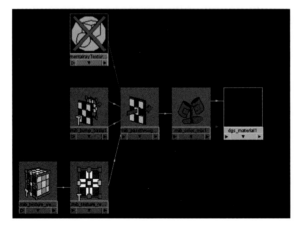

Bump map network

7 Test the bump

- Select the *mib_passthrough_bump_map1* node and open its **Attribute Editor.**
- Change the **factor** attribute to **-2.0.**

This defines the orientation of the bump along with its depth.

- **Render** the scene.

mental ray bump map

Conclusion

Custom mental ray shaders can allow you to create complex shading and lighting effects. Custom shaders can be used with standard Maya texture and utility nodes, and their rendering is fully supported.

In the next project, you will start the dynamics section of the book, learning about rigid bodies.

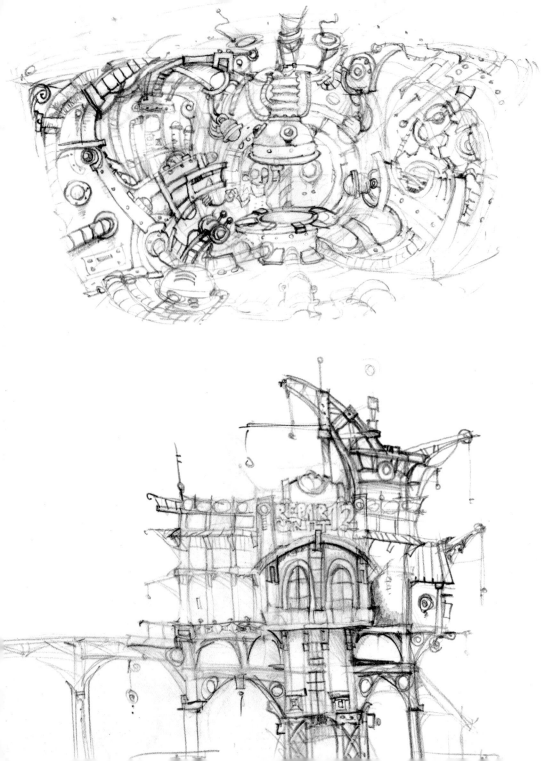

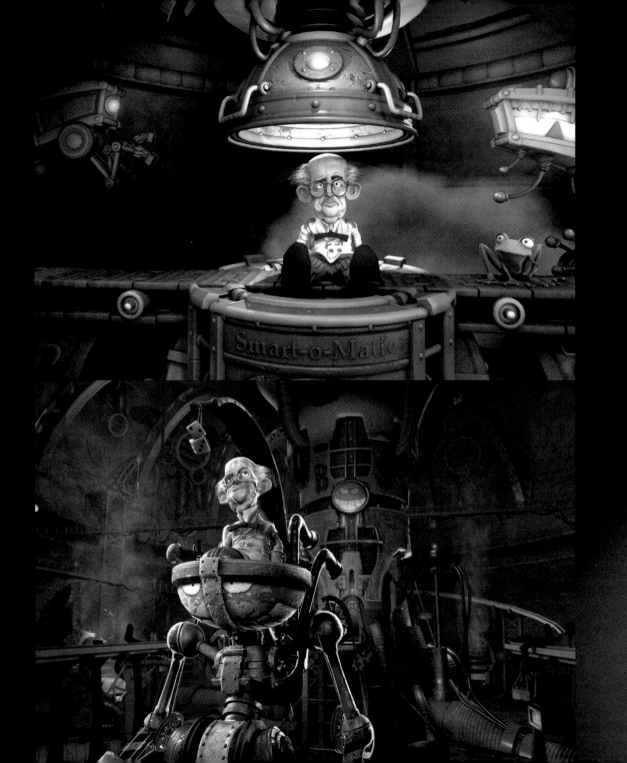

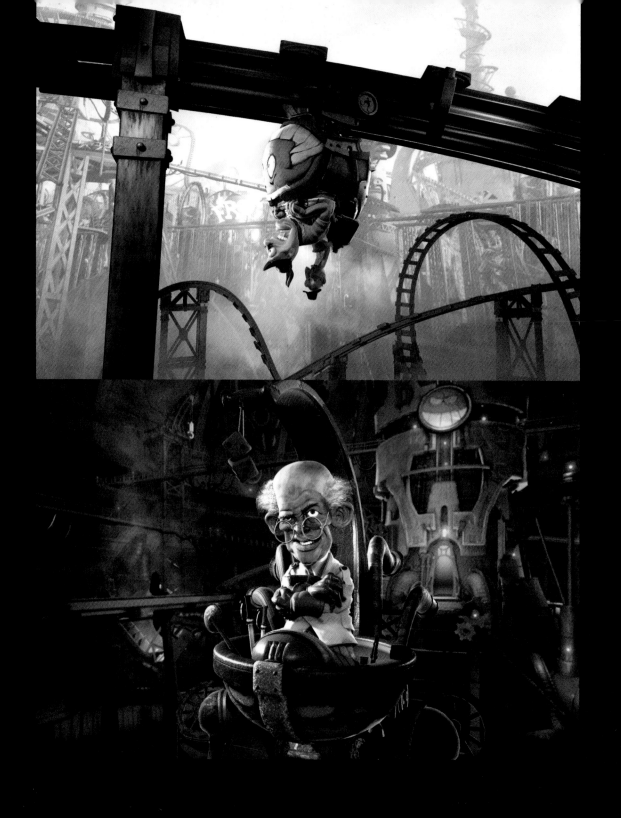

Project 05

In Project Five, you will start the overview of the Maya dynamic system by learning about rigid bodies. Rigid bodies are objects that can collide and interact with each other, resulting in dynamic animation. Such animation can add a good amount of realism to a scene, which would be extremely difficult to recreate by hand.

Maya Dynamics

Dynamics in Autodesk® Maya® uses rules of physics to let you simulate natural forces in your animation. Effects with complex motion, such as smoke, rain, fire, or colliding objects, lend themselves well to dynamically controlled animation. This animation is typically achieved by creating elements in a scene that react to the forces applied to them. By creating an environment of fields, expressions, goals, etc., the animator has artistic control over the affected objects, balancing the need for realism and animation requirements.

In this lesson, you will learn the following:

- About the different types of rigid bodies
- About the terminology of particles
- About the different clip effects available
- About particle instancing terminology
- About particle goals
- About particle rendering

Dynamics

Maya dynamics is the animation of rigid bodies, soft bodies, and particles; the use of dynamic constraints; and the rendering strategies for hardware and software particle types.

This brief lesson provides a quick overview of some of the key topics discussed in the upcoming dynamics section of the book.

Rigid bodies

The rigid body system in Maya provides animation of geometric objects in a dynamically controlled, collision-based system (Lessons 16–18).

Active and passive rigid bodies

Active and passive rigid bodies are created to collide and react with one another in a realistic manner. Active objects typically fall, move, spin, and collide with passive objects.

Rigid body constraints

Rigid body constraints (Lesson 17) allow dynamic objects to be constrained or constrain each other. Spring, hinge, pin, etc., are some of the constraint types that will be explored.

Particles

Particles (Lessons 19-27) are objects that have no size or volume. They are reference points that are displayed, selected, animated, and rendered differently than other objects in Maya.

Particle object and Array attributes

Like other nodes in Maya, particles can be thought of as objects with a collective transform. They also contain attributes that control the individual particles using Array attributes. Individual particle behavior can be controlled with ramps, scripts, and expressions.

Fields

Fields such as gravity, turbulence, air, and others provide an easy way to move particles around your scene without the use of MEL and expressions.

Particle expressions

Particle expressions (Lesson 22) are a powerful and almost limitless method of controlling particle parameters. Particle expressions share the MEL syntax and methodology. Functions such as `linstep()`, `sin()`, and `rand()` provide mathematical control over particle appearance and motion.

Particle collisions

Particle collision events (Lesson 21) provide a method for creating and killing particles when they collide with geometry. Particle collision event procedures can be used to trigger specific MEL-scripted commands at collision time.

Emit function

The emit function (Lesson 23) allows the user to create and position particles based on information directly derived from MEL and expressions. It requires an ample amount of MEL knowledge, as more complicated usage of the emit function can be MEL-intensive.

Clip effects

Clip effects provide you with powerful and flexible tools for creating common dynamic effects. These are typically MEL scripts and expressions that automate the setup of the effect for the user. They also provide an excellent set of MEL and expression examples.

Fire

This clip effect will light an object on fire for both hardware and software rendering.

Smoke

The smoke clip effect makes use of hardware sprites and is a good example of how to set-up hardware sprites.

Fireworks

The fireworks effect allows you to make fireworks that are set-up for software rendering quickly and easily.

Lightning

The lightning clip effect lets you create an electrical arc between two or more objects.

Shatter

The shatter clip effect lets you break up objects into parts you can use for dynamic simulations.

Curve flow

The curve flow clip effect allows you to select a curve as a motion path for particles.

Surface flow

The surface flow clip effect allows you to use a surface as a path for particles.

Particle instancing

With particle instancing (Lesson 26), you can use particles to control the position and motion of instanced geometry.

Animated instance

Particle instancing is only part of the functionality. You can instance a keyframed object to particles in the scene.

Cycled instance

With the particle instancer, you can cycle through a sequence of snapshot objects to create the instanced motion.

Software sprites

The particle instancer also provides aim control of the instanced object. If this instanced object is a textured plane, it can be aimed at the camera, creating a software renderable sprite method.

Goals

Goals are a very powerful method of animating particles. A goal is a destination point that a particle wants to achieve. Particles can have multiple goal objects and per particle attributes designed specifically for goal-based interaction.

Goal weight and smoothness

Goal Weight and **Smoothness** can be animated to provide particle movement that would be otherwise difficult to create with fields or expressions.

Per Particle Goal attributes

Goal attributes such as **parentU** and **goalPP** provide individual particle control. With the use of the **parentId** attribute, these values can be transferred from one particle to another.

Particle rendering

What good is all this particle animation if you cannot render it out to contribute to the final shot?

Hardware rendering

Hardware rendering of particles provides a quick method of image creation. Typically, these images are taken to the compositor who sweetens and integrates them with the rest of the scene elements.

Software rendering

Software rendering allows for scene integration of particles and rendered objects. Volumetric particle rendering is also created with software rendered particle types. Shadowing, glows, and other lighting effects are also combined.

Compositing

Without compositing, much of this process would not be possible. Dynamics should always be viewed as another contributor to the elements that will make up the final image.

Conclusion

Maya dynamics can be quite simple or very complex. The topics presented in the following lessons are shown in a progressive manner, in order to take you through as many tools and techniques as possible. Plenty of self-experimentation will be required in order to fully control the dynamic simulations and create astonishing results.

In the next lesson, you will learn about rigid bodies.

Rigid Body Dynamics

This lesson introduces the fundamental tools and techniques required to achieve realistic solid collisions in Autodesk® Maya® using rigid bodies.

In this lesson, you will learn the following:

- The differences between active and passive rigid bodies
- How to create rigid bodies
- How to create and connect fields to rigid bodies
- Stand-ins
- How to work with the rigid body solver and its attributes
- How to combine keyframing with rigid body dynamics

What is a rigid body?

A rigid body is defined as any object whose surface does not deform when a collision occurs. Common examples in nature would be billiard balls, floors, and ceilings. (Of course, in the real world these surfaces do actually deform very slightly when a collision occurs. This minimal deformation will be overlooked and the objects will be considered as either rigid or not rigid to simplify the process.)

Any NURBS or polygonal surface can contain rigid body properties. Curves, particles, and lattices, for example, cannot become rigid bodies since they contain no surface information. Surfaces, however, that are made from curves, particles, or lattices, for example, can be rigid bodies.

Active vs. passive rigid bodies

Rigid bodies are divided into two categories: *active* and *passive*. There are important distinctions between these two types of rigid bodies.

	Active	Passive
Can be key framed	No	Yes
Responds to collisions	Yes	No
Causes collisions	Yes	Yes
Affected by fields	Yes	No

A comparison of active vs. passive rigid bodies

The Soft/Rigid Bodies menu

The **Soft/Rigid Bodies** menu is used to create rigid and soft bodies, create dynamic constraints, and keyframe the active and passive states of objects.

Soft/Rigid Bodies menu

Important rigid body nodes

The rigid body command you choose will create several new important nodes and attributes for each selected object. These nodes and their associated attributes can be viewed in the Channel Box, Hypergraph, Outliner, or Attribute Editor. In the Channel Box, you will notice that the following nodes are created for each selected object:

rigidBody

The *rigidBody* node is located under the **Shapes** section for each selected rigid body object in the Channel Box.

To view and select a *rigidBody* node from the Outliner, you may first need to display shapes by selecting **Outliner** → **Display** → **Shapes**. The *rigidBody* node will appear as a child of the object's transform node.

The attributes within this node contain information that determines the active or passive status of the rigid body and various controls relating to the properties of each specific rigid body object.

rigidSolver

The *rigidSolver* node provides control over the evaluation of the rigid body dynamics. This node is listed under both the **Inputs** and **Outputs** sections within the Channel Box for the selected item. By default, one *rigidSolver* node is used to control the evaluation of all rigid bodies in the scene.

time

The *time* node determines when the *rigidSolver*'s evaluations will take place. This is useful if you wish to have multiple simulations running within the same scene based on different time parameters.

Rigid body example

This example incorporates the use of active and passive rigid bodies and is intended to familiarize you with the process of setting up a simple rigid body simulation.

1 **Scene file**

- **Open** the file named *16-dynamics_01.ma*.

  This scene contains the Constructor with his buggy. You will use it to simulate the dynamics of a buggy rolling on the track, hitting rocks on its way.

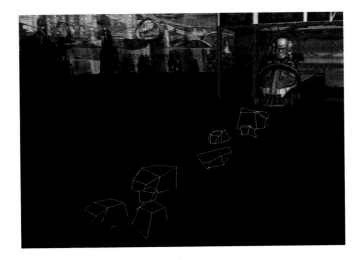

The Constructor and his buggy with the rocks in his way

2 **Create the active rigid bodies**

- From the Outliner, select all the rock surfaces.

- Click **F5** to choose the **Dynamics** menu set.

- Select **Soft/Rigid Bodies** → **Create Active Rigid Body** → ❑.

- In the Rigid Options, select **Edit** → **Reset Settings** to set the options to their default states.

- Click **Create**.

  An active rigid body is created for every selected piece of geometry.

Note: *If you have selected a group of objects, that group is now considered as one big object to be used with dynamics. For this reason, you must make sure that you have selected all the individual objects so they can be calculated on their own.*

3 **Create the passive rigid bodies**

In this example, the track, ground surface, and the buggy will be used as passive rigid bodies.

- Select the track, ground, and buggy surfaces.

- Select **Soft/Rigid Bodies** → **Create Passive Rigid Body** → ❑.

- In the Rigid Body options window, select **Edit** → **Reset Settings** to set the options to their default states.

- Choose **Create**.

  Passive rigid bodies are created for the selected pieces of geometry.

> **Note:** *When creating a passive rigid body for an object with animation, such as the buggy, the animation is passed to the rigid body node, allowing you to keep that animation. If you had created an active rigid body with the buggy, the animation would have also been passed to the rigid body node, but the animation would have been overriden by the dynamic simulation.*

4 Set rigid body attributes for the buggy

- Select the *buggy*.
- Locate the *rigidBody* node for this object in the **Shapes** section of the Channel Box.
- Set the **Mass** attribute to **100**.

5 Set rigid body attributes for the rocks

- Select all of the *rock* surfaces.
- Enter the following attribute values for the *rigidBody* nodes:

  Mass to **5**;

  Bounciness to **0.2**;

  Static Friction to **0.05**;

  Dynamic Friction to **0.05**;

  Apply Forces At to **verticesOrCVs**.

The specific definitions of these attributes will be discussed in a later lesson. For now, your goal is to have collisions occur at a decent playback speed.

> **Note:** *When multiple items are selected, changing an attribute value in the Channel Box will change the value for every selected item that contains that same attribute.*

6 Set rigid body attributes for the water

- Select the *ground* and *track* surfaces.
- Enter the following attribute values for the *rigidBody* node:

  Bounciness to **0.5**;

  Static Friction to **0.5**;

  Dynamic Friction to **0.5**;

7 Enable dynamic labels

In some cases when dealing with complex scenes containing large numbers of rigid bodies, it is difficult to keep track of which rigid bodies are passive and which are active. When set to **On**, the **displayLabel** attribute will display a small label next to each rigid body in the viewport, indicating whether it is an active or passive rigid body.

> **Note:** *Other dynamic components, such as dynamic constraints, also have labels associated with them.*

- Select any *rigidBody* object in the scene.
- Click on the *rigidSolver* node near the bottom of the Channel Box.
- Set the **displayLabel** attribute to **On**.
- Select the objects to better see the dynamic labels.

  The labels are placed at the object's center of mass, which is represented by a small **x** *on each object.*

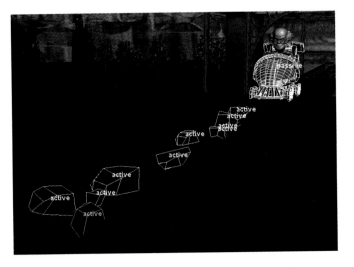

Displaying rigid body labels at the object's center of mass

8 Test the animation

- Make sure the **Playback Speed** in the preferences is set to **Play every frame**.

> **Tip:** *It is very important to play every frame when using dynamics because it allows time for the solver to calculate the dynamics correctly.*

- **Playback** the animation to see how the dynamics react.

9 **Create a gravity field**

- Click in the viewport to deselect any currently selected objects.

- From the Dynamics menu, select **Fields** → **Gravity** → ❏.

- In the Gravity options, select **Edit** → **Reset Settings**.

- Click **Create**.

  A new gravity field is created at the origin.

- **Move** the *gravityField* up above the scene so that it is easily selectable and visible.

10 **Connect the objects to gravity**

- Select all the rocks.

- **Shift-select** the *gravityField* last.

- Select **Fields** → **Affect Selected Object(s)**.

Tip: *The same results could have been achieved by selecting the rigid bodies, then creating the* **Fields** → **Gravity**. *This process would automatically connect the selected items to the chosen field. You could also use the Relationship Editor to connect fields and surfaces.*

11 **Test the results**

- **Rewind** and then **playback** the scene.

  The Constructor and his buggy are riding the track, while colliding with the rocks. Notice that the rocks also collide together and that the track and ground remains stationary because it is a passive rigid body.

The simulated dynamics

Note: *When rigid bodies interpenetrate, they are flagged by the rigidSolver to tell you that a interpenetration has occurred. This is normal and can be ignored at this stage.*

12 Save your work

• **Save** the scene as *16-dynamics_02.ma.*

Stand-ins

All the rigid body nodes have a **Stand-in** attribute, which allows you to speed up simple collisions by telling the rigid solver to calculate the piece of geometry as a simple primitive. By default, this attribute is set to **None**, which tells the solver to calculate the dynamics for each vertex of the geometry. Although it will be much slower to calculate the simulation, the dynamic animation will be accurate.

The attribute can also be set to **Cube** or **Sphere** stand-ins delimited by the bounding box of the geometry. This can really speed up the dynamic simulation, but you might notice that the rigid bodies will not react exactly the same as if the full geometry was taken into account.

Another solution is to create a low resolution version of the models for dynamics and link their dynamic animation to the high resolution model. This will be discussed in Lesson 18.

Caching

Caching allows the dynamic solver to evaluate calculations once per frame and store the results of those calculations in memory (RAM) where they can be accessed during subsequent playback at much faster speeds. In addition to providing improved performance, caching allows you to scrub through the animation without problems.

When caching is enabled, the solver will continue to use the cached version of the data until the cache has been deleted. For this reason, any modifications made to the simulation after caching the data will not exist in the currently cached version of the playback, since those changes were not part of the original calculations that were computed during the cache run-up.

It is best to tweak values and then cache the scene. Once you have evaluated those changes and wish to make more, delete the cache, make the new changes, and then re-cache the scene again.

Note: *The first playback cycle where the solver records the calculations into RAM is commonly referred to as a run-up.*

1 **Scene file**

- **Continue** with your own scene.

  OR

- **Open** the scene file called *16-dynamics_02.ma*.

2 **Cache the playback**

- In the timeline, set the playback range to start at frame **0** and end at frame **100**.

- Select one of the rocks.

- Click on the *rigidSolver* node in the Channel Box and set **cacheData** to **On**.

> **Tip:** *You can also enable or disable caching by selecting* **Solvers** → **Memory Caching** → **Enable** *or* **Disable**.

- **Rewind** and then **play back** the scene.

  You should be able to scrub in the timeline where the simulation was played once.

3 **Delete the cache**

- Select **Solvers** → **Memory Caching** → **Delete** to clear the previously cached data from memory.

- If caching is no longer required, highlight the *rigidSolver* node in the Channel Box again and set **cacheData** to **Off**.

4 **Modify the attribute values**

- Experiment with different values for CenterOfMass, Mass, and Bounciness to see how the simulation results differ.

- **Re-cache** the scene so you can see the result play back in real time.

- **Repeat** this process until you have achieved the desired motion.

Combine keyframes with dynamics

In some cases, relying solely on the influence of fields, initial forces, and other dynamic attributes to animate objects may not provide the required level of control. In these cases, it is useful to combine keyframing techniques with dynamic techniques to tune the motion of the animation. You will learn how to ignore dynamics while an object is controlled by keyframes, and how to combine keyframes and dynamics.

1 **Scene file**

- **Continue** with your own scene.

  OR

- **Open** the scene file called *16-dynamics_02.ma*.

2 Disable the rigidSolver

You will be setting up animation on the buggy now and it will be an easier task if the dynamics do not interfere with the keyframing. A quick way to do this is to disable the state of the *rigidSolver*.

- With any rigid body selected, look under the **Inputs** section in the Channel Box and click on *rigidSolver*.

- Set the **State** attribute to **Off**.

3 Keyframe the active and passive state of the buggy

In order for the buggy to be either active or passive at different frames in the animation, you will keyframe its active state attribute using special menu items.

- **Rewind** to frame **0**.

- Select the *buggy* node.

- Highlight the *rigidBody* node for *buggy* in the **Channel Box** if it is not already.

- Select **Soft/Rigid Bodies** → **Set Passive Key** to key this as a passive body.

- Go to frame **14**.

  This is a good spot to change the rigid body state to active since the buggy is not yet colliding with the rocks.

- Select **Soft/Rigid Bodies** → **Set Active Key** to key this as an active body.

Note: *Keying the active/passive state using these menu items is the most reliable method for keyframing rigid bodies.*

4 Enable the state of the rigidSolver

Now that you have completed the keyframe animation, you can enable dynamics again.

- With the *rigidBody* still selected, look under the **Inputs** section in the Channel Box and click on *rigidSolver*.

- Type **1** in the **State** attribute to set it back to **On**.

5 Connect the buggy to gravity

- Select the *buggy*.

- **Shift-select** the *gravityField*.

- Select **Fields** → **Affect Selected Object(s)**.

Tip: *If the effect of the gravity does not seem to be strong enough, you can increase its Magnitude attribute from the Channel Box. The default magnitude of 9.8 reflects the earth's gravity, but your scene might require a different setting in order to create the intended movement.*

6 Test the scene

- **Play back** the animation.

The buggy will translate and rotate with its original animation as a passive rigid body. It will then continue its animation as an active rigid body. This continued motion is the combined result of the gravity field, motion inherited from the animation, and keyframed rotation.

The buggy colliding with the rocks

Tip: *When no collisions occur until many frames into the simulation, you can keyframe the ignore state of a rigid body until near the time of collision to speed up playback. To do so, simply keyframe the* **Ignore** *attribute to* **On** *or* **Off**.

Tip: *You can also playblast the scene in order to see a movie of the animation in real-time. To do so, simply* **RMB** *in the Time Slider and select* **Playblast**.

7 Save your work

- **Save** the scene as *16-dynamics_04.ma.*

Tips and traps

The following are some additional tips to consider for this exercise and for rigid bodies in general:

- The **Ignore** attribute may cause some problems if it is keyframed **On** or **Off** at the same time some other important operation is done, such as a keyframed active state. To fix this, keyframe **Ignore** one frame before the other important action.

- Keyframing the **Ignore** flag while the simulation is cached or vice-versa may cause some unexpected behavior. Choose one or the other but avoid doing both simultaneously, or the simulation may produce unexpected results. These results may include offsetting objects' positions, or objects spinning off into space at the wrong time, etc.

- Avoid keyframing the **Active** attribute using the Channel Box on any objects containing hierarchies. Instead, use the **Set Active Key** or **Set Passive Key** menu items under the **Soft/Rigid Bodies** menu.

- If you play back the scene after an object has been animated, the object may offset itself from the intended animation. To avoid this behavior, reopen the scene. After the **Ignore** attribute has been keyframed, select the *rigidSolver* node in the **Channel Box** and set the attribute **State** to **Off**. After the active and passive states of the objects have been keyframed, select the *rigidSolver* node and set the **State** attribute back to **On**.

- Verify that your **Undo Queue** in the **Preferences** is set to **Infinite** or to a high number. Realize that Undo does not always work reliably with dynamics, because of the way dynamic simulations are computed in the software. In general, when working with dynamics, you must work methodically and think about each step before progressing. Also, avoid scrubbing playback in the timeline if your scene is not cached.

- Changing the **Mass** attribute of an object will not affect how it falls under the force of gravity. However, it will affect how much force is exerted when a collision occurs. Also, changing the mass will affect how a non-gravity field (i.e., turbulence) will move the object around in the scene.

- The file *16-friction.ma* has rigid body books that slide down a table. You can use this file to get a clear idea of how the **Static** and **Dynamic Friction** attributes work.

  These attributes provide general changes and are not precision controls. Valid values normally range from 0 to 1, although you can use higher values. Static friction controls a threshold as to how high the angle will need to be before the object begins to slide. Dynamic friction controls the slipperiness (energy loss) of the object once it is in motion along the table surface. Values closer to 1 correspond to more energy lost or more stickiness in the collision.

  It is important to remember that the friction values on the books and the table need to be taken into consideration since both contribute to the final simulation. Try adjusting the static and dynamic friction attributes for both objects and compare the different results.

The long arrows displayed from the rigidBodies in this file during playback show the direction of the velocity of the traveling rigidBody. This is a display feature called **displayVelocity** *on the rigidSolver node that can be enabled or disabled.*

The **scaleVelocity** *attribute also on the rigidSolver simply scales the length of this arrow and has no control of the motion of the objects on the solver.*

- Can a rigid body be deformed? By definition a rigidBody is rigid, which means non-deformable. You can apply a deformer to a rigid body, however, the collision calculations will be based on the shape of the original, non-deformed object also known as the intermediate object. This will not likely be the effect you are after. One exception to this rule is particle collisions. You can make particles collide with deforming geometry and deforming rigid bodies. Particle collisions are discussed in greater detail in later lessons.

Building a house of cards

Use what you have learned so far to build a house of cards on a table. Apply fields to the cards to make them collide with each other and the table.

Remember that the normal orientation of a surface is important in rigid body collisions. If you build the cards as a single-sided polygonal surface, you will find that some cards will not collide correctly. You can fix this quickly by selecting all the rigid body objects and selecting **Edit Mesh → Extrude Face**, then extruding a little to give the card some thickness. You can do this even after you have created the rigid bodies.

Conclusion

You now have a basic understanding of how rigid body dynamics work. Rigid bodies are objects that can cause and respond to collisions. Active rigid bodies cause and respond to collisions and fields, but cannot be keyframed. Passive rigid bodies cause, but do not respond to collisions, and they do not respond to fields, but can be keyframed.

Rigid bodies are controlled by the *rigidSolver* and the *time* node. Important attributes of the *rigidBody* and the *rigidSolver* can be adjusted in the Channel Box. It is possible to keyframe the active and passive state of the *rigidBody* to combine keyframing and dynamic animation together.

In upcoming lessons, you will learn about the various rigid body attributes and solver attributes in greater detail.

In the next lesson, you will learn about rigid body constraints.

Rigid Body Constraints

This lesson focuses on working with rigid body constraints. These special constraint types are meant to be used solely with rigid bodies and will mimic the behavior of nails, hinges, springs, and other real-world tools in the way they limit the movements of constrained objects.

In this lesson, you will learn the following:

- About the rigid body constraint types
- How to parent constraints
- How to animate constraint parameters
- How to set the initial state
- The different applications for dynamic and non-dynamic constraints
- About the rigid body groups

Dynamic constraint types

Rigid body constraints are created using **Soft/Rigid Bodies** → **Create Constraint**. There are six dynamic constraint types divided into two categories:

Dual-body constraints

The dual-body constraints allow for the constraining of a rigid body to a point in space or to another rigid body:

- **Pin**
- **Hinge**
- **Directional Hinge**
- **Spring**

Single-body constraints

The single-body constraints allow for the constraint of a rigid body to a point in space or, in the case of the barrier, to a plane in space:

- **Nail**
- **Barrier**

Constraint descriptions

Pin

Constrains two active rigid bodies to each other, or an active and a passive rigid body to each other. It does not allow constraining to a point in space. The pinning point or pivot is adjustable and can be keyframed On and Off.

Hinge

Constrains an active rigid body to another active or passive rigid body, with a user-defined pivot orientation. The orientation of the hinge axis will change depending on the motion of the object(s) to which it is connected. So, if you rotate an object that has a hinge attached, the constraint will orient its axis to match. It can also constrain a rigid body to a point in space.

Directional hinge

Works just like a hinge constraint. The difference is that this pivot constrains the motion to one world axis. To use a directional hinge, create a constraint and then set its constraint type to **directionalHinge** in the **Attribute Editor**.

Spring

Constrains an active or passive rigid body to another active rigid body or to a point in space. The spring constraint contains attributes that control the elastic properties: **Stiffness, Restlength,** and **Damping**.

Nail

Constrains an active rigid body to a point in space. This point can be grouped and translated under another object as a child.

Barrier

Creates a planar boundary that an active rigid body cannot pass through.

Auto create rigid body

When you select an object to be dynamically constrained to a point or another object, Autodesk® Maya® will automatically turn the necessary objects into rigid bodies, if they are not already rigid bodies. This feature is controlled by the **Auto Create Rigid Body** flag in the **Dynamics** section of **Window → Settings/Preferences → Preferences...**

Constraint examples

The scene file *17-constraintExamples_01.ma* contains a sample application of each constraint type.

Constraint examples

Rag doll

In this exercise, you will use a modified version of the Constructor's rig to create a simple rag doll using rigid body constraints. Doing so will allow you to animate the character with dynamics to simulate a rag doll effect.

1   Scene file

- **Open** the file called *17-constraints_01.ma*.

  This scene contains a simplified version of the Constructor's geometry made out of simple primitives. The scene already has its rigid bodies created and linked to a gravity field.

- Make sure to hide the *geometryLayer* and show only the *rigLayer*.

The rag doll geometry

- **Rewind** *and* **play back** *the simulation.*

At this time, the individual parts of the geometry are falling straight to the ground without any kind of relationship with each other.

2   Create a nail constraint to support the entire structure

You will now add rigid body constraints to hang the rag doll. A nail constraint will let you hang the structure from a point in space.

- Select the head rag doll surface.

  This will be the surface used to hang all the other pieces of the rag doll.

- Select **Soft/Rigid Bodies → Create Nail Constraint**.

- **Translate** the *rigidNailConstraint1* pivot up above the rag doll.

- **Play back** the animation.

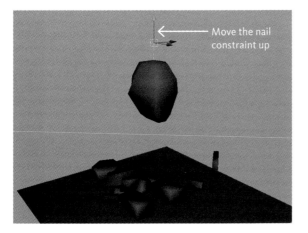

Move the nail constraint point up above the rag doll

Tip: *Moving the nail constraint's pivot in space will allow you to move the entire rag doll once it is hanging.*

3 **Create pin constraints for the hanging arms**

Each arm should be freely hanging from the top torso surface. A pin constraint will be used to simulate the shoulder ball joint. Pin constraints will also influence the rotation of the torso because of the weight of each arm.

- Select the left upper arm piece, and then **Shift-select** the torso piece.

- Select **Soft/Rigid Bodies** → **Create Pin Constraint**.

  Notice that the pin constraint is created between the two objects' centers of mass.

- **Translate** *rigidPinConstraint* if required so the pivot is located at the shoulder.

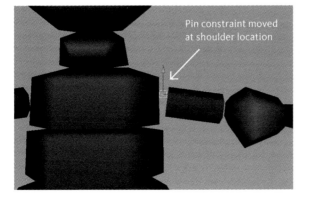

Move the pin constraint's pivot to the articulation location

4 Forearm hinge

In order to have a realistic bend at the elbow area, you will need to use a hinge constraint. Hinge constraints allow the rigid bodies to move only on a single axis, just as an elbow would.

- Select the left upper arm and the left forearm.
- Select **Soft/Rigid Bodies → Create Hinge Constraint → ❏.**
- In the options window, set the **Initial Orientation** to **90.0, 0.0,** and **0.0.**

  Doing so will allow the elbow to bend only in the proper orientation.

- **Move** and **rotate** the pin's pivot to the elbow area if required.

5 Wrist hinge

- **Repeat** step **4** to create a hinge constraint for the left wrist, but set the **Initial Orientation** to **0.0, 0.0,** and **90.0.**

6 Repeat for the other arm

- **Repeat** the process to create the required pin constraints on the right arm pieces.

7 Play back the simulation

- **Play back** the simulation to see how the arms react.

  The arm surfaces will stick together while all the other, unconstrained pieces fall individually to the ground.

The arms are now constrained together

8 Save your work

- **Save** the scene as *17-constraints_02.ma.*

Rest of hanging rag doll

You will now continue to create pin constraints for the rest of the rag doll pieces. Only the knees will require hinge constraints.

1   **Scene file**

   • **Continue** with your own scene file.

   OR

   • **Open** the scene called *17-constraints_02.ma.*

2   **Create a pin constraint for the neck and back of the rag doll**

   • **Create** pin constraints between each of the rag doll's neck and back surfaces.

   • **Move** the constraints' pivots appropriately between the objects.

   Tip: *Use the g hotkey to repeat the last command and speed up constraint creation.*

3   **Constrain the legs of the rag doll**

   • **Create** pin constraints between the lower torso piece and the upper leg pieces.

   • **Create** hinge constraints for the knees and the ankles, but set the **Initial Orientation** to **0.0, 0.0,** and **0.0**.

4   **Play back**

   • **Play back** the simulation.

   Tip: *If a simulation takes too long to calculate, you can press **Esc** to stop the simulation.*

The completed rag doll constraints

- **Toggle** the *rigLayer* and the *geometryLayer* to see the simulation while looking at the Constructor's geometry.

The simulation played with the Constructor model visible

Tip: *The fewer constraints you use, the faster playback you will get out of the dynamic simulation. This is why you will not use dynamics for any other body parts.*

5 Save your work

- **Save** the scene as *17-constraints_03.ma*.

Initial state

You will now adjust the mass of the rag doll pieces and then play the simulation until the rag doll stabilizes. Once that is done, you will be able to set this pose as the initial state of the rag doll.

1 Scene file

- **Continue** with your own scene file.

  OR

- **Open** the scene called *17-constraints_03.ma*.

Note: *There might be warnings in the Script Editor upon the opening of this file. This is normal and can be ignored.*

2 Adjust the rag doll pieces' mass

Keep in mind that the mass of all rigid body pieces directly affects the motion of the simulation. The Attribute Spreadsheet is a great way to compare values of many objects and quickly make changes.

- Select the rigid body objects by selecting **Edit → Select All by Type → Rigid Bodies**.
- Select **Window → General Editors → Attribute Spread Sheet...**
- Click the **Shape Keyable** tab in the spreadsheet, and then scroll down to locate the *rigidBody* nodes.

Tip: *If you want to select the rigidBody only, you can use the following MEL command:*
`select 'ls -typ "rigidBody"';`

- Locate the **Mass** attributes of the selected objects and adjust them as desired.

Attribute Spreadsheet

Tip: *You can **click+drag** to select multiple cells in single or multiple columns to make simultaneous value changes. You can use **Ctrl** or **Shift** in selecting cells. Entire rows or columns can be selected by clicking on the row or column header.*

3 Initial state

- **Play** the animation until the rag doll stabilizes and then stop the playback.
- Select **Solvers → Initial State → Set for All Dynamics**.

Doing so will save the current pose of the rigid bodies as the initial state.

- **Rewind** the animation to frame **1**.

Notice that the pose of the rag doll at frame 1 is now the one you have just saved.

The stabilized rag doll and initial state

> **Tip:** *If you feel that a stable initial state is not perfectly reached, you can play the simulation again and save the initial state a second time.*

4 **Save your work**

- **Save** your scene as *17-constraints_04.ma*.

Animating the rag doll

At this point, you can start playing with your new rag doll. For instance, you can animate the top nail constraint and see how the rag doll reacts. You can change the height and orientation of the floor, and change the floor's friction and bounciness to see how the rag doll will react.

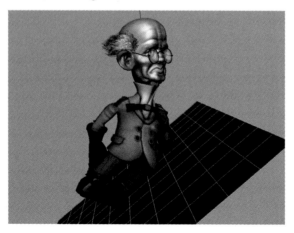

The rag doll colliding with an inclined floor

> **Tip:** *You can set the Constrain attribute of a rigid body constraint to Off to disable its effect. When disabled, the constraint will display in the viewport as a dotted line.*

Tips and Traps

Some of the following issues may arise as you go through the examples of this lesson:

- Cycle warning messages are often displayed when you use dynamics. These messages can usually be ignored. Type `cycleCheck -e off` in the Command Line to disable this warning.

- Sometimes objects will not move back to their original position correctly upon rewinding the scene. If you notice that problem, check first whether caching is enabled for the *rigidBody* solver. This problem can also be caused if you are scrubbing in the timeline or using Undos. This can be partially caused by the fact that there are dynamic and non-dynamic constraints working together. The Undo queue may not be able to record all complex interdependent functions. In some cases, simply zeroing out the transforms on the offset geometry can serve as a temporary fix. A rule of thumb when doing dynamics is to save under-incremented versions often. If you do not do so, you may have to restart and do your setup again. Try to keep scrubbing and undoing to a minimum.

- When geometry pieces are in the same hierarchy, you cannot make a parent surface a rigid body if one or more children are rigid bodies. You can only have one rigid body controlling a given hierarchy. The next lesson, on optimization, will discuss some alternatives to this limitation.

- It is recommended to make most of your dynamic changes while at frame 1. Not doing so might create unexpected results.

- Take advantage of the fact that you can keyframe a rigid body constraint On and Off in the Channel Box. For example, you can have a leaf dangling from a tree using a pin constraint, and then disable the constraint to allow the leaf to fall to the ground at a specific time.

- If a lot of collisions are happening in your scene, try dividing the rigid bodies up, on different collision layers. Although some interpenetration could happen, it might still be much faster for the solver to calculate the scene.

Conclusion

Rigid body constraints are an important part of working with dynamically animated geometry. Understanding the various advantages of using a specific constraint for a specific application can greatly affect how you approach a shot. Alternative methods outlined here for building and controlling hierarchies of objects through parenting and constraints are important to consider as you build scenes that are more complicated or require more control.

In the next lesson, you will learn about rigid body optimization.

Rigid Body Optimization

This lesson covers some fundamental tools and techniques for ensuring that your rigid body simulations are as efficient as possible.

In this lesson, you will learn the following:

- The importance of stand-in geometry
- Rigid body and solver optimization settings
- Collision and interpenetration troubleshooting
- Baking simulations

Optimization

When should you think about optimizing your scene's dynamics? The following guidelines can help you determine if you should consider optimizing your scene:

- When the scene runs at an excessively slow pace.
- When the dynamic simulation fails because of interpenetration errors.
- When the dynamics behave erratically and unpredictably.

You generally expect performance problems when running simulations in dense environments and expect lighter scenes to present less of a challenge to the interaction and playback.

The first objective in optimizing rigid body dynamics is to ensure that a scene progresses through the simulation, only stopping or slowing down during an intensive calculation.

The second objective is to achieve playback as close to real-time as possible without having to render or playblast the scene. This is a good goal, but in many cases cannot be attained because of hardware and software performance limitations.

To achieve these objectives, you will look at some typical problem areas and the necessary steps to ensure that the solver is not driven into an unsolvable situation.

The rigid solver

The rigid solver calculates the transformation attributes for rigid bodies using the attributes on the *rigidBody* nodes and the global attributes set on the rigid solver node as input. The attributes on the rigid solver node control the accuracy of the solution. The following material will help you find the right balance of accuracy versus speed.

Unpredictable or wild results

These typically occur when the solver is fed values that are wildly changing or exceeding the proper expected range. The expected range encompasses values that make sense for the solver on a given attribute or dynamic state. If the solver encounters a value that is much larger or smaller than it was expecting, it may tell an object to travel much faster or farther than the other objects around it are prepared to do.

The solver must make assumptions to increase its performance. When you intentionally or unintentionally stress the simulation, you may exploit an assumption that the solver is making. This can result in errors. Remember, the simulation is only an approximation.

The goal is to set the approximation to an appropriate trade-off between accuracy and interaction.

Solver grinding or failing

When a scene is grinding or no longer making forward progress, it is time to take a closer look at what is going on. The Script Editor is the first place to look for errors and information that may be produced by the solver. Even seemingly unimportant warnings can provide a clue about why a solver is failing farther on. Your first step should be to investigate all warnings and errors.

You should learn to associate warnings and errors with symptoms and conditions that lead to solver problems.

Slow playback

In order to speed up playback, the load on the solver must be reduced. The solver attempts to determine where every rigid body vertex is at any given frame.

The first step is usually reducing the number of vertices that the solver must keep track of. Using stand-ins will accomplish this, as will tuning rigid body tessellation to more coarse values. A stand-in is a less complex shape that is used to represent a more complex shape, essentially an object with less data for the solver to monitor.

Reducing the overhead of other scene components and display functions can go a long way toward improving playback. Think about displaying in wireframe, or hiding other unused objects, for instance.

Caching the animation is necessary for optimizing rigid bodies that have an unavoidable geometry density. Caching can use a lot of memory in scenes with dense geometric objects. Caching will not make it easier for the solver to calculate a solution, but it will help speed up your work because it reduces the time you have to wait for the solver.

Interpenetration errors

An interpenetration error occurs when the solver can no longer guarantee the accuracy of the simulation after one object's geometry has passed through another object's geometry. Typically, the solver stops or slows down the simulation if this error occurs.

The solver slows down and tells you about the problem because resolving this error is important in order for the dynamics to be properly simulated. This type of feedback is very important. You can use it to your advantage to help adjust simulation properties so that the solver does not enter into a corrupt or inaccurate situation.

Imagine if a sharp piece of geometry spiked into another object, creating an interpenetration. The only way for the object to continue on would be to reverse its direction, back itself out and continue in a less penetrating fashion. This would be a very laborious and computationally intensive moment and one that you want to avoid completely, if possible.

Avoid interpenetration errors by:

- Anticipating objects that are at risk;
- Using stand-in geometry with only quads or triangles;
- Adjusting tessellations;
- Adjusting *rigidSolver* **Step Size** and **Collision Tolerance** attributes in the **Attribute Editor**;
- Increasing **Damping** to avoid wild velocities;
- Using surfaces with closed geometry;
- Checking the surface normal orientations;
- Positioning objects to have gaps between them before the simulation starts.

Scene optimization example

This exercise steps you through some common scene problems that lead to optimization and troubleshooting. It is a very simple scene that has been constructed to demonstrate some of the more common things you can check for when optimizing a more complex scene.

1 Scene file

- **Open** the file called *18-battleTops_01.ma*.

  This scene contains an arena with four battle tops.

2 Play back the scene

The scene is mostly set-up, but it needs some optimization. It also has some warnings that are creating problems. You can often learn about the problem by opening the Script Editor. Then you should ask yourself:

- What do you notice about performance?
- What do you notice in the Script Editor?
- What do you notice about the arena object?
- What do you notice about the tops?

3 Display the normals of the objects

- Select the *base* area and the four *tops*.

Tip: *Make sure that you are in shaded mode to see the normals.*

- Select **Display → NURBS → Normals**.

  The base's normals are pointing inward. This is a common problem that should be checked for with both NURBS and polygonal surfaces.

> **Tip:** *It may be difficult to see that the normals are facing inward. It helps to dolly your camera inside one top's geometry to see the surface normals direction clearly.*

> **Note:** *When you first open the file, error messages are shown in the Script Editor, telling you that some objects' surfaces might be reversed.*

4 Reverse the surfaces

- Select the *base* area and the four *tops*.
- In the **Surfaces** menu set, select **Edit NURBS → Reverse Surface Direction → ❏**.
- **Reset** the options.
- Click the **Reverse** button.

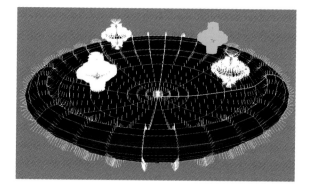

Normals with correct orientation

Although this may improve performance and alleviate interpenetration problems, for this particular scene it has not solved our slow performance problem yet. Sometimes, it is just one or two things that affect the entire situation. Nonetheless, having the normals facing outward is important.

- Select **Display → NURBS → Normals** again to hide the normals on the selected objects.

5 Rebuild the geometry

Another reason for hampered playback can be geometry that is needlessly overbuilt. Therefore, you will rebuild the tops' geometry to see if that will fix the slow playback.

- Select the four tops.
- Select **Edit NURBS → Rebuild Surfaces → ❏**.

- Set the following options:

  Rebuild Type to **Reduce**;

  Parameter Range to **0 to 1**;

  Direction to **U and V**;

  Keep Originals to **Off**;

  Use Tolerance to **Local**;

  Positional Tolerance to **1.0**;

  Output Geometry to **NURBS**.

- Click the **Rebuild** button.

- **Play back** to check for improvements.

  Once again, this step will not make a huge performance increase, but it is still recommended to help prevent other problems that could be introduced.

Tessellation factor for NURBS rigid bodies

As you may know, when you render a NURBS object, the renderer tessellates the NURBS geometry into polygons prior to rendering. A similar process occurs when the dynamics engine encounters a NURBS rigid body object. The solver assigns a tessellation factor to the NURBS object that determines the polygonal approximation of the shape. You can adjust the accuracy of this approximation by adjusting the **Tessellation Factor** attribute under **Performance Attributes** for each rigid body object. This attribute has no effect on polygonal rigid body objects.

By default, the **Tessellation Factor** is **200**.

If you have a highly detailed NURBS object, 200 polygons may not be enough for the solver to accurately represent that shape when calculating collisions. Although lower tessellation factors will mean less computation work for the solver, you will also have a less accurate representation of your NURBS geometry. Being aware of this attribute can help you tune your simulations to add more or less accuracy where necessary.

By rebuilding the top objects, you have reduced the geometric load on the solver. Another way is to adjust the **Tessellation Factor** attribute. The main drawback is that you do not have control over where the tessellation is most needed. In this example, you want more tessellation at the tips to avoid a sharp interpenetrating point, and also at the sides to avoid interpenetration when tops collide.

Another strategy might be to convert your rigid bodies to polygons during the rebuilding process, thus creating a stand-in object for collisions and simulation.

Stand-ins

One of the best ways to clean up the performance of rigid bodies is to use stand-in objects. This is very useful when you have dense or irregular objects that you want to attach rigid body dynamics to. The *rigidBody* node provides a choice of cube and sphere stand-ins that you can select from. Alternatively, you may wish to create your own stand-in geometry, then make it a rigid body and simply parent your higher-resolution object to that stand-in and hide the stand-in.

1   **Substitute the base with the lower-resolution object**

One needlessly complex object in the scene is the base object; it has geometry not involved in collisions.

- Select the *base* object.

- Select **Edit → Delete by Type → Rigid Bodies**.

- Select *lowResBase* from the Outliner and make it visible by showing selection.

  This object was created by duplicating the base object, and then detaching the surface at the appropriate place and deleting the unnecessary geometry.

- Select **Soft/Rigid Bodies → Create Passive Rigid Body**.

  Now the collisions will be computed only for the area of the base that is important for this particular simulation.

- **Hide** the *lowResBase*.

- **Play back** the scene.

  There should still be no major improvements.

Optimizing a dynamics scene is often like optimizing for rendering. You can try several different options until you find what works. During this process, you have cleaned up a lot of things and will continue to do so.

2   **Set tessellation for the tops' rigid bodies**

The rigid body dynamics are determined by an approximation of the rigid body object's shape. This approximation is controlled by the tessellation of the rigid body unless a stand-in object is specified.

- Select the *top1*.

- Open the **Attribute Editor** and locate the **Performance Attributes** section under the *rigidBody* tab.

Performance Attributes

Stand In	sphere ▼
Apply Force At	boundingBox ▼
Tessellation Factor	200
Collision Layer	0
	☐ Collisions ☐ Ignore

Performance Attributes section

- Following are explanations about the attributes found in this section:

Stand-in

Selects a stand-in object, such as **Sphere** or **Cube**.

Apply Force At

Dynamic forces can be applied at either **Center of Mass**, **Bounding Box,** or **VerticesOrCVs**. **VerticesOrCVs** is the most accurate, but the slowest.

Tessellation Factor

Adjusts geometric approximation of rigid body object.

Collision Layer

Selects the collision layer participation. Objects on the same collision layer number will collide with each other. Objects on different collision layer numbers will not collide with each other. An object on collision layer **-1** will collide with objects on any collision layer.

- Set the **Stand In** attribute to **none**.

- Set the **Apply Force At** attribute to **VerticesOrCVs**.

- Set the **Tessellation Factor** attribute to **100**.

*Below are the equivalent tessellations for the top1 object set to **100**, **150**, **200**, and **500**.*

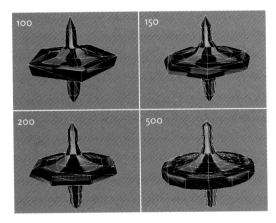

Tessellation values

Note: *At low tessellation values, the point of the top is much sharper. This affects how the top spins and also increases the likelihood of interpenetration. At low tessellation values, the interaction of the edge of the top with other tops is less predictable.*

- Set the **Collisions** attribute to **On**.
- **Repeat** the above steps for the remaining tops.

3 Use the Attribute Spreadsheet

You have tried all of these things but nothing has solved the problem yet. When this happens, it is a good idea to have a look at the *rigidBody* nodes themselves and compare them to each other. You want to look for differences between the rigid bodies or values that stand out as excessively large or small.

- Select all the tops' *rigidBody* nodes.

Tip: *A quick way to select the rigid bodies is to select the surfaces, and then press the* **down arrow** *followed by the* **right arrow** *on your keyboard.*

- Select **Window → General Editors → Attribute Spreadsheet...**
- Make sure the **Shape Keyable** tab is selected.
- Compare the attribute values.

The **InitialSpinY** *settings are very high, with some at 15000 and -30000 units per frame. This is potentially the root of the problem for this scene.*

- Lower the **InitialSpin** values around **2000** units.

With practice, you will learn valid ranges for the different attributes and also learn how many attributes rely on each other. In other words, if you change mass, you may have to change friction to compensate for the new motion.

- In order to make the tops more aggressive in their movement, set the **Bounciness** value to **0.9**, and the **Damping** value to **0**.
- **Play back** the simulation again.

You should notice much faster performance in the playback.

349

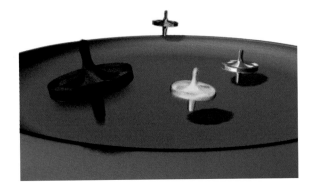

Playback is now real-time

4 Save your work

- **Save** the scene as *18-battleTops_02.ma*.

Working through this process usually is not too much fun, but knowing what to check and being methodical about checking things will help you track down and solve problems. It will also help you design things correctly when starting from scratch to avoid potential problems.

Obviously, the scene file shown here is very simple by design. Chances are that your production scenes will not be this simple. Design your work smartly from the ground up and also know what you can reasonably expect as good performance from the solver. Always look for ways to keep the number of rigid body calculations to a minimum.

Bake animation

Autodesk® Maya® is much faster at evaluating animation curves than at evaluating dynamic motions because it knows where the object is going to be at any given point in time. This is not true for a rigid body simulation. The position and orientation of all rigid bodies are calculated using rules inside each frame to produce the final result.

In the following example, you will learn some additional optimization techniques. You will learn how to produce animation curve data from objects that are dynamically controlled. This process is called *baking*.

> **Tip:** *Baking animation is not limited to dynamics animation; for instance, you can also bake objects driven by constraints.*

In the following example, you will optimize the scene of the Constructor rag doll falling on a floor.

Another challenge here will be getting these interdependent objects reacting to each other without stalling the solution due to interpenetration. Hopefully, you can use what you learned in the previous section of this chapter to overcome any such interpenetration problems encountered.

1 **Scene file**
   - **Open** the file called *18-ragdollOptimized_01.ma*.

   This scene consists of a fully functional rag doll above an inclined floor surface.

2 **Play back the scene**
   As the rag doll is falling on the floor, notice any interpenetrations that occur or reasons that could cause the simulation to slow down.

The played scene

3 **Solver attributes**
   The solver attributes of **Step Size** and **Collision Tolerance** will need to be slightly lowered.
   - Set the following for the floor *rigidSolver* within the **Attribute Editor**:

     Step Size to **0.02**;

     Collision Tolerance to **0.03**;

     Rigid Solver Method to **Runge Kutta Adaptive**.

   *The solver settings are very important and are a good place to start in reaching a solution. If your scene generates persistent interpenetration problems, the solver settings of **Step Size** and **Collision Tolerance** should be lowered slightly.*

*The solver method also influences performance. The **Runge Kutta Adaptive** method is the default calculation method and is generally the most accurate setting. Experiment with these methods so that you are comfortable with their respective strengths and weaknesses.*

As you will learn, one small change in your scene can change all the interdependent and subsequent elements of the simulation. Having patience and being methodical are important. Also, slight adjustments in the initial starting position of your simulation can have profound effects.

Controlling interpenetrations and collisions

Sometimes when creating a dynamic system, you might want to allow some rigid bodies to interpenetrate. Doing so can greatly speed up playback, at a minimal cost.

The following shows you how you can control the collisions between some of the rigid bodies on the Constructor rag doll.

1   **Allow interpenetration**

- Select the neck and head rag doll surfaces:

Select the objects that are allowed to interpenetrate

- Select **Solvers → Set Rigid Body Interpenetration**.

Those two objects are now allowed to interpenetrate.

2   **Repeat**

- **Repeat** the previous steps to allow interpenetration between the neck and torso.

- **Repeat** the previous steps for any other objects that could interpenetrate without any major degradation of the results.

3   **Play back the animation**

You should notice a slight difference in the animation and in the playback since there are fewer collisions to be handled by the solver.

4   **Enable collisions**

If you wish to enable the collisions again, do the following:

- Select the objects for which you would like to enable collisions.

- Select **Solvers → Set Rigid Body Collision**.

5   **Save your work**

- **Save** the scene as *18-ragdollOptimized_02.ma*.

Bake the rag doll

Once you have a decent simulation for all the rigid bodies, you can simplify things by baking the simulation. Baking converts the dynamics-induced animation to animation curves. These curves can then be tweaked and manipulated like any other animation curve.

The baking process also provides other performance benefits and functionality. You will bake the dynamic motion of the rag doll and delete the *rigidBody* nodes.

1   **Scene file**

- **Continue** with your own scene file.

   OR

- **Open** the file called *18-ragdollOptimized_02.ma*.

> **Tip:**   *It is recommended to save a version of the dynamic scene before baking the animation. Doing so will allow you to go back in the dynamic scene if needed.*

2   **Bake the rag doll falling down**

- Select all of the rag doll objects.

- In the **Channel Box**, highlight the **Translate** and **Rotate** attributes.

> **Tip:**   **Click+drag** *across these attributes in the Channel Box to highlight them black.*

- Select **Edit → Keys → Bake Simulation → ❏**.

- **Reset** the options in the dialog box and then set them as follows:

  Hierarchy to **Selected**;

  You only want to bake the selected object, not the entire hierarchy.

  Channels to **From Channel Box**;

  You will highlight the appropriate transform attributes in the Channel Box.

  Time Range to **Start/End**;

  Start time to **1**;

  End time to **200**;

  You only need to bake about **200** frames.

  Sample by to **1.0**.

  The resulting animation will have **1** key per frame.

354

Bake Simulation options

- Click the **Bake** button.

  The animation will be played through, and keyframes will be set for each frame of the simulation for all selected objects. This will result in animation curves.

Tip: *In order to bake any objects faster, prevent the viewport from updating its display by hiding everything in the scene with **Show → None.***

3 Delete the dynamics

Since the rigid bodies and rigid body constraints are no longer required, you will now delete them.

- Select **Edit → Delete All by Type → Rigid Bodies**.
- Select **Edit → Delete All by Type → Rigid Constraints**.
- **Delete** the *gravity* field.

4 **Delete static channels**

Baking animation often creates static animation channels, which slow down the playback.

- Select **Edit → Delete All by Type → Static Channels**.

5 **Play back**

Confirm that the bake is accurate. Problems with baking can arise when either you are sampling with too coarse a **Sample Rate** or you are trying to bake too many channels from **Control Points** or **Shape** nodes' animation. Treat these other nodes and channels as separate passes.

Also, notice that if you select any animated objects, the timeline shows a series of red tick marks. These are the keyframes that now control the motion of the objects. You can also view and edit these keys using the Graph Editor.

Baking is strongly recommended as the last step before rendering any rigid body scene. It is a good idea to keep an unbaked dynamic version of your scene and a baked version that is used for rendering. Time-based rendering options, such as motion blur, work much more reliably with baked animation data than with dynamically driven animation.

6 **Save your work**

- **Save** the scene as *18-ragdollOptimized_03.ma*.

Creating multiple rigid solvers

Using multiple rigid solvers gives you the ability to adjust solver settings independently. If you have groups of colliding objects that will not collide with each other (perhaps they are not in close proximity), putting them on different solvers helps optimize the scene and hasten the playback.

To select the current solver:

- Select **Solvers → Current Rigid Solver → rigidSolver**.

To create a new solver:

- Select **Solvers → Create Rigid Body Solver**.

To move rigid bodies to another solver, simply select the objects and type the following command in the Command Line:

```
rigidBody -edit -solver rigidSolver1;
```

New solvers can have separate settings while maintaining the settings already in place for the existing simulations. Any new rigid bodies you create in the scene will be assigned to the selected current rigid solver and will only collide with other rigid bodies that are part of that solver. In a way, this is like using collision layers. The difference is that you can control each solver's accuracy level independently.

Optimization reminder list

Tuning and troubleshooting rigid bodies can usually be approached by keeping the following in mind:

- Adapt the tessellation of NURBS and polygons so that the solver can minimize the amount of calculation to be done.
- Double-check the normals of your surfaces, which can solve many problems.
- Use stand-ins for both NURBS and polygonal objects to help the solver work with this geometry.
- Bake the simulation to increase playback speed and add control to complex scenes.
- Use collision layers to separate objects for which the solver should not calculate collisions.
- Use multiple solvers to help localize control over a specific simulation, collision, or interaction.
- The rigidBody and rigidSolver MEL commands can be used for creation and modification of rigidBodies and rigidSolver nodes in MEL scripts. Refer to the online MEL command reference for a list of all available flags for these commands.
- Use caching when possible to speed things up.

Solver accuracy

It is important to remember that the solver is an approximation of real-world physics. The solver does not evaluate detailed information about subtle surface properties. This detailed level of calculation (as done by some systems specifically designed for engineering purposes), would be unacceptably slow for other applications. The solver is not intended to give you accuracy down to the millionth decimal point. However, there is a decent level of accuracy control there if you need it. Use rigid bodies to get some dynamic motion happening, bake and modify where necessary, and be glad you do not have to keyframe it all by hand!

Units

You should always keep in mind your scene scale and units when working with dynamics and fields. In physics, gravity is measured in meters per second squared. In Maya, the same is true; however, usually people work in centimeters, not meters. Therefore, the effect of gravity seems to be off by a factor of 100. You will often see rigid body objects floating through the scene seemingly in slow motion because of this. Things may appear okay in your hardware playback, but when you view it in real time, you notice this floating motion.

For example, if you are trying to match live action motion, you will most likely need to crank your gravity much higher than a magnitude of **9.8**, for instance, **980**. In practice, it is best to keep the scene units at centimeters; you will find that you will have fewer problems. Using reference footage is very important.

The movie *dropBall.mpg* included with the *support_files* is reference footage that was shot to compare real-world gravity with the Maya gravity in centimeters. Importing this movie footage into Maya via an image plane and mimicking the motion with rigid bodies is a good way to get an idea of how Maya dynamics relate to real-world physics.

Bake before render

Baking is highly recommended before you render rigid bodies or soft bodies, especially if you are rendering with motion blur. This is especially true when rendering using multiple computers, where each machine has different frames to render and where slight differences in the dynamic simulation can make the object flicker and ruin a render.

Note: *When baking animation, you should be aware of gimbal lock, where an object can do a 360 degree rotation between two frames. This behavior might cause motion blur to create a flicker, as it thinks the object is moving at an incredible speed.*

Conclusion

You are now experienced with dynamic optimization. Knowing about the different topics discussed here can greatly improve your animation, playback, and renders.

In the next project, you will learn about particles.

Project 06

In Project Six, you will learn about particles and their different uses. Particles are the heart of special effects such as fire, snow, rain, and smoke. They can also be dynamic and collide with geometry and even affect rigid bodies. In this project, you will also learn about writing MEL expressions that can improve the creation and animation of your particle effects.

By the end of this project, you should feel comfortable creating, emitting, and controlling particles' animation and appearance.

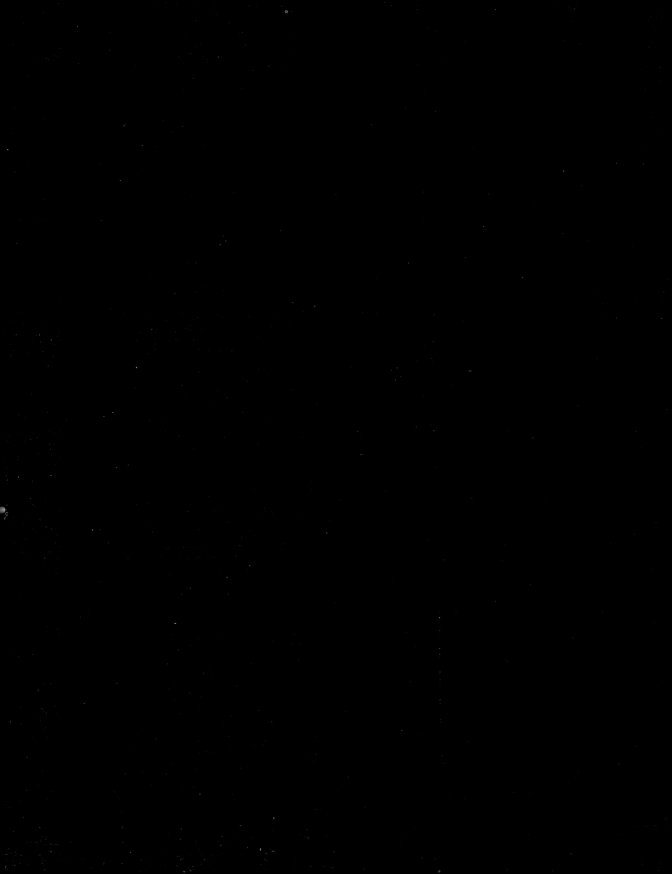

Introduction to Particles

This lesson focuses on the basic concepts required to understand and work efficiently with particles. It should be considered an essential framework to build upon for more advanced concepts that are discussed throughout the upcoming lessons.

In this lesson, you will learn the following:

- The particle shape node
- The basic particle attributes
- Fields
- Emitters

Particle structure

Particles differ from geometry in the following ways:

- Particles are points in space. They require special handling at render time because they do not contain surface information.

- Particles can be rendered using hardware or software rendering methods. The particle's **Render Type** attribute controls which of these two methods is used.

- Individual particles belong to a common collection referred to as the *particleShape* object, just as vertices of a geometric object belong to their shape node. Individual particles can be thought of as components of the *particleShape* node.

- Particle attributes are commonly categorized into two types: per particle (array) and per object.

- Particles do not have volume, which means that you will not be able to stack particles on each other. For instance, if you pour water particles into a glass, the glass will not fill up.

Applications of particles

Particles are commonly used to simulate complex natural phenomena. Common examples include smoke, rain, sparks, gases, dust, snow, fire, and other motions that consist of complex or random movement of many individual components.

Particles can be keyframed or controlled dynamically as a group.

Creating a particle galaxy

There are several methods for creating particle objects. In this first example, the focus will be on using the **Particle Tool**.

The **Particle Tool** provides a quick and easy way of creating individual particles, particle grids, and random collections of particles. This can be useful for generating some particles to begin working with. The tool also enables you to place particles interactively, exactly where you want them.

1   Sketch some particles
- Select **Particles** → **Particle Tool** → ❏.
- In the options, set the following:

  Particle Name to *galaxy*;

  Number of Particles to **20**;

  Maximum Radius to **3**;

  Sketch Particles to **On**;

  Sketch Interval to **5**.
- **Click+drag** to sketch a cross-like shape in the *top* view, and click **Enter**.

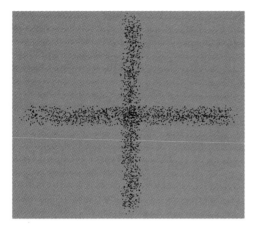

A cross of particles

- Open the Outliner to see the newly created particle object called *galaxy*.

  You will need to display shapes in the Outliner to see the galaxyShape node.

- In the Outliner, enable the option **Display → Shapes**.

2 Vortex field

To make the particles spin like a galaxy, you will apply a vortex field.

- Select the *galaxy* particle object.
- Select **Fields → Vortex**.
- **Play back** to watch the particles spin.

Tip: *Increase the playback range as needed.*

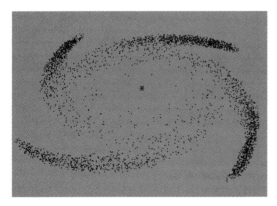

The vortex field effect on the particles

3 Set initial state

Every time you rewind, the galaxy returns to the cross shape. To prevent this, you can set the **Initial State** of the particles.

- **Playback** until the particles are in a galaxy-like shape.
- With the particles selected, select **Solvers → Initial State → Set For Selected**.

   Now when you rewind, the galaxy has the shape it had when you set the initial state.

4 Adjust conserve on the particles

To prevent the particles from immediately spinning out of control, you can lower the **Conserve** attribute on the particle object.

- Select the *galaxy* particle object.
- Under the galaxyShape node in the **Channel Box**, set **Conserve** to **0.8**.
- Set the *vortex*'s **Magnitude** attribute to **200**.
- **Rewind** and **play back** the animation.

   Conserve *is a very important particle attribute. "Conserve" is short for conservation of momentum. By default it is set to* **1,** *which means the particles will never lose any of their motion as they move through space. This is a very sensitive attribute so lowering it in very small increments is usually best. Normally, lowering* **Conserve** *just a little, such as* **0.99,** *will give your particles' motion a more realistic appearance.*

5 Keyframe the particles

Traditionally, particles have been animated exclusively through fields and dynamic expressions. You also have the option to animate the particle objects' transform like any non-dynamic object. Translate, scale, and rotation can be keyframed to provide many common effects.

- Select the *galaxy* particle object.
- Set **Rotate Z** to about **-25** degrees so the galaxy is tilted at an angle.
- **Play back** the animation.

   Things look fine at the first frame of the simulation, but as you play back, you may notice that the particles are not orbiting relative to the new rotation you introduced. Instead, they are revolving around the world axis defined by the vortex field's axis attributes, which is **0, 1, 0** *(the Y-axis).*

Note: *The axis of the vortex is specified to be* **0, 1, 0** *because of its attributes* **Axis X, Axis Y,** *and* **Axis Z**. *These attributes define the direction of the force, in this case around the Y-axis.*

- To make the particles orbit with respect to their new angle, **parent** the *vortexField* into the galaxy particle object.

- Set **Forces In World** to **Off** in the **Channel Box** for the *galaxyShape* object.

  Now, the vortex's axis is being calculated in the particle object's local space instead of the world space. Also, the field is conveniently parented into this effect so you can keyframe the entire galaxy's translation, rotation, and scale as you wish.

6 Save your work

- **Save** your work as *19-galaxy_01.ma*.

> **Note:** *It is also possible to create an empty particle object by setting the number of particles to **0** in the Particle Tool options, or by typing* `particle;` *in the Script Editor or Command Line. Empty particle objects are commonly needed when working with particle emitters, which are discussed in the next section.*

Emitters

An emitter is like a cannon that projects particles into space. Below is a list of the different kinds of emitters available to you:

Directional

Omni

Volume

Curve

Surface

Per-Point

Texture

- **Open** the file *19-emitterTypes_01.ma* to see an example of each of these types.

> **Tip:** *Shaded mode display is recommended to see the colored particles. You may also want to use the display layers provided in the scene to keep the viewport from getting overly cluttered.*

Sparks example

1 Scene file

Sparks are a very simple effect that you will create to learn how to get around the particle system.

- **Open** the file *19-sparks_01.ma*.

  This file contains the Constructor's buggy without any dynamics. You will add a directional emitter and modify some of its attributes so there are sparks behind the metal wheels.

> **Tip:** *You can mute the translation of the buggy in order to complete the lesson in the same location. To do so, simply highlight the Translate attribute in the Channel Box for the buggy, and select Mute Selected.*

2 Create a directional emitter

A directional emitter allows you to specify exactly what direction in world space to emit the particles.

- Select **Particles → Create Emitter → ❑**.
- Set the following options:

    Emitter Type to **Directional**.

- Click **Create**.

    This creates two new objects: a directional emitter named emitter1 that emits particles, and the particle object named particle1.

3 Position and name the emitter

- Select *emitter1* in the Outliner and position it behind the buggy and slightly below one of the rear wheels.
- **Rename** *emitter1* to *spray*.
- **Rename** *particle1* to *sparks*.

4 Play back the animation

- Set the playback range to start at frame **0** and end at frame **500**.
- **Play back** the animation.

    *By default, the particle emitter direction occurs along the **X-axis**.*

5 Modify the emitter's attributes using manipulators

- With the *spray* emitter selected, press the **t** key to switch to the **Show Manipulator Tool.**

> **Tip:** *You may need to hide the surfaces to see the emitter.*

The small circular icon below the emitter is a toggle switch that cycles the manipulator through different emitter attributes, so that each attribute can be quickly edited graphically. This manipulator functions similarly to manipulators on spot lights, which you may already be familiar with. The value manip will change based on the attribute manip selection. It can be click+dragged to change the attribute value.

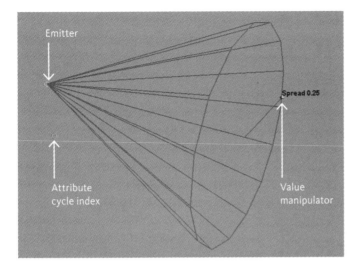

emitter

- Use the manipulators or the **Channel Box** to adjust the **Direction**, **Speed**, **Rate,** and **Spread** of the emitter.
- The following values work well for the *spray* emitter:

    Rate to **100**;

    Direction to **0, 0.75, 1.0**;

    Spread to **0.25**.

Emitter spraying in the appropriate direction

> **Note:** *A **Spread** value of 1 corresponds to a 180 degree emission cone. **Rate** is a measurement of the number of particles per time unit that are emitted. The default time unit is seconds. **Speed** determines how fast the particles initially leave the emitter.*

6 Change the particle render type

- Select the *sparks* object.

- Open the **Attribute Editor**, and select the *sparksShape* tab.

- Under the **Render Attributes** section, set the following:

   Particle Render Type to **MultiStreak**;

   Depth Sort to **On**.

- Click the **Current Render Type** button and set the following:

   Color Accum to **Off**;

   Use Lighting to **On**.

   These options determine the draw, shading, and lighting properties of this particle object. These settings make the particles appear somewhat more like sparks in motion. The specific details of these options will be discussed more in the upcoming rendering lesson.

7 Add gravity and turbulence to the sparks

Adding fields will help better define the particles' motion.

- With *sparks* still selected, select **Fields** → **Gravity**.

- Select *sparks* again, and select **Fields** → **Turbulence**.

- **Play back** the scene to test the gravity and turbulence fields.

   At this point, the particles will fall straight down since they do not have enough speed to spray up in the air behind the buggy.

> **Note:** *When a field is chosen from the Fields menu, all selected objects will be connected to that field automatically. If nothing is selected, the field is created in the scene and objects can be connected to it using the Dynamic Relationship Editor. Another method is to select the object(s) and then the fields, and then select **Fields** → **Affect Selected Object(s)**. If you want the field to be automatically parented to the selected object, use **Field** → **Use Selected as Source of Field**.*

8 Increase spray's Speed attribute

Using a higher speed value causes the particles to leave the emitter faster, which in turn allows them to travel higher before being overcome by gravity.

- Select *spray*.

- Set **Speed** to **10** in the **Channel Box**.
- **Play back** the scene.

The effect of the fields on the sparks

9 Save your work

- **Save** the scene as *19-sparks_02.ma*.

Add a second particle object

To give the impression of incandescent points within the sparks, you will now add a second particle object for the emitter to emit into. The attributes of this particle object can be controlled independently from the *sparks* particles.

1 Scene file

- **Continue** with the previous scene file.

2 Create an empty particle object

An empty particle object will be created to provide an empty storage place for the emitter to later emit into. The particles will be created by the emitter, using the attributes set on the *particleShape* node.

- In the Command Line, type the following:

```
particle -name points;
```

- Press **Enter**.
- Check the Outliner to make sure the *points* particle object was created.

3 Establish emission for points

Currently, there is no relationship between *points* and *spray*. You will now establish a connection between the two.

- Select *points* in the Outliner.
- **Ctrl+select** to select *spray*.
- Select **Particles → Use Selected Emitter**.
- **Rewind** and **play back**.

The spray emitter now emits into both sparks and points.

4 Set display attributes for points

Just as you defined descriptive attributes for *sparks*, you can do the same for *points*.

- In the **Attribute Editor**, set the following attribute values for *points*:

  Particle Render Type to **MultiPoint**;

  Depth Sort to **On**;

  Color Accum to **On**;

  Point size to **3**;

  Use Lighting to **On**.

Turning **Color Accum** *On for points creates contrast with the sparks particles whose* **Color Accum** *setting was turned Off. Depth sorting simply draws the particles on the screen from back to front.*

Tip: *When* **Color Accum** *is On, overlapping particles within the same particle object have their RGB values added together. This creates a more washed-out or additive appearance. You will only notice the Color Accum effect later, once the particles have an opacity attribute.*

5 Connect points to the existing gravity

- Select *points* in the Outliner.
- **Ctrl-select** *gravityField1*.
- Select **Fields → Affect Selected Object(s)**.

Note: *You can also use the Dynamic Relationship Editor to connect fields, emitters, and particles together.*

- **Repeat** for the *turbulenceField1*.
- **Play back** the scene.

The points particles should fall along with the sparks.

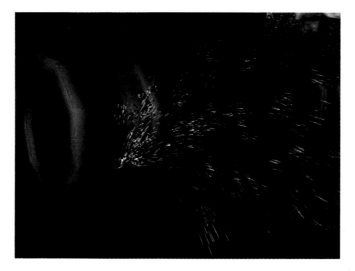

The spray emitter emitting sparks and points particles

6 Save your work

- **Save** the scene as *19-sparks_03.ma*.

Understanding particle attributes

The next step is to add more specific controls to the *sparks* and *points*. This requires a clear understanding of some important concepts that will be discussed here briefly before you continue with the sparks:

- The most commonly used particle attributes exist on the *particleShape* node. The transform node contains the traditional transform attributes such as translate, scale, and rotate.

- All particle objects use position, velocity, acceleration, and mass attributes. Therefore, these attributes are part of the *particleShape* node.

- There are many other attributes, such as lifespan, radius, color, and incandescence that can be added to particles if needed. This allows you to customize each particle shape to your specific needs and also keeps things more efficient.

- Some attributes are intended to be used for only specific particle render types. For example, *spriteNum* is only intended to be used with sprite particles.

Per particle vs. per object attributes

It is important to understand the difference between the *per particle* and *per object* attributes.

- **Per Particle Attribute** allows each particle to store its own value for a given attribute.
- **Per Object Attribute** assigns one attribute value to the entire particle object.

  It is a common convention to name per particle attributes with a PP at the end. For instance: radiusPP, rgbPP, etc. However, it is not an absolute requirement.

Tip: *For more information regarding various particle attributes, visit the Autodesk® Maya® online documentation.*

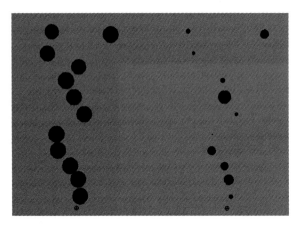

Per object radius vs. per particle radius

In the picture above, the particles emitted from the left emitter were given a per object radius attribute (**radius**). The particles emitted from the emitter on the right are in the same relative position as those emitted from the emitter on the left. However, each particle has its own radius value (**radiusPP**).

Color, lifespan, and opacity attributes

You will now add per object attributes and per particle attributes.

1 **Scene file**
   - **Continue** with the previous scene file.

2 Per object attributes for the points

The **Lifespan** attribute gives you control over how long the particles stay in the scene before they disappear. For now, you will assign the same **Lifespan** value to all the particles to keep things simple.

- Select *points* and open the **Attribute Editor**.
- In the **Lifespan Attributes** section, in **Lifespan Mode,** select **Constant**.
- Set **Lifespan** to **0.5.**

This is the number of seconds that the particles will live. This number means the particles will die (disappear) quickly after they have been emitted.

- In the **Add Dynamic Attributes** section, click **Color** and select **Add Per Object Attribute**.
- Click **Add Attribute**.

Fields for editing **RGB** *are added in the* **Render Attributes** *section and in the Channel Box for this particle object as shown below.*

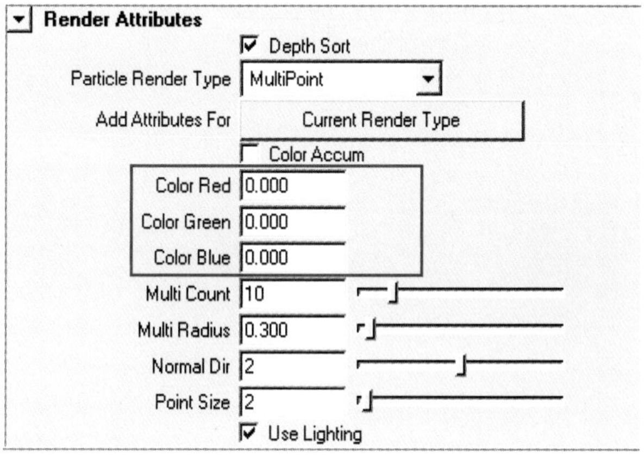

```
┌─▼─ Render Attributes ─────────────────────────────────────┐
│                            ☑ Depth Sort                     │
│      Particle Render Type │ MultiPoint        ▼│            │
│      Add Attributes For        Current Render Type          │
│                            ┌ Color Accum                    │
│         Color Red  │0.000                                   │
│       Color Green  │0.000                                   │
│        Color Blue  │0.000                                   │
│       Multi Count  │10        ┌─┐────────────               │
│       Multi Radius │0.300    ┌┘────────────────             │
│        Normal Dir  │2         ┌────────┐─────────           │
│         Point Size │2        ┌┘──────────────────           │
│                            ☑ Use Lighting                   │
└─────────────────────────────────────────────────────────────┘
```

Color per object attribute

- Set the following attributes for **Color:**

    Color Red to **1.0;**

    Color Green to **1.0;**

    Color Blue to **0.0.**

3 Sparks life span

The **Lifespan** attribute of the sparks particles should be the same as the points.

- Select *sparks* and open the **Attribute Editor**.
- In the **Lifespan Attributes** section, in **Lifespan Mode,** select **Constant**.
- Set **Lifespan** to **0.5.**

4 Per particle attributes for the sparks

You will now add a per particle opacity attribute, which will control the fading out of each particle as it falls.

- In the **Add Dynamic Attributes** section, click **Opacity** and select **Add Per Particle Attribute**.

- Click **Add Attribute**.

  This adds an **opacityPP** *field in the* **Per Particle (Array) Attributes** *section of the Attribute Editor.*

- **RMB** in the **opacityPP** field and select **Create Ramp**.

  A ramp texture now controls the opacity of each particle.

- **Rewind** and **play back** the scene.

  Notice that the sparks particles are opaque when emitted and fully transparent just before dying.

- **RMB** in the **opacityPP** field, then select **arrayMapper1.outValuePP** → **Edit Ramp**.

  The Attribute Editor will display the ramp that controls the particles' opacity. The sparks will be opaque when emitted and transparent toward the end of the particles' life.

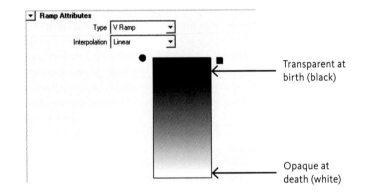

Transparent at birth (black)

Opaque at death (white)

Opacity during life of a particle

The vertical axis of the ramp represents the particle's normalized age, thus going from 0 to 1. The bottom of the ramp corresponds to the particle's birth and the top of the ramp corresponds to its death.

Tip: *It is usually recommended to set-up the ramp as you want it, and then add color handles to make the particle fully transparent at birth and just before death. Doing so will prevent the particles from "popping" when they appear and die.*

- **Repeat** the previous steps to control the transparency of the *points* particles.

5 **Test the animation**

- **Rewind** and **play back** the animation.
- If necessary, adjust the lifespan so that the particles live longer.

> **Note:** *The unit for* **Lifespan** *is seconds, so it is important to be aware of your frames-per-second settings and the different results that can occur if the same file is used on two different machines with different time settings. This can happen when you use Import instead of Open. When you use* **File → Open Scene**, *the time setting will be read from the scene file. To check the time setting, open* **Window → Settings/Preferences → Settings...**

- **Create** a directional light.
- Press **7** on the keyboard to display the scene with hardware lighting.
- **Play back** the animation.

Now the particles are displayed with color and lighting.

6 **Experimentation**

- **Duplicate** the spray emitter and place it behind the other set of wheels.
- Select the *sparks* particles, then Shift-select the new emitter and select **Particles → Use Selected Emitter**.
- **Repeat** for the *points* particles.
- **Parent** the emitters to the *buggy*.
- **Unmute** the *buggy* animation through the **Channel Box**.
- Experiment on your own to get interesting effects.

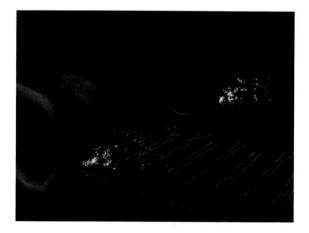

The refined particles

You may notice that the particles do not collide with the rail in this example. Particle collisions will be discussed in a later lesson.

7 **Save your work**
   - **Save** the scene as *19-sparks_04.ma*.

Omni emitters

An omni emitter causes particle emission to occur equally in all directions. Adding an omni emitter to a NURBS surface, polygon, or curve will cause particles to be emitted from the vertices of the object the emitter is added to.

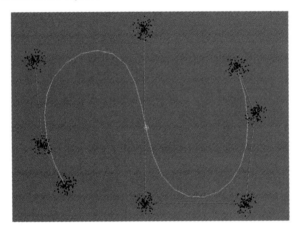

An omni emitter emitting from a curve's CVs

Curve emitters

Although it is possible to add a directional or omni emitter to a curve, doing so will cause emission to occur only from the CVs of that curve, not from the portions of the curve between the CVs or from points on the curve.

A curve emitter is designed to allow omni emission to occur along the entire curve, instead of only from the CVs.

1 **Create a simple curve emitter**
   - Create your own curve using the **EP Curve Tool**.
   - Select the curve and add a curve emitter by selecting **Particles → Emit from Object → ❑**.
   - In the option window, set the **Emitter Type** to **Curve**.

2 **Test the animation**

- **Play back** the animation to view the curve emission.

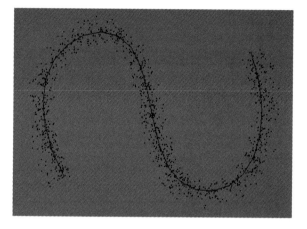

Curve emission

> **Tip:** *It is possible to change the emitter type after the emitter has been created by editing the* **emitterType** *attribute in the Channel Box or the selected emitter's Attribute Editor.*

Curve emitter example

The following quick example illustrates the use of curve emitters and also introduces you to more per particle attributes.

1 **Open the scene file**

- **Open** the scene file called *19-curveEmit_01.ma*.

  This simple scene contains dynamite barrels and a fuse which you will set on fire.

2 **Add a curve emitter to the wire**

- **Rewind** to frame 1.

- Select the *fuse* curve from the Outliner.

  This is the curve that was used to create the fuse geometry.

> **Note:** *If the curve is not available, you could also select an isoparm and then use* **Edit Curves → Duplicate Surface Curves**.

- Add a curve emitter to it by selecting **Particles** → **Emit from Object** → ❏.
- In the options, set the **Emitter Type** to **Curve**, and then click the **Create** button.
- **Rename** the resulting particle object *fire* and the resulting emitter *fireEmitter*.

> **Tip:** *You can also add curve emitters to a curve on surface. You can create a curve on surface by using tools like* **Intersection** *or* **Project Curve**, *or by making the surface live using* **Modify** → **Make Live**, *and then drawing a curve directly on the geometry.*

3 Adjust Lifespan attribute

- Select the *fireShape* particles and change the **Particle Render Type** to **Cloud (s/w)** in the **Channel Box** or **Attribute Editor**.
- In **Lifespan Attributes,** change **Lifespan Mode** to **Constant**.

  The default setting of **1.0** *is fine for now.*

4 Add a radiusPP attribute

Adding a **radiusPP** attribute will provide control over the radius of each cloud particle emitted.

- Click the **General** button in the **Add Dynamic Attributes** section of the **Attribute Editor**.
- Click on the **Particle** tab and select **radiusPP** from the list of particle attributes.
- Click **OK**.

  A **radiusPP** *attribute field is added to the* **Per Particle (Array) Attributes** *section of the*

Adding a radiusPP from the Add Attributes window

5 Add a ramp to control each particle's radius

- **RMB** on the **radiusPP** field in the **Per Particle (Array) Attributes** section.
- Select **Create Ramp** from the pop-up menu.
- **RMB** on the same **radiusPP** field and select **arrayMapper1.outValue1PP → Edit Ramp**.

  The ramp is displayed in the Attribute Editor.

6 Edit the ramp color

- Edit the ramp so that there is a white handle at the bottom of the ramp and a black handle at the top, as shown here:

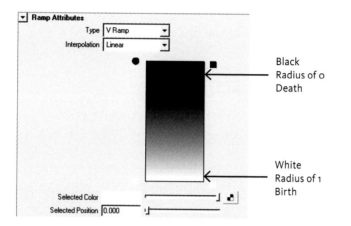

Black
Radius of 0
Death

White
Radius of 1
Birth

The ramp of radiusPP over age

*Black corresponds to a radius value of **0**, white to a value of **1**. Therefore, with the current ramp configuration, the radius will be **1** when the particle is born and decrease to **0** when the particle dies by the end of its lifespan. The age of a particle is normalized, so you are sure that each particle will go from the bottom of the ramp all the way to the top.*

Note: *Normalized age is the relationship between a particle's age and its lifespan* **(age / lifespan)**.

Tip: *In order to assign values greater than 1 for float attributes such as* **radiusPP** *with a ramp, open the Color Chooser window and switch to* **HSV** *mode, then simply enter the desired value in the* **V** *field.*

7 Test the animation

- **Rewind** and **play back** the animation.

  The radius decreases smoothly over the particle's age.

- Using what you have seen so far, try to make the particles emit with a radius of o.o, then quickly increase to **1.2**, stay at **1.2** until halfway through their life, and finally decrease to a radius of **o.o** when they die.

Tip: *You may want to decrease the emission rate of the emitter while you adjust the effect and then boost it back up when you have satisfactory settings.*

Note: *Adjusting* **Noise** *and* **Noise Frequency** *in the ramp is an interesting way to achieve randomness. This works better with some attributes than others.*

8 Adjust the Inherit Factor of the particles

The **Inherit Factor** attribute controls how much of the emitting object's velocity is transferred to the particles during emission. This is a good thing to know when you emit from animated objects.

- Select the emitted particles and set **Inherit Factor** in the **Channel Box** to **1.0.**

  When **Inherit Factor** *is* **0***, the particle velocity is not affected by the emitting object's motion. A setting of* **1** *causes the particles to emit with the same velocity as their emitting point.*

9 Add reverse gravity

In order to have the particles flying up, as real fire would do, you will create a gravity field and invert its magnitude.

- Select the *fire* particles.

- Select **Field → Gravity.**

- Change the new *gravity*'s **Magnitude** to **-9.8.**

10 Tweak the fire particles

You will now tweak the particles so they look more like fire.

- Open the **Hypershade.**

- In the Create bar, create a **Particle Cloud** shader from the **Volumetric Materials** section.

- Select the *fire* particles.

- **RMB** on the new *particleCloud* shader and select **Assign Material to Selection.**

- Open the **Attribute Editor** for the *particleCloud* shader.

- Set the following:

    Color to yellow;

    Incandescense to white;

    Glow Intensity to **0.2**;

    Density to **0.2**.

- Click on the **map** button for the **Blob Map** attribute.

- Create a 3D **Crater** texture.

- Set the following:

    Shaker to **1.0**;

    Channel1 to white;

    Channel2 to black;

    Channel3 to black;

    Melt to **0.2**.

11 Test render the scene

- **Increase** the number of emitted particles.

- **Play** the animation until there are some particles visible.

- **Render** the scene using the software renderer.

The fire emitted from the wire curve

> **Note:** *Curve emission is also useful for simulating effects like shockwaves or energy pulses, by adding an emitter to a curve and scaling the curve over time. This could be a stand-alone effect or a grayscale rendering used as a displacement effect in compositing.*

12 Save your work

- **Save** the scene as *19-curveEmit_02.ma*.

Surface emitters

Surface emitters can be applied to NURBS and polygonal surfaces and cause emission to come from the entire surface rather than just from the vertices.

1 Scene file

- **Open** the file *19-glass_01.ma*.

  This scene contains a drinking glass with ice cubes.

- Press **4** to go into wireframe mode.

2 Add a surface emitter

- Use the Outliner to select *glassBase*.

- Choose **Particles → Emit from Object → ❏** and set **Emitter Type** to **Surface**.

- Click the **Create** button.

- **Rename** the emitter *bubbleEmitter* and the particles *bubbles*.

3 Change the render type

- Select *bubbles* and open the **Attribute Editor**.

- In the **Render Attributes** section of the **Attribute Editor**, set **Particle Render Type** to **Spheres**.

- Click the **Current Render Type** button.

  This displays the attributes specific to that type of particle.

- Set **Radius** to **0.06**.

4 Test the animation

- Set the playback range to go from **1** to **500**.

- **Play back** the animation.

  The particles emit from the base towards the top of the glass, but remain in the scene indefinitely.

Note: *The particles are emitting upward because the normals of the surface point in that direction.*

5 Add a turbulence field

Turbulence will add some fluctuation to the movement of the particles to add realism.

- Select *bubbles*.
- Select **Fields → Turbulence**.
- Position the field near *glassBase*.
- In the **Channel Box**, set the following:

  Magnitude to **2**;

  Attenuation to **2**;

  Frequency to **2**.

  Attenuation *controls an exponential relationship between the strength of the field and the distance between the affected objects and that field. For instance, imagine a curtain being blown by the air from a fan. In reality, as the distance between the fan and the curtain increases, the effect of the air from the fan on the curtain diminishes. It is this relationship between distance and field strength that attenuation controls. An attenuation of* **0** *causes a constant force, regardless of the distance between the field and the affected object.*

6 Set the Per Object Lifespan attribute

- Set the **Lifespan** attribute to **Constant** for the *bubbles*.

  Choose a **Lifespan** *value that causes the particles to die before they reach the top of the glass.*

7 Add color to the particles

- Use the **Attribute Editor** to add an **rgbPP** attribute to *bubbles*.

Note: *If an* **rgbPP** *attribute is added without a specified lifespan,* **Lifespan** *will automatically be set.*

- Add a default *ramp* to the **rgbPP** attribute.
- Make the *outerGlass* layer a template.
- Press **5** to switch to shaded mode.

8 Test the animation

- **Rewind** and **play** the animation.

  As a particle's age approaches its lifespan, its color corresponds to a color higher along the vertical axis of the ramp.

- Edit the ramp so the color smoothly interpolates from white to a slightly blue light tint.

The bubbles going up

9 Save your work

- **Save** the scene as *19-glass_02.ma*.

Tangent speed and normal speed

Two attributes that are noteworthy when working with surface emission are **Tangent Speed** and **Normal Speed**.

These are closely related to the **Speed** attribute that was previously discussed. **Normal Speed** controls the particle's speed along the vector that is normal to the point of emission. **Tangent Speed** controls the particle's speed along a randomly selected vector that is tangent to the surface of emission.

A good way to see what normal speed and tangent speed do is to create a NURBS sphere and add a surface emitter to it. Increase the rate to around **300** and play back. If you view the sphere from the top view, you will see a radial emission pattern.

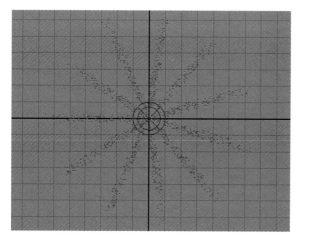

Radial emission pattern

This pattern emerges because the particles are emitted from tessellated geometry. The default **Tangent Speed** is **0**, causing the particles to move perpendicularly to the faces of the tessellated geometry from which they were emitted. Adding a bit of tangent speed eliminates this problem. Select the emitter and increase the tangent speed, and the particles will now be given some velocity along the surface tangent from which they originate. This causes them to shoot off the surface at angles and gets rid of the radial emission pattern.

> **Tip:** When both the **Normal Speed** and **Tangent Speed** are set to **0**, the emitted particles will have no speed.

1 Scene file

- **Continue** with your own scene.

   OR

- **Open** the scene called *19-glass_02.ma*.

2 Add water sparks to the glass surface

- Untemplate the *outerGlass* layer.
- Add a surface emitter to the *drinkingGlass*.
- **Rename** the new emitter *glassEmitter*.
- **Rename** the corresponding particle object *sparks*.
- Set the following attributes for the *glassEmitter*:

   Tangent Speed to **0**;

   Normal Speed to **0**.

3 **Change the sparks' render type**

- Select *sparks* and open the **Attribute Editor**.

- In the **Render Attributes** section of the **Attribute Editor**, set **Particle Render Type** to **Spheres**.

- Click the **Current Render Type** button.

  This displays the attributes specific to that type of particle.

- Set **Radius** to **0.08**.

4 **Test the animation**

- **Rewind** and **play** the animation.

  The emitted particles are emitted without any speed, and thus appear to stick to the glass.

5 **Adjust the Max Count attribute**

At this time, there are too many particles being emitted on the glass. Adjusting the emitter rate and particle lifespan to get the precise number of particles can be difficult. Fortunately, the **Max Count** attribute can control the number of particles directly to limit the emission.

- Open the **Attribute Editor** for the *sparks*.

- Set **Max Count** to **50** near the top of the **Attribute Editor**.

- Set **Rate** of the *glassEmitter* to **10**.

  Since the maximum number of particles is 50, a rate larger than that would cause the 50 particles to all be emitted around the same frame and then die all at the same time. Lowering the rate will randomize the particle emission.

6 **Test the animation**

- **Rewind** and **play** the animation.

  *As you can see, the **Max Count** attribute limits the total number of particles the selected particle object is allowed to hold.*

Note: *When a particle object is created, **Max Count** is set to **-1** by default. This means there is no limit on the number of particles it can hold.*

7 **Use a ramp to control acceleration**

Currently, the *sparks* remain stationary during playback. It is possible to control their acceleration using a ramp. This is an alternative to attaching a gravity field.

- Open the **Attribute Editor** for *sparks*.

- In the **Per Particle (Array) Attribute** section, **RMB** in the **rampAcceleration** field and select **Create Ramp** from the pop-up menu.

- Adjust the ramp so there is only a single color handle at the bottom of the ramp.

- Open the Color Chooser for that handle's color.
- Set the **RGB** values for the color entry to **o**, **-o.5**, **o**, respectively.

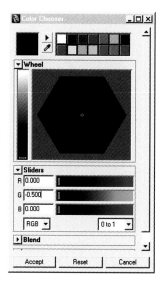

Setting a vector quantity (acceleration) using RGB

> **Note:** *When using the Ramp Editor to control **vector** quantities such as position, acceleration, and velocity, RGB corresponds to the particle's X,Y,Z values respectively.*

Controlling particle motion with ramps is not really all that common. This example is very simple as it is intended to show you the purpose of this feature and also help give you some ideas of other ways to move particles around. You could potentially use textures that are mapped to the ramp handles to push particles around your scene. This would require some additional setup, but it is a technique that some studios are currently using to help modify existing motion of particles without changing too much in the simulation.

8 Map radiusPP

- Use what you have learned so far to map a ramp to the sparks' **radiusPP**.
- Have the particles grow in size as they move down the glass and then vanish.

9 Save your work

- **Save** the scene as *19-glass_03.ma*.

Texture emission

With surface emitters, it is possible to control emission rate and location based on characteristics of a texture file or any 2D procedural texture. Texture emission works with textures only, not materials.

1   Scene file

- Open the file *19-paperBurn_01.ma*.

2   Add a surface emitter

- Select the *paper* surface, and then choose **Particles → Emit from Object → ❏**.

- In the options, **Rename** the emitter *textureEmitter* and the particle object *textureParticles*.

3   Set tangent and normal speed

- Select *textureEmitter*.

- Set the **Tangent Speed** to **0.5** and **Normal Speed** to **1.0**.

   This prevents the particles from emitting directly at the normal of the surface, providing a more randomized emission appearance.

4   Add an rgbPP attribute to textureParticles

An **rgbPP** attribute is required for the **Inherit Color** option of texture emission to work. This is a common oversight when setting up texture emission.

- In the **Attribute Editor** for *textureParticles*, add an **rgbPP** attribute.

5   Set the rate of textureEmitter

- Select *textureEmitter*.

- Set the **Rate** to **200** particles per second in the **Channel Box**.

- Set **scaleRateByObject Size** to **On**.

   If this attribute is enabled, the size of the object emitting the particles affects the rate of the particles emitted per frame. The larger the object, the greater the rate of emission.

6   Specify a texture for coloring the particles

Now you will connect a pre-made animated procedural texture to the emitter, which will determine the color of the particles emitted.

- Open the **Attribute Editor** for *textureEmitter*.

- Select **Window → Rendering Editors → Hypershade...** and position it next to the **Attribute Editor**.

- In the **Hypershade**, select the **Textures** tab.

  This displays all of the textures currently in the scene file. An animated fireRamp texture has already been prepared for this example and should be visible in the Hypershade window.

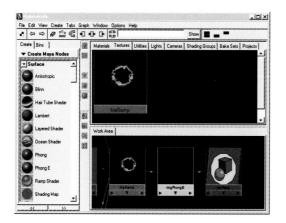

Displaying the fireRamp texture in the Hypershade window

- With the *textureEmitter* still selected, locate the **Texture Emission Attributes** section of the **Attribute Editor**.

- **MMB+drag** and **drop** the *fireRamp* texture icon from the **Hypershade** window onto **Particle Color** in the **Attribute Editor** for *textureEmitter*.

- Turn **Inherit Color** to **On** for the emitter.

- Press **6** to switch to hardware texture mode.

7   **Test the animation**

- **Rewind** and **play** the animation.

  Notice that the emitted particles have inherited the RGB values from the texture at the location where they were emitted. Notice that black particles are emitting from the outer edge of the texture where the color is not present. You will be fixing this shortly.

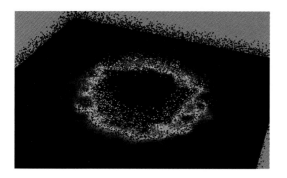

Using an animated ramp texture to color the emitted particles

Note: *To use a 3D texture for texture emission, you will first need to convert it to a 2D UV mapped image using* **Convert To File Texture** *in the Hypershade.*

8 Change Lifespan attribute

- Set the **Lifespan Mode** to **Constant**.

9 Add opacity so the particles fade out

Now you will add opacity and a ramp to control it based on the age of the particles.

- Create a **Per Particle Attribute** for **Opacity**.

- Add a ramp to **opacityPP**.

- Edit the ramp handle position so it has the following properties:

   Color entry 1: **Selected Position** to **0**; **RGB** to **0.9, 0, 0**;

   Color entry 2: **Selected Position** to **1.0**; **RGB** to **0, 0, 0**.

10 Save your work

- **Save** the scene as *19-paperBurn_02.ma*.

Scaling emission rate with a texture

Similar to the way you mapped a color image to control the color of emitted particles, you can also use the values of a grayscale image as multipliers on the emission rate of the emitter. This provides control over which portions of the surface will emit more than others. In this example, you want to shut off emission from the black areas of the ramp texture and leave emission on for the areas where there is color in the burning ring.

1 Scene file

- **Continue** with your own scene.

   OR

- **Open** the scene called *19-paperBurn_02.ma*.

2 Connect a ramp to the rate

Since the areas of emission that you are interested in controlling correspond exactly to the color ramp that is being animated, the same ramp can be mapped to **Texture Rate**.

- Use the same method used in Step 6 above to **MMB+drag** the *fireRamp* from the **Hypershade** onto the **Texture Rate** slider of the *textureEmitter*'s **Attribute Editor**.

- Set **Enable Texture Rate** to **On**.

3 **Test the results**

• **Rewind** and **play back**.

*Although fireRamp is a color image, when mapped to **Texture Rate**, the luminance values are extracted from the texture and those values are used as multipliers against the emission rate at the corresponding location of the surface.*

Areas of the color map with a luminance of 0 (black), use a 0 emission rate. Areas of the color map with luminance of 1 use 100% of the emitter's rate.

Once rendered, this fire ring could be rendered with a matte channel and combined with other textured surfaces using compositing software. These techniques will be discussed in later lessons.

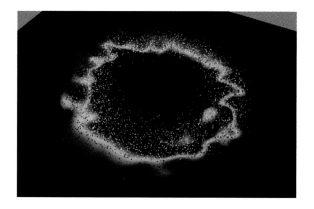

Texture mapped to texture rate

4 **Save your work**

• **Save** the scene as *19-paperBurn_03.ma*.

Per point emission

When working with particles, you may want to have some points on a curve or a surface emit at a different rate than other points. This can be achieved to some extent using texture emission controls. Another option that offers some additional control is **Per Point Emission**.

1 **Scene file**

• **Open** the scene called *19-perPointEmit_01.ma*.

This scene is the same scene you worked with when using curve emission, except that the curve emitter was deleted, leaving the fire particles in the scene to be reused.

2   Create an emitter

- Select the *wire* curve.

- Press **F8** to go into Component mode.

- Set the selection mask to have only the **NURBS Edit Points** available for selection.

- **Click+drag** over the entire *wire* curve to select all of its edit points.

- Select **Particles → Emit from Object → ❑**.

- In the options, change the **Emitter Type** to **Omni**, and click the **Create** button.

- **Rename** the new emitter to *perPointEmitter*.

3   Test the animation

- **Rewind** and **play back** the animation.

    An even emission rate occurs from the edit points, as illustrated here:

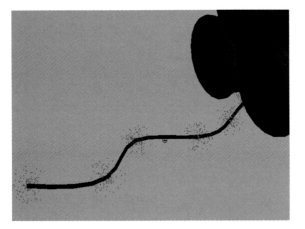

An even omni emission from the curve's edit points

4   Per point emission control

You can easily vary the emission rate for each edit point using per point emission:

- Select the *perPointEmitter*.

- Select **Particles → Per Point Emission Rates**.

    *The **Use Rate PP** attribute of perPointEmitter is automatically unlocked and set to **On** in the Channel Box.*

- Select the *wire* curve and change the **RatePP** for each edit point in the **Channel Box** as follows:

wireShape	
Per Point Emitter Rate PP[0]	0
Per Point Emitter Rate PP[1]	0
Per Point Emitter Rate PP[2]	0
Per Point Emitter Rate PP[3]	0
Per Point Emitter Rate PP[4]	100
Per Point Emitter Rate PP[5]	500

Per point emission rates in the Channel Box

5 Reconnect the fire particles

In order to reuse the fire particles created earlier, you must use the Relationship Editor.

- Select the *fire* particles.
- Select **Window** → **Relationship Editors** → **Dynamic Relationships**.
- In the **Relationship Editor**, change the selection mode to **Emitters**.
- Click on the *perPointEmitter* to highlight it.

  Doing so will allow the emitter to release the fire particles.

- **Delete** the *particle1* object, since it is no longer required.

6 Test the animation

- **Rewind** and **playback** the animation.

  The emission rates of each edit point correspond to the changes made in the Channel Box. This style of emission can be combined with the curve emitter to add some variation to the overall effect.

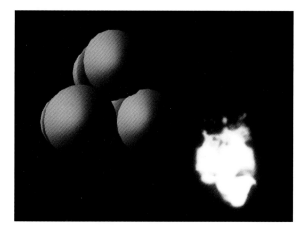

Per point emission rates

7 Save your work

- **Save** the scene as *19-perPointEmit_02.ma*.

There are more practical examples of when you might use per point emission, but these often require the use of particle expressions, which you will learn about in a later lesson.

For example, perhaps you have a car crashing into a wall. Points that collide with the wall at a higher velocity could be made to emit more particles at the collision point.

Tips and Traps

The following tips and traps will give you some additional information relating to these lessons, and also some possible explanations for things you may run into while working with the provided examples:

- People often ask about the **currentTime** attribute found on particles. By default, a particle system is plugged into the default scene time. As you advance the timeline, the particles evaluate. It is possible to break the connection from the main scene time and create your own custom time curve for the particles to evaluate from.

  The file 19-reverseTime.ma demonstrates a simple example of this. For instance, perhaps you want to have particles shoot out into a scene and freeze in space while other animation continues; a custom time curve will help with this.

- To set-up a reverse time, do the following:

  Create an emitter.

  Set the timeline to end at frame **100** and advance to frame **100**.

  Select the associated particle object and cache it using **Solvers → Memory Caching → Enable**, then **rewind** and **play back**.

  Select the particle object and **RMB → Break Connection** on the **Current Time** attribute in the Channel Box.

  Set a key at frame **1** on *currentTime* to **1**.

  Set a key at frame **50** on *currentTime* to **25**.

  Set a key at frame **100** on *currentTime* to **50**.

  Play back and see that particles play at half speed.

  Now select the particle object and edit its time curve in the Graph Editor. Since the data is cached, you can actually make the time curve cause the particles to get sucked back into the emitter by pulling the time keyframes down near values of **1** at frame **100**. You can also add keyframes in the Graph Editor and adjust the curve however you want.

- To connect the particle object back to the default time, break its connection from time again, then select **Particles → Connect to Time**.

- The *geoConnector* node on the surface associated with the emitter has a **Tessellation Factor** control. This is very similar to the tessellation factor used with rigid bodies. However, it controls the level of detail of the surface that the emitter uses to emit particles from. Increasing this attribute will slow things down but provide more even and accurate emission from the surface. If you have a highly detailed surface from which you need very accurate emission, increasing this number will likely be necessary.

- Patchy or sputtering emission can also be caused by the **Real-time** playback setting in your general preferences. Set the playback to **Play Every Frame** in the animation preferences to correct the problem.

Conclusion

You have now been introduced to some different ways of creating and working with particles. At this stage, you have experimented with the basics of particles, and you have learned where everything is and the basic particle and dynamic terminology. You also worked on controlling simple motion and characteristics of particles using per object and per particle attributes. There are many more attributes specific to particles that can be used. Several will be discussed in greater detail throughout the rest of this book. Keep in mind that they are all created, accessed, and manipulated in the same way.

In the next lesson, you will learn how to combine particles with rigid bodies.

Rigid Bodies and Particles

Now that you have been introduced to particles and rigid bodies, you will combine the two into one exercise to learn some ways they can work together. It is common for particles to collide and interact with rigid bodies. Getting the two to work together can help create realistic movement that otherwise would require intensive keyframing.

In this lesson, you will learn the following:

- How to add particle and rigid body collisions
- How to set particle mass in a creation expression
- How to change geoConnector attributes
- How to set collision layers

A particle-driven mechanism

In this example, you are going to create a particle-driven mechanism. You will be incorporating some of the tools that you have been working with up to this point, as well as some new techniques.

1 Scene file

- **Open** the scene called *20-particleRigidBodies_01.ma.*

   This scene consists of some simple geometry already placed to create a simple mechanism.

2 Active rigid bodies

In order for the mechanism to move, some pieces need to be made into active rigid bodies.

- Select the three flat pieces of geometry and the big cylinder.

- Select **Soft/Rigid Bodies → Create Active Rigid Body**.

3 Hinge constraints

- For each active rigid body, create a **Hinge** constraint.

4 Passive rigid bodies

- Select the prism and the plane surfaces.

- Select **Soft/Rigid Bodies → Create Passive Rigid Body**.

5 Emitter

- Select **Particles → Create Emitter → ❑**.

- In the options, make sure **Emitter Type** is set to **Omni,** then click the **Create** button.

- **Move** the new *emitter* on the **Y-axis**, above all the geometry.

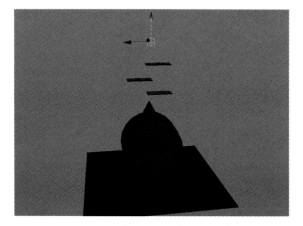

The emitter position

6 Gravity field

- Select the particle object.
- Select **Fields** → **Gravity** → ❑ and **reset** the options.
- **Play back** the animation.

  At this time, the particles are falling down, straight through the geometry.

7 Make the particles collide

- Select the *particle* object, and then **Shift-select** the first flat surface at the top of the mechanism.
- Select **Particles** → **Make Collide**.
- **Play back** the animation.

  The particles now collide with the first rigid body.

- **Repeat** the previous steps in order to make the particles collide with all the other rigid bodies in the scene.

8 Enable the rigid bodies' particle collision

- Select all of the rigid bodies.
- In the **Channel Box**, scroll down and set **Particle Collision** to **On**.
- **Play back** the animation.

  The particles now collide with all the rigid bodies, which in turn react to the collisions. You will notice that the particles fly unexpectedly and that the collisions are much too pronounced. You will now fix this.

9 Change the particles' settings

- Select the *particle* object.
- From the **Attribute Editor**, change the **Particle Render Type** to **Spheres**.
- Set the **Lifespan Mode** to **Constant**.
- Set the **Lifespan** to **7**.
- Set the **Conserve** attribute to **0.99**.

10 Change the particles' mass

- Still in the **Attribute Editor**, scroll down to the **Per Particle (Array) Attributes**.
- **RMB** in the **Mass** field and select **Creation Expression**.

  The Expression Editor will appear.

- Type the following in the **Expression** field:

```
particleShape1.mass = 5;
```

- Click on the **Create** button, and then click on the **Close** button to close the editor.

  *Each particle will now have a weight of **5** assigned when it is born. But, if you play back the scene, the dynamics are still chaotic.*

11 Change the mass of the rigid bodies

- Select the top three rigid bodies.

- In the **Channel Box**, set their **Mass** to **200**.

- Select the big cylinder rigid body.

- In the **Channel Box**, set its **Mass** to **1000**.

12 Change the geoConnector settings

- Select the *particle* object.

- In the **Inputs** section of the **Channel Box**, locate the geoConnector nodes.

  *There is one geoConnector node per surface, which the particles collide into. This node defines some dynamic attributes, such as **Resilience** and **Friction**. The following diagrams illustrate these attributes:*

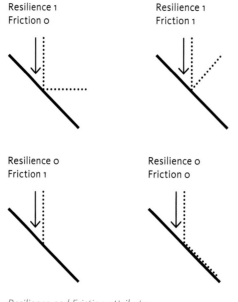

Resilience 1
Friction 0

Resilience 1
Friction 1

Resilience 0
Friction 1

Resilience 0
Friction 0

Resilience and Friction attributes

- For each geoConnector node, set the following:

  Resilience to **0.2**;

  Friction to **0.2**.

13 Play back the results

- **Play back** the results.

  You should see the particles going through the first three flaps, and then being distributed in the big cylinder's grooves. When there is enough weight at the top of the cylinder, it starts rotating.

  Spend some time adjusting the various rigid body and field attributes to change the motion to your liking. You can also try incorporating some of what you learned in previous lessons to add more interesting characteristics to the particles, such as color or opacity.

The simple mechanism is now working

Tips and Traps

- **Resilience** controls how much rebound occurs in the particle collision. You can even use negative numbers with **Resilience**; however, it is rare that you would need this.

- If rigid bodies keep colliding together and you do not want them to, you can change their **Collision Layer** attribute to be different values. Doing so will prevent them from colliding and could increase the solver's calculation speed, especially in scenes with heavy dynamics.

- You can also use the **Set Rigid Body Interpenetration** and **Set Rigid Body Collision** menu options under the **Solvers** menu to produce the same basic result of placing different objects on different collision layers. Set **Rigid Body Interpenetration** has the same effect as putting all selected objects on different collision layers. Set **Rigid Body Collision** has the effect of all selected objects being on the same collision layer. This is just another way of doing the same thing, but it is faster since you do not have to manually change all the numbers. However, it can be tricky to keep track of which things are set to collide and which things are not. The advantage of collision layers is that you can very clearly see which objects will be colliding just by looking in the Attribute Spreadsheet.

Conclusion

You should now have a good idea how to set-up and work with particle collisions, as well as understand methods for integrating particles with rigid bodies. You also learned how to produce a creation expression to control the mass of each particle.

In the next lesson, you will take this a step further to work with particle collision events, which cause a user-defined action to occur when a particle collision occurs.

Particle Collisions

In this lesson, you will learn how to create and fine-tune particle collisions. Such a task can involve creating particle collision events and defining a collision procedure. The straightforward examples in this lesson will teach you how to use this approach to create refined dynamic simulations.

In this lesson, you will learn the following:

- How to create particle surface collisions
- How to create and edit particle collision events
- How to use the Particle Collision Event Editor
- How to implement particle collision event procedures
- Different applications for particle collision

Particle to surface collisions

As you saw in the previous lesson, it is possible to implement particle collisions on rigid bodies, but you are not limited to rigid bodies. To enable a particle to collide and interact with any geometric object (including soft bodies, trimmed objects, and deforming geometry), you can use the **Particles** → **Make Collide** command.

Note: *Particles can collide with geometry but cannot collide with each other.*
*Only **nParticles** can collide with each other and will be covered in the last lesson of this book.*

Particle collision events

With the particle collision event, you can trigger the following events when a particle collides with a collision object:

- Emit new particles from the colliding point;
- Execute a MEL script procedure;
- Kill (delete) the colliding particles.

Note: *The collision can be caused either by moving particles or by moving or deforming geometry.*

Raindrops

This exercise will introduce you to the Collision Event Editor.

1 **Scene file**
   - **Open** the scene file called *21-rainDrops_01.ma.*

     This scene file contains three pieces of geometry:

     rainCloud - polygonal plane;

     rainSurface - NURBS surface obtained from trim;

     mounds - NURBS surface.

2 **Add a surface emitter**
   - Select the *rainCloud* plane.
   - Select **Particles** → **Emit from Object** → ❑.

- In the option window, set **Emitter Type** to **Surface**.
- Click the **Create** button.
- Set the new *emitter*'s **Rate** to **2** and **Speed** to **10**.

> **Tip:** *The rain particles will move down because the surface's normals are pointing down.*

3 Set attributes for the particles

- Set the following attributes for *particleShape1*:

    Particle Render Type to **Streak**;

    Line Width to **1**;

    Normal Dir to **2**;

    Tail Fade to **0.5**;

    Tail Size to **0.5**;

    Use Lighting to **On**.

4 Make rainSurface a collidable object

- Select the *rainSurface*.

- Select **Particles → Make Collide**.

    This will create a geoConnector node and connect it to the rainSurface object. The rainSurface geometry will now appear as an option for connecting the particle object as a collision through the Dynamics Relationship Editor.

5 Connect rainSurface to particle1

- Open the Dynamic Relationships Editor by selecting **Window → Relationship Editors → Dynamic Relationships...**

- Select the *particle1* object.

- Select **Collisions** under **Selection Modes.**

- Highlight *rainSurfaceShape1*.

    The connection is made between the rainSurfaceShape1 and the particleShape1 nodes via the geoConnector node. Now, the particles will collide with that surface.

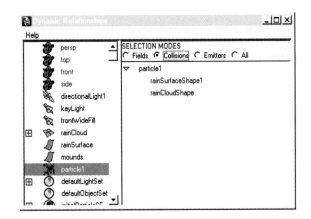

Connecting collisions to rainSurfaceShape1

> **Tip:** You can also do this collision and connection in one step by first selecting the particle, and then the surface it is to collide with, and then selecting **Particles →**
> **Make Collide**.

6 Test the scene

- **Play back** the scene.

  You should see the particles now colliding with rainSurface.

- Adjust the **Resilience** and **Friction** attributes as desired on the *rainSurface1's geoConnector.*

7 Create an empty particle object

You will soon make the colliding particles split into new particles. Creating an empty particle object now will allow you to emit those new particles.

- Type **particle** in the Command Line, and then press **Enter**.

  An empty particle object is created.

8 Set the new particle object to collide

You can set-up collision and connection in one step without using the Dynamic Relationship Editor.

- Select *particle2*, and then **Shift-select** the *rainSurface* object.

- Select **Particles → Make Collide**.

Using the Particle Collision Event Editor

This Particle Collision Event Editor is the graphical interface to the **event** MEL command. From this editor, you can choose actions to occur when a particle collides with its collision objects.

The top two panes provide selection of valid objects to create and edit events for the selected particle object. The next section provides fields that give information about the selected event and allow for editing the event name.

You can create multiple events for each particle object selected in the left list. You can also update the list of particle objects by clicking the **Update Object List** button.

Below that section is an area that displays whether you are in edit or creation mode, with a button to add a new event to the particle object you are working with.

The next section lets you define the collision event to occur when any of the particle objects collide.

Particle collision events

Emit vs. Split

In an **Emit** event, the particle emits new particles, while **Split** is when the particle emits new particles and dies. If a new target particle is not specified for **Split**, it uses the same particle object as the colliding particle. Also, when **Emit** is used, the age of the new particles starts at **0**. When **Split** is used, the age of the new particles is inherited from the colliding particle.

Random # Particles

Checking this option will create a random number of emitted particles with a min range of **0** and a max range of the **Num Particles** attribute.

Num Particles

Sets the number of particles emitted at collision time, or the max range of particles if **Random # Particles** is enabled.

Spread

Controls the spread of emitted particles. Valid values are from **0** to **1**, where 0 is narrowest and 1 is the widest.

Target Particles

The **Target Particles** field is where you can choose the particleShape that you want to emit upon the collision event. If you do not select a particle, the colliding one is used.

Inherit Velocity

This value controls the percentage of the parent particle velocity that will be transferred by the new particles.

Original Particle Dies

This option specifies whether the original particle dies upon collision.

Event Procedure

With an event procedure, you can call a MEL script procedure at the time of collision. You will use this option later in this lesson.

1   Open Collision Event Editor

- Select **Particles → Particle Collision Event Editor.**

2   Set event options

- Highlight *particle1* in the **Objects** section.
- Set the following options as directed:

> **All Collisions** to **On**;
>
> **Type** to **Split**;
>
> **Num particles** to **20**;
>
> **Spread** to **1**;
>
> **Target Particle** to *particleShape2*;
>
> **Inherit Velocity** to **0.8**.

3   Create Event

- Click the **Create Event** button.

4   Play the animation

- Select *particle2* and then select **Fields → Gravity**.
- **Play back** the simulation.

5   **Add two events to the particle2**
   - Select **Particles → Particle Collision Event Editor.**
   - Select *particle2* in the object list.
   - Click the **Create Event** button.
   - **Rename** this event from *event0* to *firstEvent* in the **Set Event Name** field.
   - Click **New Event**.

     You are now in creation mode.
   - Choose **Create Event** at the bottom of the window.

     You have now created another new event for particle2, called event1.
   - **Rename** this event to *secondEvent*.

6   **Event options for firstEvent**
   - Highlight the *firstEvent*.
   - Set the following options:

        All Collisions to **Off**;

        Collision Number to 1;

        Type to **Split**;

        Num Particles to 2;

        Spread to 0.5;

        Target Particle to **particleShape2**;

        Inherit Velocity to 0.5.

7   **Event options for secondEvent**
   - Highlight the *secondEvent*.
   - Set the following options:

        All Collisions to **Off**;

        Collision Number to 2;

        Type to **Split**;

        Num Particles to 1;

        Spread to 0.5;

        Target Particle to **particleShape2**;

        Inherit Velocity to 0.5.
   - **Close** the editor.

8 Test the scene and tune

- **Play back** the scene.
- **Adjust** the lifespan and render attributes for *particle1* and *particle2* to help refine the simulation.

The particles splash as they collide

9 Save your work

- **Save** the scene as *21-rainDrops_02.ma*.

Raising dust while walking

The following example scene contains the Constructor running through particles (dust) on a floor. You will make the Constructor kick up a cloud of particles as he runs through the scene.

1 Scene file

- **Open** the scene file called *21-run_01.ma*.
- **Play** the animation.

  You will see the Constructor running through an array of particles.

2 Create a radial field

- Select *particle1*.
- Select **Fields → Radial → ❑**.
- In the options, set the following:

  Magnitude to **1**;

  Attenuation to **1**;

  Use Max Distance to **On**;

  Max Distance to **5**;

  Volume shape to **none**.

- Click the **Create** button.

3 **Point constrain the field**

  - Select the *LeftToeBase* joint and **Shift-select** the radial field.

  - Select **Constrain** → **Point** → ❑.

  - In the options, make sure **Maintain Offset** is set to **Off**.

  - Click the **Add** button.

4 **Radial field on the other foot**

  - **Repeat** the last two steps to create another radial field and point constrain it to the other foot.

5 **Test the animation**

  - **Play back** the scene to ensure that the fields and particles are interacting.

6 **Set the floor particles to collide with the floor object**

  - Select the *particle1* object, and then **Shift-select** the *stage* object.

  - Select **Particles** → **Make Collide**.

7 **Create a collision event for the floor particles**

  - Select **Particles** → **Particle Collision Event Editor**

  - Highlight *particle1* in the **Objects** section.

  - Click **New Event**.

  - Highlight *event1* in the **Events** list for *particle1*.

  - Set the following options:

    All Collisions to **On**;

    Type to **Emit**;

    Random # Particles to **On**;

    Num Particles to **10**;

    Spread to **1**;

    Target Particle to *particleShape2*;

    Inherit Velocity to **1**;

    Original Particle Dies to **On**.

  - Click the **Close** button.

8   **Tweak the secondary particles**

- Select the *particle2* object.

- Select **Fields** → **Gravity**.

- Set the new *gravity*'s **Magnitude** to **−9.8**.

- Change the *particle2*'s **Render Type** to **Sprites**.

- Set the *particle2*'s **Lifespan** to **Constant 1.0**.

9   **Texture the sprites**

- **Assign** a **lambert** material to the *particles2* object.

- **Map** a **File Texture** to the **Color** of the material you have just created.

- **Browse** for the file *smoke.tga*.

10 **Play back the scene**

There are various places to fine-tune this example. The particle **Lifespan** and **Max Count** attributes on *particle2* control how many particles are in the scene. Adjusting the field attributes, such as **Magnitude** and **Max Distance**, will also make a big difference.

The particles raise as the character is walking

11 **Save your work**

- **Save** the scene as *21-run_02.ma*.

Particle collision event procedure

You have learned how to create and edit collision events. Now, you will take things further and explore the options for triggering a more complex animation at the time of collision.

The particle collision event also has a section called **Event Actions**. From this section you can enter an *Event Procedure*. An event procedure is typically a MEL script that is called when a collision occurs and the event is triggered. There are a multitude of applications that can utilize this functionality. For example, perhaps you want to move an object to the location of a particle collision, or perhaps you want to query the UV coordinates and determine or modify the shading information at a collision point. In many production environments, there may be other proprietary rendering systems or software applications that require you to pass information on to them. Having access to this level of information and being able to modify that information is what makes this a powerful feature.

One requirement for the script that is called by the particle collision event is that it must have the following format and argument list:

```
global proc myEventProc
        (string $particleName, int $particleId, string $objectName)
```

Where **myEventProc** is the name of the MEL procedure and also the name of the script file (*myEventProc.mel*), **$particleName** is the name of the particle object that owns the event, **$particleId** is the particle number of the particle that has collided, and **$objectName** is the name of the object that the particle has collided with.

These arguments, which are also variables, are the placeholders for the information that is passed to the script from the particle collision event.

1 **Scene file**

- **Open** the scene called *21-collisionScript_01.ma*.

   This scene contains a rainy backdrop and will be set-up to execute a specific particle collision event procedure.

2 **MEL commands**

Enter the following commands in the Script Editor to create a special node and establish the connection to the *ground* surface:

```
createNode closestPointOnSurface;
connectAttr -f groundShape.worldSpace[0]
        closestPointOnSurface1.inputSurface;
```

Note: *The closestPointOnSurface node is very useful for querying the world and UV position of a point on a surface.*

3 **Set particle1 to collide with ground**

- Select *particle1*, and then **Shift-select** the *ground* surface.

- Select **Particles** → **Make Collide**.

4 **Add a script procedure to the particle collision event**

- Select **Particles** → **Particle Collision Event Editor**.

- Click the **New Event** button.

- Set **Original Particle Dies** to **On**.

Note: *Do not select* **Emit** *or* **Split** *as the* **Event Type**.

- Enter *partCollisionPrnt* into the **Event Procedure** field under the **Event Actions** section.

  This is the name of a script that is included as part of the support files for dynamics.

- Click the **Create Event** button and close the editor.

- In order to make sure that Autodesk® Maya® knows about the script, **click+drag** the *partCollisionPrnt.mel* file from the *project6/mel* folder into the viewport.

  Doing so will automatically source the script.

Note: *Another way to source a script is to open the Script Editor and choose* **File** → **Source Script**.

Tip: *You can also copy the script file partCollisionPrnt.mel from the support directory to your current Maya script folder, such as the \My Documents\maya\scripts\ directory. The next time you launch Maya, the script will be automatically found.*

5 **Create a point light in the scene**

The script that will be executed at collision time will do two things: first, it will print out the collision information; then, it will take a point light and move it to the X,Y, Z location of the collision. You will thus need to create a point light for the script to execute without error.

- Select **Create** → **Lights** → **Point Light** .

- Make sure the name of the light is *pointLight1*.

- Press **7** on your keyboard to switch to hardware lighting mode.

6 Test the scene

- Open the Script Editor .

- **Play back** the scene .

The partCollisionPrnt script is executed each time a particle collides with the surface. The script then prints the position on the surface where the collision occurred. The script also moves the point light you created to these world coordinates.

Sample output from the Script Editor:

```
partCollisionPrnt("particleShape1", 0, " ground");
CPOS XYZ         10.51686562 2.943025257e-15 -10.38921561
CPOS UV          0.9370036721 0.9316994754
POS Position     10.51686562 2.943025257e-15 -10.38921561
POS UV Position  0.9370036721 0.9316994754
```

7 Save your work

- **Save** the scene as *21-collisionScript_02.ma.*

8 Open the partCollisionPrnt.mel script

Optionally, you can use a Text Editor or the Script Editor to read through the *partCollisionPrnt.mel* script. Unless you know some MEL, this script may not make a lot of sense to you. But, you will be able to see the basic framework of the collision event procedure and get an idea of how this type of effect is set-up.

The procedure *partCollisionPrnt* does a few things. First, it takes the arguments given to it from the particle collision event and puts these values into global variables:

```
$particlePositions
$particleVelocitys
$hitTimes
$particleHitCount
$currentHitTime
```

These variables can then be accessed from other procedures or expressions. Use this upper portion of the script as a template for your own particle collision event script.

The second portion uses two types of point-on-surface nodes to get and maintain collision information as it pertains to the surface.

closestPointOnSurface returns information about a point on the surface in relation to the world space position information that the **$particlePositions** variable is getting from the particle collision event each time a particle collides with the surface.

pointOnSurface is an operation that can create a *pointOnSurfaceInfo* node. This node will maintain information about a point on a surface even if the surface is animating and deforming.

The script then moves the point light into position.

Finally, it does some clean up to delete nodes no longer required by the scene. This last step is optional, but it will optimize this specific example.

> **Note:** *Several lines in the partCollisionPrnt.mel script are only included to generate human-readable feedback and are not neccessarily useful to the script's task.*

Tips and traps

- People often ask about the difference between **Emit** vs. **Split**. The two functions determine what happens to the particle that originally collided. **Emit** keeps it in the scene, while **Split** will kill the particle. This also affects what happens to the age of the new particle. **Emit** resets the age of the new particle to **0** and **Split** starts the age of the new particle at whatever value the old particle's age was when the collision occurred.

  The file 21-emitVsSplit.ma is a very basic demonstration of this.

- As the Constructor runs through the grid of particles, everything may appear to work fine for the first part of the run, but then particles can stop emitting later in the cycle. This is because there is a **Max Count** set for *particle2*, included just to keep the number of particles in the scene to a reasonable level. If you want, you can set the value to **-1** and use the **Level Of Detail** attribute on *particle2*, instead of **Max Count**.

- When you enter the name of a script to be executed by the collision event procedure, do not type the *.mel* portion of the script name into the Particle Collision Event Editor.

- If errors occur, check to make sure the script is in your scripts directory. If you make any changes to the *partCollisionPrnt.mel* script yourself, make sure to source the script by dragging the script file in the viewport. Always check the output to the Script Editor to help track down problems.

- A great way to find out where Maya is looking for your scripts is to type the following line in the Script Editor:

  ```
  internalVar -userScriptDir;
  ```

- The file *21-dieOnFrustumExit.ma* shows how to make particles die when they leave the camera frustum. This is a very simple file in which a polygon has been fit to the camera frustum and a collision event is used to kill the particles. This can be useful when dealing with very large numbers of particles for memory management.

- The **event** MEL command can be used in MEL scripts and expressions to customize the behavior of particle collision events beyond what is in the Particle Collision Event Editor. Additionally, particles have **Event** attributes that keep track of how many collisions each particle has had. For more information on this and many other particle attributes, refer to the *particle node* entry in the Maya online documentation.

Conclusion

Particle collision events are a very powerful method of controlling particles and their behavior. They provide a logical method of particle emission or death, based on collision. The ability to execute a procedure at collision also opens up a wide range of possibilities for creating geometry or manipulating virtually any other part of the scene, or even your system, at times of collision.

In the next lesson, you will learn about particle expressions.

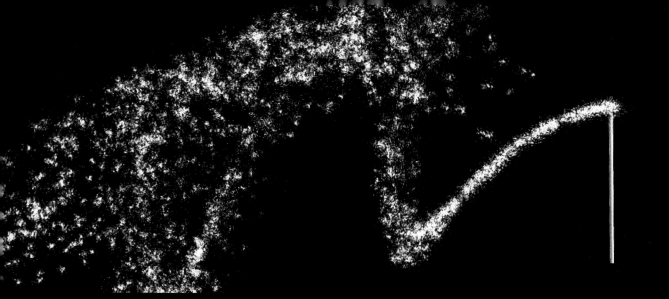

Particle Expressions

This lesson focuses on different techniques for controlling particle motion, with special attention placed on particle expressions.

In this lesson, you will learn the following:

- Fundamental physics concepts
- The Autodesk® Maya® particle evaluation process
- Initial state
- The difference between creation and runtime expressions
- The linstep and smoothstep functions
- How to use the particleId attribute
- Absolute value
- The sine function

Fundamental physics concepts

Some of the basic rules that govern the motion of objects in the universe are directly applicable to a discussion of particles. Newton's first law states the following:

```
Force = Mass x Acceleration
```

 Note: *This is more commonly written as* **F** = **ma**.

Force and **Mass** are known quantities when dealing with particles. Acceleration is calculated by the dynamic system based on these values. The resulting values are used to control the particle's motion.

Force

A generated quantity that can come from things like fields, springs, and expressions.

Mass

An attribute that exists by default on particle objects. Therefore, since two items in the equation are known, the third item, the acceleration, can be determined through the following simple division:

```
a = F/m
```

This rule forms the basis of the underlying architecture that Maya uses to calculate particle attributes such as position, velocity, and acceleration. Understanding this relationship is not always necessary, but it can be useful when deciding how to set something up, or when troubleshooting.

Some useful definitions

There are some common terms and definitions that come up frequently regarding particle attributes and quantities related to particles:

Scalar

A numerical quantity with only one specific component. Time and mass are examples of scalar values, represented by values like 20 or –3.5.

Vector

A quantity with magnitude and direction. This is represented as three distinct numerical components grouped together in brackets, such as «1,2,3» or «5,–2,1».

Float

A decimal ("floating—point") numerical value, such as 2.3, 0.001, 3.14, etc.

Integer

A non-decimal whole number, such as. −1, 0, 57, etc.

String

A collection of alphanumeric characters, such as "*hello123.*"

Boolean

A value that is either true or false, on or off, 1 or 0.

Variable

A location in memory used to store information that is one of the above data types. For example, `float $hello` defines `$hello` as a storage space for decimal numerical information that can be accessed in expressions and scripts.

Position (vector)

A particle's location in the world is its **position**.

Velocity (vector)

A particle's change in position over time. This is a measurement of both **rate** and **direction**. To visualize velocity, imagine an arrow pointing in the direction of the object's motion with the arrow's length proportional to the speed of the object compared to the previous frame.

Speed (scalar)

A particle's measurement of rate, only without respect to direction.

Acceleration (vector)

A particle's measurement of the change in velocity over time.

Propagation: the evaluation process

Propagation is the method Maya uses to determine a particle's attribute values by basing the calculations for the current frame on the result that was determined from the previous frame.

Propagation is like a *piggy-back* effect. For example, frame 2 gets information from frame 1, does some calculations, and then positions the particles. Next, frame 3 gets the result from frame 2, does its calculations, positions the particles, and moves to frame 4. The cycle continues throughout the playback of the animation.

So what happens at frame 1?

Frame 1 in the above example is the **Initial State** of the system. Initial state refers to the values that exist in any dynamic object's attributes at the initial frame of a dynamic simulation. It is from this initial state that propagation occurs.

Note: *The **Initial State** of a simulation is not necessarily the first frame in the playback frame range, but instead, is determined by the **Start Frame** attribute on each particle object.*

Creation vs. runtime expressions

It is important to understand the difference between creation and runtime expressions.

Each particle object stores all of its expressions in one of two places: the **Creation Expression** or the **Runtime Expression**.

Creation Expression

Evaluated only once for each particle in the particle object when the particle is born.

Runtime Expression

Evaluated at least once per particle per frame, but not at particle birth. There are two types of runtime expressions available: **Runtime before Dynamics** and **Runtime after Dynamics**.

The Expression Editor can toggle between displaying the runtime and creation expressions for the selected *particleShape* node. The expressions are evaluated in the order they appear in the Expression Editor.

The Expression Editor

All **Creation Expressions** are stored in the creation portion of the Expression Editor for that particle object.

Likewise, all **Runtime Expressions** on a given particle object reside in the runtime segment of that particle object.

> **Tip:** *Runtime and creation will be greyed out unless the particleShape node is the selected item. If you select the particle object, you can press the **down arrow** on the keyboard to navigate to the particleShape node.*

Expression examples

The following exercise will take you through the process of creating both types of particle expressions.

1   Scene file

- **Open** the file called *22-expressions_01.ma*.

    This file contains two pre-made directional emitters.

2   Creation expression

Now you will write a simple particle expression.

> **Tip:** *Remember that typing the expression is good practice and is recommended if this is new territory for you.*

- **Play** the scene.

    *The emitters both have an **rgbPP** attribute already added to both particleShape nodes. Right now, the rgbPP value is <<0,0,0>>, so the emitted particles are black.*

- Open the Attribute Editor for *particleShape1*.
- **RMB** on the **rgbPP** attribute and select **Creation Expression**.
- Enter the following expression in the Expression Editor:

    ```
    rgbPP = <<rand(1),0,0>>;
    ```

    In the above syntax, the double brackets indicate a vector quantity. There are three entries in a vector quantity: the X, Y, and Z components. The components are separated by commas. In this case, the X component corresponds to a red color, the Y component to a green color, and the Z component to blue.

> **Note:** *It is common to see many different attributes assigned values on the same line in the Expression Editor. Each should be separated by semicolons as follows:*
>
> `rgbPP = <<1,0,1>>; lifespanPP = rand(4,6);`

- Click the **Create** button.

3 Runtime expression

- Select *particleShape2*.
- **RMB** on the **rgbPP** attribute and select **Runtime Expression Before Dynamics**.
- Enter the following expression in the Expression Editor:

  `rgbPP = <<0,0,rand(1)>>;`

- Click the **Create** button.

4 Test the results

- Press **5** to switch to shaded mode.
- **Rewind** and then **play back** the scene.

The particle shape with the creation expression gets a random red color assigned to it only once during the animation. The particle shape with the runtime expression reassigns a new random blue value on each frame of the animation.

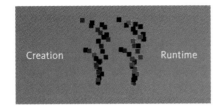

The resulting particle color

> **Note:** *The syntax* `rand(1)` *picks a random value between* **0** *and* **1**. *The result is always greater than* **0** *and less than* **1**. *You can also define a more specific range by using two numbers. For example,* `rand(20, 30)` *picks a random value greater than* **20** *and less than* **30**. *This example uses a range from* **0** *to* **1**, *since RGB values range from* **0** *to* **1**.

- Use the same techniques to create additional creation and runtime expressions to control other attributes, such as **radiusPP** or **opacityPP**.

5 Save your work

- **Save** the scene as *22-expressions_02.ma*.

Applied particle expressions

You should now have a better understanding of the difference between runtime and creation expressions. The next step is to use these concepts in conjunction with normalized age to establish a relationship between time and the attribute values.

The following template can be used when writing a particle expression to animate from **quantity A** to **quantity B** over the particle's **age**:

```
A+((B-A)*(age/lifespan))
```

1 **Scene file**

• **Open** the file called *22-sparksExpression_01.ma*.

This file contains the Constructor's buggy and the sparks done in a previous lesson.

2 **Mimic a ramp behavior with a particle expression**

So far, you have learned to change the color of a particle over its age based on a ramp. This exercise teaches you how to do the same thing using an expression. This is handy if you need some specific control that you cannot get from a ramp.

• Open the Attribute Editor for *points*.

• Add an **rgbPP** attribute to *points*.

• **RMB** in the **rgbPP** field and choose **Runtime Expression Before Dynamics...**.

• Type the following in the Expression Editor, which will change the color of the particles to go from yellow to red:

```
$normAge = age/lifespan;
vector $startColor = <<1,1,0>>;
vector $endColor = <<1,0,0>>;
rgbPP = $startColor + (($endColor - $startColor) * $normAge);
```

• **Highlight** the text you have just entered, and then **MMB+drag** the contents of this expression to the shelf as a **MEL** script.

Doing so will save the expression to your shelf so that you can later reuse it.

• Click **Create** and **Close** the Expression Editor.

• Press **5** to switch to shaded mode.

• **Rewind** and **play** the animation.

The expression causes the particles to transition slowly from yellow to red over the particles' age in the same way ramps controlled their related attribute. You can adjust the start and end colors in the expression to your liking once you see the effect the expression is having.

The resulting particle color

3 Save your work

- **Save** the scene as *22-sparksExpression_02.ma.*

Linstep and smoothstep

`linstep` and `smoothstep` are MEL commands that return a value between **0** and **1** over a specified range for a given unit (frames, fps, lifespan, age, etc).

`linstep` produces a linear curve, while `smoothstep` produces a linear curve with an ease-in and ease-out appearance at the tangents.

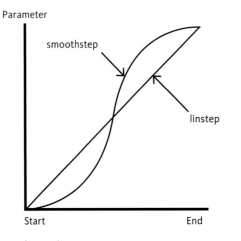

Resulting value curves

The syntax template for a `linstep` or `smoothstep` statement is as follows:

```
linstep (start, end, unitParameter);
smoothstep (start, end, unitParameter);
```

One advantage of using `linstep` and `smoothstep` is that the range of the effect can occur over any defined interval instead of being limited to the particle's age.

It is also possible to make the range of the values for `linstep` or `smoothstep` extend beyond the range of **0** to **1**. For example, to make a particle's radius increase from **0** to **5** over the course of frames **8** to **20**, the following runtime expression could be used:

```
radiusPP = 5 * linstep(8, 20, frame);
```

To make a `linstep` curve decrease instead of increase, subtract the `linstep` statement from **1**. Below is a common `linstep` function that will cause opacity to fade out linearly over the particle's age if placed in the runtime expression.

```
opacityPP = 1 - (smoothstep(0, lifespanPP, age));
```

Taking it a step beyond ramps

So far, what you have done could be done using ramps. The idea has been to make you familiar with entering expressions and how their evaluation works. Now, you will control a particle attribute such as **radiusPP** using a dynamic attribute like velocity. This is more difficult to accomplish with ramps and lends itself well to an expression.

1   **Scene file**

   • Continue with the previous sparks example file.

2   **Sphere render type**

   • Change the *points* particle **Render Type** to **Spheres**.

   Although you may not want to render the final shot in sphere mode, for this example you will use the sphere render type, since the effects of the expression are easiest to see with that render type.

3   **Add a radiusPP attribute and enter a runtime expression**

   • Add a **radiusPP** attribute to the *points* by clicking the **General** button and going to the **Particle** tab.

   • Add to the existing runtime expression as follows:

```
float $startRadius = 0.1;
float $endRadius = 0.5;
vector $vel = velocity;
float $y = $vel.y;
radiusPP = $y / 10 * ($startRadius + ($endRadius -
$startRadius) * $normAge);
```

Tip: *You may want to enter a few carriage returns below the existing rgbPP expression to make things more readable.*

*The above expression changes the radius of the spheres based on a factor of their velocity in the **Y** direction and also based on their normalized age. Notice when you play back the scene and thus run the expression, that the radius decreases when the particle drops slow down and increases as they speed back up.*

Problem with the particle's radius

4   Problem with the radiusPP values

While in shaded mode, you will notice that the spheres begin very big, but shrink at some point. The numeric render type is useful for determining what values a specific particle attribute holds.

- Select the *points* particles.

- Set **Particle Render Type** to **Numeric**.

- Press the **Current Render Type** button and enter *radiusPP* in the **Attribute Name** field.

This displays the numeric radius value held for each particle. During playback, the values start as positive, and then become negative. Since the expression used is returning negative radius values, the spheres could get turned inside out.

5   Correct the expression

- Open the Expression Editor for the expression written in the previous step.

- Edit the last line of the expression so it appears as follows:

```
pointsShape.radiusPP = abs($y / 10 * ($startRadius +
($endRadius -

$startRadius) * $normAge));
```

The only difference is that you enclosed what you previously had within **abs()**. *The* **abs** *function takes the absolute value of whatever is within parentheses. This tells the expression to check the value and always make it positive.*

- Click **Edit** and **Close**.

6   Creation radius

The other problem with the particles' radius is that when the particle is first emitted, it receives a default radius size, in this case **1.0**. In order to correct this, you need to make sure the particles are emitted with a small initial radius.

- Switch **Render Type** back to **Sphere**.

- Click the **Current Render Type** button and set **Radius** to **0**.

- **Play** your scene.

The corrected particles

7   Save your work

- **Save** the scene as *22-sparksExpression_03.ma*.

Particle motion examples

The file *22-expressionExamples.ma* contains several particle objects in different display layers. Each particle object has its own creation and runtime expression illustrating a common or interesting technique used with particle expressions. Here's an example:

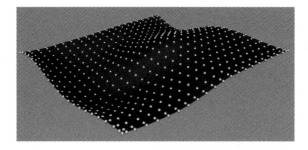

A wave example

Magic wand

This example is an application for controlling particle color over time to create the common pixie dust effect.

1   Scene file

- **Open** the file *22-magicWand_01.ma*.

  This scene consists of an animated cylinder object called wand and some standard lighting.

2   Create an emitter and parent it to the wand geometry

- **Create** a directional emitter with default values.

- **Rename** the emitter *dustEmitter*.

- In the Outliner, **MMB+drag** *dustEmitter* onto *wand*.

- Select *dustEmitter* and **translate** it to the end of the *wand* geometry.

3   Set the emitter to emit dust particles

- **Rename** *particle1* to *dust*.

- Select *dust*.

- Select **Particles → Emit from Object**.

  This creates an emitter that will emit particles from the dust particles. It also creates another particle object.

- **Rename** the added emitter *trailEmitter*.

- **Rename** the new particle object *dustTrail*.

4   **Emitter attributes**

  • For the *dustEmitter* set the following:

    Emitter Type to **Directional**;

    Rate to **800**;

    Direction X, Y, Z to **0, 1, 0**;

    Spread to **0.5**;

    Speed to **2**.

  • For the *trailEmitter* set the following:

    Emitter Type to **Directional**;

    Rate to **1**;

    Direction X, Y, Z to **0, 1, 0**;

    Spread to **0.2**;

    Speed to **0**.

5   **Create fields for the pixie dust**

  • Add **Gravity** to *dust* and decrease **Magnitude** to **1**.

  • Add a separate **Gravity** field to *dustTrail* with **Magnitude** to **1**.

  • Add **Turbulence** to *dust* and set **Magnitude** to **2**.

6   **Adjust dust particle shape attributes**

  • For the *dust* particle object, set the following:

    Particle Render Type to **Points**;

    Normal Dir to **2**;

    Point Size to **2**.

7   **Adjust dustTrail particle shape attributes**

  • For the *dustTrail* particle object, set the following:

    Particle Render Type to **Streak**;

    Line Width to **1**;

    Normal Dir to **2**;

    Tail Fade to **1**;

    Tail Size to **0.05**.

8   **Add per particle attributes to the dust particle**

  • Select the *dust* particle shape.

  • Add an **rgbPP** attribute.

9 Add per particle attributes to the dustTrail particle

- Select the *dustTrail* particle shape.

- Add an **rgbPP** attribute.

- Add an **opacityPP** attribute.

10 Creation expression for the lifespanPP of the dust particle

- Select the *dust* particle shape.

- Set **Lifespan Mode** to **LifespanPP Only**.

- Use the following creation expression to control the dust particle lifespan on a per-particle basis:

```
lifespanPP = rand(1,3);
```

*This expression assigns a random lifespan value greater than **1** second and less than **3** seconds to each particle.*

- Click the **Create** button.

11 Runtime expression for the rgbPP of the dust particle

- Switch the Expression Editor to its **Runtime Before Dynamics** mode.

- Enter the following twinkle expression to control the color of the particles on a per-particle basis:

```
rgbPP = <<1,1,1>> * (sin(0.5 * id + time * 20));
```

Following is a breakdown of what it is doing:

<<1,1,1>> : *This is the rgb vector value of white. The expression multiplies a number against this value to change its overall value by <<0,0,0>> (black) and <<1,1,1>> (white).*

sin(0.5 * id + time * 20) : `sin` *is a function that can create an oscillating value between **1** and **−1**.*

By multiplying `sin` *by variables like* `particleId` *and* `time`*, we can get values that are unique and changing rhythmically. This is a very important function of expressions, especially particle expressions.*

0.5 * id : *When working with per particle expressions, the* `particleShape.particleId` *attribute is useful. This attribute, as you have seen, gives us a unique value for each particle the runtime expression is applied to.*

0.5 * id + time * 20 : *Again, time is a great incrementer. Multiplying by 20 in this case dictates the frequency or how fast this* `sin` *functions repetitively.*

- Click the **Create** button.

Alternate expression #1:

Here is an alternate expression that does not use negative values against the RGB vector:

```
rgbPP = <<1,1,1>> * ((sin(0.5 * id + time * 20) * 0.5) + 0.5);
```

This example offsets the **sin** function to provide values that fall between 0 and 1. To do this, the **sin** value is multiplied by 0.5 to cut the amplitude in half. An offset has also been added to keep its values above 0.

Alternate expression #2:

How about an even simpler method? Just like tossing a coin, we can make some of the particles dark grey and some white to cause a blinking effect:

```
if (rand(1)> 0.5)
      rgbPP = <<1,1,1>>;
else
            rgbPP = <<0.3,0.3,0.3>>;
```

There are always many different ways to do similar things. Be careful about making things overly complicated when you do not really need to. But, at the same time, you should allow enough control in your expressions to be able to achieve the effects you want.

12 Creation expression for the lifespanPP

- Select *dustTrail* particle shape.
- Enter the following creation expression:

```
lifespanPP = rand(2,5);
```

  This will cause these particles to live a little longer.

- Click the **Edit** button.

13 Runtime expressions for the rgbPP and opacityPP of the dustTrail particle shape

You will create the same type of expression for **rgbPP** and **opacityPP** to control not only the **Color** but also the **Transparency** of the particles.

- Select the *dustTrail* particle shape.
- Update the runtime expression for the following:

```
rgbPP = <<1,1,1>> * ((sin(0.5 * id + time * 20) * 0.5) + 0.5);
opacityPP=(1 - ((linstep(0, lifespanPP, age))) * 0.0005);
```

  1–linstep (0, lifespanPP, age) : *The* linstep *function is used here to provide a linear change of value between 0 and 1 over time.* **1–linstep** *gives us the reverse, returning values from 1 to 0 over the particle's age. This value is different for each particle based on the lifespanPP creation expression you already made.*

- Click the **Edit** button.

14 Play back

Experiment with field attributes, render types, or multiplier values in the expressions to tune the results.

Pixie dust

15 Save your work

- **Save** the scene as *22-magicWand_02.ma*.

Tips and traps

- In the sparks exercise of this lesson, the emitter may emit black particles on the first frame. To fix this, add a creation expression that sets the color to white. The runtime expression does not evaluate when the particle's age is equal to **0** (birth).

- **mag** is a function that finds the magnitude of a vector, also known as the length. This is useful for representing a three-component vector with a single value. **mag** does the following math automatically for the user:

  ```
  distance^2 = (x2-x1)^2 + (y2-y1)^2 + (z2-z1)^2
  ```

  mag is often useful to help determine the distance between two points in space. For an example of this, look at the 22-waveDistCam.ma file. The **mag** *function is used to determine the distance from each wave particle to the camera. When the camera moves closer to the surface, the waves diminish in intensity, and vice versa.*

- People often look through some of the expression examples and see things like **position0** and **velocity0** and wonder what they are.

  When you save **Intial State** *on a particle object, that information needs to be stored somewhere. Most static particle attributes (i.e., position, velocity, acceleration, mass, etc.), have an* **Initial State** *attribute that is designated by the 0 as in* **position0***. Also, when you add a new array attribute to a particle object via* **Modify → Add Attribute...***, there is an option to* **Add Inital State Attribute***. When you check this* **On***, it adds a 0 attribute for the custom attribute.*

- Expressions are evaluated in the order in which they are typed in the Expression Editor, from top to bottom. For more specific information about the order of evaluation of dynamics, refer to Lesson 24.

- Lesson 24 provides a more in-depth explanation of each expression type and shows more specific expression syntax.

Conclusion

You now have a foundation for creating some of your own particle expressions. Keep in mind that applications for particle expressions are limitless, and are comprehensive topics on their own. In this lesson, you have seen how to get started with some basic examples.
Particle expressions should be considered as an entire tool within the Maya dynamic system. Not all situations lend themselves well to using expressions. However, they give you access to a lower level of information that, in some cases, is not accessible through graphical methods such as ramps or the Attribute Editor. Expressions can also provide a solution for getting results that would be difficult or impossible to keyframe and can enable your simulations to have decision-making built into them.

In the next lesson, you will learn about the particle `emit` function.

The emit Function

In this lesson, you will learn about additional control provided for particle placement and emission using the MEL command called emit.

In this lesson, you will learn the following:

- Common uses for the emit function
- Common emit syntax and options
- How to use simple conditional statements
- How to add and work with custom attributes
- How to construct MEL commands with strings
- How to use the eval MEL command
- How to emit particles when rigid body collisions occur

Emitting particles

Up to this point in our exploration of particles, the examples have relied on the Particle Tool and predefined emitters such as surface, directional, and omni to place particles in the scene. For most applications, these provide an adequate starting point.

Some cases may require additional control that is difficult or impossible using the default emitters.

For example, if you create a cloud of particles with the Particle Tool and realize you need to add a few more particles to change its shape, one common practice is to use the `emit` command.

Emit function with position flag

1   Create a particle object

- Type `particle` in the Command Line, and then press **Enter**.
- **Rename** the particles *addParticles*.
- Set the **Particle Render Type** to **Sphere**.
- Click the **Current Render Type** button and set the **Radius** to **0.3**.

2   Add three particles to the existing particle object using emit

- Select **Window** → **General Editors** → **Script Editor**.
- Enter the following lines in the lower window of the Script Editor:

```
emit -object addParticles -position 1 1 1;
emit -object addParticles -position 2 2 2;
emit -object addParticles -position 3 3 3;
```

- Press **Enter** on the numeric keypad or select **Script** → **Execute**.

   Each line above adds one particle to the existing addParticles particle object. The `position` *flag is followed by the world space coordinate where the particle will be placed in the scene.*

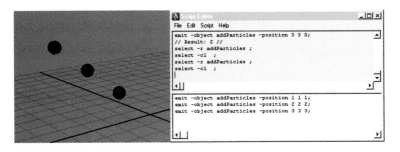

Emitting individual particles

> **Tip:** *Individual particles cannot be removed from a particle object. However, you can set an individual particle's* **opacityPP** *to* **0** *or its* **lifespanPP** *to* **0** *using its* **particleId** *in an expression, or by setting the value in the Component Editor.*

Define particle placement with a locator

You can make particle placement more interactive by setting it up so the `emit` command places the particle at the coordinates of a locator.

- Select **Create → Locator**.
- Type the following in the Script Editor:

```
float $locX = `getAttr locator1.tx`;
float $locY = `getAttr locator1.ty`;
float $locZ = `getAttr locator1.tz`;
string $partObject[] = `ls -type "particle"`;
emit -object $partObject[0] -position $locX $locY $locZ;
```

- Highlight and **MMB+drag** the script to the shelf.
- **Move** the locator to a point in space where you want to add a new particle.
- Click the shelf button.

  This will automatically add a new particle into the particle object at the locator position.

- **Repeat** the process as desired.

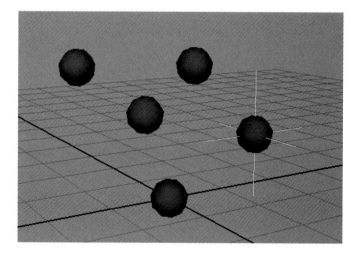

Particles created at the locator position

Emitting based on other particles

The `emit` function can set any attribute for a particle, not just its position. In the following example, `emit` is used to set position and velocity on newly spawned particles to make it appear as though the dying particles are emitting new particles.

1   Create a directional emitter

- In a new scene, select **Particles → Create Emitter → ❑**.
- In the options, set the **Emitter Type** to **Directional**.
- **Rename** the emitter *primaryEmitter*.
- **Rename** the particles *primaryParticles*.
- Set the following attributes for *primaryEmitter*:

    Rate to **100**;

    Direction to **0, 1, 0**;

    Spread to **0.25**;

    Speed to **10**.

- Set the following attributes for *primaryParticles:*

    Particle Render Type to **Spheres**;

    Radius to **0.2**;

    Lifespan Mode to **lifespanPP only**.

2   Create an empty particle object

- In the Command Line, type the following and press **Enter**:

    ```
    particle -n secondaryParticles;
    ```

    This will create an empty particle object named secondaryParticles.

3   Set a render type for secondaryParticles

- Select *secondaryParticles*.
- Set the following:

    Particle Render Type to **Multi-Streak**;

    Lifespan Mode to **lifespanPP only**.

4 **Connect gravity to primaryParticles**

  • Select *primaryParticles*.

  • Select **Fields → Gravity**.

5 **Add a runtime expression to lifespanPP for primaryParticles**

  • Add the following to *primaryParticles'* runtime expression:

```
$pos = position;
$vel = velocity;
if ($vel.y < 0)
{
        lifespanPP = 0;
        emit -object secondaryParticles
                -position ($pos.x) ($pos.y) ($pos.z)
                -at velocity -vectorValue ($vel.x) ($vel.y)
($vel.z);
}
```

  • Click the **Create** button.

6 **Test the expression**

  • Set the playback range to go from **1** to **500**.

  • **Rewind** and **play back**.

Just as primaryParticles begin to fall, the emit function is invoked and new secondaryParticles replace them with the same velocity and position.

New particles emitted thanks to runtime expression

> **Tip:** *Full descriptions of flags used by the* **emit** *function are listed in the online MEL documentation, in the Scene Commands section.*

7   Edit the expression to add color to secondaryParticles

- Add an **rgbPP** to *secondaryParticles*.

- Edit the runtime expression on *secondaryParticles* as shown:

```
$pos = position;
$vel = velocity;
$col = sphrand(1);
if ($vel.y < 0)
{
    lifespanPP = 0;
    emit -object secondaryParticles
        -position ($pos.x) ($pos.y) ($pos.z)
        -at velocity -vectorValue ($vel.x) ($vel.y) ($vel.z)
        -at rgbPP -vectorValue ($col.x) ($col.y) ($col.z);
}
```

- Click the **Edit** button.

8   Test the results

- Press **5** for shaded mode.

- **Rewind** and **play back**.

  A random color is assigned to each particle in secondaryParticles.

Colored particles

Fireworks

In the last lesson, you created the framework for a fireworks effect.

You can take the `emit` function a step further by repeatedly invoking the command in a looping structure to create a fireworks effect. Here you will create a fireworks effect and will also learn how to add custom attributes to the particle object and emitter. This will allow you to customize the launching and explosion characteristics.

1   Create the emitting cannon

- Open a new scene.
- Create a **Directional** emitter with the following settings:

    Rate to **5**;

    Direction X to **0**;

    Direction Y to **1**;

    Direction Z to **0**;

    Spread to **0.25**;

    Speed to **10**.

- **Rename** the emitter *launcher* and the particle object *fireworks1*.

2   Add custom attributes to launcher

Custom attributes are attributes that the user can tailor to his or her specific needs. Below you will add several custom attributes to the emitter that will later be used in particle expressions to modify the motion of the particles and the amount of emission that occurs.

To add custom attributes to the emitter, follow these steps:

- Select *launcher* and choose **Modify → Add Attribute...**

The Add Attributes window

- Add the following custom attributes to *launcher*:

  antiGrav with a **Default Value** of **5**;

  showerUpper with a **Default Value** of **30**;

  showerLower with a **Default Value** of **30**;

  streamUpper with a **Default Value** of **1**;

  streamLower with a **Default Value** of **1**;

Note: *All the custom attributes should be* **Integer**, **Scalar**, *and* **Keyable**.

3 **Add and adjust attributes for fireworks1**

- Add a per object **Color** attribute to *fireworks1*.

- Set the attribute values for *fireworks1* as follows:

  Max Count to **3**;

  Particle Render Type to **Streak**;

  Red to **0.8**;

  Green to **0**;

  Blue to **0**;

  Line Width to **1**;

  Tail Fade to **0.1**;

  Tail Size to **3.6**;

  Lifespan Mode to **lifespanPP only**.

4 **Connect fireworks1 to gravity**
   - Select *fireworks1*.
   - Select **Fields → Gravity**.

5 **Save your work**
   - **Save** your scene as *23-fireworks_01.ma*.

Create the secondary particle object

The secondary particle object represents the small projectiles that leave the initial projectile when its velocity reaches 0. These will be created using the `emit` function.

These secondary particles will act as leading particles for the long streaks of sparks that will be added later. Wherever the leading particles go, the streaks of sparks will follow. The secondary particles are the glowing tips of the streaks.

1 **Scene file**
   - Continue working with the scene from the last exercise.

2 **Create the "leading" particle object**
   - Enter the following into the Script Editor:

     ```
     particle -n fireworks2;
     ```

     This will create an empty particle object named fireworks2.

Lesson 23 | The emit Function

3 Add and modify attributes for fireworks2

- Select the *fireworks2* particles.
- Change the **Particle Render Type** to **Spheres**.
- Set a **Radius** value of **0.05**.
- Set **Lifespan Mode** to **lifespanPP only**.

4 Create and connect gravity

- Select *fireworks2*.
- Select **Fields** → **Gravity**.

Create the final particle object and emitter

Now you will create the stream of sparks that follow behind the leading particles.

1 Add a directional emitter to fireworks2

- Select *fireworks2*.
- Select **Particles** → **Emit from Object**.
- Make sure the new emitter is **Directional**.
- **Rename** the emitter *sparkEmitter* and the new particle object *fireworks3*.

2 Adjust attributes for sparkEmit

- Select *sparkEmitter* and set the following attributes:

    Rate to **40**;

    Direction to **0, 1, 0**.

    Spread to **0.25**;

    Speed to **1**;

3 Set the attributes for fireworks3

- Select *fireworks3* and set the following attributes:

    Depth Sort to **On**;

    Particle Render Type to **MultiPoint**;

    Color Accum to **On**;

    Multi Count to **15**;

    Multi Radius to **0.2**.

- Set **Lifespan Mode** to **lifespanPP only**.

Add expressions to the particle objects

Now that the particle objects have been built and the appropriate fields are connected, you can add expressions to the various particle objects.

1 Use emit to spawn the leading particles

- Select **Window** → **Animation Editors** → **Expression Editor**.
- Select *fireworks1Shape*.
- In the Expression Editor, make sure to select the **Runtime Before Dynamics** option.
- Add the following runtime expression to *fireworks1*:

```
vector $pos = fireworks1Shape.position;
vector $vel = fireworks1Shape.velocity;

float $antiGrav = launcher.antiGrav;
int $upperCount = launcher.showerUpper;
int $lowerCount = launcher.showerLower;
int $upperLife = launcher.streamUpper;
int $lowerLife = launcher.streamLower;

if ($vel.y < 0)
{
    fireworks1Shape.lifespanPP = 0;
    int $numPars = rand ($lowerCount, $upperCount);
    string $emitCmd = "emit -o fireworks2Shape ";
    for ($i = 1; $i <= $numPars; $i++)
    {
        $emitCmd += "-pos " + $pos + " ";
        vector $vrand = sphrand(10);
        $vrand = <<$vrand.x, $vrand.y + $antiGrav, $vrand.z>>;
        $emitCmd += "-at velocity ";
        $emitCmd += "-vv " + $vrand + " ";
        float $lsrand = rand ($lowerLife, $upperLife);
        $emitCmd += "-at lifespanPP ";
        $emitCmd += "-fv " + $lsrand + " ";
    }
    eval ($emitCmd);
}
```

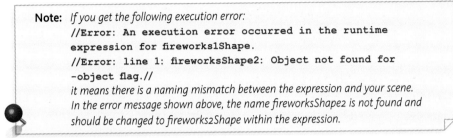

Note: *If you get the following execution error:*
```
//Error: An execution error occurred in the runtime
expression for fireworks1Shape.
//Error: line 1: fireworksShape2: Object not found for
-object flag.//
```
it means there is a naming mismatch between the expression and your scene. In the error message shown above, the name fireworksShape2 is not found and should be changed to fireworks2Shape within the expression.

This expression creates the flares at the tips of the fireworks trails.

- Click the **Create** button.

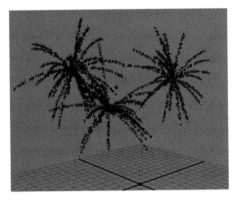

The rough fireworks expression

2 **Create a non-dynamic expression to control launcher's rate**

A non-dynamic expression is one that is not contained within a runtime or creation expression. Non-dynamic expressions are evaluated once per frame.

- Select *launcher* and add the following in the Expression Editor:

```
launcher.speed = rand (12,18);
if (frame%20 == 0)
        launcher.speed = 22;
```

This expression varies the speed at which a particle leaves the cannon so the fireworks explode at different heights. Every 20th frame, a particle is launched much higher.

- Click the **Create** button.

Note: *The **Creation** and **Runtime** options are greyed out in the Expression Editor because the expression is being added to launcher, which is not a particle shape object.*

3 Assign a random lifespan to the spark trails

- To control how long the spark trail burns, add the following to the creation expression of *fireworksShape3*:

```
fireworksShape3.lifespanPP = rand (0.3, 0.7);
```

This causes each particle in the spark trails of the fireworks to die before they are one second old.

- Click the **Create** button.

4 Play back

- **Play back** the animation.

Now that you are comfortable with how this process works, try setting different values for lifespanPP and other particle and attribute values, including the custom attributes you added to the emitter.

5 Save your work

- **Save** your scene as *23-fireworks_02.ma*.

Final fireworks effect

Note: *On the DVD, the files 23-fireworks_03.ma and 23-fireworks_04.ma are finished versions of this example.*

Emission on contact

In the following exercise, you will learn how to emit particles at the location where rigid bodies collide. To test this functionality, you will drop an active rigid body object on the passive rigid body ground and you will emit particles at the contact points.

1   Open File

- **Open** the scene *23-crash_01.ma*.

   This file contains the Constructor in his buggy, just about to jump over the broken track. A simplified version of the buggy is set-up to jump and collide with the track and ground. The rigid bodies and field have already been set-up.

2   Create an empty particle object

- Type `particle` in the Command Line and press **Enter**.

   This empty particle object will be used later to hold the particles that are emitted when a collision occurs.

- Set the following attributes:

   Max Count to **500**;

   Lifespan Mode to **lifespanPP only**.

   Particle Render Type to **MultiStreak**;

   Color Accum to **On**;

   Line Width to **2.0**;

   MultiCount to **7**;

   MultiRadius to **0.3**;

- Add an **rgbPP** attribute.

- Add an **opacityPP** attribute and add the default ramp to it.

3   Enable contact data attribute on the rigidSolver

The rigidSolver has an attribute called *contactData*. If this attribute is **On**, you can use MEL to get information about when and where rigid body collisions occur. This attribute is **Off** by default since it requires extra work for the solver to manage this data.

- Select the *standinBuggy*.

- Locate the *rigidSolver* node in the Channel Box and set the **contactData** attribute to **On**.

4   Add a non-dynamic expression

An expression applied to the lure will be used to check the velocity of the rigid body, find out when and where a contact has occurred, and emit particles into *particle1* at that location.

- Select *standinBuggy* and open the Expression Editor.

Project 06

450

- Enter the following expression:

```
if(frame > 80)
{
    float $vel[] = `rigidBody -q -vel standinBuggy`;
    float $speed = mag(<<$vel[0],$vel[1],$vel[2]>>);
    int $num = $speed * 1;
    int $contact = `rigidBody -q -cc standinBuggy`;
    string $cPos[];
    string $each;
    if(($contact > 0) && ($num > 0))
    {
        $cPos = `rigidBody -q -cp standinBuggy`;
        for ($each in $cPos)
        {
            string $emit = ("emit -o particle1 -pos " +$each);
            for ($x = 1; $x < $num; $x++)
            {
                $emit += (" -pos " + $each);
            }
            $emit += (" -attribute velocity");
            for ($x= 1; $x <= $num; $x++)
            {
                vector $rand = (sphrand(3) + <<0,5,-5>>);
                $emit += (" -vectorValue " +
                    $rand.x + " " +
                    $rand.y + " " +
                    $rand.z);
            }
            eval($emit);
        }
    }
}
```

- Click the **Create** button.

This expression does the following:

Checks if the current frame is after frame 80, so the buggy is in the air.

Finds the velocity of the buggy so it does not emit if the buggy is stopped.

For each collision point, generates an emit command with a certain number of particles and gives them a random velocity.

Finally, it executes the emit command.

5 Connect particles to gravity

- With the particle node selected, select **Fields** → **Gravity**.

6 Add creation expression to particles

- In the Attribute Editor for the *particleShape1*, **RMB** any **Per Particle Attribute** and select **Creation Expression**.
- Enter the following expression:

```
mass = 50;
lifespanPP = rand(0.8,1);
rgbPP = <<1.0,1.0,0.0>>;
```

- Click the **Create** button.

7 Play back the scene

- **Hide** the *standinBuggy* and **show** the Constructor *geometry* and *buggy* in the Layer Editor.
- **Play** the simulation.

  Particles are emitted wherever the buggy rigid body collides with the second portion of the track or the ground.

Collision emit

8 Experiment

Experiment by changing various values in the expressions created earlier. Also try to change the values of friction on the buggy and tracks. Move the second portion of the track a little bit to see the new simulation.

9 Save your work

- **Save** the scene as *23-crash_02.ma*.

Conclusion

In this lesson, you learned about several key concepts, such as using the **emit** command to add and place new particles, building complex MEL expressions using loops and **eval** commands, and emitting particles from other particles and at rigid body collision points. Now that you have had some exposure to the **emit** command, you have another tool available to achieve the effects you are working on.

You will likely come across cases where the methods discussed here are applicable to a situation you are trying to simulate. Be careful about getting sidetracked by the more technical approach of using **emit** if the same effect is easily accomplished using the particle tools already available.

In the next lesson, you will go even more in-depth with particle expressions.

Advanced Particle Expressions

This lesson provides a more in-depth discussion of the expressions and steps used to build some examples contained in the file *22-expressionExamples.ma*. You will now learn how they were built and obtain a description of how some expressions work. This section also discusses the order of evaluation for the various elements in the dynamics system. Lastly, you will find more detailed descriptions of the expressions using the emit command in the fireworks example.

In this lesson, you will learn the following:

- How to move particles with expressions

- How to create random motion

- How to change the color of particles based on their motion

- How to vary the emission rate with expressions

- How to use particleId

- The order of evaluation

Moving particles with expressions

You have been dealing primarily with expressions to control rendering attributes such as color or opacity. Here, you will apply similar methods on position, velocity, and acceleration attributes to dynamically control the motion of the particles.

Note: *If you do not feel comfortable with expressions and algorithms, this lesson can help you understand some fundamental concepts.*

Position control expression

1 **Create a particle in the scene**
   - Use the **Particle Tool** to create a single particle near the origin.
   - Set **Particle Render Type** to **Spheres**.

2 **Add a runtime expression**
   - Enter the following runtime expression for **position**:

     ```
     position = <<0, time, 0 >>;
     ```
   - Click the **Create** button.

3 **Test the results**
   - Set the frame range to go from **1** to **300**.
   - **Rewind** and **play back**.

     The particle moves up on the **Y-axis** *as* time *increases. As the animation plays back,* time *is a constantly changing value determined using the following relationship:*

     ```
     Time = Current Frame Number / Frames Per Second
     ```

Random motion expression

   - **Create** a cloud of **100** particles.
   - Try each of the following on their own in the **Runtime Expression** to see the interesting effects they produce:

     ```
     velocity = dnoise (position)
     acceleration = dnoise (position)
     velocity = sphrand(10)
     acceleration = sphrand(10)
     position = position + dnoise(position)
     ```

> **Note:** sphrand *returns a random vector value that exists within a spherical or ellipsoidal region of your choice.* dnoise *returns a vector with each component containing a random number from −1 to 1.*

Acceleration using variables and magnitude

1 **Create a new scene file with a cloud of particles in it**

- Select **File → New Scene**.
- Create an **Omni** emitter.
- Set **Rate** to **10**.
- Set **Particle Render Type** to **Spheres**.
- Set **Radius** to **0.3**.

2 **Add a runtime expression for acceleration**

- Enter the following in the runtime expression for **acceleration**:

```
int $frequency = 65;
float $distance = mag (position);
int $limit = 3;
if ($distance > $limit)
        acceleration = acceleration - (position * $frequency);
```

- Click **Create** in the Expression Editor.

3 **Play back the animation**

The particles move in a swarming pattern. Watch one particle to see what it is doing. It is swinging between a range in 3D space defined by **$limit**.
When the *magnitude* of the position is greater than the limit, the expression begins subtracting acceleration from the particle, which increases its acceleration in the opposite direction.

If this is unclear to you, try the same expression on a single particle instead of an emitter. Also, try changing the values used for **frequency** and **limit**.

Swarming particles

Noise position expression and custom attribute

1 Create a grid of particles

- Select **File** → **New Scene**.

- Select **Particles** → **Particle Tool** → ❏.

- Set the following in the options:

  Create Particle Grid to **On**;

  Particle Spacing to **1.0**;

  Placement to **With Text Fields**;

  Minimum Corner to **5, 0, 5**;

  Maximum Corner to **-5, 0, -5**.

- Press **Enter** in the viewport to create the grid.

- Set **Particle Render Type** to **Spheres**.

- Set **Radius** to **0.3**.

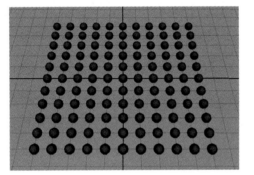

A grid of particles

2 Add a custom vector attribute

Adding a custom vector attribute will give us a place to store the original position of each particle.

- Select *particleShape1* and open its Attribute Editor.

- In the **Add Dynamics Attributes** section, click the **General** button.

- Set the following:

    Attribute Name to *origPos*;

    Data Type to **Vector**;

    Attribute Type to **Per Particle (Array)**;

    Add Initial State Attribute to **On**.

- Click the **OK** button.

An origPos field is added to the **Per Particle (Array) Attributes** *section of the Attribute Editor. Since the* **Attribute Type** *was set to* **Array***, you just made your own custom per particle attribute.*

▼	Per Particle (Array) Attributes	
	position	
	rampPosition	
	velocity	
	rampVelocity	
	acceleration	
	rampAcceleration	
	mass	
	lifespanPP	
	origPos	
	worldVelocity	

Your custom per particle attribute

3 Add a creation expression for origPos

- Add the following creation expression to **origPos** to store the position of each particle at the initial frame:

```
origPos = position;
```

Note: *Because it is a creation expression, the original position will be saved only on the first frame of the simulation.*

- Click the **Create** button.

- Make sure to **rewind** the scene in order to execute the creation expression.

4 Add a runtime expression for position

- Click the **Runtime Before Dynamics** radio button in the **Expression Editor**.
- Enter the following Runtime Expression to control **position**:

```
position = origPos +
                << 0, (0.8 * noise (origPos *
3+time*<<0,1,2>>)), 0>>;
```

- Click the **Create** button.

5 Test the results

- **Rewind** and **play back**.

*Each particle moves in a wave-like fashion up and down along only the **Y-axis**. The above expression is just adding a vector to **origPos**. The Y component of that vector is a statement that generates a random stream. **0.8** controls the amplitude of that stream, **3** controls the frequency, and <<0,1,2>> controls the direction of the phase.*

The noise *function produces a smoother random number stream than the previously discussed* rand *function.*

*Notice how you are setting a value for **origPos** in the creation, and then modifying that value again in the runtime expression. This is a very common technique for working with particle expressions.*

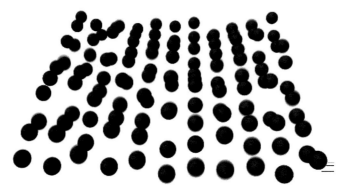

The noise expression effect

Change color based on position

- In a new scene, create an **Omni** emitter.

- Add an **rgbPP** attribute.

- Add the following runtime expression to **position**:

```
vector $pos = position;
if ($pos.y >=0)
        rgbPP = <<1,0,0>>;
else
        rgbPP = <<0,0,1>>;
```

- Switch to shaded mode.

- **Rewind** and **play back**.

This expression stores the position for each particle in a vector variable called $pos.
The if statement checks the Y component of that vector to see if it is above or below the
Y-axis. If the particle is above, it is red; otherwise, it is blue.

You can try the same idea with acceleration or velocity instead of position.

Tip: *The individual elements of a vector (<<x, y, z>>) are called components.*

Emitter examples

Although emitters are closely related to particles, they *do not* use creation and runtime
expressions. The following example is good for obtaining a randomized emission rate that can
be used to simulate an eruption, geyser, or puffing smoke effect. This example shows you a
concept you can build upon when working with emitters.

1 **Start with an empty scene file**

- Select **File → New Scene**.

2 **Create a directional emitter**

- Create a **Directional** emitter.

- Set the following for the emitter:

  Direction to **0, 1, 0**;

  Spread to **0.25**;

  Speed to **10**.

- Set the following for the particles:

  Particle Render Type to **Clouds (s/w)**;

  Radius to **0.2**;

  Lifespan to **Constant**.

3   Add gravity to the particles

- Select the particles, and then select **Fields** → **Gravity**.

4   Add an expression to control the rate

- Select *emitter1*.

- Open the Expression Editor and enter the following expression:

```
emitter1.rate = 200*noise (time*1000);
```

- Click the **Create** button.

This expression uses `noise` *as opposed to* `dnoise`, *since* `rate` *is a scalar quantity. You would only use* `dnoise` *if you were working with a vector quantity such as position or color. You would then multiply* `noise` *and* `time` *by* **1000** *to increase the amplitude and frequency of the* `noise` *values, since they are far too small without these multipliers.*

Particle ID

Just as each building on a street has its own address number, each particle in a particle object has its own unique numerical identity called the **particleId**. ParticleId is an integer value ranging from **0** to **n−1**. The **particleId** attribute makes it easier to control attributes of specific particles independently of other particles within the same particle object. This is especially useful for adding variation to attributes of a particle object.

The following example will control color based on particleId.

1   Create a new scene file

- Select **File** → **New Scene**.

2   Create an Omni emitter

- Select **Particles** → **Create Emitter**.

- Set **Emitter Type** to **Omni**.

- Change the render type to **Sphere**.

3   Add an rgbPP attribute to particleShape1

4   Add a runtime expression to rgbPP

- Add the following to the runtime expression for *particleShape1*:

```
if (particleId == 10)
      rgbPP = <<0,1,0>>;
```

- Click the **Create** button.

- Make sure you are in shaded mode.

- **Rewind** and **play** the animation.

  *The first particle in a particle object is always particleId **0**. Therefore, the 11th particle emitted into particleShape2 is particleId **10** and is colored green because of the conditional statement of the expression.*

- Below is another particleId example you can add as a runtime or creation expression for **rgbPP** to produce some interesting results.

```
if (particleId % 10 == 0)
        rgbPP = sphrand(1);
```

  The **%** *symbol stands for the modulus operation, which is the remainder produced when two numbers are divided. The above expression divides the particleId by 10. If the remainder of that division is **0,** then the* sphrand *function picks a random vector value between <<0,0,0>> and <<1,1,1>>. In other words, every 10th particle will get a random color assigned.*

Order of evaluation

The following is a breakdown of the order in which the dynamics system evaluates the elements of a simulation.

- First, the **acceleration** is cleared at the beginning of each frame or evaluation.

- Particle **Runtime Expressions before Dynamics** are then evaluated. The expressions can get, set, or add to the current values of the particle's attributes.

- Next, the **forces** are computed. Forces include **fields, springs,** and **goals**. These forces are added to whatever is currently in the acceleration, which includes whatever a particle expression may have put there.

- The **velocity** is computed from the **acceleration**. This also just adds to whatever value is currently in the velocity, which may have previously been set in an expression.

- The **positions** are computed from the **velocity**. Just as with acceleration and velocity, `position` is added to whatever is currently stored in `position` from expressions or forces already computed.

- Finally, the **Runtime Expressions after Dynamics** are evaluated.

The expressions do not override the dynamics. The dynamics happen after the expressions are evaluated, and their results are added together. It is possible to have expressions calculated before dynamics on a per object basis by disabling the **Expressions After Dynamics** checkbox of the *particleShape* object.

An emit expression in detail

Below is the runtime expression used for the *fireworks1* particles in the scene called *23-fireworks_03*. The short command flags have been replaced with the long flag names for additional clarity. A detailed description is provided after the expression.

```
vector $pos = fireworksShape1.position;
vector $vel = fireworksShape1.velocity;
float $antiGrav = launcher.antiGrav;
int $upperCount = launcher.showerUpper;
int $lowerCount = launcher.showerLower;
int $upperLife = 0.8 ;  //launcher.streamUpper;
int $lowerLife = 2 ;  //launcher.streamLower;

string $emitCmd = "emit -object fireworks2 ";
if ($vel.y < 0)
{//opening bracket for the if statement
    // kill this particle
    fireworksShape1.lifespanPP = 0;

    // emit a shower of new particles in this particle's place
    int $numPars = rand($lowerCount, $upperCount);

    for ($i = 1; $i <= $numPars; $i++)
    {//opening bracket for the for loop
            $emitCmd += "-position " + $pos + " ";
            vector $vrand = sphrand(60);
            $vrand = <<$vrand.x, $vrand.y + $antiGrav, $vrand.z>>;
            $emitCmd += "-attribute velocity ";
            $emitCmd += "-vectorValue " + $vrand + " ";
            float $lsrand = rand($lowerLife, $upperLife);
            $emitCmd += "-attribute lifespanPP ";
            $emitCmd += "-floatValue " + $lsrand + " ";
    }//closing bracket for the for loop

    eval($emitCmd);
}//closing bracket for the if statement
```

Step-by-step explanation

```
vector $pos = fireworksShape1.position;
vector $vel = fireworksShape1.velocity;
```

- These lines store the values for the position and velocity of a particle to be used later in the expression.

```
float $antiGrav = launcher.antiGrav;
```

- This stores the value for **antiGrav** into a **float** (decimal) variable called **$antiGrav**. This variable is one of the custom attributes added to the *launcher* object.

  *The **$antiGrav** variable will be used later in this expression to add or remove velocity in the Y-axis as particles fall. This provides a way to enhance or counteract the effect of gravity.*

```
int $upperCount = launcher.showerUpper;
```

```
int $lowerCount = launcher.showerLower;
```

- **showerLower** and **showerUpper** are two custom attributes previously added to *launcher.*

   These attributes define a range (lower and upper bound) out of which a random number will be picked later in the expression. That random number will then be used to control the number of fireworks2 particles emitted.

```
int $upperLife = launcher.streamUpper;
```

```
int $lowerLife = launcher.streamLower;
```

- **streamUpper** and **streamLower** are two more of the custom attributes previously added to *launcher.*

   These attributes define a range (lower and upper bound) out of which a random number will be chosen later in the expression. That random number will then be used to control the **Lifespan** *of fireworks2 particles emitted.*

```
string $emitCmd = "emit -object fireworks2 ";
```

- The expression is designed to piece together the **emit** command and execute it once it has been fully assembled.

- Each particle created in *fireworks2* will be the result of using the same basic syntax framework for the **emit** command. The only difference will be in the attribute values (position, velocity, etc.) for each particle.

- **$emitCmd** stores the **emit** command while it is being constructed in the expression. The text between quotes is the first piece of the **emit** command. The remaining elements will be appended in the looping structure.

```
if ($vel.y < 0)
```

- This is a conditional statement that needs the velocity on the Y-axis of the particle to become negative in order to return true and execute the portion of the expression between its brackets.

```
fireworksShape1.lifespanPP = 0;
```

- This line will kill the particle from which the explosion is happening on the next frame by setting its lifespan to **0**.

```
int $numPars = rand($lowerCount, $upperCount);
```

- Choose a random integer number from within the range of values defined by **$lowerCount** and **$upperCount** and assign that random value to **$numPars**.

- **$numPars** will be used in the next line to control the number of times the commands within a loop will be executed.

```
for ($i=1; $i<=$numPars; $i++)
```

- This is a looping structure that will execute the commands enclosed between its brackets.

- The random value assigned to `$numParts` controls the number of times those commands are executed. .

- The basic syntax of a `for` loop is:

```
for (startValue; endValue; increment)
{
        statements;
}
```

- In the expression's loop, `$i` is the *startValue* and represents how many times it has cycled through the loop to this point.

  The first time through the loop, `$i` has the startValue of 1.

  Then, `$i` is incremented by 1, by the `$i++` in the increment portion of the loop.

  Therefore, the second time through the loop `$i = 2`.

  *As long as the condition `$i <= $numParts`, which defines the endValue, is **true**, `$i` will be incremented and the loop will continue.*

  *When the endValue condition is **false**, the loop is exited and the next line in the expression is evaluated.*

```
$emitCmd += "-position " + $pos + " ";
vector $vrand = sphrand(60);
$vrand = <<$vrand.x, $vrand.y + $antiGrav, $vrand.z>>;
$emitCmd += "-attribute velocity ";
$emitCmd += "-vectorValue " + $vrand + " ";
float $lsrand = rand($lowerLife, $upperLife);
$emitCmd += "-attribute lifespanPP ";
$emitCmd += "-floatValue " + $lsrand + " ";
```

- The syntax `+=` will take what is currently stored in `$emitCmd` and append what is on the right side of the symbol to the end of `$emitCmd`.

- `$vrand` uses the `sphrand` function to select a random vector value between `<<0,0,0>>` and `<<60,60,60>>`. This provides a random value to use for velocity.

- The expression constantly appends to `$emitCmd`. Each line is setting a different attribute for the emit command.

```
eval($emitCmd);
```

- So far in the expression, you have entered and constructed the `emit` command in the `$emitCmd` variable. After the loop is finished, the `emit` command is complete and ready to be executed.

- `eval` is a command that is much like the `=` button on a calculator. It will execute the content of the `$emitCmd` variable. This will actually place particles in the correct locations and assign them the correct attribute values.

Conclusion

In this lesson, you have taken a deeper look into ways of using advanced expressions to control particles and emitters. You learned about several new MEL commands and also how to add custom per particle attributes. You also experimented with using particleId to add an extra level of control to your particles.

In the next lesson, you will learn about particle goals, which can be very useful as they provide a way to have particles move towards a specific position in space.

Goals

This lesson focuses on working with particle goal functionality. A goal is an object that particles follow or move toward. You can use goals to give trailing particles a flowing motion that is difficult to generate with other animation techniques. The trailing particles move as if connected to the goal by invisible springs.

In this lesson, you will learn the following:

- How to create goal objects
- The different goal parameters
- How to animate goal attributes
- Per particle goal attributes and their functionality

Particle goals

One of the most powerful methods for controlling particle position and motion is the use of goals. A goal is a location in space that a particle will move toward. You can create goals out of curves, lattices, polygons, NURBS surfaces, particles, or transform nodes. A particle can also have multiple goal objects.

When a goal is created, new attributes are added to the *particleShape*. In the Attribute Editor, under the **Goal Weights and Objects** section, you will see an attribute with the name of the goal. This is the **Goal Weight**. In the **Per Particle (Array) Attributes** section, you will see a **goalPP** attribute. Together with the **Goal Smoothness** attribute, these attributes control how each particle moves toward the goal.

Creating particle and non-particle goals

Creating a particle goal object involves selecting the particles, selecting the object or objects that will be used as the goal objects, and then selecting the menu item **Particles → Goal**. You have the option of using particles or geometry objects as the goal objects. In the Goal options, you can specify if you want to use the transform of the object as the goal. By default, this option is Off, and the components of the goal object will be used as the goal. When more than one object is an active goal for a particle, the resulting goal will be a combination of the goal objects' positions and the **Goal Weights** that have been set for each goal on the *particleShape*.

A goal object in the Attribute Editor

Goal weights and goalPP

Goal weights can be set for all particles at the same time or on a per particle basis. The per particle goal weight is controlled by the **goalPP** attribute. This is a dynamically added attribute. It is automatically added when a goal is created for a particle object. The **goalPP** weight is then multiplied by the **Goal Weight** of the particle object for a total particle goal weight. A **Goal Weight** of 1 means the particle will stick to its goal immediately. A **Goal Weight** of 0 means it will not move toward the goal at all.

Goal smoothness

Goal Smoothness controls how particles accelerate toward a goal object. A low **Goal Smoothness** value will make the particle take large steps toward the goal; a higher value will cause the particle to take smaller steps. The ratio between **Goal Smoothness** and **Goal Weight** controls how far the particle will travel toward the goal in each step.

Simple example

In this example, you will learn the basics of creating goal weights.

1   **New scene**
    - Open a new scene.
    - Create an **Omni** emitter with default attributes.
    - Select **Create → Polygon Primitives → Sphere**.
    - **Move** the *sphere* by **5** on the **Z-axis**.

2   **Add a goal object**
    - Select the *particles*, and then **Shift-select** the *sphere*.
    - Select **Particles → Goal**.

    A goal object was added to the particles.

3   **Play back**
    - Set the playback range to go from **1** to **1000**.
    - **Play back** the scene.

    You will notice that as the particles are being emitted, each one is attracted by the component on the sphere with the same identification number. For instance, the particleId 0 moves toward its goal, which is the vertex 0 of the sphere.

Particles with a sphere goal object

Note: *Once the same number of particles as the goal object's number of vertices have been emitted, the particles start over at the first vertex of the goal object. If a particle dies before a certain goal point, a new one will be emitted.*

4 Goal attributes

- Select the particles.
- In the Channel Box, locate the **Goal Smoothness** attribute.
- Experiment with different values for the **Goal Smoothness**, **Goal Weight[0]**, and **Goal Active[0]** attributes.

Note: *These attributes have the* **[0]** *suffix because they represent the first goal object. Particles can have multiple goal objects.*

5 Add another goal object

- Select **Create** → **Polygon Primitives** → **Torus**.
- **Move** the *torus* beside the *sphere*.
- Select the *particles*, and then **Shift-select** the *torus*.
- Select **Particles** → **Goal**.

6 Change the goal weight

- Set both **Goal Weight[0]** and **Goal Weight[1]** to **0.5**.
- **Play back** the scene.

  Since the particles are influenced by both goal objects equally, they will be exactly between the two goal objects.

- Experiment with different values for the **Goal Weight** attributes.

7 Per particle goal

A **goalPP** attribute is automatically added to the particles when a goal is created. This attribute allows you to set **Goal Weights** on a per particle basis. The total **Goal Weight** per particle is the object **Goal Weight** multiplied by the **goalPP** value. The default value of **goalPP** is **1**.

- Select the particle object and open its Attribute Editor.
- Under the **Per Particle (Array) Attributes**, **RMB** in the **goalPP** field and select **Create Ramp**.

Note: *Doing so automatically changes the* **Lifespan** *of the particles to* **Constant**.

- **RMB** in the **goalPP** field again and select **arrayMapper** → **Edit Ramp**.
- Set the bottom (birth) of the ramp to white and the top of the ramp (death) to black.
- **Play back** the scene.

The particles will first be attracted to their goal because of the white section of the ramp. They will then fly off because of the black section of the ramp.

- Set the bottom (birth) of the ramp to black and the top of the ramp (death) to white.
- **Play back** the scene.

The particles will first be emitted normally, and then be attracted to their goal object.

GoalPP used with a ramp

A ray gun

In this example, you will control particle movement with goal objects to create a ray gun effect. You will notice that using goals instead of expressions and fields has many advantages.

1 Scene file

- **Open** the file *25-goal_01.ma*.

This scene file consists of a ray gun and a target object. The rayGun_group has several objects underneath as children:

> *Gun* - This is the group that holds the *rayGun* geometry.
>
> *targetFocus* - This is the goal for the particles.
>
> *circleEmitter* - This is the particle emitter curve.
>
> *coneControl* - This is another object that is used for particle control.

2 Curve emitter

- Select the *circleEmitter* object.
- Select **Particles** → **Emit from Object** → ❑.
- In the options, set **Emitter type** to **Curve**.
- Click the **Create** button.

This emitter will serve as the particle source.

3 Add targetFocus as a goal object

- Select the particle object, and then **Shift-select** the *targetFocus* object.

- Select **Particles → Goal**.

The targetFocus object will be the main destination for the emitted particles.

 Note: *Notice that the targetFocus object is animated to rotate on itself to give an added effect.*

4 Play back to see the results

- Open the **Goal Weights and Objects** section in the Attribute Editor for the particle object.

- Experiment with these values to see their effect on the particles.

- Also experiment with the attributes that affect particle motion in general, such as:

> **Dynamics Weight**;
>
> **Conserve**;
>
> **Inherit Factor**.

Dynamics Weight *may not have much effect, but note that if it is* **0***, the simulation will not compute. This is a global control for the particle object, scaling how much the various dynamic contributors, such as fields, affect this particle object. If you want to scale the effect of all fields by a little, it is much easier to lower this value than to try to adjust all field magnitudes, especially if they are all keyframed.*

Conserve *is a very important attribute for controlling the acceleration of particles. If you find that particles are overshooting their goal object, you may be able to dampen their movement with this attribute.*

Inherit Factor *controls the amount of velocity inherited from the emitting object. This only comes into play here if the position of the gun is animated.*

The main attributes to use in the case of the ray gun are **Conserve, Goal Weight,** *and* **Goal Smoothness***.*

Ray of particles

Note: *You can hide the goal objects using the pre-made display layers.*

5 Add coneControl as another goal object

- Add *the coneControl* object as another goal object for the particles.

- Experiment with the particle **Goal Weight[0]** and **Goal Weight[1]**.

A different ray look

Tip: *To remove a goal object's influence, set the object's* **Goal Active** *to* **Off** *for the particle object.*

6 Experiment with different animation, scale, and position settings on the goal objects

- Note that if you set the **goalWeight** to **0.5** for the coneControl object and **0** for the targetFocus object, the particles line up on the CVs of the coneControl. Conversely, if you set the **goalWeight** to **0.5** for targetFocus and **0** for coneControl, the particles gather on the CVs of the *targetFocus* object.

- You can animate the goal objects around the scene if you want. Notice in this case that the *targetShape* object is already animated.

- Mixing the **Goal Weights** between the two objects produces some very interesting results.

Tip: *Do not forget to also lower* **Conserve** *and adjust* **goalSmoothness** *values.*

7 Animate the rayGun_group

 • Animate the *rayGun_group* as if it was trying to disintegrate a moving target.

8 Parent the particle object

When you animate the *rayGun_group* transform, all of the child objects, including the goal objects, will translate and rotate together. The particles will move toward their respective goals, but will react in world space.

 • **Parent** the *particle* object into the *rayGun_group*.

Note: *If you get strange offsetting of the particles after you parent them, toggle the* **Emission In World** *attribute for the particle object.*

9 Save your work

 • **Save** your work as *25-goal_02.ma*.

Goal U and goal V

In this example, you will make particles travel along a NURBS surface as though they are water droplets. You will keep track of where the particle is emitted on the surface and move it along the surface by incrementing the goal values for each particle on each frame of the animation.

In the previous example, the particles traveled directly to the CVs of the goal objects.
Now, you will learn how to move them on the surface using the **Goal U** and **Goal V** attributes in a runtime expression.

1 Scene file

 • **Open** *25-faucet_01.ma*.

2 Surface emitter

 • Select the *faucetSpout* surface.

 • Create a **Surface** emitter with a **Rate** of **15**.

3 Adjust attributes

 • Select the *emitter* and set **Need Parent UV** to **On**.

 • Select the *particles* and set **Lifespan Mode** to use **lifespanPP only**.

4 Goal object

 • Select the *particles*, and then **Shift-select** the *faucetSpout*.

 • Select **Particles → Goal**.

 • Set the new **Goal Weight** attribute to **0.9**.

- **Play back** to watch the particles build up on the surface of the faucet.

Particles building up on the faucet

5 Add per particle attributes

- Select the particles and click the **General** button in the **Add Dynamics Attributes** section of the Attribute Editor.
- Select the **Particles** tab and add **goalU**, **goalV**, **parentU**, and **parentV** attributes.

6 Add expressions

The **parentUV** attributes establish the UV coordinates where a particle is emitted from the surface. At birth, the goal and the parent should be the same, so the particle has a goal on the surface instead of at the CV of the surface.

- **RMB** in one of the new attributes' fields and select **Creation Expression**.
- Enter the following creation expression:

```
goalU = parentU;
goalV = parentV;
```

- Click the **Create** button.

To get the particles to move along the U direction of the surface, you will change the **goalU** attribute on each frame.

- Select the **Runtime Before Dynamics** option in the Expression Editor.
- Enter the following runtime expression:

```
goalU = goalU - 0.1;
```

- Click the **Create** button.

7 **Test the scene**

- **Play back** the simulation to see the effect of the expressions.

   The particles are emitted on the surface and move toward the tip of the faucet.

8 **Refine region of emission and make particles drip off**

The expressions below have some new lines added to them, allowing particles to exist only on a specific part of the faucet. The runtime expression has been modified to have the **Goal Weight** for each particle shut off when the particle reaches a certain U location on the surface.

- Modify the existing creation expression with the following:

```
goalU = parentU;
goalV = parentV;
if ((parentU > 10) || (parentU < 2))
        lifespanPP = 0;
else
        lifespanPP = 5;
```

Note: *The double pipe* || *stands for the* **Or** *operator. In this case, if the particle was emitted between U values of* **10** *and* **2**, *which is the lower part of the faucet, it will stay alive for* **5** *seconds. Otherwise, it will be killed.*

- Click the **Edit** button.

- **Modify** the existing runtime expression so that it looks as follows:

```
goalU = goalU - 0.1;
if (goalU <= 2)
        goalPP = 0;
else
        goalPP = 1;
```

- Click the **Edit** button.

9 **Add gravity to the particles**

Adding gravity gives the particles downward motion after the **Goal Weight** has been set to **0**.

- Select the particles.

- Select **Fields** → **Gravity**.

10 **Play back**

- **Play back** the animation.

- Tweak the look of the particles as wanted.

Sphere particles with increasing radiusPP and a ramp1

11 Save your work

  • **Save** the scene as *25-faucet_02.ma*.

Tips and Traps

  • Errors might occur if **Dynamic Weight** is set to **0**, so set it above 0 when using goals.

    *Dynamics weight allows you to scale the effects of dynamics (fields, collisions, springs, goals). A value of **0** causes fields, collisions, springs, and goals connected to the particle object to have no effect. A value of **1** provides the full effect. A value less than **1** sets a proportional effect. For example, **0.6** scales the effect to 60% of full strength.*

Note: *Expressions are unaffected by* **Dynamics Weight**.

  • The **Min Max Range U** and **Min Max Range V** attributes in the Attribute Editor of a NURBS surface make it easy to determine the UV range of a surface. This is useful when working with **goalUV** expressions. Also, the feedback line will show you this information to select isoparms on the surface.

  • In the faucet example, the runtime expression is what moves each particle along the surface. Incrementing the goal on each frame of the simulation is what moves it along the U or V direction. This expression also determines when the **goalPP** value will be set to **0**. This is what causes the particle to drip off the end of the faucet. You may want to add a collision object beneath the faucet that makes the particles die on contact rather than setting their lifespan.

- When setting a value using **goalPP**, it is good practice to set the **Goal Weight** slider to **1** when creating the goal. This is important because the **goalPP** attribute always gets multiplied by that number. Therefore, if the goal is created with a value of **0** and **goalPP** is set to **0.5**, the resulting **goalPP** value will be **0**, not **0.5** as would normally be expected.

- By default, the first particle will go to the first CV or vertex of a goal object. This mapping cannot be changed.

- People commonly ask if there is an *easy* way to apply a black-and-white ramp to the surface and have the grayscale of the ramp control the particle **Goal Weight**. Currently, this involves quite a convoluted workaround to accomplish, so the short answer is no. Applying a ramp to **goalPP** will change the **goalPP** weight of all particles in that particle object with respect to the particle's lifespan, not the surface UV coordinates. This does not mean that it is not doable; it just is not a quick and simple solution.

Normalize goalPP

The file *25-goalNormalized.ma* is a simple example of a more advanced use of goal weights. It shows how to use an expression to check to see if a given particle has reached its goal. The particles are colored using the values of a ramp. The particle's color is at the bottom of the RGB ramp at birth and at the top of the ramp once it reaches the goal.

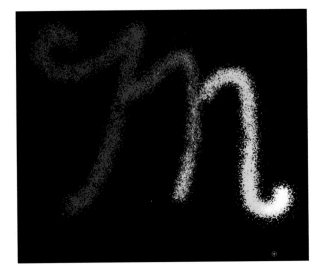

their goal

Tip: *Make sure to display this example scene in shaded mode.*

Goal from point A to point B

The file called *25-goalAtoB.ma* shows an interesting application of **goalPP**, particle expressions, and blobby surface rendering. Here is how the effect was achieved:

- First, two polygonal letters were created with the **Text Tool**.

- A surface emitter was added to each letter.

- The scene was played until the A surface filled up with particles.

- The **Max Count** of the B particles was set to the **Count** of the A particles.

- B particles were made to be a goal for A particles.

- A locator was animated in the scene to check the distance between the B particles and the moving locator. This distance check was done using a runtime expression. As the locator moves further from the B particles, the **goalPP** value of the A particles is set to **1**. The **goalPP** value is multiplied by the number at which the original goal was created. The **goalPP** is set to **0** until the locator gets closer to the A particles; then they transition over to a setting of **1**, which makes the particles jump to stick to B particles.

- The particles were set to be blobby surfaces, and an expression was added to control the radius size.

Particles moving from point A to point B

Conclusion

Goals are an intuitive, fun, and powerful method of particle manipulation. They can be used to solve particle movement problems, a feat shared only by complex expressions. Mixing goals with fields and other animation is often the best way to achieve good control over your particles.

In the next lesson, you will learn about particle instancing.

Particle Instancing

This lesson focuses on particle instancing, a tool for placing geometry at the
location of individual particles.

In this lesson, you will learn the following:

- How to make geometry match particle movement
- How to add animated geometry to particles
- How to use cycles to instance a sequence of geometry
- How particle instancing uses custom attributes
- How to add randomness to particle instanced geometry
- Important qualities of hardware sprites
- How to use the velocity as an aim vector

Instancing

An instance is similar to a duplicated object. The primary difference is that an instance contains no actual surface information, but is just a redrawn version of an original object. That original object acts like a master to all of its instances. The instance takes on all shading and surface characteristics of the original and will update as the original is updated. Since instances contain less information than duplicates, they can be handled and redrawn faster.

Particle instancing

Particle instancing is the process of using the position and behavior of particles to control the position and behavior of instanced geometry. For example, you could model a bee, animate it flapping its wings, and then use particle instancing to apply that flapping bee to a number of particles. By replacing each particle with a piece of instanced geometry, you could then easily create a scene with swarming bees at a decent playback rate.

Although complex results can be obtained using particle instancing, it is important not to interpret it as a full-featured behavioral animation system or flocking system. For example, you could build a fish swimming, and then instance that swimming fish onto particles to simulate a school of fish. However, each fish would just follow its own particle; there are no behavioral relationships established between the individual instanced elements.

The instancer node

The *instancer* node can be considered the *engine* to perform particle instancing. Although use of the instancer node is not limited to particles, the most common inputs it receives are from particles and from the geometry that will be instanced to those particles.

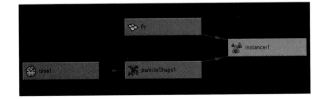

Inputs to the instancer node in the Dependency Graph

Instancing example

1   Scene file

- **Open** the scene file called *26-dragonFly_01.ma*.

2 Animate the wings flapping

- Select *lWing*, and then **Shift-select** *rWing*.
- Use **Shift+e** to keyframe the rotation attributes of both wings as follows:

  Frame **1**, wings down;

  Frame **2**, wings straight;

  Frame **3**, wings up;

  Frame **4**, wings straight;

  Frame **5**, wings down.

Tip: *You can **MMB+drag** in the timeline to advance frames without scrubbing through the animation. This makes it easier to set-up one position at two different frame numbers for cycling. You can also use the **RMB** menu in the timeline to **Cut**, **Copy**, and **Paste** keyframes.*

The dragonfly with animated wings

- With both wings selected, open the Graph Editor and set both **Pre-Infinity** and **Post-Infinity** to **Cycle**.

  Doing so will make the dragonfly flap its wings repeatedly.

485

3 Create a grid of particles

- Select **Particle → Particle Tool → ❏**.
- In the options, set the following:

    Particle Name to *flyParticles*;

    Conserve to **1**;

    Create Particle Grid to **On**;

    Particle Spacing to **12**;

    Placement to **With Text Fields**;

    Minimum Corner to **-25, 0, –25**;

    Maximum Corner to **25, 0, 25**.

- Click anywhere in the viewport and press **Enter**.

    *Setting particle spacing to **12** allows enough space between each particle so that the instanced dragonflies do not intersect.*

4 Randomly offset the particles

- Add the following creation expression to the position attribute of **flyParticles**:

```
float $randY = rand (-3,3);
float $randXZ = rand (-1,1);
vector $offset = <<$randXZ, $randY, $randXZ>>;
position = position + $offset;
```

- Click **Create**.
- Click the **Rewind** button to offset the particles.

Tip: *You can repeatedly execute the creation expresion and offset the particles by clicking the Rewind button several times.*

- With the *flyParticles* selected, select **Solvers → Initial State → Set for Selected**.
- **Delete** the creation expression created earlier, and close the Expression Editor.

Initial state of the offset particles

5 Instance the dragonfly to the particles

- In the Outliner, select *dragonFly* group.

- Select **Particles** → **Instancer (Replacement)** → ❑.

- In the options, set **Particle Instancer Name** to *flyInstanced.*

- Make sure that *dragonFly* is the only object in the **Instanced Objects** list.

```
┌──────────────────────────────────────────────────┐
│ 🔳 Particle Instancer Options              _ □ ×  │
│ Edit  Help                                         │
│         Particle Instancer Name │flyInstanced│  ▲  │
│                Rotation Units │ Degrees  ▼ │       │
│                Rotation Order │ XYZ  ▼ │           │
│                Level Of Detail │ Geometry    ▼ │   │
│                      Cycle │ None     ▼ │          │
│              Cycle Step Units │ Frames    ▼ │      │
│               Cycle Step Size │1.0      │──┘───    │
│ ─────────────────────────────────────────────     │
│ Instanced Objects                                  │
│ ┌──────────────────────────────────────────┐      │
│ │ 0: dragonFly                               │      │
│ │                                            │      │
│ │                                            │      │
│ │                                            │      │
│ └──────────────────────────────────────────┘      │
│ │ Add Selection │ Remove Items │ Move Up │ Move Down │
│          Allow All Data Types  □                   │
│   Particle Object To Instance │ flyParticlesShape ▼ │
│ General Options                                     │
│              Position │ worldPosition    ▼ │     ▼ │
│ │   Create   │ │   Apply   │ │   Close   │          │
└──────────────────────────────────────────────────┘
```

Particle instancer options

- Click the **Create** button.

  This creates an instancer node in the scene and creates an instanced version of the dragonfly for each particle.

The instanced dragonflies

6 Hide the original dragonfly

Since the original object is still in the scene and there is one instance per particle, you will need to hide the original dragonfly.

- Select the *dragonFly* group.
- Press **Ctrl+h** to hide it.

7 Add a vector attribute to the particles

Now, you will add some variation to the size of each of the instanced dragonflies. Since the radiusPP of the particles does not affect the size of the instanced geometry, you will need a custom attribute.

- Open the Attribute Editor for *flyParticlesShape*.
- Click the **General** button in the **Add Dynamic Attributes** section.
- Set the following under the **New** tab:

  Attribute Name to *flyScaler*;

  Data Type to **Vector**;

  Attribute Type to **Per Particle (Array)**;

  Add Initial State Attribute to **On**.

- Click the **OK** button.

8 Assign values to the attribute with a creation expression

- **RMB** in the new **flyScaler** field in the Attribute Editor, and select **Creation Expression**.
- Add the following to the Expression Editor:

```
$rand = rand (0.4, 1.5);
flyScaler = <<$rand, $rand, $rand>>;
```

  *This expression picks a random number greater than **0.4** and less than **1.5** for each particle and assigns that value to the **flyScaler** attribute.*

- Click **Create** and close the Expression Editor.

9 Set the instancer to use flyScaler

- Select *flyParticlesShape*, and then expand the **Instancer (Geometry Replacement)** tab in the Attribute Editor.
- Under **General Options**, set **Scale** to **flyScaler**.

  Any attribute added to the particle object can be fed into the various control attributes of the instancer node. In this case, you are computing a value with an expression, storing that value in the flyScaler attribute, and then assigning flyScaler to the scale option in the instancer node. The ability to use any attribute value for any of the connections to the instancer is what gives the instancer its flexible control, since you are able to control the contents of those attributes with expressions.

Instanced dragonflies with random positioning and scaling

10 Comment out the expression and set the initial state

Since the value of *flyScaler* changes in a creation expression, the scale of the bugs will change every time you click the **Rewind** button. Once you are satisfied with the scale of the bugs, you can delete or comment out the expression and set the initial state of the particles. Use two forward slashes (//) at the beginning of each line to comment out the expression.

> **Note:** *Commenting lines of code allows you to easily reuse the lines without retyping them.*

> **Tip:** *If the bugs disappear upon rewind, that means that the flyScaler attribute resets to o and that you probably forgot to set the initial state for the particles.*

- Select the particle shape and open the Expression Editor.
- **Comment** out the creation expression by placing // in front of the expression lines.

  OR
- **Delete** the expression.

> **Tip:** *It is a good idea to save your file before setting the initial state.*

- Select **Solvers** → **Initial State** → **Set for Selected**.

11 **Apply a uniform field to the particles**

- Select the particle object, and then select **Fields** → **Uniform**.

- Use the following settings for the uniform field:

    Direction X, Y, Z to **1, 0, 0**, respectively;

    Magnitude to **15**;

    Attenuation to **0**.

- **Play back** the animation.

    The flies are now moving forward and flapping their wings according to the original dragonfly. Because the instances are animated in the same way as the original object, they flap their wings all together. In the next exercise, you will learn how to create different animation cycles for the instances.

Tip: *If you want each particle to move differently, you could apply an acceleration runtime expression to the particles instead of using a uniform field.*

12 **Save your work**

- **Save** your scene as *26-dragonFly_02.ma*.

Instance cycling

One way of having different animation cycles for all the instances is to create duplicates of the different poses of the original object, and then tell the instances to use different sequences for the animation cycle.

In this example, you will see how to randomly animate a flock of butterflies.

1 **Scene file**

- **Open** the scene file called *26-butterfly_01.ma*.

    This scene contains one butterfly with no animation. You will create an animated cycle using the instancer and several duplicates of the butterfly.

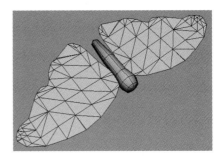

A simple butterfly

Note: *Since there could possibly be many butterfly instances in the scene, the butterfly used here is quite low resolution.*

2   Set-up a cycle using duplicated butterflies

- Select the *butterfly* group from the Outliner.
- **Duplicate** the butterfly eight times.
- **Move** each butterfly on the **Y-axis**.

Note: *Do not select the butterfly geometry when translating. You must move the butterfly's top group. If you move the geometry, it causes the items to be offset from the base object's coordinate system and will cause offsetting from the particles during instancing.*

- **Hide** the original *butterfly*.
- **Rotate** the wings of each duplicate as shown here:

Tip: *You can rotate both wings simultaneously. They have been set-up to have inverse rotations.*

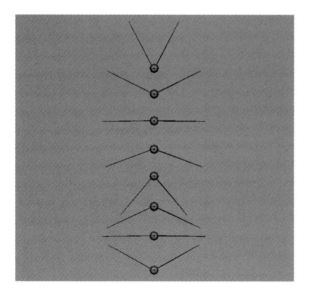

Eight butterflies producing a complete flap cycle

- Make sure the duplicated butterfly's groups are named from *butterfly1* through *butterfly8*.

Tip: *It is important to have the groups correctly named in sequence. That will make it easier to place the different positions in order.*

3 Create particles in the scene

- Use the **Particle Tool** to create a cloud of **20** particles within a radius of **40**.
- **Rename** the particles *butterflyParticles*.

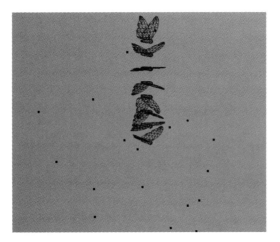

Cloud of twenty particles to be used for butterfly instancing

4 Set basic instancer options

- Use the Outliner to select *butterfly1* through *butterfly8* in order.

  The order in which they are selected will determine the cycling order used by the instancer.

- Select **Particles** → **Instancer (Replacement)** → ❑.
- Set the following options:

  Particle Instancer Name to *butterflyInstancer*;

  Cycle to **Sequential**;

  Cycle Step Size to 1.

- Click the **Create** button.

  *The list of objects the instancer will use is shown in the **Instanced Objects** list. The number beside the object is called the **Object Index**. The first object in the list is always index **0**. The instancer uses this index value to determine which object in the sequence of butterflies to display at a given point in time.*

  *A cycle setting of **Sequential** causes the instancer to cycle through the object indices in sequence (rather than not using any cycling at all). A **Cycle Step Size** of 1 causes the instancer to display each object index for **1** frame before changing to the next item in the list.*

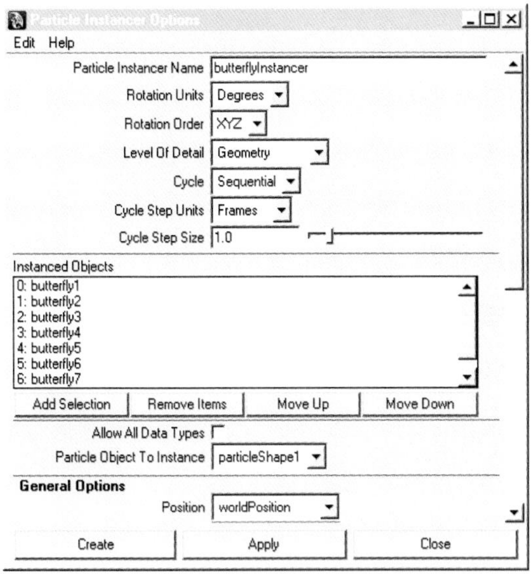
Particle Instancer Options
Edit Help
Particle Instancer Name butterflyInstancer
Rotation Units Degrees
Rotation Order XYZ
Level Of Detail Geometry
Cycle Sequential
Cycle Step Units Frames
Cycle Step Size 1.0
Instanced Objects
0: butterfly1
1: butterfly2
2: butterfly3
3: butterfly4
4: butterfly5
5: butterfly6
6: butterfly7
Add Selection
Remove Items
Move Up
Move Down
Allow All Data Types
Particle Object To Instance particleShape1
General Options
Position worldPosition
Create
Apply
Close

The list of instanced objects and their object indices in the instancer options

5 Make a test run

- **Hide** *position1* through *position8*.
- **Play back** the scene to view the instanced objects cycling.

  All butterflies cycle through the eight positions in exactly the same fashion.

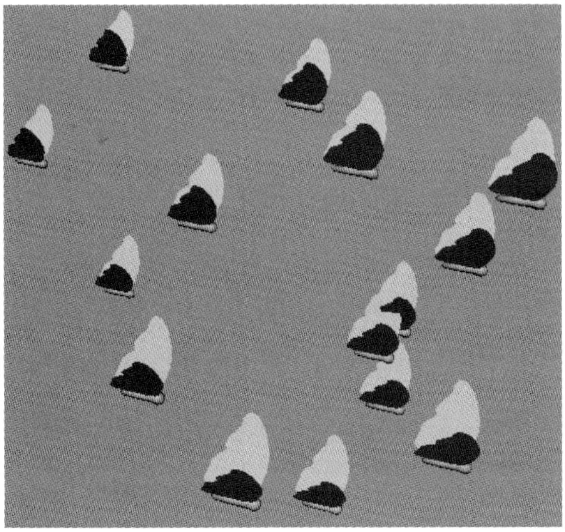

Instanced butterflies all with the same initial object index

6 Add a custom attribute to control cycling on a per particle basis

Recall that the **Cycle Step Size** determines how long the instancer will display each object index before switching to the next item in the list. Since the particleId is unique for each particle, it can be used to control this duration on a per particle basis. This is accomplished by multiplying the particleId by the age and storing the result in a custom attribute that, in turn, is fed into the **Age** control of the instancer's cycling options as explained below.

- Select *butterflyParticles* and open the Attribute Editor.
- Click the **General** button in the **Add Dynamic Attribute** section.
- Set the following options:

     Attribute Name to *customAge*;

     Data Type to **Float**;

     Attribute Type to **Per Particle (Array)**;

     Add Initial State Attribute to **On**.

- Click the **OK** button.

7 Assign values to customAge with a runtime expression

Now that you have added the custom age attribute, you need to assign values to it for each particle. Because age changes over time, you will use a runtime expression instead of a creation expression.

- **RMB** on the *customAge* field and select **Runtime Expression Before Dynamics**.
- Enter the following runtime expression:

```
if (particleId == 0)
        customAge = age;
else if (particleId == 1)
        customAge = age * 0.5;
else if ((particleId % 2 == 0) && (particleId % 3 == 0))
        customAge = age * 0.25 * particleId / 4;

else if (particleId % 2 == 0)
        customAge = age * 0.4 * particleId / 4;
else if (particleId % 3 == 0)
        customAge = age * 0.35 *particleId / 4;
else
        customAge = age * 0.2 * (particleId) / 4;
```

This expression assigns a different value to customAge based on multiplication of the particleId. Since these particles are not being emitted, they have the same age. To get around this, age is multiplied by a decimal value arbitrarily selected to provide variation in age for each particle. This value is then multiplied by the particleId, which is, again, another unique value. The particleId is divided by four to keep the values small. If this division was not done, the values in customAge would grow rapidly and cause the cycle to occur too quickly.

8 Set particle render type to numeric

To get a better idea of which portion of the expression is controlling which particles, you can use the **Numeric** render type.

- Select *butterflyParticles*.

- Set **Particle Render Type** to Numeric.

*By default, the **Numeric Render Type** displays the particleId attribute for each particle. This makes it easier for you to see which particle will be affected by which portion of the expression. For example, particleId 12 is evenly divisible by both 3 and 2, so it will therefore be set by the following portion of the expression:*

```
else if ((particleId % 2 == 0) && (particleId % 3 == 0))
        customAge = age * 0.25 * particleId / 4;
```

> **Tip:** *You can change the attribute displayed by the **Numeric Render Type** by clicking the **Current Render Type** button in the Attribute Editor, and then typing in the name of the attribute to display in the field provided. Attributes such as **rgbPP** and **Mass** are other useful attributes to view in numeric mode.*

9 Set the cycle options

- In the **Instancer (Geometry Replacement)** section of the *butterflyParticles* Attribute Editor, choose **customAge** from the **Age** pull-down menu in the **Cycle Options** sub-section.

If you play back the simulation, you should now see the butterflies update with various cycle speeds.

10 Add a float array attribute to control the starting object index

Currently, all butterflies begin their sequence from object index 0 (position1). They all cycle through the instanced object list starting from *position1* and ending at *position8*, and then repeating.

You can change the sequence an object index starts on by setting the **CycleStartObject** attribute in the instancer. In this case, you will create another custom attribute, called *startPick,* to control **CycleStartObject** on a per particle basis, similar to the way you set-up *customAge*.

- Using what you have learned so far, add a custom particle **Float Array** attribute with initial state to *butterflyParticles* and name it *startPick*.

- Add the following creation expression to *startPick*:

```
if (particleId == 0)
        startPick = 0;
else if (particleId == 1)
        startPick = 1;
else if ((particleId % 2 == 0) && (particleId % 3 == 0))
        startPick = 2;
else if (particleId % 2 == 0)
        startPick = 3;
else if (particleId % 3 == 0)
        startPick = 4;
else
        startPick = 5;
```

Note: *The value chosen for* `startPick` *in this expression will determine which butterfly the instancer chooses to begin the cycle on.*

11 Set the cycle options

- In the **Instancer (Geometry Replacement)** section of the *butterflyParticles* Attribute Editor, choose **startPick** from the **cycleStartObject** pull-down menu in the **Cycle Options** sub-section.

The butterflies' intial frame is now more random.

Tip: *The above method shows you a certain approach to selecting a starting object. A similar result can be achieved by setting* **cycleStartObject** *to* **particleId**.

12 Add uniform and radial fields to move the particles

- Add fields or expressions to control the motion of the individual particles as desired.

13 Play back

- **Hide** the particle object.
- **Play back** the simulation.

496

Butterflies animated with different cycle starts and speeds

Planning, optimizing, and rendering considerations

You have used the instancer with an animated object and a cycled sequence of snapshots. There are advantages and disadvantages to both methods. Using an animated object allows you to use 2D and 3D motion blur when rendering. Motion blur is not available when cycling through a sequence of instanced objects. Therefore, it is best to consider rendering requirements when setting up shots requiring instancing.

It is also important to keep your geometry as simple as possible. Making your surfaces single-sided and keeping the number of NURBS patches or the poly count low will make a big difference.

One advantage to using a sequence of snapshots is that you have control over the duration of each snapshot and also the starting point of the cycle.

Note: *You can also instance Paint Effects' strokes to particles.*

Hardware sprites

The **Sprite** render type is used for displaying 2D file texture images on particles.

The scene file *26_snowHW.ma* illustrates a simple application of hardware sprites. Open this file and play back the animation to see its effect.

The scene contains a phongE shading group with a file texture of a snowflake that has an alpha channel assigned to the particles. If you tumble the camera, the sprite images will always aim at the camera. This is a built-in feature of hardware sprites. You cannot make the hardware sprite type aim at some other object or direction.

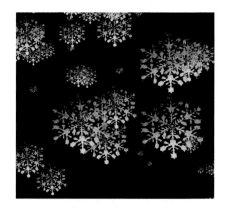

Hardware sprites

Software sprites using the instancer

The hardware sprite render particle type is only available for rendering using the hardware renderer or the Hardware Render Buffer. Therefore, you cannot render 3D motion blur, reflections, refractions, or shadows with hardware particles as you can when using software rendering. The *swSprite.mel* script, found in the *MEL* directory of the current project in the *support_files,* uses a method for creating software-renderable particle sprites via the instancer. This will allow you to take advantage of these important software rendering features while maintaining the core functionality that the hardware sprite render type provides. The scene *26_snowHW.ma* illustrates the usage of this script.

Particle instancing tips and traps

- In this lesson's first exercise, dragonflies may disappear when the scene is rewound. This happens if the initial state is not set after the expression has evaluated once, or if you have not set the scale pop-up menu to *flyScaler* in the instancer section of the *particleShape* node.

  Make sure the initial state is set immediately after the creation expression is evaluated once. If you cannot get your dragonflies to come back, delete the creation expression and try entering a runtime expression like this:

  ```
  bugScaler0=<<1,1,1>>;
  ```

  Play the animation back to see if the dragonflies reappear, but do not rewind. If they do appear, set the initial state and delete the runtime expression. Now you are back where you started before the problem arose and you can add the creation expression back in. Click **Edit** *and then* **Delete** *for the creation expression and set the initial state one final time.*

> **Tip:** *Restarting the example from scratch may be easier.*

- If nothing happens after expressions are entered, it is usually because you forgot to hook up the custom attribute from within the instancing section's pop-up menus in the Attribute Editor.

- If the custom attribute you created does not show up in the pop-up menus, you probably created the custom attribute as a different data type than the pop-up menu expects. Enabling **Allow All Data Types** refreshes the menus and allows the attribute to show up. The better solution is to recreate the attribute as the correct data type: float for object index numbers and vector for nearly all other instancer attributes.

- A very quick way to make each particle start on a different cycle index is to set *CycleStartObject* to *particleId*. This is faster than typing in an expression and gets the same basic results. It is still good, however, to understand the expression used in the butterfly example.

- The file *26-arrows.ma* is good for illustrating how to make an object aim in the direction of its velocity.

  To do so, you simply need to set the **AimDirection** *of the instancer to* **Velocity** *on the particle object.*

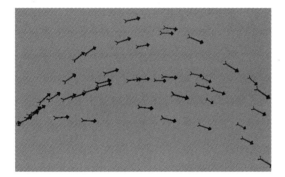

Arrows aiming at velocity

- If the snowflake texture does not appear with the example files, reassign the file *snowflake_wAlpha.rgb* found in the *sourceImages* directory of the **Color** attribute of the phongE material shader.

- The *swSprites.mel* script does the camera set-up, instancing, and shader set-up automatically. It is normal for you to have to rewind and play back to get the sprites to align properly. It is also normal for the sprites not to align on the first frame until the expressions are evaluated.

- To play different sequences of images on software sprites, you need to animate the file texture for the plane. In addition, each poly plane needs to be a duplicate rather than an instance, so the current setup would not suffice.

- People often ask if there is a way to fade instanced objects out based on the **opacityPP** of the master particle. This is a limitation of particle instancing, since there is currently no direct connection between shading attributes of the particles and the objects that are instanced to them.

- The different aim attributes on the particle instancer can be confusing. Here's a quick breakdown:

  AimPosition

  Where the polygon plane will point.

  AimAxis

  Determines which axis of the polygon plane will point at the AimPosition.

  AimUpAxis

  Determines which axis of the polygon plane is considered the up axis.

  AimWorldUp

  Determines which axis of the polygon plane is considered up in world space.

- **Particles** → **Sprite Wizard** is a script that automatically sets up animation of file textures on sprite particles.

Sprite Wizard

- One trick for keeping particles away from each other is to use each particle as an individual radial field. To do so, do the following:

  With nothing selected, create a radial field with **Attenuation** *of* **0** *and* **Volume Shape** *set to* **none**.

  Select the particles, then the field, and choose **Fields** → **Use Selected as Source of Field**.

  Connect the radial field up to the particles by selecting **Fields** → **Affect Selected Object(s)**.

  Select the radial field and enable **Apply per vertex** *in the Attribute Editor under the* **Special Effects** *section.*

  Now each particle is a small repelling field. You do not have control over the individual field magnitudes for each particle, but this is at least a start in keeping all the particles pushing away from each other. You can experiment with different **Max Distance**, **Attenuation**, *and* **Magnitude** *settings for better results.*

Conclusion

Particle instancing is a built-in way to move geometry around using particles. Although the geometry will not detect the other instanced geometry, you can still come up with some pretty good effects using particle instancing. The fact that each parameter of the instancer is open to MEL scripting is a big benefit for customizing the parameters you use for your instanced animations.

In the next project, you will learn about rendering and compositing particles.

Project 07

In Project Seven, you will learn about the various particle rendering types, particle caching, and useful particle rendering attributes. You will also get a glimpse of how to render a complex scene with layers on a composite workflow.

By the end of this project, you should feel comfortable rendering both software and hardware particles and compositing rendered layers together.

Rendering Particles

This lesson covers rendering types and techniques used for particles.

In this lesson you will learn the following:

- Hardware particle rendering types;
- Software particle rendering types;
- Particle caching in memory and on disk;
- How to use the Particle Sampler Info utility node;
- Particle cloud rendering.

Particle render types

Autodesk® Maya® provides two types of rendering for particles: hardware and software.

Hardware rendering uses the graphics buffer and graphics memory of your computer to draw the image to the display and then take a snapshot of this image. This snapshot is then written to a file as a rendered image. This technique of using the hardware rendering capabilities of your computer has the advantage of being very fast, but also the limitation of few rendering features, such as shadows, reflections, or post-process effects like glow. Often particles are rendered using the Hardware Renderer only for the positional and matte or alpha information. The actual look of the particle effect is then obtained by adding color, shadows, reflections, or environment lighting in the compositing stage of production. Again, this pipeline of image creation is used when speed and the flexibility for aesthetic change of mind are the top priorities.

The hardware render types are:

Numeric;

Points;

Spheres;

Sprites;

Streak.

As a subset of these types, there are also two versions of Point and Streak that utilize multi-pass rendering. These are the MultiPoint and MultiStreak particle render types. It is probably safe to say that these two are the most commonly used hardware render types for most of the effects you create. Sprite comes in at a close second. As you saw in the preceding lesson, on particle instancing, the Sprite render type is used for displaying 2D images on particles. The Sphere and Point render type are more commonly used just to visualize where the particles are in space, while the Numeric type is used especially to debug particle values. The Point render type is the simplest and the one that the display draws the quickest.

The software render types are:

Blobby Surface;

Cloud;

Tube.

These render types allow for various combinations of surface and volumetric shading techniques, which will be discussed in an upcoming section of this lesson. Their shaders are constructed from the similar shading nodes that are applied to geometry and lights.

When you software render, any hardware-render -type particles are skipped. When you hardware render, software-render-type particles are rendered as their respective hardware display appearance and filled circles.

Hardware rendering

Maya has two hardware renderers: the Hardware Render Buffer and the Hardware Renderer.

The Hardware Render Buffer

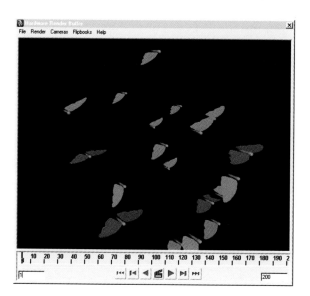

Hardware Render Buffer

The Hardware Render Buffer can be found under **Window → Rendering Editors → Hardware Render Buffer**. This window will assume the size of the selected resolution format. It is recommended that you make sure there are no windows beneath or in front of this window when you are rendering to it. It is also suggested to use an absolute black desktop background if you are going to be doing a lot of hardware rendering. Also, shut off your screen saver. The Hardware Render Buffer simply snapshots what is on the screen; therefore, you should avoid moving the window around during rendering.

Hardware rendering can also be used as a quick animation test. Geometry can be hardware-rendered with lighting and textures, but without shadows or advanced lighting effects. There are also many options that allow geometry matting to be generated to aid in the compositing process.

The Hardware Renderer

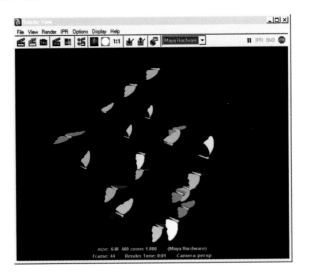

Hardware Renderer

The Hardware Renderer is one of the renderers listed in the Render Settings under **Render Using**. While it doesn't provide all the same options as the Hardware Render Buffer, it has significant advantages. Most importantly, it can render depth-mapped shadows for hardware particle types. The exception is the Sprite render type, because sprites cannot cast shadows. A workaround for rendering sprites that cast shadows is to use instanced geometry.

Starting and stopping the Hardware Render Buffer

You invoke a render in the Hardware Render Buffer using **Render → Render Sequence** or by clicking the test button in the bottom center of the window to test a single frame. You can cancel a render by pressing and holding the **Esc** key, or by clicking the mouse inside the Hardware Render Buffer window.

Multipass hardware rendering

Multipass hardware rendering creates a softer rendered look for your particles. It can also anti-alias the geometry that is being hardware rendered. Multipass rendering requires you to use a multipass render type as your particle render type. As mentioned earlier in this lesson, you have the choice of MultiPoint or MultiStreak.

For each of these render types, you have several particle attributes that control the multi-pass effect:

Multi Count

Controls the number of added and offset pseudo-particles to distribute around the original particle.

Multi Radius

Controls how far away from the actual particle the additional pseudo-particles are drawn.

Hardware render attributes:

Render Passes

Controls the number of times a render is averaged.

Edge Smoothing

Controls anti-aliasing of geometry.

Motion Blur

Controls samples of time taken to blur particles and geometry. The values and approach used differ from Maya software motion blur.

Motion blur and caching

Motion blur allows you to average the look of particles over time. To use motion blur, it is strongly recommended that you cache your particle motion. Otherwise, you will often get strange and unpredictable results.

Cigarette smoke

In this example, you will create and render particles for cigarette smoke using hardware rendering techniques. The file contains props and dynamic elements ready for particle rendering. The animation of this setup is interesting as well. The main trick to the particle movement is two turbulence fields that have their phase animated with a simple `sin` expression. The only difference between the two fields is that the second turbulence field has a slightly lower frequency. These two fields work to reinforce each other while moving the particles. Rotation is obtained with a vortex field.

1 Scene file

- **Open** the scene file called *27-cig_01.ma.*

  This scene file consists of a cigarette, an ashtray, and several fields. There are two emitters parented under the cigarette group. You will use these emitters as your source for the particle smoke.

- **Play** the scene to get an idea of how the particles are moving.

Cigarette smoke

2 Open the hardware render window

- Select **Window** → **Rendering Editors** → **Hardware Render Buffer...**

This will open the Hardware Render Buffer.

Note: *This window cannot be minimized or sized.*

3 Set hardware render attributes

- In the Hardware Render Buffer window, select **Render** → **Attributes...**
- Set the following in the **Image Output Files** section:

    Filename to *cigSmokeTest*;

    Extension to **name.0001.ext**;

    Start Frame to **1**;

    End Frame to **100**;

    By Frame to **1**;

    Alpha Source to **Luminance**.

- Set the following in the **Render Modes** section:

    Lighting Mode to **All Lights;**

    Draw Style to **Smooth Shaded;**

    Texturing to **On;**

    Line Smoothing to **On**.

*The **Line Smoothing** option helps smooth out the particle tails when rendering Streak or multiStreak particles.*

Note: *Hardware rendering has a maximum limit of eight lights.*

- Set the following in the **Multi-Pass Render Options** section:

    Multi Pass Rendering to **On**;

    Render Passes to **9**;

    Anti-alias Polygons to **On**;

    Edge Smoothing to **1.0**;

    Motion Blur to **4.0**.

- Following are descriptions of additional options:

    Full Image Resolution

    Turn this **On** if you are rendering at a resolution larger than screen resolution. An example would be rendering large images for film. The render will split the image into tiles, render each tile, and then sew the tiles together into one image.

    Geometry Mask

    If this is turned **On**, you will only get particles in the final rendered image; no geometry is included. This can be useful when rendering a particle pass that will be composited over a separately rendered geometry pass.

    When this is on, the geometry will not be rendered into the hardware rendered image. However, the geometry will mask the appropriate particles so that layering occurs correctly during the compositing stage.

    You should be aware that geometry masking is not perfect. For example, if you are layering your particles over a software-rendered geometry pass, and that geometry pass has software motion blur, it is unlikely that the geometry masking of the hardware particle pass will match the motion blurred alpha channel from the software render. This is because the Software Renderer is much more accurate than the Hardware Renderer. Changing your object's tessellation will not necessarily increase the quality of the geometry masking. Also, geometry masking is not anti-aliased. Often you will need to use matte creation or modification tools in your compositing software to adjust how the particles will layer over the geometry.

    Display Shadows

    Some graphics cards support hardware shadowing. If your graphics card supports this feature, enabling this option will allow you to render shadows into your hardware-rendered images.

4 Test render

- **Play back** the simulation until you are happy with the particle position.

- In the Hardware Render Buffer, select **Render → Test Render**.

    This will render a single frame of the particles at the current time slider position.

> **Tip:** *While rendering in the Hardware Render Buffer, if the rendered image doesn't stay in the view, make sure to clear the selection before rendering.*

5 Set Particle Render Type to MultiStreak

This render type will provide streaking and multiple jittered pseudo-particles.

- Select the *particleShape*.
- Change the **Particle Render Type** to **MultiStreak**.
- In the Attribute Editor, click the **Add Attributes For Current Render Type** button.
- Set the following:

  Depth Sort to **On**;

  Color Accum to **On**;

  Line Width to **1**;

  Multi Count to **5**;

  Multi Radius to **0.1**;

  Normal Dir to **2**;

  Tail Fade to **–0.5**;

  Tail Size to **0.75**;

  Use Lighting to **On**.

- **Render** the scene in the Hardware Render Buffer to see the difference.

MultiStreak cigarette smoke

6 Fine-tune lighting of particles

For hardware rendering, you will find that lighting values are often different than what is appropriate for software rendering.

> **Note:** *You may want to use separate light sets for hardware and software rendering. You can then use light linking to limit the number of lights affecting the objects in the scene.*

- Toggle **Color Accum** to see its effect on the particle rendering.

  When transparent particles are in front of one another they can either render the nearest particle or add the overlapping particle's colors. By using color accumulation, you can more closely simulate transparent particle effects.

  Color accumulation also works to hide orphaned particles that are not contributing to the overall smoke trail. This adds to the smooth look of the smoke.

> **Note:** *Color accumulation does not work with sprite particles.*

- Toggle **Normal Dir** to see its effect on the particle rendering.

  *The **Normal Dir** attribute on the particles is available on many of the hardware render types. Normal Dir affects how particles are lit. Usually you won't need to adjust this unless your particles are moving in and out of lighting.*

- To maximize particle illumination, set **Normal Dir** as follows:

  Set to **1** if most or all particles are moving towards the light. Example: smoke rising toward a light.

  Set to **2** if most or all particles are stationary or passing in front of the light. Examples: rain passing in front of headlights, or stationary particles creating a glow around a point light.

  Set to **3** if most or all particles are moving away from the light. Example: rain falling down past a street light.

7 Save your work

- **Save** the scene as *27-cig_02.ma*.

Caching particles

In order to apply hardware motion blur to a sequence of rendered images, you will need to cache the simulation. Motion blur requires knowing where the particle is and was, in order to determine the correct motion of the particle and determine the correct tail shape. Because future particle position is evaluated as the dynamic simulation calculates each frame, the renderer will not be able to predetermine the motion blur for future frames unless the calculations have already been performed and stored in memory or on disk. Caching also makes it easier to evaluate timing, since you can scrub in the timeline once the particles have been cached.

Memory caching vs. Disk caching

You have two choices for caching particles: *Memory caching* and *Disk caching*. Memory caching for particles works very much like memory caching of rigid bodies. You select the particle objects you want to cache and enable caching via a menu. The particle information is stored in RAM the first time. Subsequent playbacks are read from the RAM, making evaluation much faster, but the cache can only be used by the current Maya session. Disk caching is similar to memory caching, except that it writes the cache on your computer's hard drive. Doing so thus makes the cache accessible between Maya sessions and between computers.

Memory caching workflow

Memory caching is good to use when you have a short simulation that doesn't have a huge number of particles. It is also useful when you know you will not be using distributed rendering across multiple computers. Currently, hardware rendering cannot be distributed in this manner but software rendering can. Memory caching provides a quick way of caching your particles without having to keep track of cache data files on your hard disk. However, memory caching can quickly eat up your computer's available RAM, so be aware of that before using it.

Following is a typical memory caching workflow:

- Select the particle object(s).
- Select **Solvers** → **Memory Caching** → **Enable**.

  The particleShape will now show **Cache Data** *attribute as* **Enabled**.

  To disable caching for a particular particle, you can deselect this attribute.

Note: *Each time you make a change to your scene, either to field values or particleShape attributes, you will need to delete the cache. To delete the cache, select each affected particle and* **Solvers** → **Memory Caching** → **Delete**.

Disk caching workflow

Disk caching creates particle disk cache files (*.pdc*) on your hard drive, containing all the particle attribute information in your scene. One *.pdc* file is written for each particle object on each frame of playback. These files can be read very quickly, so near-real-time scrubbing is still possible. You are only limited by available disk space, rather than available RAM. The *.pdc* files can be transferred to other machines if necessary, or accessed remotely, such as when using distributed rendering.

Following is a typical disk cache workflow:

- **Save** your scene.
- Choose **Solvers → Create Particle Disk Cache → ❑**.
- Read the dialog description, and set the appropriate options.
- Click the **Create** button.

    Maya will not draw the particles on the screen but will record all their attribute information to disk.

- **Save** the file again.

    You are doing this so Maya knows this file has a disk cache going with it.

Following is how to disable or delete a particle disk cache:

- To disable the cache temporarily, select **Solvers → Edit Oversampling or Cache Settings**, and then disable the **Use Particle Disk Cache** option.
- To remove the disk caching permanently, you need to locate the *particles* directory in your current project using your operating system. The subdirectories inside *particles* contain all the *.pdc* files for the various particle objects you have cached.

> **Tip:** For more specific control of which particle attributes will be written to disk cache, refer to the `dynExport` command in the MEL documentation.

1 Scene file

- Continue with your own cigarette smoke scene.

    OR

- **Open** the scene file called *27-cig_02.ma*.

2 Cache the particles

- Set the playback range to go from **1** to **200**.
- **Cache** the particles to disk using the workflow stated previously.

3   Adjust the motion blur

Now that you have cached the particles, experiment with different values of hardware motion blur.

- Open the Hardware Render Buffer attributes.

- In the **Multi-Pass Render Options** section, set **Motion Blur** to a value of **6**.

Note: *Some older hardware graphics configurations do not support hardware motion blur.*

4   Adjust opacity over lifespan

The opacity of the particles should thin out as they get older.

- Add the **opacityPP** attribute and add a ramp to control the particle opacity.

5   Save your work

- **Save** the scene as *27-cig_03.ma*.

Graininess

Graininess is to be expected in your final smoke renders. You should smooth and blur this during the compositing stage, so at this point you should not work too hard to get rid of it. Anticipate that the small particles that are orphaned or not contributing greatly to the effect will get removed during the blurring and softening that takes place in the compositing stage.

Using low opacity values with a lot of particles can really help your hardware renders avoid a computer-generated look and appear less flat. Also, you can simulate self-shadowing in hardware rendered smoke by using expressions to randomly assign gray values to the particles at creation time.

Glow and incandescence

People often ask if you can make hardware particles glow or produce self-illumination. **Color Accumulation** is currently the closest possible effect. This task is much better suited for compositing effects that let you make this adjustment very quickly. Even the most basic compositing packages generally have some nice tools for adding in incandescence and glowing effects. For hardware rendering, focus more on the motion and shadowing qualities inside of Maya. Sweetening effects like blurs, halos, glows, etc., are traditionally easier to add during compositing.

Final composited render

Software rendering

Software rendering of particles will allow you to do post-process effects such as glow and incandescence, as well as interactive effects of reflection, object occlusion, and shadows. These particles are really nice to work with, but they are expensive in rendering time.

There are three types of software particle render types. They each serve a separate purpose but can be combined as well.

Blobby particles

Blobby particles depend on each other to form blobs or connected shapes based on their radius and proximity to each other. There are two attributes related to the Blobby particle object that control this behavior:

Radius

Sets the diameter of the blob particle.

Threshold

Sets the amount of flow between adjacent particles. The resultant blobbiness is a function of the particle radius, threshold and distance between particles. A setting of **0** generally means no blending. Values closer to **1** will normally produce more blending, assuming that there are particles close to each other. All of these factors are interdependent, so experimentation is almost always necessary.

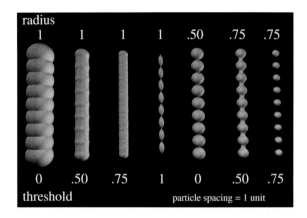

radius						
1	1	1	1	.50	.75	.75
0	.50	.75	1	0	.50	.75
threshold				particle spacing = 1 unit		

Blobby particle comparison of Radius vs. Threshold

To see a comparison of **Radius** vs. **Threshold**, open the scene file *27-blobCompare.ma*.

> **Note:** *A high* **Threshold** *with big gaps between particles or a* **Threshold** *value that is larger than the particle's* **Radius** *may result in invisible particles.*

Blobby particles are also the only render type to which you can assign shading groups and render in the same way you would assign shading groups to geometry.

It is generally recommended that you avoid depending on 2D mapping on blobby particles, as blobbies use an averaging of UV space to calculate their respective mapping coordinates. This can result in artifacts or incorrect mapping of the resulting blobby surface. 3D mapping works the same as you would expect for any surface. It is often best to keyframe your 3D texture placement nodes to approximate the motion of your particles, as this helps to reduce the appearance of texture swimming during rendering. However, it can be difficult to eliminate completely the appearance of swimming when rendering blobbies using 3D textures, since particles may be moving at different speeds.

Bump mapping can be used with blobby surfaces, but displacement mapping might not work as you would expect.

Motion blur is not supported by any software particle render types.

Cloud particles

The Cloud particle render type, as its name implies, is designed to create volumetric rendering effects. It has an additional attribute called **Surface Shading,** which controls how much blob the cloud will have. There are three attributes related to the Cloud particle render type that control this behavior:

Radius

Sets the diameter of the cloud particles.

Threshold

Works like the blobby surface.

Surface Shading

Adjusts the degree of surface shading applied to the *particleCloud* shader via the **Surface Material** input on the shading group.

Tube particles

Tube particles are the software counterpart to the hardware Streak particle render type. The tube particle has attributes to control the size of either end of the particle as well as tube length. The Tube particle type does not have the surface shading capability that the Cloud and Blobby type have. The tube particle is velocity-dependent, like the hardware Streak types. The **Tail Length** and **Direction** are dependent on the velocity and direction of the particle.

Radius0

Controls the tail size.

Radius1

Controls the head size.

Tail Size

Controls the tail length, but is also proportional to the particle velocity.

> **Note:** **Radius0** *and* **Radius1** *are per-object attributes only.*

Shading group organization

The software rendering engine accepts three basic types of shader information: **Surface Material**, **Volume Material**, and **Displacement Material**. These three types are passed to the rendering partition through the shading group node. This node acts as a placeholder that tells the rendering partition what will be rendered and which shaders are to be used on which objects. The light linking partition also looks to the shading group to determine which lights will work with which shaders or objects.

Software particle rendering makes use of the **Surface** and **Volume** inputs to the shading group node. You can connect surface shaders and volume shaders to the three different types of particle render types via the *particleCloud* shading group (*particleCloudSG*). Surface shading is plugged into the **Surface Material** input of the shading group and volumetric shading is plugged into the **Volume Material** input.

Blobby particles make use of the standard surface material shaders, such as anisotropic, phong, lambert, blinn, etc.

Cloud particles make use of the surface materials and the volumetric *particleCloud* shader by plugging the *particleCloud* into both the **Surface Material** input and the **Volume material** input.

Tube particles make use of the volumetric shader *particleCloud* only. The *ParticleCloud* shader is plugged into the **Volume Material** input of the shading group.

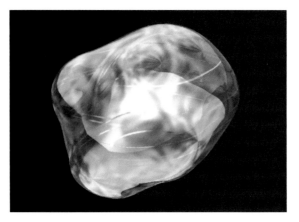

Blobby particles with phong shader and reflection map

Water bucket

In this exercise, you will create a very simple blobby water rendering. This will give you a chance to experiment with the blobby attributes and shading parameters.

1   Scene file

   • Open the file *27-waterBlob_01.ma*.

   This scene consists of a bucket falling on the ground. The bucket contains water, deformed with an animated wave deformer. You will have water to splash around using blobby surfaces.

   • **Play** the scene to see the animation.

Note: *The bucket starts falling on the ground only at frame 20, giving you time to fill the bucket with particles.*

The dynamic bucket

2 **Emit from surface**

- Select the hidden *waterEmitter* surface from the outliner.

- Select **Particles → Emit from Object**.

- Set the emitter attributes from the Channel Box as follows:

  Emitter Type to **Surface**;

  Rate to **1000**;

  Spread to **0.5**;

  Speed to **0**;

  Direction to **0, 1, 0**.

- Set the particle attributes as follows:

  Conserve to **0.95**;

  Inherit Factor to **3**;

  Particle Render Type to **Blobby Surface**.

- **Add Attributes** for the **Current Render Type** in the Attribute Editor.

- Set the following:

  Radius to **0.2**;

  Threshold to **0.75**.

3 **Keyframe the emission**

- Keyframe the **Rate** of the emitter as follows:

  Frame **15** to **1000**;

  Frame **16** to **0**.

4 Collisions and gravity

- Select the particle object, and then **Shift-select** the gravity field.
- Select **Fields → Affect Selected Object(s)**.
- Select the particle object, and then **Shift-select** the *bucket*.
- Select **Particles → Make Collide**.
- **Repeat** so the particles also collide with the *background* and the *water* surface.
- Select the *water* surface and set its *geoConnector* as follows:

    Resilience to 1;

    Friction to 0.8.

5 Apply phong shader to the blobby particles

You will use a phong material as the basis for the blobby particle shader. From this material, you will add other rendering nodes to control color, reflection and specularity.

- In the Hypershade window, create a **phong** material.
- Select the particles, **RMB** on the new phong material, and select **Assign Material To Selection**.

6 Create the color and specular map

Because you want the blob to mimic clear, water-like material, it will get most of its color from its environment. But, you will still want some method to control the color and specularity. The 3D texture marble makes a good sky texture.

- Open the Attribute Editor for the phong.
- Click the **Map** button for the **Color** attribute.
- In the Create Render Node window, click **Marble** in the 3D Textures section.
- Adjust the values as shown here:

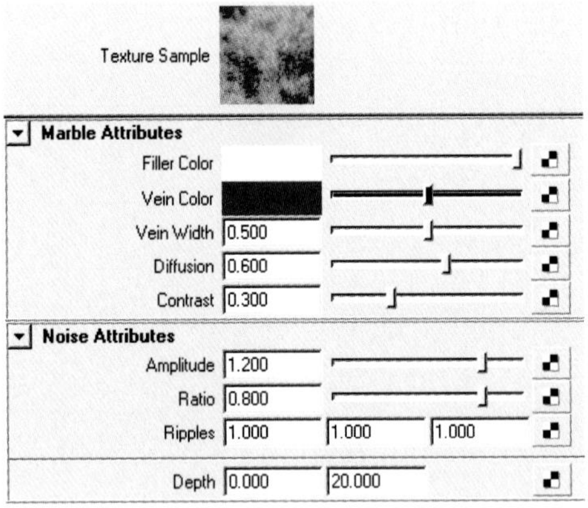

Texture Sample	

▼ Marble Attributes

Filler Color	
Vein Color	
Vein Width	0.500
Diffusion	0.600
Contrast	0.300

▼ Noise Attributes

Amplitude	1.200
Ratio	0.800
Ripples	1.000 1.000 1.000
Depth	0.000 20.000

Marble settings

- **Rename** the marble node to *skyMarble.*

- **MMB+drag** *skyMarble* and **drop** it on to the **Specular Color** of the phong.

7   Environment map reflection

An environment map is a quick method for mimicking raytraced reflections and refraction.

- Set the following values for the phong material node:

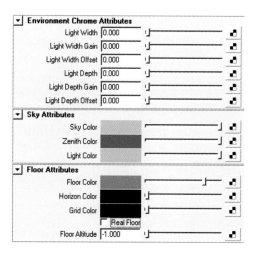

Phong settings

- **Map** the **Reflected Color** attribute with an **Env Chrome** texture.

- Set the following values for the *chromeEnv* node:

EnvChrome settings

- Also set the **Grid Placement** attributes to **o** as follows:

Grid Placement		
Grid Width	0.000	
Grid Width Gain	0.000	
Grid Width Offset	0.000	
Grid Depth	0.000	
Grid Depth Gain	0.000	
Grid Depth Offset	0.000	

Grid settings

8 Map 3D textures into the chromeEnvironment inputs

The chrome environment map has several inputs for sky and floor color values. You will create a new texture for the floor.

- **Map** the **Floor Color** with a **Rock** texture.
- Set the values to approximate what your ground will look like:

Rock Attributes	
Color1	
Color2	
Grain Size	0.040
Diffusion	2.000
Mix Ratio	0.600

Rock color

- From the Hypershade window, **MMB+drag** the *skyMarble* texture onto the **Horizon Color** input of the *envChrome* node.

Your shading network should look like this:

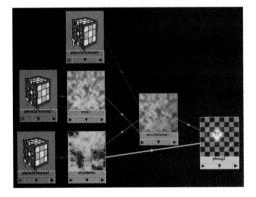

Blobby environment shader network

Project 07

524

9 Adjust values

Experiment with Radius and Threshold settings for the particles. Also experiment with lighting and texture parameters to see how they affect the look of the render.

10 Render the scene

- Add lights and render the scene starting from frame **20**. You should notice that the particles behave with a nice waving effect and react in a similar way to water.

Final water render

525

11 Save your work

- **Save** your scene as *27-waterBlob_02.ma*.

Particle cloud shader

The *particleCloud* shader provides tools for many particle rendering effects. This is the most flexible shader mechanism for software particle rendering. The *particleCloud* shader provides volumetric density control and surface material attributes like color, transparency, glow, and incandescence. You can create a new *particleCloud* shader in the Hypershade using: **Create → Volumetric Materials → Particle Cloud**.

This section outlines some of the most important *particleCloud* and particle sampler info node attributes, so you can learn their functions before putting them to work in a practical application.

Note: *The particleCloud material works with Cloud and Tube particle render types only.*

Density and transparency

Density is closely related to **Transparency** and will interact with the method you choose to drive the particle opacity. The Density attributes allow you to control how a particle will look at its edges and where it overlaps with other particles. Density can be thought of as the volume transparency or as another series of inputs that add greater control over several aspects of shader transparency. It is important to understand how Density works, as the Transparency attribute alone will only get you part of the look you may be anticipating. The Transparency attribute will work as the base of particle transparency, whereas the Density attribute applies to the volumetric portion of the shading. The third component is the **Blob Map**, which allows a texture to be added to the internal structure of the particles' appearance. Typically, the less Blob Map is applied, the less of the particle surface outline is visible. The Blob Map will also affect how the shapes of the individual clouds are drawn in the render.

Particle Cloud attributes

Density

This attribute controls how dense the particle shading appears inside the volume. This attribute is also necessary, for example, to increase the shading if there is a lot of noise. If you are using the Transparency attribute to drive the surface shading, you may find that the Density attribute can control the volume portion independently. Typical values between **0** and **1** provide slight density but values up to **10** can create interesting internal density for a very transparent particle. Also, keep in mind that the number of overlapping particles is going to affect the range of the Density attribute. If you have a lot of particles overlapping, you can set density values lower.

Noise

This attribute controls the amount of random noise applied to the modification of the density. **Noise** can give you control over how extremely the density will diffuse across the particle. Typical values range from **0** to **4,** but will also depend on how much density is being used and, again, on the number of particles and the specific effect.

Noise Freq

This attribute controls the spacing of the **Noise** maps across the particle. Typical values can be quite small, around **0.01** to **0.1**, for low-frequency noise.

Noise Aspect

This attribute controls at what angle or *shear* the noise will appear to exist in the volume. Typical values of **–1** to **2** will change the noise direction from horizontal to vertical.

Blob Map

This attribute controls the mixture of surface shading and volume shading, independent of the presence of a **Surface Material**. Surface shading is controlled by the **Surface Shading Properties** section in the Attribute Editor, in particular the **Diffuse Coefficient**. **Blob Map** can have a texture applied through it to give a more interesting internal structure to the particle appearance. It will interact with the overall density and transparency. If you turn this value very low, you may need to increase the density, noise, or transparency to see the particles. A minimum value above **0** for **Blob Map** is necessary for particles being rendered with no surface material shading. Otherwise, they will be invisible. **Blob Map** is a scaling factor for density. You can think of it as volume transparency. To see how this works, try mapping a **Cloud** texture to the default *particleCloud* shader and then rendering some cloud particles with different **Blob Map** values.

Self-shadowing

Self-shadowing is an important part of getting realistic cloud-like particle rendering. To achieve self-shadowing on particles you must:

- Enable **Raytracing** in the Render Settings.
- Set the appropriate lights to **Use Ray Trace Shadows**.
- Enable the *particleShape* attributes for **Better Illumination**.
- Enable **Casts Shadows** under the **Render Stats** section of the Attribute Editor.

> **Note:** **Better Illumination** *is not required for shadowing; however, this option will produce a higher-quality image and higher-quality shadowing. Better Illumination will increase the number of lighting samples the renderer is using. It is best to leave this option Off until you are at the final tweaking stages of rendering.*

Particle Rendering Tips and Traps

- When fading particles out, it is usually a good idea to fade them all the way out before they die; otherwise, you will notice popping in your renders. If you are using opacity or transparency to fade them out, move the top handle of the ramp down from the top a little bit. You may want to do the same thing for particles fading in to avoid popping.

- If particles stay opaque throughout their entire life, you might want to increase the **radiusPP** starting from **0** when the particles are born and then diminish the radius to **0** before the particles die. Otherwise, you might notice a pop when the particles show up and die.

- You can control the shading samples rendered for particles by changing the number in the **Particles** field in the Render Settings. This option is listed under **Anti-aliasing Quality → Number of Samples**. Increasing this may improve image quality, but it will also slow your rendering down, so only increase it if you cannot get rid of aliasing using other methods.

- Motion blur and IPR are not supported for software rendering of particles.

- The resolution of sphere particles is constant; you cannot change the detail of the sphere. Also, you cannot cause particle collisions to occur at the edge of a sphere particle or at the edges of sprite particles. As shown in the instancing lesson, if you need to change the resolution of the sphere render type, try instancing geometric spheres to point particles as a workaround.

- In the support files, some additional undocumented files related to rendering are *27-blobbyBlended.ma* and *27-blobbyFadeOut.ma*. The first file shows how to mix colors between blobby particles that are intersecting. The second file shows how to fade the transparency of blobby particles according to age.

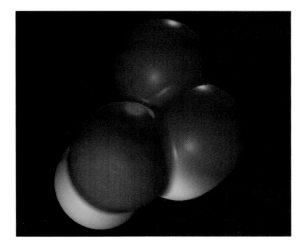

27-blobbyBlended.ma

27-blobbyFadeOut.ma

Conclusion

This lesson has introduced you to some ideas and processes involving particle rendering. Now that you have learned some of the advantages of each method, you may begin to understand the difference between hardware and software rendering. Remember the importance of color, lighting, and shadow in your imagery. Often, it is these elements that make the biggest difference.

The next lesson is an overview of the compositing stage. It also introduces some other methods for improving the look of your images.

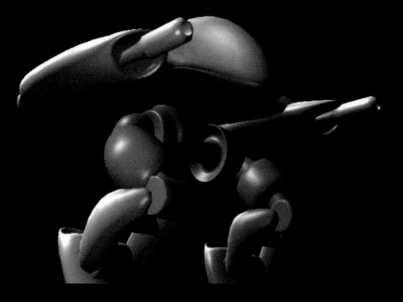

Compositing

This lesson covers rendering strategies for compositing dynamic effects.

In this lesson, you will learn the following:

- Workflow using layers
- The rendering options for compositing
- Workflow using the UseBackground shader
- Workflow using shadow passes
- Workflow using geometry masking

Compositing is a timesaver

One method of optimizing your production time is to plan and prepare your project around compositing. Compositing has been an integral part of image creation since artists first began committing their images to some form of media. Filmmaking pioneers were quick to grasp the power of combining image elements into a seamless sandwich of layers to produce final projected images that would not be possible otherwise.

Computer graphics is not different and has, in fact, been a prime beneficiary of this process.

Separating your image elements into distinct rendered passes has the following advantages:

- Faster render times;
- Flexibility of version injection and artistic control;
- Faster and more precise color matching;
- Sweetening processes and post-process effects;
- Lower resolution demands for inserted elements;
- Hardware particle rendering;
- Combining software and hardware rendered particles;
- Object and material options for visibility and lighting;
- Integration of shadow and glowing effects;
- Control of timing and editing.

Larger and more elaborate concepts are made possible by compositing. For this reason, all major studios have centered their image creation pipeline around the compositing process. The compositing station is the hub that all elements are fed into.

Autodesk® Maya® provides tools to support the process of image creation for compositing:

- Render layer management;
- Shading options for matte opacity, blackHole, useBackground;
- Geometry masking;
- Z-depth and alpha rendering;
- Object visibility;
- Render passes.

Extensive example

The scene called *28-gunbot.ma* contains an exploding robot. This example utilizes much of what you have learned and applies it to a scene that is in the process of layer creation and manipulation for the compositing process.

In this scene, you have a mechanical biped that is to lose its upper torso in a most violent manner. Although the scene file has been broken down into layers for easy display management, some of the actual rendered layers are derived from set management/rendering flags as well.

Following is a breakdown of the important display layers found in the scene:

gunbotPieces

These are the upper torso pieces that are shattering and flying away. They are rigid bodies that have been animated with various dynamic fields.

ground

This is the ground plane. It is a passive rigid body.

legs

This is the *gunbot* without the upper torso.

blastWave

This is a sphere that is animated to mimic the initial shock wave and act as a guide for pyro timing.

gunBotBody

This is the upper torso intact. This object will be swapped for the exploding pieces.

gutsLeaders

This is a particle layer that consists of leading particle emitters.

gutsSmoke

This layer is made up of the particles emitted from the *gutsLeaders*. They are software rendered clouds.

chunkSparks

This is a layer of particles that has been emitted from the exploding surface of the *gunbotPieces*.

MattePieces, MatteLegs, MatteGround

These three layers consist of duplicated geometry that is parented to the gunbot and ground surfaces. These objects have useBackground shaders applied to them for use in creating mattes and alpha channels of render passes.

Fields and lights

These two layers contain the various fields using dynamics and scene lighting.

Layers breakdown

Now you will learn about the individual rendering passes in the gunbot example and how they fit together. Typical effects shots are usually much more complex. The emphasis here is on how the rendering passes were conceived, not on the steps involved in actual compositing.

Note: *All the following renders can be found in the support files images directory.*

Layer1 render: pieces

The *gunbotPieces* are a layer of *rigidBody* NURBS surfaces. They were derived from detached surfaces obtained from the original gunbot body. The guns are included as children of stand-in spheres that make up the actual active rigid bodies.

These pieces were animated using a radial field and gravity. The radial field attributes, as well as the *rigidBodies,* have keyframes on several attributes to add control to the accelerations.

These objects were rendered in software by themselves with the ground visibility turned **Off** via its layer. The ground still acts as a passive rigid body collision for the *gunbotPieces* when hidden.

These objects are also rendered with Z-depth to aid in compositing. However, this is a technique that you do not want to rely on as it can lead to accuracy problems for objects that overlap, or are very close, or are transparent. Z-depth is only an 8-bit channel, so you do not have a lot of detail to rely on if using Z-depth as a compositing aid.

The pieces render layer

Layer2 render: ground

This is simply the ground plane, software rendered. The ground shadow pass is derived from this layer by applying the useBackground shader to the ground object, and then rendering with primary visibility turned **Off** on all of the gunbot objects.

The ground render layer

Layer3 render: shock

This layer is an animated NURBS sphere. It is software rendered with an X-ray or ghost shader applied. This shader creates the soft edge effect by using the facing ratio of the *SamplerInfo* utility node to drive the transparency of the material. This layer is useful for initially timing the rate of explosion and helps to coordinate all the elements of the explosion.

The shock render layer

Layer4 render: smoke

These particles are emitted from the guts particles and have only a slight amount of inherited velocity. They also have their own gravity, which is very slight. The intended effect is that they are trailing smoke. These are rendered in software. The geometry of the gunbot and ground are masked by using the useBackground shader with **Matte Opacity** set to **blackHole**.

The smoke render layer

Layer5 render: sparks

This layer of particles is surface-emitted from the rigid body pieces. They emit pixie dust, so they sparkle and flash. The sparks collide with the ground and the gunbot. They have a collision event that emits other sparks at the point of collision. They are hardware-rendered.

The sparks render layer

Layer6 render: particles

Stock footage of a fireball explosion was inserted into the composite. Because these images did not contain Z-depth information, the images were scaled and positioned inside the compositing application. A time warp was also used to sync the timing and duration for this effect.

The particles render layer

Layer7 render: shadows

A few different shadow pass sequences were rendered separately, and then composited into the final movie. The shadow pass layers were created using the useBackground shader on the gunbot and the ground. With their **Primary Visibility** set **Off**, the geometry acts as shadow catchers. This information is only visible in the matte channel. To see your matte information when test rendering, select **Display → Alpha Channel** from the Render View. Use a compositor to manipulate this information further by using it as a mask input channel, thus recreating the shadows as darker areas on the images. Using this technique, you can also render the shadows at a lower quality and then blur and add color to them in compositing. This can significantly shave off time when rendering large scenes.

Once all these layers are composited together in the compositing software, you could get a result similar to the following:

Final composited image

Compositing

As the layers or passes are rendered, they should be tested together in a compositing application.

Images that have been rendered should be used in the compositing application as references only. As subsequent improvements or versions are created, it is recommended to keep the different versions and not directly replace referenced images. Doing so will allow you to go back and forth between the different image sequences as needed.

Images can undergo drastic manipulation during compositing with much less rendering time. Lighting effects and manipulation of shadow, color, intensity, and softness are prime examples. Rendering shadows separately and with coarse resolution with the intention of softening during composition can be a huge time- and effort-saver in itself.

These are some popular effects achieved by compositing:

- Color correction and contrast balance;
- Edge anti-aliasing;
- Film grain;
- Camera shake;
- Lighting effects such as glow and lens flare;
- Fake depth of field by blurring certain layers.

Compositing is also the stage where elements created in other applications are brought together. These packages are also a great way to bring in external plates or video source footage for rotoscoping interaction with image plane or texture elements.

Maya has render layer management that can be used to organize your rendered images into separate color and shadow passes automatically. Render layers can be set-up inside the Render Layers Editor.

Render Layer Editor

> **Tip:** *Each render layer can have its own Render Settings overrides and materials assignment.*

Conclusion

Compositing is an important part of pulling your scene elements together. It is an especially common part of the process for dealing with the look and integration of particle rendering. Hopefully, the extended movie example and descriptions in this lesson have given you a clear idea of what is happening at the compositing stage, as well as showing you how to construct your scenes for this process. Taking advantage of the additional speed and flexibility that compositing offers will not only expand the options you have for controlling the look of your imagery, but will also help you organize your work and make changes efficiently.

Project 08

In Project Eight, you will learn about the advanced Autodesk® Maya® Unlimited features. The lessons in this project only scratch the surface of the very powerful tools used to create fluids, fur, hair, and dynamic particles and surfaces such as clothes.

By the end of this project, you should have a basic understanding of the Autodesk® Maya® Unlimited features and how you could potentially use them.

Maya Fluids

This lesson is the first of four on the advanced Autodesk® Maya® Unlimited features. You will now experience the Maya Fluid effect, which is based on mathematical equations (Navier-Stokes), to realistically simulate fluid motion. With fluids, you can create a wide variety of 2D and 3D atmospheric effects, such as clouds or mist, pyrotechnic effects such as explosions or smoke, or any other dynamic surfaces that would be otherwise almost impossible to reproduce with the usual modeling techniques. Later in the lesson, you will also create an open water surface using the ocean shader.

In this lesson, you will learn the following:

- How to create 2D and 3D fluids
- How to affect geometry with fluids
- How to create an ocean
- How to create a dynamic boat
- How to create a pond

Fluids classification

There are three basic types of fluid effects: dynamic, nondynamic, and open water.

Dynamic fluid effects

These behave according to the natural laws of fluid dynamics, and Maya simulates the effects by solving fluid dynamics equations for each time step. You can texture dynamic fluids, have them collide with and move geometry, affect soft body geometry or cloth objects, and interact with particles.

> **Note:** *The effects you can produce are single-fluid effects, which means you cannot have two or more fluids interacting to produce liquid-like effects (for example, pouring water where water and air are the two fluids).*

Non-dynamic fluid effects

These use textures and animation to simulate fluid and fluid motion. Effects of this type do not use fluid dynamics equations. You can create fluid motion by animating texture attributes. Because Maya does not solve the equations, rendering this type of fluid is much quicker than rendering a dynamic fluid.

Open water fluid effects

You can create ocean and pond fluids to simulate large realistic water surfaces, such as stormy oceans with foam and swimming pools. Oceans are NURBS planes with ocean shaders assigned to them. Ponds are 2D fluids that use a spring mesh solver and a height field. Also, you can add wakes to oceans and ponds to create boat wakes, add additional turbulence, or generate bubbling and ripples.

About fluid containers

The fluid container is the basis for any dynamic or non-dynamic fluid effect. A fluid container is in fact a rectangular 2D or 3D boundary that defines the space in which the fluid can exist. Without boundaries, a dynamic fluid could conceivably deform into an infinite space and your scenes would take forever to render. You can create fluid containers as either 2D or 3D containers. A 2D fluid container is really a 3D fluid container with a depth of one voxel. The size of that voxel is determined by the Z size of the container. The benefit of using a 2D container is the considerably shorter rendering time, so in situations where you do not have geometry traveling through the container (such as an airplane flying through clouds), you should use a 2D container instead of a full-fledged 3D fluid. Because of the extra data necessary to define them, 3D containers can be quite heavy, thus resulting in a very slow solution for the fluid dynamic behavior.

Note: *Fluid containers can be placed within each other, but their contents will not interact with each other. Oceans do not require a fluid container, although they can interact with containers.*

Contents Method

The **Contents Method** defines how a fluid property is defined in the container, if at all. There are two basic ways to define a fluid property in a fluid container:

- As a **Preset Gradient**;
- As a **Grid**.

Defining a fluid property as a **Preset Gradient** will maintain that property as a constant over time, and it sets a ramp of values from 1 to 0 on the selected axis.

Defining a fluid property as a **Grid** allows you to place individual values in each grid unit called a voxel (volume pixel), thus giving you more precise control over that property.

Grids can be defined as static or dynamic. **Static Grids** are used when you do not want the fluid property values to change over time (even if used in a dynamic simulation).

Dynamic Grids are used to simulate dynamic behavior where the values in each voxel are recalculated at each step using the fluid dynamics solver. In many cases, you will combine static properties with dynamic properties to achieve a certain fluid effect (for example, clouds moving in one direction would have a constant velocity acting upon a dynamic density).

Fluid states

The state of a fluid is a collection of its grid property values (the values in the **Density**, **Velocity**, **Temperature**, **Fuel**, **Color**, and **Texture Coordinate** grids). The state of an uncached dynamic fluid in any frame other than the first one is based on its state in the prior frame.

Note: *You have to cache a fluid simulation in order to be able to scrub through the timeline.*

Initial state

The initial state represents the grid property values defined in a fluid container at the first frame of a simulation. When you play a simulation up to any frame, you can use the current state at that frame as the initial state.

For example, if you have an empty fluid container but you want to start the simulation with fluid already in it, you could add an emitter to the container, play and stop the simulation at the frame containing the desired amount of fluid, and then set the emitted fluid values as the initial state.

To set the initial state:

- Select the fluid container.
- In the **Fluid Effects** menu, select **Set Initial State**.

Modifying the behavior and contents of a fluid

By modifying the attributes of the fluid container, you change the appearance and behavior of the fluid. For example, if you change the **Gravity** value (found in the **Dynamic Simulation** section of the Attribute Editor for the fluid container) to a negative value, the **Density** will fall instead of rise.

Note: *No matter what changes you make to the attributes, the fluid can never leave the container.*

You can also edit the contents of a fluid container using the **Paint Fluids Tool** found under **Fluid Effects → Add/Edit Contents**.

To paint contents into a container:

- With the container still selected, choose **Fluid Effects → Add/Edit Contents → Paint Fluids Tool → ❑.**

  The Tool Settings window opens and a slice appears at the origin of the fluid container. The slice is represented by a plane with dotted edges and fluid sub-volume manipulators at one corner. When you move the pointer over the slice, the pointer changes to a brush, indicating that you can paint.

- At the top of the Tool Settings window, click **Reset Tool** to set the **Paint Fluids Tool Settings** to the default values.

- In the **Paint Attributes** section of the Tool Settings window, select the fluid properties you want to paint.

  You could paint each property separately, but in some cases it is more efficient to paint two of them at the same time.

Tip: *You can display numeric values for **Density**, **Temperature**, or **Fuel** in the grid by changing the **Numeric Display** in the **Display** section of the fluid Attribute Editor. This way you can visualize the values as you paint.*

Container size and resolution

Over the course of the following exercises, you will look at several combinations of methods that will help achieve the desired result. There are situations when you will want to modify the size of the fluid container. Scaling the container will change the size of the voxels but not their content; thus the fluid content will look less dense. Changing the container size in the Attribute Editor for the *fluidShape* node changes the size of the voxels and the voxel content, scaling everything proportionally.

If you need finer detail for your fluid simulation, you will have to increase the resolution.

The size should be proportional to the resolution to get consistent quality on all axes. For example, if the container size is 10, 5, 2, then a valid resolution would be 20, 10, 4. If the size is not proportional to the resolution, the quality will be higher along one axis than on another axis.

To increase the fluid resolution:

- Select the fluid container.
- In the **Dynamics** menu set, select **Fluid Effects** → **Edit Fluid Resolution** → ❑.
- In the options, enter the desired number of voxels and click **Apply** and **Close**.

   Be aware that increasing the fluid resolution will considerably increase the rendering time because of the larger number of voxels that need to be evaluated by the fluid solver.

Creating fire effects

In this exercise, you will use a 3D fluid container that has the **Contents Method** set to **Dynamic Grid**. The motion of the flame is controlled by the **Buoyancy, Swirl, Turbulence, and Reaction Speed attributes. Incandescence**, which controls the amount and color of light emitted from regions of **density**, is driven by the **temperature**. Opacity uses density as an input, and there is no texturing assigned. The opacity ramp determines the shape of the flame, particularly the edges.

Incandescence controls the color, and the actual color ramp is set to black. In this example, the incandescence ramp uses *super white* color entries (values greater than 1). The interpolation to black will produce intermediate orange and red colors similar to the color variation from flames of varying temperature.

1   **Scene file**
- **Open** the scene called *29-fireEffect_01.ma* from the *support_files*.

   This scene contains a simple environment, along with a campfire ready to be lit up.

The rendered camp fire scene

2 **Create a 3D fluid container with an emitter**

 • From the **Fluid Effects** menu, select **Create 3D Container with Emitter**.

 • **Rename** the fluid to *fire*.

 • **Translate** the container up by **5** units on the **Y-axis**.

3 **Adjust the resolution and size**

 • Select the 3D container and open the **Attribute Editor**.

 • In the **Container Properties** section, enter the following values:

  Resolution to **30**, **30**, and **30**;

  Size to **10**, **10**, and **10**.

 Changing the resolution and size proportionally will maintain a uniform look for the rendered fluid.

4 **Move the 3D fluid emitter**

 • In the *Perspective* view, select *fluidEmitter1* and **move** it on the **Y-axis** until it is under the wood geometry.

5 **Adjust the 3D fluid emitter attributes**

 • With the *fluidEmitter1* still selected, go to the **Fluid Attributes** section in the **Attribute Editor** and set the following values:

  Density/Voxel/Sec to **1**;

  Heat/Voxel/Sec to **2**;

  Fuel/Voxel/Sec to **4**.

- Open the **Fluid Emission Turbulence** section and set **Turbulence** to **1.2**.

  These values control how the fluid will be emitted in the fluid container.

6 Adjust the fluid contents

- In the **Attribute Editor** for the *fire* fluid, open the **Contents Method** section and choose the following settings:

  Density to **Dynamic Grid**;

  Velocity to **Dynamic Grid**;

  Temperature to **Dynamic Grid**;

  Fuel to **Dynamic Grid**;

  Color Method to **Use Shading Color**.

- Press **6** on your keyboard to see the fluid in hardware texturing mode.

- **Play back** the scene to see the emitted fluid.

7 Simulation rate scale

The *Simulation Rate Scale* changes the time step used in emission and in solving, making the playback a little faster.

- In the **Attribute Editor** for the *fire* fluid, open the **Dynamic Simulation** section and set the **Simulation Rate Scale** attribute to **2**.

The basic behavior of the fluid

8 Tweak the fluid's behavior

- In the **Attribute Editor** for the *fire* fluid, open the **Contents Details** section, open the **Density** subsection, and set the following:

    Buoyancy to **9**;

    Dissipation to **0.2**.

  Doing so will change the speed at which the fluid moves up and changes the rate at which it dissipates in the container.

- In the **Velocity** subsection, set **Swirl** to **10**.

- In the **Turbulence** subsection, set **Strength** to **0.01**.

- In the **Temperature** subsection, set the following:

    Temperature Scale to **2**;

    Buoyancy to **9**.

- In the **Fuel** subsection, set the following:

    Fuel Scale to **2**;

    Reaction Speed to **1**.

9 Tweak the fluid's shading

- Open the **Shading** section and set Transparency to a pale gray.

- Set the **Dropoff Shape** to **Sphere**.

- Set the **Edge Dropoff** to **0.5**.

- Within the **Shading** section, open the **Color** subsection and set the color to **black**.

10 Adjust the fluid's incandescence

The *Incandescence* controls the amount and color of light emitted due to self-illumination from regions of density.

- In the **Shading** section under the **Incandescence** subsection, select the first color entry on the left in the incandescence ramp.

- Set its **Selected Position** to **0.65** and then change its color to a super white as follows:

    HSV to **15, 0.8,** and **15**.

- Set the **Interpolation** to **Smooth** for the first color entry.

- Delete the second color entry in the incandescence ramp.

- Set the color entry on the right as follows:

    HSV to **15, 0.8,** and **0**.

- Make sure that **Incandescence Input** is set to **Temperature**.

- Set the **Incandescence Input Bias** to **−0.3**.

11 Adjust the fluid opacity

Opacity represents how much the fluid blocks light.

- Under the **Opacity** subsection of the **Shading** section, make sure that **Opacity Input** is set to **Density**.

- Set the **Opacity Input Bias** to **0.3**.

- Set the **Selected Position** for the first entry on the left of the opacity graph to **0.1** and the **Selected Value** to 0.000.

- Set the **Interpolation** to **Spline** for the first entry.

- Click inside the opacity graph to add a new entry and set the following values:

  Selected Position to **0.14**;

  Selected Value to **0.5**.

- Set the **Interpolation** to **Linear** for the second entry.

- Click inside the opacity graph to add a new entry and set the following values:

  Selected Position to **0.3**;

  Selected Value to **0.25**.

- Set the **Interpolation** to **Spline** for the third entry.

- The last entry in the opacity graph should have the following values:

  Selected Position to **0.85**;

  Selected Value to **0.02**.

- Set the **Interpolation** to **Spline** for the last entry.

12 Adjust the Shading Quality

- Within the **Shading** section, open the **Shading Quality** subsection and set the **Quality** to **5**.

  This setting will increase the number of samples per ray used to render, thereby increasing the quality of the render.

13 Test render your fluid

- **Play back** the animation up to a point where you can clearly see a flame.

- **Render** the scene.

The final fluid fire

Note: *The fluid does not emit light in your scene. A point light was placed at the fire location to create the illusion that the light comes from the fire.*

14 Save your work

- Save your scene as *29-fireEffect_02.ma*.

Colliding geometry with fluids

With the force of a fluid you can move or modify geometry, move cloth objects, or particles. You can also make the contents of a fluid container collide with geometry. Over the following exercises you will take a look at some of these features.

The following steps illustrate how to get the contents of a fluid container to collide with geometry.

1 Create a dynamic fluid container

Colliding fluids with geometry works with any type of fluid containers. In this example, you will use a 3D container.

- Under the **Fluid Effects** menu, select **Create 3D Container with Emitter**.
- Make sure that under the **Contents Method** section in the **Attribute Editor**, **Density** and **Velocity** are set to **Dynamic Grid**.

2 Move the geometry inside the fluid container

- Select any piece of geometry and **move** it inside the fluid container.

3 Create the dynamic connection between the geometry and the fluid

- Select both the geometry and the fluid container, and then select **Fluid Effects** →
  Make Collide.

Note: *For better results, increase the* **Tessellation** *on the geoConnector node found under the* **Outputs** *for the geometry in the Channel Box.*

---

4 Watch fluid colliding

- **Play back** the simulation.

  You will see that the fluid collides and avoids the geometry intersecting with the container.

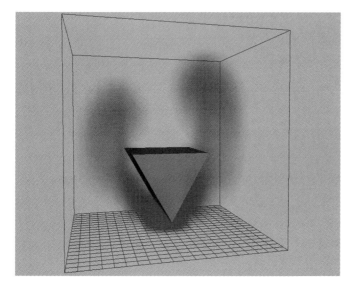

Colliding fluids

Tip: *Set the fluid* **Render Interpolator** *to* **Linear** *in the* **Shading Quality** *section of the Attribute Editor if you notice the fluid passing through the geometry.*

Using fluids to move geometry

In this exercise, you will use the force of a fluid to move geometry by making the geometry a rigid body.

1 Create a fluid container with an emitter

Colliding geometry with fluids works with any type of fluid container. In this example, you will use a 3D container.

- Under the **Fluid Effects** menu, select **Create 3D Container with Emitter**.
- Make sure that under the **Contents Method** section in the **Attribute Editor**, **Density** and **Velocity** are set to **Dynamic Grid**.
- Select the fluid emitter and **move** it close to the bottom of the container.

2 Move the geometry inside the fluid container

- Select the geometry that will be affected by the fluid force and **move** it inside the fluid container, above the emitter.

3 Make the geometry an active rigid body

- Select the geometry and select **Soft/Rigid Bodies** → **Create Active Rigid Body**.

4 Adjust the rigid body performance

- In the **Channel Box** for the *rigidBody* node, set the **Apply Force At** attribute to **centerOfMass**.

5 Make the connection between the fluid and the rigid body

- Select both the fluid container and the geometry.
- Go to the **Fields** menu and choose **Affect Selected Object(s)**.

6 Play back the simulation

- Modify the simulation to your liking by modifying either the fluid attributes or the rigid body, adding fields, etc.

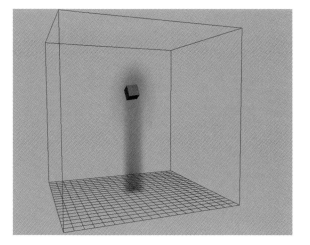

The affected geometry

Creating open water effects

With Fluid Effects, you can easily create a variety of realistic water surfaces, from high seas with foam to ponds or swimming pools. Although fluid containers are not necessary when creating oceans, both oceans and ponds can interact with them.

There are two ways to create open water effects:

- Creating oceans, which are defined by a flat surface with an ocean shader assigned to it. Fluid Effects simplifies the process by providing a single command that creates a plane optimized for best results and an ocean shader with the appropriate connections.
- Ponds are 2D fluids that use a spring mesh solver and a height field. With the pond options and attributes, you can set the size and color of your fluid surface. Ponds are good for creating swimming pools or smaller bodies of water.

Overview of oceans

The *ocean shader* can be used to simulate a wide range of water wave patterns, from stormy sea swells to bathtub waves, and it generates the waves through displacement. The shading of the ocean surface has been turned off for hardware playback since it would slow down the playback considerably, and the only way to preview the animation is a *heightField* node used as a *Preview Plane*. This allows you to adjust the look of the displaced waves interactively without having to render the file. The Preview Plane can be scaled only on the X and Z-axes, and moved anywhere across the NURBS surface used by the ocean shader. It will not appear in renders. It can also be parented to an object floating on the ocean surface, thus allowing for previewing the animation of the waves at the location of any floating object. The resolution of the Preview Plane can be adjusted if necessary, but any substantial increase will result in a slower playback of the ocean simulation.

Fluid Effects also allow you to create floating objects such as regular boats or motor boats through the help of dynamic locators. They also provide a large number of parameters including throttle, rudder, and roll that allow for controlling the animation and appearance of the floating objects. You can animate the floating objects either by using the above-mentioned attributes for the dynamic locators or by keyframing the X and Z positions of the locators over time.

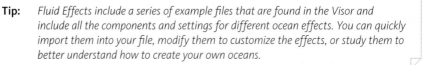

Tip: *Fluid Effects include a series of example files that are found in the Visor and include all the components and settings for different ocean effects. You can quickly import them into your file, modify them to customize the effects, or study them to better understand how to create your own oceans.*

Creating a motor boat

In the following exercise, you will create an ocean and make geometry into a motor boat using the Make Motor Boats menu option. Then, using the attributes found in the Extra Attributes section of the motor boat locator, you will animate the boat across the ocean surface.

1   **Scene file**

• **Open** the scene file named *29-ocean_01.ma*.

2   **Create the water surface**

• In the Dynamics menu set, select **Fluid Effects** → **Ocean** → **Create Ocean** → ❏.

• Set the following options:

> **Create Preview Plane** to **On**;
>
> **Preview Plane Size** to **100**.

• Click the **Create Ocean** button.

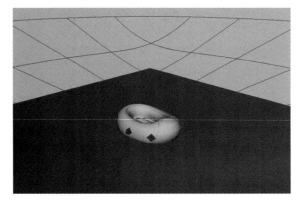

The ocean preview

3   Make the boat geometry into a motor boat

- Select the *boat* geometry.

- Press **Ctrl+g** to group the boat.

- In the **Dynamics** menu set, select **Fluid Effects** → **Ocean** → **Make Motor Boats**.

  This will create a dynamically charged locator, to which the boat group node will be parented.

Note: *If you want to animate the X and Z positions of the motor boat across the water surface through keyframing and not by using the locator attributes, turn on* **Free Transform** *in the* **Make Motor Boats** *options window before applying it to the geometry.*

- **Play** the simulation.

  You will see how the boat's default buoyancy will keep the boat floating on the ocean surface.

4   Adjust the locator's attributes

- Select the *locator1* node.

- Open the **Extra Attributes** section in the **Attribute Editor** for the *locatorShape1* node.

Tip: *In the Attribute Editor under the Notes section, you will find explanations about the usage of the boat locator.*

- Set the **Buoyancy** to **0.5**.

  Lowering the buoyancy will sink the boat deeper into the water. **Air Damping** *and* **Water Damping** *models the effects of air viscosity and friction, respectively, on the object's motion.*

- For natural motion, set the **Boat Length** and the **Boat Width** equal to the actual length and width values. The **Roll** sets the rolling motion of the boat from side to side. The **Pitch** sets the pitching motion of the boat so that the front end rises or falls in relation to the back end. You will leave these attributes at their default values for now.

5   Animate the boat

- Change the Time Slider range to go from **1** to **1000**.

- **Play** the simulation in order to see the effects of the upcoming steps.

- Start increasing the **Throttle** value while the simulation is playing.

  You will see the boat starting to move across the water. This attribute sets the velocity of the boat.

- Set the **Throttle** value to **15**.

- Change the **Rudder** value to a positive value and the boat will start turning toward its left. If you choose a negative value, it will turn the boat to its right.

  The Rudder sets the angle of the rudder to make the boat turn.

- Set the **Throttle Pitch** to **10**.

This attribute sets how much the front of the boat rises when the throttle is open.

- The **Turn Roll** attribute sets how much the boat rolls to the side as it turns.

6 Scene file

- **Save** the scene as *29-ocean_02.ma*.

Interactive boat simulation

MEL shelf buttons can be created for a more interactive boat simulation. To make one of the following MEL script examples into a shelf button, type the script into the input section of the Script Editor, highlight it, and then **MMB+drag** it onto the shelf. While you play back the simulation you can use the shelf buttons to modify the way the boat moves across the water's surface.

Following are some MEL button examples.

1 Increase Throttle

```
float $t = `getAttr locator1.throttle`;
setAttr locator1.throttle ($t + 0.5);
```

Tip: *Execute this script multiple times to gradually increase the throttle.*

2 Decrease Throttle

```
float $t = `getAttr locator1.throttle`;
$t -= 0.5;
if( $t < 0 ) $t = 0.0;
setAttr locator1.throttle $t;
```

3 Rudder Left

```
float $t = `getAttr locator1.rudder`;
$t += 2.0;
if( $t > 20 ) $t = 20;
setAttr locator1.rudder $t;
```

4 Rudder Right

```
float $t = `getAttr locator1.rudder`;
$t -= 2.0;
if( $t < -20 ) $t = -20;
setAttr locator1.rudder $t;
```

5 Stop Boat

```
setAttr locator1.throttle 0;
setAttr locator1.rudder 0;
```

Adding wake and foam to the boat

In this exercise, you will add a wake and foam to the motor boat simulation. This will create two 3D fluid containers (used as textures) and an emitter that will interact with the ocean surface by overriding the Wave Height Offset and Foam Offset, respectively, of the *oceanShader1* node. The intensity of the wake effect can be adjusted by either modifying the values for the Density/Voxel/Sec of the *OceanWakeEmitter1*, or adjusting the Density attributes of the *OceanWakeTexture1*, found in the Contents Details section of the Attribute Editor. The intensity of the foam emission can be adjusted by either modifying the values for Heat/Voxel/Sec of the *OceanWakeEmitter1*, or adjusting the Temperature attributes of the *OceanWakeFoamTexture1*, also found in the Contents Details section of the Attribute Editor.

1 Scene file

- **Open** the scene file named *29-ocean_02.ma* or use the file that you saved at the end of the previous exercise.

2 Add wake and foam to the boat

- Select the *locator1* node.
- In the **Dynamics** menu set, select **Fluid Effects** → **Ocean** → **Create Wake** → ❑.
- **S**et the following options:

  Wake Size to **100**;

  Wake Intensity to **3**;

  Foam Creation to **3**.

- Click the **Create Ocean Wake** button.

  This will create two 3D containers, one for the wake and the other for the foam emission.

3 Adjust the Preview Plane Resolution

- Select the ocean Preview Plane and open the **Attribute Editor** window.
- Set the **Resolution** to **40**.

  This will provide a better preview quality for the wake and foam effects.

4 Adjust the shape and position of the wake emitter

- Select the *OceanWakeEmitter1* node, which is parented to the *locator1* node.

- Open the **Attribute Editor**, and in the **Volume Emitter Attributes** section set the **Volume Shape** to **Cone**.

- In the **Channel Box**, adjust the emitter transform attributes as follows:

  Translate Z to **−4**;

  Rotate X to **−90**;

  Scale X to **5**;

  Scale Y to **5**.

  Scale Z to **3**.

  Doing so places the wake emitter at the back of the boat with an appropriate shape.

5   Tweak the results

- Tweak the wake and foam effects by adjusting the **Density** content of the *OceanWakeTexture1* node or the **Temperature** content of the *OceanWakeFoamTexture1* node in the **Contents Details** section of the **Attribute Editor**.

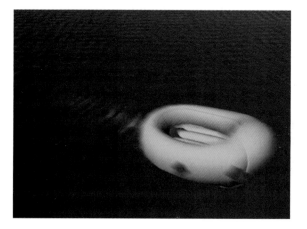

The rendered wake

6   Save your work

- **Save** the scene as *29-ocean_03.ma*.

Overview of ponds

Ponds are 2D fluids that use a spring mesh solver and a height field to generate the water simulation. They are better suited for creating smaller bodies of water. A pond functions in almost the same manner as an ocean. The exception is that when you create wake and foam for a floating object, no new fluid containers are created, but an emitter will be created that will affect the pond fluid.

The following emitter attributes control wake behavior:

- **Density/Voxel/Sec** controls the wake intensity.
- **Heat/Voxel/Sec** controls foam creation if the **Temperature Method** on the pond is set to **Dynamic Grid**.

The appearance of the pond surface can be modified using the pond options and attributes. You can set the **Size**, **Resolution**, **Color**, and **Transparency** of your fluid surface the same way as for any other 2D fluid container.

To create wakes in a pond fluid:

- Select the object you want to create a wake for and **Shift-select** the *pond*.
- In the **Dynamics** menu set, select **Fluid Effects** → **Pond** → **Create Wake** → ❑.
- Set the wake options.

The **Wake Intensity** will set the emission value for the **Density/Voxel/Sec** attributes of the *PondWakeEmitter*. The **Foam Creation**, if not zero, will set the **Temperature** content of the pond fluid to **Dynamic Grid**, and will set the emission value for the **Heat/Voxel/Sec** attributes of the *PondWakeEmitter*.

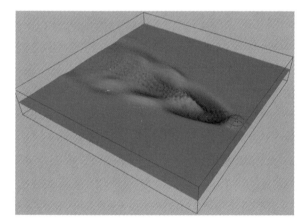

Pond example scene

Conclusion

Fluid containers allow you to create a wide variety of 2D and 3D effects, which can be affected by geometry or can affect any rigid bodies. With ocean shaders or ponds, you can create open water effects, float objects, create motor boats, and add wake and foam to the simulation.

In the next lesson, you will look at how to add fur to the bunny from Theme Planet.

Maya Fur

Maya Fur is a great tool for creating fur on animals. In this lesson, you will create fur for the bunny from Theme Planet, a multiple-surface NURBS model. The fur will then be modified and fine-tuned to simulate realistic animal fur.

In this lesson, you will learn how to do the following:

- Work with fur on a multiple-surface NURBS model
- Offset fur so all patches flow in the same general direction
- Work with the Fur Paint Tool
- Comb the direction, modify the length, and set the baldness of the fur
- Apply color to the Base and Tip Color attributes of a fur description
- Fine-tune fur descriptions
- Add fur shading effects for additional realism
- Define fur renders using the Fur Render Settings

Apply fur to a patch model

You will now apply fur to the bunny model and experiment with the different fur tools and settings.

1 **Scene file**

   • **Open** the file called *30-bunny_01.ma*.

      The bunny model is made up of several NURBS patches. 3D textures have been assigned to color the surfaces.

The bunny model

2 **Create a fur description**

   • Select **Edit** → **Quick Select Sets** → **HeadSet** to select the surfaces that belong to the bunny's head.

   • In the **Rendering** menu set, select **Fur** → **Attach Fur Description** → **New**.

      A fur description is created and attached to the selected surfaces. Fur feedback automatically displays on the selected surfaces, providing you with a visual representation of the default fur attributes for the fur description.

The head fur feedback

> **Note:** *When creating fur on a polygonal object, you must make sure to have a clean UV layout so the fur is created and reacts as expected. You can use* **Automatic Mapping** *to achieve this quickly.*

3 Rename the fur description

Changing the names of the fur description and fur feedback nodes to something meaningful is useful for easy identification if more than one fur description is created.

- Select **Fur → Edit Fur Description → FurDescription1...**
- In the **Attribute Editor**, rename *FurDescription1* to *headFur*.

4 Fur feedback

- **Rename** the *FurFeedback* group node to *headFurFeedback* from the Outliner.
- Expand the *headFurFeedback* node.

  Note that there is a fur feedback node for each head surface.

- Select every fur feedback node within the *headFurFeedback* node.

- In the **Channel Box** under **Shapes**, set the following:

    U Samples to **6**;

    V Samples to **6**;

    Fur Accuracy to **1**;

    Color Feedback Enable to **On**.

The number of **U** *and* **V samples** *on the surface determines how many feedback hairs display. However, this does not change how many hairs actually render on the surface.*

Fur Accuracy *sets how closely the fur feedback resembles the appearance of the final rendered fur. A value of* **0** *represents the hairs as straight lines, while a value of* **1** *will give a good indication of what the final fur render will look like but can slow interaction.*

Lower fur feedback samples

Tip: *It is better to decrease the U and V samples on very small surfaces so you can see the effect of fur attributes more clearly while working.*

5 Reverse fur normals

When you attach fur to a model, each hair makes up the fur points in the normal direction to the surface. If your model appears to have short or invisible fur after you have attached a fur description to it, it could be because the fur normal is pointing in the negative direction.

To solve this problem, you must reverse the fur normals.

- Select any NURBS patch that seems to have reversed normals.
- Select **Fur → Reverse Fur Normals**.

Tip: *It is better practice to correct the NURBS patch directions than to reverse fur direction.*

6 Edit the head fur description

When you edit a fur description, any changes you make to the fur attributes apply to all surfaces that are assigned to the fur description.

- Select **Fur → Edit Fur Description → headFur**.
- Set the following values:

> **Length** to **0.5**;
>
> **Inclination** to **0.7**;
>
> **Roll** to **0.5**;
>
> **Polar** to **0.5**;
>
> **Base Curl** to **0.3**;
>
> **Tip Curl** to **0.7**.

7 Offset the head fur direction

When you add fur to a model and adjust the **Inclination**, **Polarity,** and **Roll**, you may find that the fur grows in different directions for some of the surfaces.

The direction fur grows in is determined by the inclination of the fur (how much the fur sticks out), the polarity of the fur (the angle each hair rotates around the fur normal), and the roll of the fur (the angle each hair rotates about the surface V-axis).

- Tear off the menu **Fur → Offset Fur Direction by**.
- Select any NURBS patch, and then select one of the **Offset Fur Direction by** menu items to rotate the fur in a proper direction so it flows with the head's fur direction.

This is only a general start-up position for the fur as you will comb it in the next exercise.

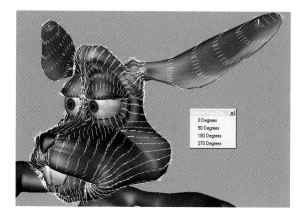

The modified fur direction

> **Note:** *All fur directions are at* **0** *by default.*

Comb the fur

1   Paint direction for the head fur

To comb fur, you will paint the direction of fur using the Paint Fur Attributes Tool.
The direction you comb sets the Polar attribute value for each hair to correspond with
the painted direction, and as a result, a map will be created for the **Polar** attribute.

- Select **Edit → Quick Select Sets → HeadSet**.
- Select **Fur → Paint Fur AttributesTool → ❏**.

  *The Paint Fur Attributes Tool Settings window opens, followed by the Paint Scripts Tool
  Attribute Editor.*

- In the Paint Fur Attributes Tool Settings window, set the following:

  Fur Attribute to **Direction**;

  Fur Description to **headFur**.

  Attribute Map Width to **256**;

  Attribute Map Height to **256**.

Note: *Only the fur descriptions attached to the selected surfaces are available
for selection.*

Tip: *The **Attribute Map** should be twice as large as the wanted number of U and V
samples, or else detail will be lost for attributes that will be painted using the Paint
Attributes Tool.*

- **Close** the Paint Fur Attributes Tool Settings window.

2   Viewing the Value Map while you paint

While you paint on a surface with an Artisan Tool, you can view the grayscale Fur Attribute
Value Map as you paint. This provides useful feedback when the changes you are painting
are not easily detected with the fur feedback. Keep in mind that this option may slow
performance.

- In the Paint Scripts Tool **Attribute Editor**, open the **Display** section.
- Set **Color Feedback** to **On**.

The paint color feedback

3 Painting with reflection

At this time if you paint on the model, you will only paint one side of the head. To speed things up, you can enable the Reflection option and paint both sides of the head at the same time.

- In the Paint Scripts Tool **Attribute Editor**, expand the **Stroke** section and enable **Reflection** and set the **Reflection Axis** to **X**.

- In the **Brush** section, set **Opacity** to **1.0**.

- In the **Paint Attributes** section, set the following:

    Paint Operation to **Replace**;

    Value to **o**.

- **Click+drag** the brush across the surface to comb the fur.

Tip: *To increase the size of the Artisan Paint Brush, hold down the* **b** *key and* **click+drag** *in the viewport to change the scale of the brush, or increase the value for* **Radius (U)** *in the Script Paint Tool Settings window.*

Because the **Polar** *values are affected only by the direction you comb, when you comb hair, none of the settings in the Script Paint Tool Editor are relevant.*

Note: *You can restore the fur direction in the fur description values by deleting the Polar Attribute Map created when you painted the direction. The map is located in the Attribute Editor for the headFur description in the* **Details** *section under* **Polar →Maps**. *While holding the* **Ctrl** *key, select all surfaces listed under the* **Surface** *tab and click the* **Remove Item** *button.*

4 **Save your work**

- **Save** your scene as *30-bunny_02.ma*.

Apply textures to the fur

A material using a ramp projection has already been assigned to all sections of the bunny model. The projection node will be mapped into the Base and Tip Color of each *FurDescription* to color the fur.

1 **Map Base Color for the headFur**

- Select **Panels** → **Saved Layouts** → **Hypershade/Outliner/Persp**.

- In the **Hypershade**, **graph** the material of any head patch.

- Make sure to frame the entire shading network.

- Select **Fur** → **Edit Fur Description** → **headFur**.

  The Attribute Editor will open to show the attributes for headFur.

- **MMB+drag** the *projection1* on the **Base Color** attribute in the **headFur Description Attribute Editor**.

  Doing so will map the projected color from the bunny's surfaces onto the base color of the head fur.

- Open the list box for the **Bake Attribute** and select **Base Color**.

- Click the **Bake** button.

  Doing so creates texture map files on your disk from which the fur can read its base color values. The fur feedback will not reflect the mapped attributes until you bake.

- In the **Attribute Editor**, you can open the **Details** section for the **Base Color** attribute, under **Maps**, to see **Base Color** maps and their respective assigned surfaces.

Note: *If you edit the texture after baking, you must bake the texture again or your changes will not take effect.*

2 **Map Tip Color for the headFur**

- **Repeat** the previous step for the **Tip Color**, which will keep the color of the fur the same from base to tip.

- Open the list box for the **Bake Attribute** and select **Tip Color**.

- Click the **Bake** button.

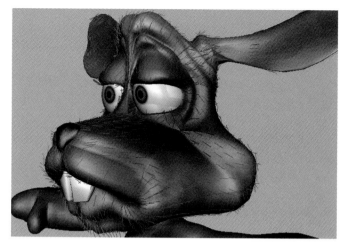

The fur's base and tip color

Paint fur length

The Fur Paint Tool will be used to edit the length of the *headFur* description. You will paint shorter hairs around the eye, mouth, and nose area.

1 Increase the FurFeedback samples

 • In the Outliner, expand the *headFurFeedback* node and select all *FurFeedback* nodes.

 • In the **Channel Box**, set the following:

> **U Samples** to **25**;
>
> **V Samples** to **25**.

The increased fur feedback samples

2 Paint fur length around the eyes

Hairs are noticeably shorter around a bunny's eyes, nose, and mouth.

- Select **Edit → Quick Select Sets → HeadSet**.

- Select **Fur → Paint Fur Attributes Tool → ❑**.

- Set the following in the Paint Fur Attributes Tool Settings:

    Fur Attribute to **Length**;

    Fur Description to **headFur**;

    Attribute Map Width to **256**;

    Attribute Map Height to **256**.

- In the Paint Scripts Tool **Attribute Editor**, set the following:

    Opacity to **1.0**;

    Paint Operation to **Replace**;

    Value to **0.1**.

- Shorten the length of the fur around the eyes.

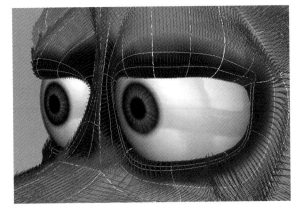

The eye fur length

> **Tip:** *You could paint the fur length on the inside of the eye with a **Value** of **0**, but instead you will paint the **Baldness** attribute later in the lesson, which completely removes fur from certain locations.*

3 Paint fur length around the nose and mouth

- **Repeat** the previous step to shorten the fur length around the nose and mouth area.

4 Smooth paint values

After you have shortened the length of hairs, you can smooth out the painted areas for a seamless transition between values:

- In the **Paint Scripts Tool Attribute Editor** in the **Paint Attributes** section, set **Paint Operation** to **Smooth**.

- Click the **Flood** button to smooth out the entire head surface at once.

5 Paint fur baldness

When there are areas where you do not want any fur, it is better to paint the Baldness attribute rather than setting the fur length to o.

- In the Paint Fur Attributes Tool Settings window, set the following:

    Fur Attribute to **Baldness**;

    Fur Description to **headFur**;

    Attribute Map Width to **256**;

    Attribute Map Height to **256**.

> **Tip:** *If the Paint Fur Attributes Tool Settings window is closed, you can double-click on the tool in the Toolbox to bring up the option window.*

- In the **Paint Fur Attributes Tool**, set the following:

    Paint Operation to **Replace**;

    Value to **o**.

- **Paint** around and inside the eye, ear, and mouth area to remove any unwanted hair.

- Set **Paint Operation** to **Smooth**.

- Click the **Flood** button to smooth out the entire head surface at once.

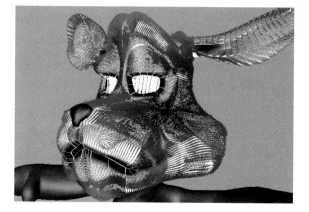

No more hair around and inside the eye, mouth, and ear

6 Fine-tune the fur

Now that you have painted the different fur attributes, you can fine-tune the look of the fur so it renders properly for your character. The following is only an example of a look you can achieve, but feel free to experiment on your own.

- Select **Fur → Edit Fur Description → headFur**.
- Set the following attributes for the FurDescription:

  Base Opacity to **1.0**;

  Tip Opacity to **0.8**;

  Base Width to **0.03**;

  Tip Width to **0.01**;

  Scraggle to **0.3**;

  Segments to **5**.

  The **Segments** *attribute defines the number of segments that make up each patch of fur. For smoother curves, use more segments. The longer the fur, the more segments are needed to produce a smoother result.*

Tip: *For a wet fur look, set* **Clumping** *to* **1**.

7 Modify details of the headFur description

- Scroll down to the **Details** section of the FurDescription **Attribute Editor**.
- Expand **Length** and set the following:

  Noise Amplitude to **0.5**;

  Noise Frequency to **12**.

- Expand **Inclination** and set the following:

  Noise Amplitude to **0.5**;

  Noise Frequency to **18**.

- Expand **Polar** and set the following:

  Noise Amplitude to **0.2**;

  Noise Frequency to **16**.

The fine-tuned fur

8 Test render the scene

- Frame the bunny's head, and then click the **Render** button in the main menu bar.

  Your first impression when the head is rendered might be to think that the fur is not dense enough to cover the entire head.

- Select **Fur → Edit Fur Description → headFur**.

- Set the **Density** attribute to **5000**.

  Doing so will increase the amount of fur at render time, but it will also take longer to generate the rendered image.

The rendered fur

Tip: *Start with a low density value for faster rendering performance while fine-turning the fur.*

- Change the color of the **Specular Color** attribute to a very **dark grey**.

  Doing so will reduce the shiny highlights on the fur.

The rendered fur with darker specular highlights

9 Save your work

- **Save** your scene as *30-bunny_03.ma*.

Adding fur shading effects

To shade fur that is relatively realistic, you will apply auto-shade lights. This can produce self-shading or back shadow effects and takes no longer to render than fur without shading effects.

Most fur roots are not exposed to light. Self-shading simulates this effect by lighting the tips of the fur, and making the roots dark. Back shadows will simulate the effect of darker regions where the fur does not receive light and lighter regions where the fur is closest to the light.

However, the best way to generate realistic-looking shadows onto fur and geometry is by creating fur shadow maps. When you render the fur, a shadow map is created for each shadow map light.

Note: *Be aware that although generating several fur shadow maps may produce more realistic results, it takes time and slows rendering.*

1   **Create a spot light**

Only spot lights can cast shadows for fur.

- Select **Create** → **Lights** → **Spot Light**.

- Place the spot light and tweak its attributes as you want.

- Set the spot light to **Use Depth Map Shadows**.

- **Delete** any other light source.

2   **Set-up a light for fur shading and shadows**

- Select the *spotlight1*.

- Select **Fur** → **Fur Shadowing Attributes** → **Add to Selected Light**.

- Open the *spotlight1* **Attribute Editor**.

- Expand **Fur Shading/Shadowing** and adjust the following:

    Fur Shading Type to **Auto-Shading**;

    Self-Shade to **1.0**;

    Self-Shade Darkness to **0.5**;

    Back Shade Factor to **2.5**;

    Back Shade Darkness to **0.3**.

- **Render** to see results.

    To generate realistic shadows onto fur and geometry, you can create fur shadow maps.
    A fur shadow map represents depth information generated from the position and
    orientation of the spot light. The depth information is used to create two types of
    shadowing: fur shadowing, where fur casts shadows on itself; and geometry shadowing,
    where fur casts shadows on geometry. In this case, you will use the Shadow Map option so
    the fur will cast shadows on itself.

The rendered fur with shadows

- Set **Fur Shading Type** to **Shadow Maps**.

> **Note:** *You might get a warning stating the following:*
> ```
> Fur shadows can be incorrectly placed when a spot light has
> Dmap Auto Focus turned on. We suggest you turn off Dmap
> Auto Focus, and instead set the Dmap Focus value to Cone
> Angle + (Penumbra * 2).
> ```
> *It is a good idea to correct your shadowing lights to respect this suggestion.*

- **Render** to see results.

The fur rendered using shadow maps

3 Save your work

- **Save** your scene as *30-bunny_04.ma*.

Fur Render Settings

Fur Render Settings are the attributes that define how fur renders. These setting must be defined before rendering.

- Select **Fur → Fur Render Settings**.

   Enable Fur *must be turned* **On**. *If this option is not turned on, the scene renders but the fur is completely ignored.*

- **Calc. Area Values** sets how the fur is distributed across surfaces.

- Since your model is made up of multiple patches, you should set **Calc. Area Values** to **Globally**.

   This option gives an even distribution of hairs across different-sized surfaces.

   The density of each fur description is distributed evenly over all surfaces that have fur descriptions attached, regardless of which fur description is attached.

- **Comp. Fur** creates a composite of the rendered fur and the rendered models. The fur and the models render separately, but if you turn this option off they are not composited. This option is useful for compositing images using another application.

- **Keep Temp Files** keeps the fur files built by the fur in the process of creating the final fur images. The intermediate files, which are fur files and shadow maps, are stored in the *furFiles* and *shadowMap* directories, respectively.

   If you turn this option off, the intermediate files are deleted when the render is complete. This can prevent your disk from filling up with fur files.

- **Keep Fur Images** keeps the fur image files created by fur. These files are useful when you want to turn on **Comp. Fur**, but still want to see the rendered fur without the model.

- Set **Equalizer Maps** to **Default Equalizer Maps**.

   An equalizer map compensates for the uneven distribution of fur caused by uneven parameterization, so that fur is evenly distributed across the surface.

- **Default Equalizer Maps** uses the equalization maps automatically created by fur.

- Open the **Advanced Options** section and set the following:

   Enable Fur Image Rendering to **On**;

   Enable Fur Shading/Shadowing to **On**.

- Open the **Fur Image Rendering** section and set the following:

   Hairs/Pixel to **5**;

   Use Fur Shading/Shadowing on Fur to **On**.

- Open the **Shadow Map Rendering** section (only if **Fur Shading Type** is set to **Shadow Maps**);**Hairs/Pixel** to **5**.

Conclusion

In this lesson you learned how to create a fur description and how to modify the fur feedback nodes. You offset the fur direction in certain areas so that the fur would flow in the proper direction. Then you modified the *FurDescription* and mapped the texture assigned to the 3D model to the base and tip color of the FurDescription. Finally, to set-up the scene before rendering, you fine-tuned each fur description and applied fur shadowing techniques using spot lights.

In the next lesson, you will use the Maya Hair feature.

Maya Hair

Maya Hair systems use a collection of dynamic NURBS curves that are generated from hair follicles. Each hair follicle contains one NURBS curve but can contain a number of hairs that make up a clump. The follicle has various attributes for modifying the appearance and style of the hair, including braiding. The Paint Hair Tool allows for creating and removing follicles, as well as painting hair attributes. With hair, you can simulate natural movement of long hair, hair blowing in the wind, hair motion when swimming underwater, and various hair styles. Because hair is a generic dynamic curve simulation, the curves can also be used to create non-hair effects such as ropes and creatures. Paint Effects brushes can also be attached to dynamic curves to give a unique style to your scene.

In this lesson, you will learn the following:

- The basics of a hair system
- How to adjust the hair attributes for achieving certain hair styles
- How to set the starting position of hair
- How to achieve realistic hair colliding with the head geometry
- How to create hair constraints
- How to create hair caches
- How to import and transplant hair from a library

Creating hair

Hair can be created on both NURBS and polygonal surfaces. Before you create a hair system, you should decide which renderer you will be using, as this will affect the type of output you select. You can render hair as Paint Effects strokes or you can convert the Paint Effects strokes to polygons and use another renderer such as mental ray.

When you create hair, the visible result in the viewport is the hair system output, but you will need to render your scene to see the final results.

Hair can be created from existing NURBS curves or from follicles, which create their own NURBS curve. You would use existing NURBS curves if you plan to use the dynamic hair system for non-hair simulations.

There are three sets of curves in a hair system:

Start position curves

This is the position of the hair at the start frame of a hair simulation (similar to the initial state for dynamics). At creation time, these curves stick out straight from their follicles' normals or are duplicates of existing curves.

Rest position curves

This is the position of the hair when no forces are affecting it. The shape of these curves can be edited to influence the look of the hair. These curves are usually used as goals for the hair so it maintains its shape.

Current position curves

These curves reflect how the hair behaves when you play the simulation.

Using the **Hair** → **Display** menu, you can choose to display any of the above-mentioned curves while you set-up your simulation.

Tip: *Never edit the current position curves, as this will produce unpredictable results.*

Steps to create hair

- Select the surface on which you want to create hair.
- From the **Dynamics** menu set, select **Hair** → **Create Hair** → ❏.
- Choose the desired options, and then click on the **Create Hairs** button.

Note: *When creating fur on a polygonal object, you must make sure to have a clean UV layout so the fur is created and reacts as expected. You can use* **Automatic Mapping** *to achieve this quickly.*

General steps for hair simulations

In order to create and animate hair for your models, in most cases you will go through the following general steps:

- Add hair to your models.
- Style the hair curves.

  This can be achieved by setting a first rest position for the curves from the start curves, and then editing the shape of the rest position curves to your liking.

- Change the hair dynamic behavior.
- Set-up the hair shading and shadowing.
- Render the scene.

Hair dynamic behavior

You can use the *Paint Hair Tool* to modify the various attributes of a hair system or follicles, or you can use the Attribute Editor window to change the values for those attributes manually. In order to be able to tweak the hair attributes, you will need to select the hair system, the hair follicles, or the dynamic curves.

To select a hair system

- Select the *hairSystem* node in the Outliner or the **Hypergraph**.

To select all the follicles in a hair system

- In the Outliner, select *hairSystemFollicles*.
- Select **Hair → Convert Selection → To Follicles**.

To select individual follicles

- Hide the **Strokes** and **NURBS Curves** in the viewport.
- Make sure the **Show → Follicles is enabled.**
- Select the follicle you want to modify.

Note: *After you modify the hair system or the follicle attributes, you may have to play the simulation in order to see the changes.*

Hair simulation

In the following steps, you will interactively move, rotate, and scale the surface with hair while the simulation is playing, as well as see the hair update as the dynamic forces are applied to it.

Interacting with the hair simulation

- Select **Hair → Display → Current Position**.

  This will change the hair curves display to the current dynamic curves, which are the ones that update when you play the simulation.

- Select the surface with hair.

- In the **Dynamics** menu set, select **Solvers → Interactive Playback**.

  This will play the hair simulation, allowing you to interact with it at the same time.

- Move the surface with hair to see how the hair will behave in response to the dynamic forces.

Making the hair collide

In order for hair to interact with a surface, you must set the surface to collide with the hair before you play the simulation. Both polygonal geometry and NURBS surfaces can collide with hair. You can also make the hair collide with the ground, itself, or both.

Make the hair collide with a surface

- Select the *hairSystem* node.

- **Shift-select** the geometry that you want to collide with the hair.

- Select **Hair → Make Collide**.

> **Tip:** It will speed up playback if you use stand-in geometry rather than high resolution objects for collisions. Alternatively, you can use either the Collide Sphere or Collide Cube from the **Hair → Create Constraints** menu, which can be evaluated much faster than geometry.

Make the hair collide with the ground or itself

- Select the *hairSystem* node and open its **Attribute Editor**.

- Open the **Collisions** section and turn on the **Collide Ground** option.

- Turn on the **Self-Collide** option if you want the hair curves to collide with each other.

Hair shadowing

Adding shadows to the hair will make it look more realistic. To achieve this effect, you can use a light with depth map shadows enabled.

Set-up hair self-shadowing

- **Create** a spot light.

- In the light's **Attribute Editor**, open the **Shadows** section and set the following:

    Use Depth Map Shadows to **On**;

    Use Mid Dist Dmap to **Off**.

- Optionally, turn **Off** the **Use Dmap Auto Focus** to get better quality shadows, and then manually set the **Dmap Focus**.

- Increase the **Dmap Filter Size** to get softer shadows.

- Set the **Dmap Bias** to **0.006** or higher.

    This sets how far the light filters through the hair.

- In the **Attribute Editor** for the *hairSystem* node, open the **Shading** section and make sure that **Cast Shadows** is set to **On**.

- **Render** your scene to see the results.

Rendering hair

If you choose Paint Effects as the hair output when you create hair, you must render it with the Autodesk® Maya® Software Renderer. In order to render the hair using mental ray, you must first convert the Paint Effects strokes to polygons. You may also output the curves to another renderer that can take care of rendering the hair.

- You can render more hairs with fewer Paint Effects strokes by using Paint Effects MultiStreaks. These attributes are found in the **Attribute Editor** for the *hairSystemShape* node under the **Multi Streaks** section.

- For more realistic results, turn on the **Oversample** and **Oversample Post Filter** options found in the Render Settings under the **Paint Effects Rendering Options** section.

Dynamic effects using hair

In this exercise, you will learn about *dynamic curves*, the basics of the hair systems. This type of curve is based on the dynamics of a hair system; such dynamic curves can be used for such things as ropes or chains, or also as deformers for geometry or as lofting profiles as shown in the following exercise.

In this exercise, you will use a hair system to generate the effect of a curtain that can interact either with the existing geometry, or with fields and forces. The hair system will use NURBS curves as output and the current position curves will be used as lofting profiles for the curtain surface. When you create the hair system, the higher the points per hair, the more accurate the simulation will be.

Note: *This example's purpose is to show the different usage and tools of the dynamic curves and hair solver. The best way to create a curtain would be to use nCloth, which is explained in the next lesson.*

1 Scene file

- **Open** the scene file named *31-curtain_01.ma*.

  This scene consists of a simple ball and floor surface, along with a curtain rod from which you will create the dynamic curves.

2 Create a hair system

- Select the curtainRod geometry.

- Select **Hair → Create Hair → ❑.**

- In the Create Hair options, set the following values:

  Output to **NURBS Curves**;

  Create Rest Curves to **Off**;

  U Count to **14**;

  V Count to **1**;

  Passive Fill to **0**;

  Randomization to **0**;

  Edge Bounded to **Off**;

  Equalize to **On**;

  Points Per Hair to **10**;

  Length to **10**.

- Click the **Create Hairs** button.

  Ten dynamic curves will be created from the curtainRod surface. The curves are pointing down because they are located in the center of the NURBS spans, for which the border is on top of the rod.

3 Lock the length of the start curves

- Select **Hair → Display → Start Position**.

- Select the hair curves.

- Select **Hair → Modify Curves → Lock Length**.

  Doing so will prevent the curves from stretching under their own weight.

4 Create the curtain surface

- Select **Hair** → **Display** → **Current Position**.

  This changes the hair curves display to the current dynamic curves, which are the ones that update when you play the simulation.

- Select the hair curves in order, starting from the left.

- In the **Surfaces** menu set, select **Surfaces** → **Loft**.

- **Rename** the new surface to *curtain*.

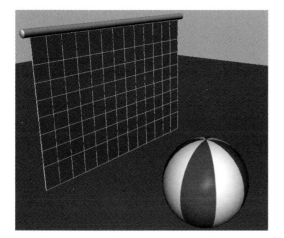

The lofted curtain

5 Make the curtain and the ball collide

- Select the *hairSystem* node.

- **Shift-select** the *ball* geometry.

- In the **Dynamics** menu set, select **Hair** → **Make Collide**.

  The ball surface will now interact with the dynamic curves.

Note: *You can also set collisions between the hairSystem and the floor.*

6 Adjust the collision attributes

- Select the *hairSystem* node and open its **Attribute Editor**.

- Under the **Collisions** section, turn on **Self-Collide**.

  This will make the curtain curves collide with themselves.

- Set **Repulsion** to **0.6**.

- Set **Num Collide Neighbors** to **5**.

7 **Hair stiffness and gravity**

- Under the **Dynamics** section, set **Stiffness** to **0.1**.

- Under the **Forces** section, set **Gravity** to **3**.

8 **Increase the geoConnector tessellation factor**

- Select the *ball* geometry.

- In the **Channel Box** under the **Inputs** section, highlight *geoConnector1*.

- Set the **Tessellation Factor** to **600**.

This improves the resolution of the collision stand-in object.

9 **Play back the simulation interactively**

- Set your playback range to **1000** in the timeline.

- Select the *curtainRod* geometry.

- Select **Solvers → Interactive Playback**.

This will play the hair simulation, allowing you to interact with it at the same time.

- **Move** the *curtainRod* geometry over the ball so the curves collide with it.

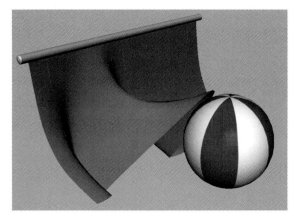

Interactive playback in action

Tip: *For better results and to avoid interpenetration between the curtain surface and the ball, you can use a stand-in object slightly bigger for the collision object and parent it to the ball. You can then hide it for a perfect illusion.*

Creating long hair

In this exercise, you will learn how to create a hair system for long hair. The hair system will be made up of several follicles, which will be influenced by dynamic fields in order to get to the proper hair style position. In addition, a hair constraint will be applied to mimic a hair clip behavior.

A hair system consists of the following elements: the *hairSystem*, *hairSystemFollicle*, and a specified *hairSystem* output. The hairSystem is the collection of the hairSystemFollicles. The hairSystemFollicles control the attributes and curves associated with a particular hair clump. Each follicle contains one NURBS curve that represents the position of the hair in that follicle. The NURBS curves can then be mapped with Paint Effects to create the actual hair.

The following scene consists of a girl's head.

1 **Scene file**

- **Open** the scene *31-girl_01.ma.*

  This scene contains a simple head for which you will create long hair.

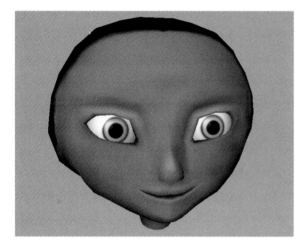

The head to use for long hair

2 **Create hair**

There are several ways to create a hair system on a piece of geometry. You can use the **Paint Hair Follicles** Tool or **Transplant Hair**. In this example, you will select polygonal faces and create a single follicle per face.

- In the Outliner, **RMB** on the *hairFaces* set and select **Select Set Members**.

  Doing so selects the faces where you want hair on the head.

- Select **Hair** → **Create Hair** → ❏.

- In the option window, select **Edit** → **Reset Settings** and then set the following:

  Output to **Paint Effects**;

  Enable **At selected points/faces**;

  Points per hair to **5**;

  Length to **6**.

Tip: *In the lesson we will keep the **U** and **V Count** to **10**. This count allows for faster performance during playback of the dynamic simulation. However, for the effect of fuller and thicker hair, you should increase these settings.*

- Click the **Create Hairs** button.

The default hair

Tip: *You can select fewer faces in order to create less hair and speed up the simulation.*

3 Tweak the hair system

- In the Outliner, select the *hairSystem1* node.

- In the **Channel Box**, change the **Display Quality** to **1**.

  *The **Hairs Per Clump** attribute controls how many hairs will be rendered per clump, while the **Display Quality** attribute controls how many are shown in the viewport. Since you are not fine-tuning the hair at this point, it is a good idea to decrease the amount of detail for each hair clump for faster performance during playback.*

- With the *hairSystem1* still selected, select **Hair → Display → Current and Start**.

   Doing so displays both the current position and the start position curves. The current curves are the dynamic curves affected by the simulation, while the start curves are the inputs to each follicle. The hair follicles control the attributes and curves associated with each Paint Effects hair clump.

4 Play the simulation

The hair will fall down, thanks to the built-in force in the Y-direction simulating gravity on the *hairSystem1*.

The hair falling down because of gravity

Note: *Your simulation might be different than the above.*

5 Make collide

In order for the hair follicles to behave properly, they must collide with the head geometry. You will now set-up this connection.

- Select *hairSystem1*, and then **Shift-select** the *head* geometry.

- Select **Hair → Make Collide.**

6 Collide sphere

Adding collisions with the head will ensure that the hairs do not go through the head but will slow down the simulation. As an alternative, you can create a collision sphere constraint, which is much faster to calculate, but will impact the precision of the hair collisions.

- **Undo** the last step to remove the head collision.
- Select the *hairSystem1* node.
- Select **Hair → Convert Selection → To Start Curves.**

  Doing so automatically selects all the current NURBS curves associated with the hair system.

- Select **Hair → Create Constraint → Collide Sphere.**
- Move the constraint node to fit the head.

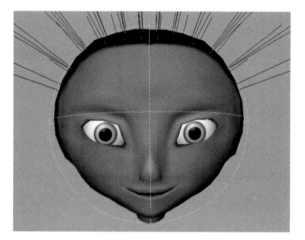

The collide sphere in place

> **Tip:** *You can parent the constraint into the character's hierarchy so it follows when animated.*

7 Set the start position

Similar to particles and other dynamics, you can set the start position of the hair so the simulation starts with a predefined hair style.

- With the *hairSystem1* selected, select **Hair → Display → Current Position**.
- **Play** the simulation up to a point where the hair follicles are in their relaxed position.
- With the *hairSystem1* still selected, select **Hair → Convert Selection → To Current Positions.**

- Select **Hair** → **Set Start Position** → **From Current.**
- Decrease the *hairSystem1*'s **Stiffness attribute** to **0.01**.

  Doing so will allow the hair to fall more freely.
- **Play** the simulation again, and then select **Hair** → **Set Start Position** → **From Current.**
- Decrease the *hairSystem1*'s **Friction attribute** to **0**.
- **Play** the simulation again, and then select **Hair** → **Set Start Position** → **From Current.**

  You should end up with something similar to the following:

The start position of the hair

Tip: *Your simulation will run much faster if you display the scene in wireframe.*

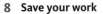

---

8   Save your work
- **Save** the scene as *31-girl_02.ma.*

Hair styling

At this point, you should start looking into refining the hairstyle. For instance, you might want to add a hair clip or shape the hair differently. The following will show how to do such tasks.

1   Create a constraint

You will now constraint the hair that's falling across the face of the character to a hair pin.
- Display the start curves.
- Select all the hairs that are falling in the character's face.

- Select one CV per hair in a diagonal as follows:

The selected CVs

- Select **Hair → Create Constraint → Transform.**

  A locator that defines the hair constraint is created.

2 Place the constraint

The following shows a way to place the constraint that requires playing the simulation as you place, and then scaling the constraint locator.

- Set the time range to go from **1** to **5000**.

- Select **Hair → Display → Current Position.**

  You will notice hashed lines that connect the constrained CVs to the locator.

- Select the constraint locator.

- Set the view to be in wireframe for a faster playback.

- Select **Solvers → Interactive Playback.**

- As the scene plays, move the locator on the upper right side of the forehead and scale it down to nearly zero.

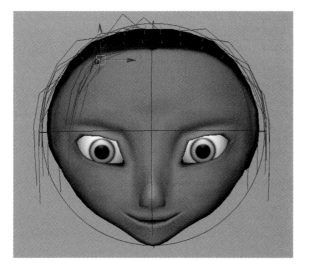

The moved hair

- **Stop** the playback.

3 **Set the initial position of the hair**

Now that you have changed the positioning of the hair, you need to save its shape so it looks as it did at the beginning of the simulation. Not doing so would simply reset the hair to its previous position.

- Select the *pfxHair1* node in the Outliner.
- **Select Hair → Set Start Position → From Current.**
- Rewind the scene.

The hair stays in position.

> **Tip:** *You might want to play the simulation again and set the start position once more to make sure the hair is in a relaxed position.*

4 **Hair pin**

- In the Outliner, set the **Visibility** of the *hairPin* to **1**.
- **Tweak** the hairpin placement and shape so it is at the location of the hair constraint.

The placed hairpin

- **Parent** the *hairConstraint2* to the *hairPin*.

  Doing so will allow you to animate the hair pin, and the hair will follow.

5 **Change the shape of the hair**

Now that the hairpin is in position, you can take some time to manually tweak the shape of the start curves so the hair looks more stylized.

- Select **Hair → Display → Start Position.**

- Select all the long hair coming down on the side and back of the head.

- Select the last two rows of CVs as follows:

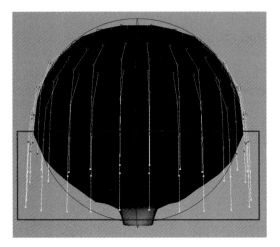

The last CVs selected

- **Scale** the CVs to shape the hair as follows:

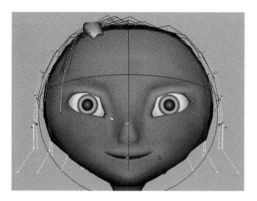

The hairstyle

Doing so shapes the initial shape of the hair when the simulation is played.

> **Note:** *On playback, you will notice the hair falling down straight. You will see how to fix this in the next exercise.*

6 Save your work

- **Save** the scene as *31-girl_03.ma.*

Fine-tuning the hair

At this point, if you were to render, you would see that the hair looks very rough and unrealistic. In this exercise, you will take some time to refine the look and behavior of the hair.

1 Test render the scene

The hair looks thin and chunky

2 Tweak the hair system

You will now experiment with the hair system and different settings. While changing the settings, make sure to test render to see the effect between each change.

- Select the *hairSystem1* node and set the following:

    Start Curve Attract to **0.1**.

    When playing the simulation, the hair will now keep some curvature of the start position curves.

    Sub Segments to **10**.

    This will increase the smooth curvature of the rendered hair.

    Clump Width to **0.6**;

    Clump Twist to **0.5**;

    Hair Per Clump to **30**;

    Thinning to **0.5**;

    MultiStreaks to **1**.

    This will increase the number of hairs and set their ends to be uneven.

    Hair Color RGB to **0**, **0**, and **0**;

    Specular Color RGB to **0.2**, **0.2**, and **0.3**.

    This will change the color of the hair.

The tweaked hair

3 Add a light with shadows

You can now proceed to add a light with shadows.

Hair casting shadows

4 Save your work

- **Save** the scene as *31-girl_04.ma*.

Hair cache

You can save your hair simulation cached in memory to reduce the number of calculations Maya performs when playing back or rendering scenes that contain hair systems.

To cache a simulation, do the following:

- Select the *hairSystem*.

- Select **Hair** → **Create Cache.**

  The simulation will play and the cache files will be saved on disk in the current project's Data directory.

> **Tip:**   *You can press the **Esc** key on your keyboard to interrupt a caching operation. The cache will have been created for every frame up to the current one.*

- Once the simulation is cached, you can scrub in the Time Slider and the hair will be properly evaluated and much faster.

To delete a cache, do the following:

- Select the *hairSystem*.

- Select **Hair** → **Delete Cache.**

Hair library

You can transplant hair coming from a hair library. This hair library contains several examples of hairstyles from which you can learn. The following shows how to import a hairstyle and transplant it to your model.

1   Scene file

  • **Open** the scene *31-transplant_01.ma.*

    This scene file contains the Constructor geometry.

2   Hair library

  • Select **Hair → Get Hair Examples...**

    The Visor will appear and show you the available hairstyle examples.

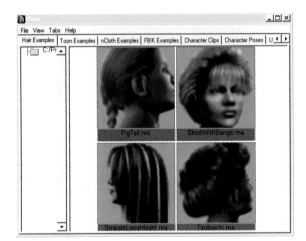

The hair library

  • **MMB+drag** a hairstyle to the viewport to import it into your scene.

3   Transplant the hair

By default, each hair follicle will be transplanted to the closest corresponding point of another model. You should then place the two heads on top of each other and transplant the hair.

  • Select the *hairBase* geometry from the example scene.

  • **Move, rotate,** and **scale** the head to fit your geometry as closely as possible.

  • Select any parts of the hair system, and then **Shift-select** the destination surface.

  • Select **Hair → Transplant Hair.**

  • **Delete** the *hairBase* model.

- Render your scene.

The transplanted hair

Conclusion

In this lesson, you learned how to create dynamic effects with hair using NURBS curves. You have modified the various attributes that belong to the hair system, and made hair collide with a surface. You also learned how to work with a hair constraint to gather the clumps into a hair bunch. Finally, you have rendered the hair with shadows, and learned about hair caches and about how to transplant hair.

In the next lesson, you will learn how to use Maya nParticles and nCloth to create volumetric particle effects and dynamic cloth simulations.

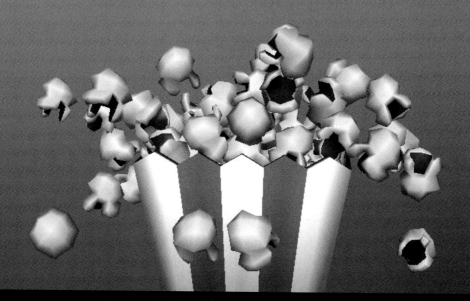

Maya nDynamics

This lesson teaches how to create volumetric particles and carry out cloth simulations within Autodesk® Maya® using the powerful nDynamic. The focus will be on establishing workflow practices on a variety of effects to explore the relevant tools and their applications. Once you have gone through this lesson, you should be able to experiment on your own and create effects such as clothing, water, tree leaves, ripping materials, balloons, etc.

In this lesson, you will learn the following:

- About nDynamics
- How to create volumetric particles
- How to create cloth pieces
- How to run clothing simulations
- How to adjust the behavior of the clothing
- How to speed up a simulation
- How to make nCloth cache files
- How to tear nCloth
- How to import nDynamics examples

Maya nDynamics

nDynamics is a dynamic simulation framework driven by Maya® Nucleus ™ technology. A Maya Nucleus system is composed of a series of Nucleus objects, which consist of nCloth, nParticle, and passive collision objects, as well as dynamic constraints, and a Maya Nucleus solver.

Nucleus dynamics allow users to create particle effects and dynamic simulations that cannot be achieved with Maya classic particles. For example, liquid simulation attributes allow you to create realistic liquid effects that can interact and drive nCloth animations and deformations.

The Maya Nucleus solver is stable, capable of handling large data sets, and it provides fast simulation results. The solver works with numerous shapes (like curves, non-manifold geometry, and meshes with holes) within the simulation framework, and its flexibility allows for less obvious nCloth applications, like flower petals or leaves.

As part of the Maya Nucleus system, the Maya Nucleus solver calculates Nucleus simulations, collisions, and constraints in an iterative manner, improving the simulation after each iteration and quickly recovering from each iteration's failure to produce accurate behavior.

Note: *Only nCloth, nParticle, and passive objects that belong to the same solver system can interact with one another.*

nParticles

nParticles use the Maya® Nucleus™ solver, which allows nParticles to interact and collide with nCloth and passive collision objects, as well as with other nParticle objects. You can use nParticles with Nucleus-based nConstraints to create particle effects and dynamic simulations that cannot be achieved with Maya classic particles. Like other Nucleus objects, nParticle objects are assigned to a Nucleus solver which calculates the nParticle simulation in an iterative manner.

In addition to Nucleus-based dynamics, nParticles can be used in place of Maya classic particles for particle goals, geometry instancing, and sprite effects. nParticles can also be manipulated by external non-Nucleus forces, including gravity and wind.

nParticles use the classic particle render types, including points, streaks, and blobby surfaces, and can be used in place of Maya classic particles for particle goals, geometry instancing, and sprite effects. nParticles does not replace Maya classic particles. Maya still uses the classic particle system to create the Dynamics preset effects, such as fire, smoke, fireworks, and lightning.

Create nParticles system

nParticles objects can be created using the following methods:

- Using the nParticle Tool;
- Creating an nParticle emitter;
- Emitting nParticles from selected objects in the scene;
- Filling selected polygon geometry with nParticles.

For each nParticle creation method, you can specify an nParticle style, which presets some nParticle attribute values, including Particle Render Type, Radius, Mass, and collision-related properties. nParticle styles provide a starting point for your nParticle effects and simulations. After you have created an nParticle object, you can adjust the object's attributes to suit your simulation.

The type of nParticle effect you want to achieve determines the method and style selected to create the nParticle object, and if applicable, emitter objects. For example, if you want to place individual spherical objects in your simulation, select the **Balls nParticle** style, and then use the **nParticle Tool** to place the objects in your scene. To create a liquid simulation effect, such as a lava flow, select the **Water** style, and then create an nParticle object and emitter using the **Create Emitter** or **Emit From Object** methods.

When you create an nParticle object, a new nParticleShape node and a Maya Nucleus System node are created. If your nParticles are emitted, an emitter node is also created.

nParticle Tool

Using the **nParticle Tool**, you can create individual nParticles, nParticle grids, and random collections of nParticles. The nParticle Tool allows you to position an exact number of particles in specific areas of your scene. These particles are static in the first frame of the simulation, but can be animated by Nucleus forces and by collisions with Nucleus objects, including other nParticle objects. You can attach static nParticles to moving Nucleus objects, such as animated nCloth, using Nucleus nConstraints. Like other Maya objects, nParticles can be manipulated by external dynamic forces.

Create Emitter and Emit from Object

Using **Create Emitter** or **Emit From Object**, you can emit nParticles into your scene as a simulation plays. When you use an emitter to create nParticles, an emitter node is automatically created and attached to the nParticleShape node.

As the simulation plays, the emitter generates nParticles and the particle count of the connected nParticle object increases. Emitted nParticles can collide with nCloth objects, passive objects, and other nParticle objects. The energy and velocity of emitted nParticles can be transferred through collisions to deform nCloth objects or other nParticle objects. Setting emitter properties, such as emission rate, speed, and direction, can determine how emitted nParticles collide and interact with Nucleus objects.

Fill Object

You can use Fill Object to fill polygon geometry, including modeled geometry, nCloth objects, or passive objects. The geometry that is to be filled must have a potential volume, meaning that it must have a concave region that can contain the nParticles. For example, polygon planes cannot be filled with nParticles.

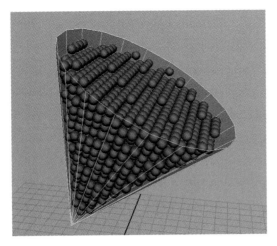

Polygonal object filled with nParticles

When filling geometry with nParticle objects, you can specify lower and upper fill boundaries along the geometry's X, Y, and Z axes. The fill boundaries are relative to the X, Y, and Z axes of the target geometry's bounding box. For each respective axis, a maximum fill setting of 1.0 completely fills the geometry along the specified axis. For example, a Max Y setting of 1.0 fills the geometry to the top of its bounding box (Y axis) with nParticles. You can also specify the total number of nParticles that fill the geometry using the Resolution control, and nParticle size using the Particle Density control.

nParticles example

In this example, you will learn to create a basic popcorn simulation using nParticles. Since nParticles can collide with each other, the complex rippling animation of numerous colliding objects will be greatly simplified.

1   **Scene file**
    - **Open** the scene file *32-popcorn_01.ma*.

    This scene contains a popped corn object and a popcorn box.

2   **Create an emitter**
    - Select the **nDynamics** menu set from the list box in the upper left corner of the interface.

> **Tip:** *The nDynamics menu does not have a hotkey assigned to it.*

- Enable **nParticles** → **Create nParticles** → **Balls**.
- Select **nParticles** → **Create nParticles** → **Create Emitter**.
- Move the emitter at the bottom of the popcorn box.

  Make sure to move the emitter high enough so the particles can emit from the inside of the box.

- Set the **Emitter Type** to **Omni** in the **Channel Box**.
- **Set** the **Emitter Rate** to **20**.

3 Change the particle style

- Select the *nParticle1* node from the Outliner and open its **Attribute Editor**.
- Under the **Shading** category, set **Particle Render Type** to **Spheres**.
- Under the **Particle Size** category, set **Radius** to **0.8**.

> **Note:** *Particles are colliding with each other because of the **Self-Collide** attribute set to* ***On*** *under the **Collisions** category.*

4 Create passive collider

The nParticles now need to collide against the popcorn box.

- Select the popcorn box, and select **nMesh** → **Create Passive Collider**.

5 Add gravity

- Select the *nParticle1* node, and select **Fields** → **Gravity**.

6 Play the simulation

- Set the timeline to go from **1** to **1000**.
- **Play** the simulation.

The corn is popping

7   **Fine-tune the simulation**

  - Set the following for the *nParticle1* node:

      Bounce to **-1**;

      Friction to **0.1**;

      Damp to **0**;

      Stickiness to **0**;

      Push Out Radius to **0.8**;

      Viscosity to **0**.

  - Set the following for the *nRigid1* node:

      Bounce to **0**;

      Friction to **1**;

      Damp to **0**.

8   **Play the simulation**

Better simulation of corn popping

9   **Particle instancer**

Just like with regular particles, you can use the particle instancer to place a piece of geometry at the location of each particle.

  - Select the *popcorn* object.

  - Select **nParticles → Instancer (Replacement) → □.**

  - Set the Particle instancer name to *popcornInstancer.*

- Click the **Create** button.
- Hide the original *nParticle1* object.

10 Add a initial per particle rotation

In order to get the popcorn to be randomly rotated upon creation, you will need to add a custom dynamic attribute to the nParticles and then write a simple expression to randomize an initial rotation vector.

- Select the *nParticle1* object and open its **Attribute Editor**.
- Open the **Add Dynamic Attributes** section and click the **General** button.
- Under the **Particle** tab, select *userVector1PP* and click the **Add** button.
- Under the **Per Particle (Array) Attributes** section, RMB in the **User Vector 1 PP** field and select **Creation Expression**.
- In the Expression Editor, type the following expression:

```
nParticleShape1.userVector1PP=<<rand(0,360),rand(0,360),rand(0,360)>>;
```

- Under the **Instancer (Geometry Replacement)** section of the **Attribute Editor**, set Rotation to **userVector1PP**.
- **Play** your simulation.

The final popcorn simulation

> **Note:** *nParticles do not hold any type of rotation information coming from the dynamic simulation. In order to have your particles fake a rotation, you will need to write a custom expression.*

nCloth

nCloth is a fast and stable dynamic cloth solution that uses a system of linked particles to simulate a wide variety of dynamic polygon surfaces. For example, nCloth is flexible enough to simulate all the following surfaces: clothing fabric, inflating balloons, shattering surfaces, and deformable objects.

nCloth can be generated from any modeled polygon mesh. You can model any type of polygon mesh and make it an nCloth object, which is ideal for achieving specific poses and maintaining directorial control.

nCloth is composed of a network of many particles connected by many links, which together create a dynamic mesh. Within this network, there are also cross-links that further connect the particles. Links maintain the distance between particles, and cross-links maintain the angles between links, stabilizing the nCloth and preventing cloth behavior like shearing.

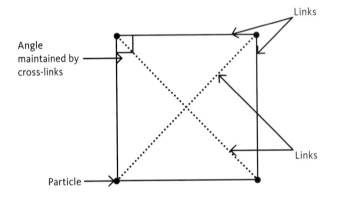

The nCloth links

When you make a polygon mesh nCloth, cross-links are automatically added to the resulting nCloth object. You can turn these cross-links on and off with the Add Cross Links attribute in the nClothShape Attribute Editor tab. Cross-links are not generated for triangulated polygon meshes, only for quad meshes.

The components in an nCloth's particle network directly correspond to its object components. For each vertex in your nCloth there is a particle, for each edge there is a link, and for each quad face there are two cross-links: one located at the quad split (tessellation) and one positioned perpendicular to the quad split.

Certain nCloth properties affect the object and particle network components of your nCloth. For example, nCloth Stretch and Compression Resistance affect links, Shear Resistance affects cross-links, and Bend Resistance affects edges. Also, Bend and Restitution Angles are measured across edges. For more information on attributes that affect the components of your nCloth, see nClothShape in the Maya Help.

You can view your nCloth's cross-links by selecting Stretch Links or Bend Links from the Solver Display drop-down list in the nClothShape Attribute Editor tab. You can view your nCloth's tessellation by turning on Display Triangles in the Mesh Component Display section of the outputCloth Attribute Editor tab. You can also change the direction of your nCloth's tessellation with the Quad Split drop-down list in the Mesh Controls section of the outputCloth tab.

nCloth workflow

The following procedure outlines a typical user workflow for creating an nCloth garment for a character. While performing these steps, you should play back your simulation so that you can see the results of your adjustments.

- Make your character's clothing nCloth.

- Make your character an nCloth collision object or passive object.

- Constrain the nCloth clothing to itself and its character.

- Adjust your nCloth clothing's properties to achieve the appearance and behavior you desire. You can also edit your nCloth's properties in a nonlinear manner by painting texture or vertex property maps.

- (Optional) Create external, non-nCloth dynamic forces to influence your nCloth's behavior.

- (Optional) Cache your nCloth.

- (Optional) Edit, merge, and blend your nCloth caches. *n Cloth*

Making a mesh nCloth

When you create an nCloth object, the following occurs: a new Maya Nucleus system of nodes is created and new connections are established for the selected mesh, and an nCloth handle appears on your new nCloth object. If the selected polygon mesh is made up of quads, the Maya Nucleus solver also tessellates the selected polygon mesh and generates cross-links. If the selected polygon mesh is made up of triangles, cross-links are not generated for the selected polygon mesh.

1   **Scene file**
- **Open** the scene file *32-cloth_or.ma.*   *semi_nude Bunny.01.mb*

   This scene contains the bunny's setup, where the bunny has pants in a separate piece of geometry.

The pants model

2 Create nCloth

- Select the *pants*.
- From the **nDynamics** menu set, select **nMesh → Create nCloth.**

   Doing so will make the currently selected geometry nCloth and will create an nCloth node visible only in the Outliner or Hypergraph. Also created is the Nucleus solver, which you can easily access in the Attribute Editor.

Note: *Any nCloth objects that should interact with each other need to be connected to the same solver along with the relevant collision objects. You can use collision layers to separate the various objects from colliding with each other. Assigning different groups of cloth to different solvers will speed up your simulation.*

3 Play the simulation

- Click the **play** button to execute the simulation.

   The Nucleus solver has an integrated gravity, which will affect all associated nCloth.

Tip: *You can tweak the Nucleus' Gravity and Wind section through the Attribute Editor. You can also enable the Ignore Solver Gravity or Wind for the nCloth object and then add your own dynamic fields.*

[Handwritten notes:] The pants fall down — select the nCloth node in the Outliner, Ctrl A. Select the nucleus node notice the gravity + wind Section. (Change gravity to 0)

4 **Collide with the floor**

- With the *pants* selected, open the **Attribute Editor**.
- Under the *nucleus1* tab, make sure the **Use Plane** option is enabled.

  Doing so with the default options will have the pants collide with an infinite ground plane located at the origin.

5 **Play the simulation**

- Set the time range to go from **1** to **1000**.
- Click the **play** button to execute the simulation.

  Notice how the pants now collide with the ground plane.

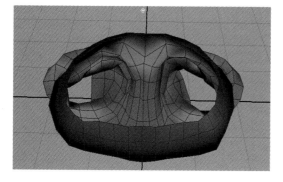

The pants colliding with the ground plane

6 **Collisions**

You will now have the pants collide with the bunny's geometry by setting the body geometry to a passive nCloth object.

- **Rewind** your scene.

  *You must always make sure to be at frame **1** for most of the dynamics-related tools and commands.*

- Select the *body* geometry.
- Select **nMesh** → **Create Passive Collider**.

  A node called nRigid1 has been created.

7 **Play the simulation**

If you play the simulation, you will notice that the pants are now falling down and colliding with the body geometry.

8 **Save your work**

- **Save** your scene as *32-cloth_02.ma*.

Speed up the nCloth simulation

If you play back your simulation at this time, you will notice a performance drop since the body geometry is quite complex, but the pants should behave pretty much as expected. As you will see, there are several things you can do to increase the play rate.

1   Pants solver display

You will now enable the display of the different objects the solver takes into consideration when calculating the simulation.

- Select the *pants* object and open its **Attribute Editor**.
- Under the *nClothShape1* tab, locate the **Solver Display** attribute located under the *in* **Collisions** section and select **Collision Thickness**.

  A yellow duplicated pants object will be displayed, showing you the collision thickness of the pants for other objects. When the simulation is played, the solver will attempt to remove any interpenetration occurring with a passive nCloth object.

- In the **Channel Box**, highlight the *nClothShape1* node.
- Change the **Collision Flag** to **Edge**.

  The solver display will update for the following:

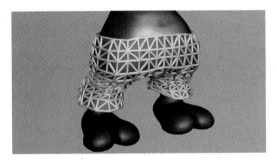

The collision surface using edges

  Since the pants already have quite dense geometry, edges will be more than enough in order to prevent any interpenetration.

- Under the *nClothShape1* tab, locate the **Solver Display** attribute and select **Self-Collision Thickness**.

  Doing so shows the collision thickness of the pant to itself.

- In the **Channel Box**, highlight the *nClothShape1* node and change the **Self-Collision Flag** to **VertexEdge**.

  There are two types of collisions on an nCloth surface: collisions with other objects and collisions with itself. In this case, these settings will suffice, but in other cases, such as where particles would collide with the nCloth, a full-face collision flag would be required.

In Attribute Editor) → Set the **Solver Display** attribute to **Off**.

2 Body solver display

- Select the *body* surface and highlight the *nRigidShape1* from the **Channel Box**.

- Set the **Collision Flag** to **Edge**.

It is also important to check the collisions on the passive nCloth objects.

> **Note:** *The **Self-Collision Flag** of a passive nCloth object is ignored.*

3 Simulation iterations

In order to speed up the simulation, you can reduce the number of iterations done by the solver to calculate the proper position of the nCloth.

> **Note:** *Doing so will also decrease the quality of the nCloth animation.*

- Select the *pants* object and highlight the *nClothShape1* object in the **Channel Box**.

- Change the **Max Self-Collision Iterations** attribute to **2**.

- Change the **Max Iterations** attribute to **200**.

You should notice an improvement in the playback rate.

4 Disable self-collision

If you believe there is no need for self-collision detection, it might be best to disable this feature. In the case of the pants, this should not make a big difference.

- Set the **Self-Collide** attribute for the *nClothShape1* object to **Off**.

5 Disable air tightness

nCloth can be used to create balloons or inflatable objects. In the case of a cloth piece, it is probably best to disable these features. → *In Channel Box (scoll down)*

- Set the **Air Tightness** attribute for the *nClothShape1* object to **0**.

- Set the **Seal Holes** attribute to **Off**.

You should notice an improvement in the playback rate.

6 Save your work

- **Save** your scene as *32-cloth_03.ma*.

Animated nCloth

In this exercise, you will animate the bunny in order to see the nCloth pants moving.

When dealing with dynamic objects, you must make sure to start animating the cloth before you actually start the animation. Doing so will ensure that the cloth has reached a proper initial state and velocity so the animation looks good from the first frame.

There are multiple techniques for getting a cloth into a proper position. The one demonstrated here will involve starting the animation from the original t-stance position at frame -50, and then playing the simulation so the cloth is well placed on frame 1. Once that is done, you can set the initial state of the cloth.

1 **Attach the pants to the body**

   When you play the animation, the pants will always be falling down since they are not attached in any way to the body geometry. While this will work for a shirt since it is stuck around the neck and stopped by the shoulders, the pants will require some sort of belt to prevent them from falling.

   • **RMB** on the *pants* and select **Vertex**.

   • Select the top border of vertices.

   • Select **nConstraint → Transform.**

     Doing so will create a new dynamicConstraint node and pin the selected vertices to their current location.

   • Parent the *dynamicConstraint1* node to the *HipsOverride* joint.

   • Hide the *dynamicConstraint1* node.

2 **Disable the nCloth solver**

   To speed up the animation process, you can temporarily disable the Nuclei in your scene.

   • Disable **Modify → Evaluate Nodes → Nuclei.**

3 **Original position**

   • Go to frame **-50**.

   • Select the *bunny* character set from the Outliner and press the **s** hotkey to set a keyframe in the current default position.

4 **Animation start pose**

   • Go to frame **1**.

   • **Pose** the character and set a keyframe.

The posed character

Tip: *You do not need to set a keyframe if the Auto Key button is enabled.*

You should now have an animation going from frame -50 to frame 1, where the character moves from the original position to a start pose.

5   Tweak the nCloth

All dynamics are set to start evaluating at frame 1 by default. In this case, you want the dynamics to start at frame -50.

- Select the pants *object* and open the **Attribute Editor**.
- Under the *nucleus* tab, open the **Time Attributes** section.
- Set the **Start Frame** to **–50**.
- Enable **Modify → Evaluate Nodes → Nuclei.**

6   Play the simulation

- **Rewind** and **play** the simulation up to frame **1**.

Tip: *Use the Step Forward button to step by only one frame at a time.*

The bunny's pants should now be properly deformed.

Note: *Before going on, make sure to tweak the nCloth behavior so the pants appear in their best position at frame 1. For instance, you can enable the Self-Collide attribute to give better deformation results.*

Select nCloth

7 Set the initial state

Now that frame 1 is properly simulated, you must save the initial state of the cloth for that frame.

- Under the *nucleus* tab, open the **Time Attributes** section.
- Set the **Start Frame** to **1**.
- With the *pants* selected, select **nSolver → Initial State → Set From Current.**

> **Tip:** *You could also manually model the pants properly deformed at frame 1 and select* **nSolver → Initial State → Set From Mesh.**

- Set the time range to start from frame 1.

The initial state of the pants

> **Tip:** *You will no longer need to run the dynamic simulation from frame -50, though it is recommended to keep the initial pose keyframe so you can return to it eventually and re-create the initial state of the cloth.*

- To relax the initial state further, select **nSolver → Initial State → Relax Initial State.**

  Doing so will simulate a number of iterations for the cloth and resave its initial state.

8 Save your work

- **Save** your scene as *32-cloth_04.ma*.

Tearing nCloth

In this simple example, you will tear a piece of cloth.

1 Scene file

- **Open** the scene *32-tear_01.ma*.

  This scene contains a round loop, a piece of cloth in its center, and a sphere to be used to tear the cloth.

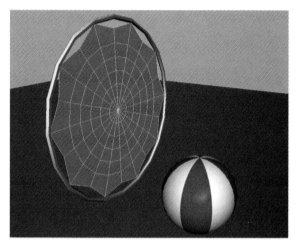

The example scene

Note: *nCloth can only be made out of polygonal objects.*

2 Create the nCloth

- Select the *cloth* object, then select **nMesh → Create nCloth.**

3 Create constraints

In order to attach the piece of cloth to the loop, you will need to create an nCloth constraint.

- **RMB** on the *cloth* object and select **Vertex**.
- Select every vertex touching the loop.

  Those are the vertices that should not move.

- Select **nConstraint → Transform**.

  This type of constraint will weld the selected vertices all together to a locator.

- **Parent** the nConstraint *dynamicConstraint1* to the *loop* object.

4 Play the simulation

Notice how the nCloth stays in position and appears to be hanging from the loop object.

Tip: *To get the cloth object to dangle from the loop, you can change its Stretch Resistance to a lower value such as 5.*

5 **Create passive**

- Select the *loop*, the *ball*, and the *floor* objects.

- Select **nMesh** → **Create Passive Collider.**

6 **Tearable surface**

You will now specify which vertices on the cloth surface can be torn.

- **RMB** on the *cloth* object and select **Vertex**.

- Select all the vertices that are not currently constrained.

   Those are the vertices that can tear.

- Select **nConstraint** → **Tearable Surface.**

   The faces of the object have been separated into individual faces and the constraint is holding the vertices together. In order to display the object as a single surface, a polyMergeVert and a polySoftEdge history node have been added to the surface.

7 **Tear the cloth**

- Set the time range to go from **1** to **1000**.

- Under the Dynamics menu set, select **nSolver** → **Interactive Playback.**

- Move the ball through the loop.

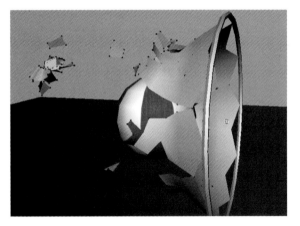

The ball tears the cloth

8 **Save your work**

- **Save** your scene as *32-tear_02.ma.*

Troubleshooting

Following are some guidelines to help you improve the accuracy of your nCloth simulations.

nCloth is vibrating

Denser meshes require more collision iterations to solve. In order to reduce cloth vibrations, you can try the following:

- Increase the number of collision iterations.
- Increase the number of substeps on the Nucleus node.
- Increase the damping of the nCloth, which will make the animation smooth.

Note: *Too much damping will make the cloth appear to float in the air.*

nCloth dynamics look wrong

Dynamics are always calculated in meters. If you want to use centimeters in your scene, set the **Space Scale** on the Nucleus node to **0.01**.

Ridges on nCloth

You may see ridges appearing on nCloth objects where perfectly aligned edges meet. To help in solving this, you can add **Bend Resistance** to the nCloth object. Even a small amount of bend resistance, such as **0.1**, provides enough resistance to prevent ridges, without changing the overall behavior of the nCloth.

nCloth cache

You can save your nCloth's simulation data to a server or local hard drive by caching your nCloth objects. nCloth caches are special Maya files that store the simulated point data of your nCloth simulations. nCloth caches also connect to the Nucleus nodes in your nCloth systems, which allows both cached and uncached nCloth objects to interact.

nCloth caches are useful when you want to reduce the number of calculations Maya performs when playing back or rendering scenes that contain simulated nCloth objects, and they allow you to easily direct, mix, and edit your nCloth simulations in an intuitive, nonlinear manner.

Note: *nCloth caches only store the XYZ positions of an nCloth object's vertices, not the translation, rotation, or scale of the nCloth's Transform node.*

You can use nCloth caches to do the following:

- Improve performance by caching an nCloth outfit (pants, jacket, and pants) so that its collisions and constraints are not calculated each time its scene is played back.
- Improve control and direct the behavior of an nCloth cape by arranging and blending its cache clips.

You can also create nCloth caches for your nCloth objects from the nCache menu, and edit them from the Attribute Editor or the Trax Editor.

Tip: *You can boost the simulation quality before creating a final cache. Doing so will ensure that you get fast playback in your scene, while getting the best possible simulation from the nCloth objects.*

Create an nCloth cache

- Select the nCloth object.

- Select **nCache** → **Create New Cache.**

Note: *If an nCloth cache file with the same name already exists in the directory specified in the Create nCloth Cache Options window, a Create Cache Warning message will appear.*

The simulation will play and the cache files will be saved on disk in the current project's Data directory.

Tip: *You can press the **Esc** key on your keyboard to interrupt a caching operation. The cache will have been created for every frame up to the current one.*

- Once the simulation is cached, you can scrub in the Time Slider and the nCloth will be properly evaluated and much faster.

Tip: *Disable the Nucleus solver to speed up playback rate once your animation is cached.*

Delete an nCloth cache

In order to delete an nCloth cache or simulate a new one, do the following:

- Select the nCloth object.

- Select **nCache** → **Delete Cache.**

The default option for deleting the cache is to delete the connection with the cache, but keep the files on disk so you can return or overwrite them if needed.

Tip: *Read the Maya Help to learn about all the possibilities of nCloth caches.*

Example scenes

There are several examples of nParticles and nCloth usage available in Maya, along with their online Web tutorials. There is a lot to learn from these tutorials if you spend the time to study them.

To import an example nParticles scene

- In a new scene, select **nParticles → Get nParticle Example...**

  The visor will be displayed and you will be able to import an example scene.

- **MMB+drag** an example scene into the viewport to import it.

To import an example nCloth scene

- In a new scene, select **nMesh → Get nCloth example...**

  The visor will be displayed and you will be able to import an example scene.

- **MMB+drag** an example scene into the viewport to import it.

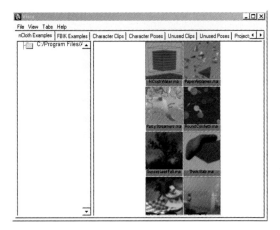

The visor with some nCloth examples shown

Conclusion

In this lesson, you have looked at creating nParticles and nCloth. Cache simulation was created so that the simulation would be calculated properly and much faster when playing back the scene. You have also learned where to get many more nCloth examples in order to become familiar with all the different possibilities of the nCloth and Nucleus solver usage.

In this book, you have built your knowledge from exploring shading networks and software/ hardware rendering, to experimenting with particles, dynamics and advanced Maya Unlimited features. There has been a plethora of information, with each exercise designed to practice your newfound skills. We wish you the best of luck using these skills in your own projects.

Index

Oh me oh Maya!

Sharpen your Maya skills with these expert guides from Sybex,
the official publisher of Autodesk Maya Press books.

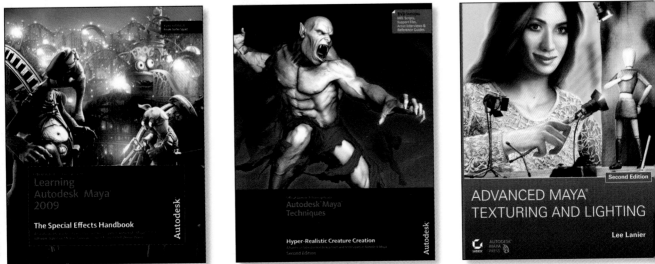

978-1-897177-51-8

978-1-897177-52-5

978-1-897177-50-1

978-1-897177-48-8

978-0-470-29273-0

Available at www.sybex.com and wherever books are sold.

AUTODESK
MAYA
PRESS

SYBEX
An Imprint of WILE
Now you know.

TurboSquid 3D Marketplace

www.TurboSquid.com

Save time and save money with 3D models from TurboSquid

With over 200,000 stock models from some of the world's greatest 3D artists, TurboSquid's goal is to revolutionize the way that 3D products are bought, sold and delivered through digital marketplaces. We offer the largest library of royalty-free products, quality guarantees on all purchases and 24/7 technical support, so give us a try today on your latest project and see how much money we can help you save.

The Tentacles plug-in

www.TurboSquid.com/tentacles

Access TurboSquid from inside your Autodesk 3ds Max or Maya applications

 Powerful search capabilities

 Side-by-side product comparisons

 Dynamic shopping cart

 Unpack and import models directly into your 3D application

Optimize your investment in Autodesk® software.

Maximize the classroom experience with the latest product downloads, one-on-one support, and access to training and the technical knowledge base when you add Autodesk® Subscription to your Autodesk® Maya® software purchase.

With Autodesk Subscription, educational institutions can extend the value of their educational offerings with the followings benefits:

- **Product Downloads** - Access all Maya software upgrades and bonus tools released during the subscription term – at no additional charge.

- **Training**—Give your students access to a complete library of high-quality, self-paced interactive tutorials developed by Maya software experts.

- **Support***—Get direct, one-on-one communication with Maya product support specialists – minimize classroom downtime.

- **Knowledge Base**—Easily access a searchable database of Maya solutions - a valuable classroom resource.

- And receive many more premium benefits. Access all of these membership benefits quickly and easily via the Subscription Center – the exclusive online membership portal.

No Worries. No Hassles. No Waiting.

Visit **www.autodesk.com/subscription** for a complete overview and online tour.
Or contact your local Autodesk authorized education reseller **www.autodesk.com/resellers**

* Available for Maya Unlimited + Subscription with Gold Support only

Autodesk Subscription

A FREE SUBSCRIPTION LETS YOU
DISCOVER MANY WAYS TO DEVELOP
YOUR SKILLS—AND IT PUTS YOU
IN TOUCH WITH THE EXCITING AUTODESK(R)
3D ANIMATION COMMUNITY.

TUTORIALS & TIPS
DOWNLOADS
ARTISTS' SHOWCASE
COMMUNITY NETWORK

AREA

WWW.THE-AREA.COM   < GO

AREA

Autodesk is a registered trademark of Autodesk, Inc. /Autodesk Canada Co. in the USA and other countries.
AREA is an Autodesk supported 3D animation community portal.
Autodesk is not responsible for any content outside of www.autodesk.com.
© 2008 Autodesk Inc. All rights reserved.

FULL ACCESS FOR ONLY $24·99/MONTH

Autodesk® Maya® eMagazine

Monthly Downloadable Learning Tools Membership
No Shipping! No Waiting! No Classrooms!

The Autodesk® Maya® eMagazine is a monthly program providing downloadable learning content for software users. This global online program delivers content presented by industry professionals, and offers step-by-step exercises and valuable tutorials, to enable you to understand the tools and workflows available in Autodesk Maya software.

Each month you can download a newly released learning tool that will introduce you to a wide range of techniques. You'll learn to make sound decisions from the beginning, to save yourself unnecessary challenges further down the pipeline. As well, you will have access to a library of previously released DVDs and books.

Support Files

Video Files

Instructor Notes

- Downloadable DVDs, each containing 1.5 hours of instruction
- New Learning Tools published each month
- Books excerpts in PDF format
- Support files, models and plug-ins
- Clear step-by-step tutorials
  And much more...

www.autodesk.com/mayaemagazine

FREE 30 DAY TRIAL

Autodesk